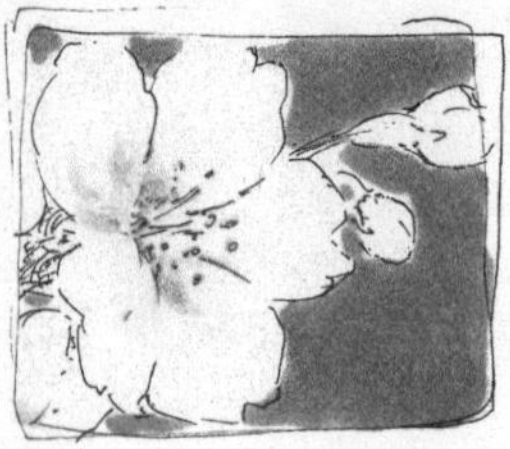

My friend from overseas visited for the first time in a while. I asked why they had come to Japan and it was to see the sakura blooming in Ueno.

I thought that coming all that way to see the sakura was a very Japanese thing, but maybe wanting to see the flowers bloom in the spring is universal. Interesting.

-Tite Kubo

Bleach is author Tite Kubo's second title. Kubo made his debut with *ZOMBIEPOWDER.*, a four-volume series for *Weekly Shonen Jump*. To date, *Bleach* has been translated into numerous languages and has also inspired an animated TV series that began airing in the U.S. in 2006. Beginning its serialization in 2001, *Bleach* is still a mainstay in the pages of *Weekly Shonen Jump*. In 2005, *Bleach* was awarded the prestigious Shogakukan Manga Award in the *shonen* (boys) category.

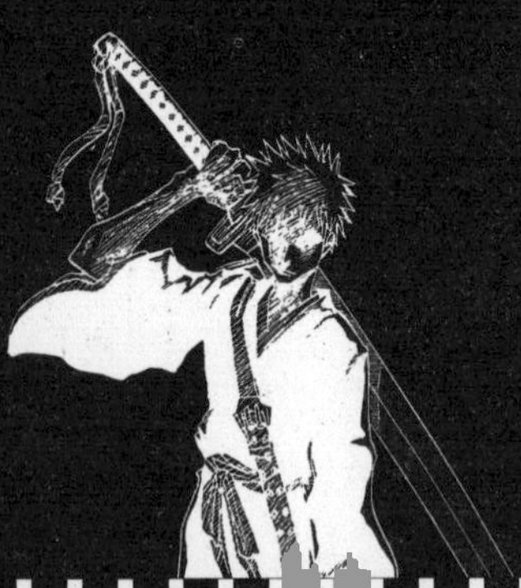

BLEACH
VOL. 68: THE ORDINARY PEACE
SHONEN JUMP Manga Edition

STORY AND ART BY
TITE KUBO

Translation/Joe Yamazaki
Touch-up Art & Lettering/Mark McMurray
Design/Kam Li
Editor/Alexis Kirsch

Printed in the U.S.A.

Published by VIZ Media, LLC
P.O. Box 77010
San Francisco, CA 94107

10 9 8 7 6 5 4 3 2 1
First printing, November 2016

Doesn't all that venom make you dizzy?

BLEACH 68 THE ORDINARY PEACE

Shonen Jump Manga

ALL STARS ★ AND

石田雨竜
イシダウリュウ

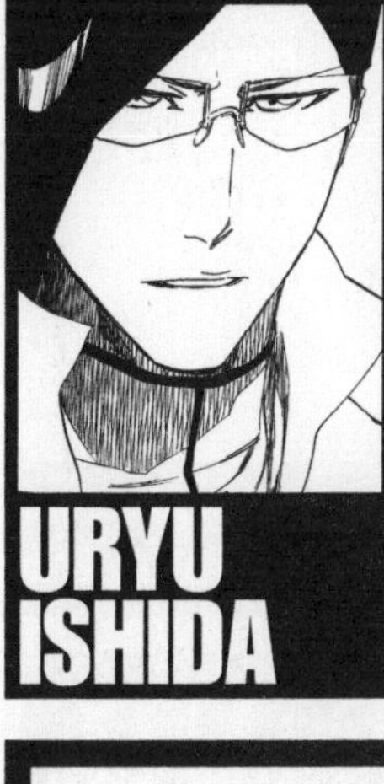

URYU ISHIDA

YHWACH

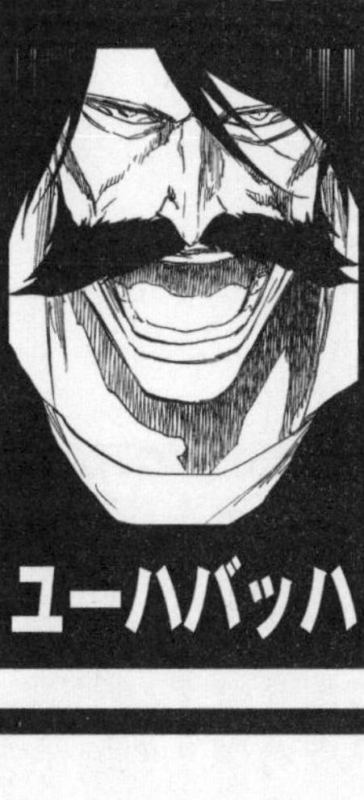

ユーハバッハ

黒崎一護
クロサキイチゴ

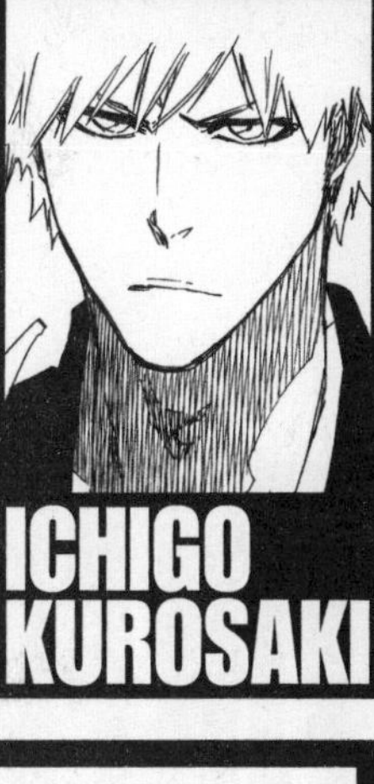

ICHIGO KUROSAKI

★plot★

Ichigo Kurosaki meets Soul Reaper Rukia Kuchiki and ends up helping her eradicate Hollows. After developing his powers as a Soul Reaper, Ichigo befriends many humans and Soul Reapers and grows as a person...

The battle between Yhwach's royal guard and Squad Zero appears to be a victory for the Soul Reapers. But Yhwach revives his fallen men and Squad Zero is defeated. Kyosube, the final line of defense, is also defeated when Yhwach regains his true powers. Ichigo and company finally arrive at the royal palace, but they are too late. And with the palace's guardians down, Yhwach closes in on his prize...

BLEACH

JUSHIRO
UKITAKE

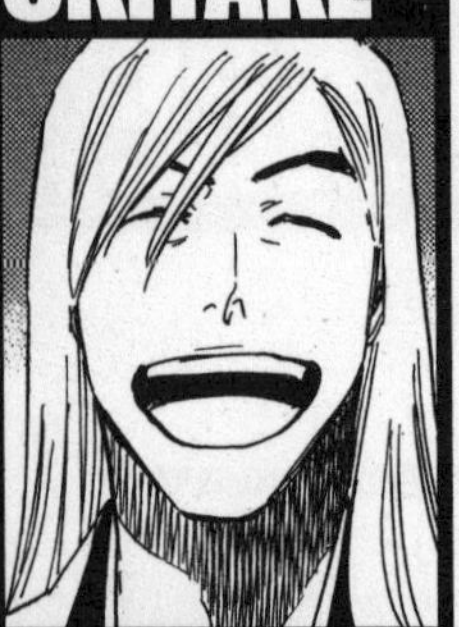

浮竹十四郎
ウキタケジュウシロウ

京楽春水
キョウラクシュンスイ

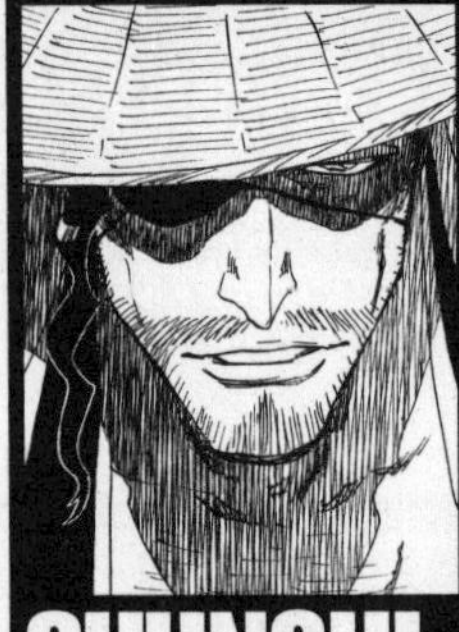

SHUNSUI
KYORAKU

KISUKE
URAHARA

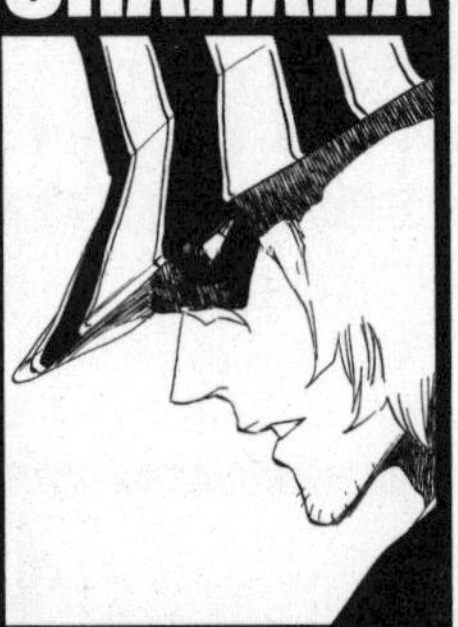

浦原喜助
ウラハラキスケ

STORIES

BLE68 ACH68

THE ORDINARY PEACE

CONTENTS

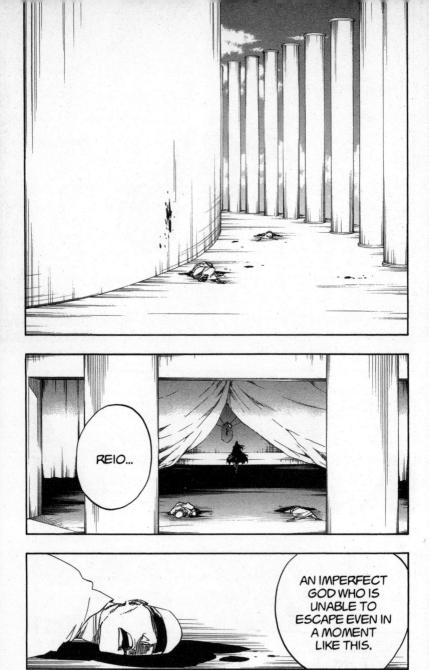

REIO...

AN IMPERFECT GOD WHO IS UNABLE TO ESCAPE EVEN IN A MOMENT LIKE THIS.

612. DIRTY

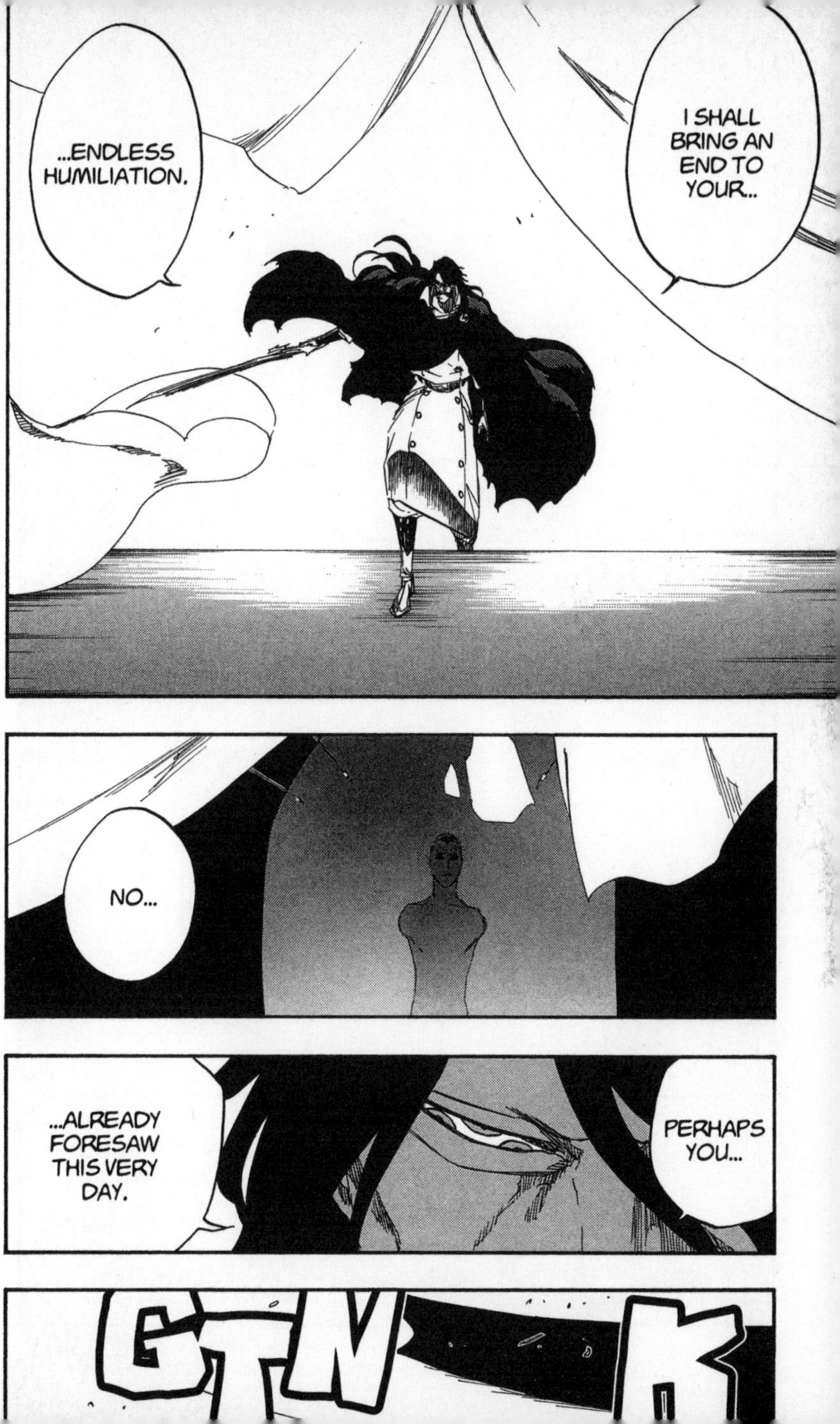
I SHALL BRING AN END TO YOUR...
...ENDLESS HUMILIATION.
NO...
PERHAPS YOU...
...ALREADY FORESAW THIS VERY DAY.
GTNK

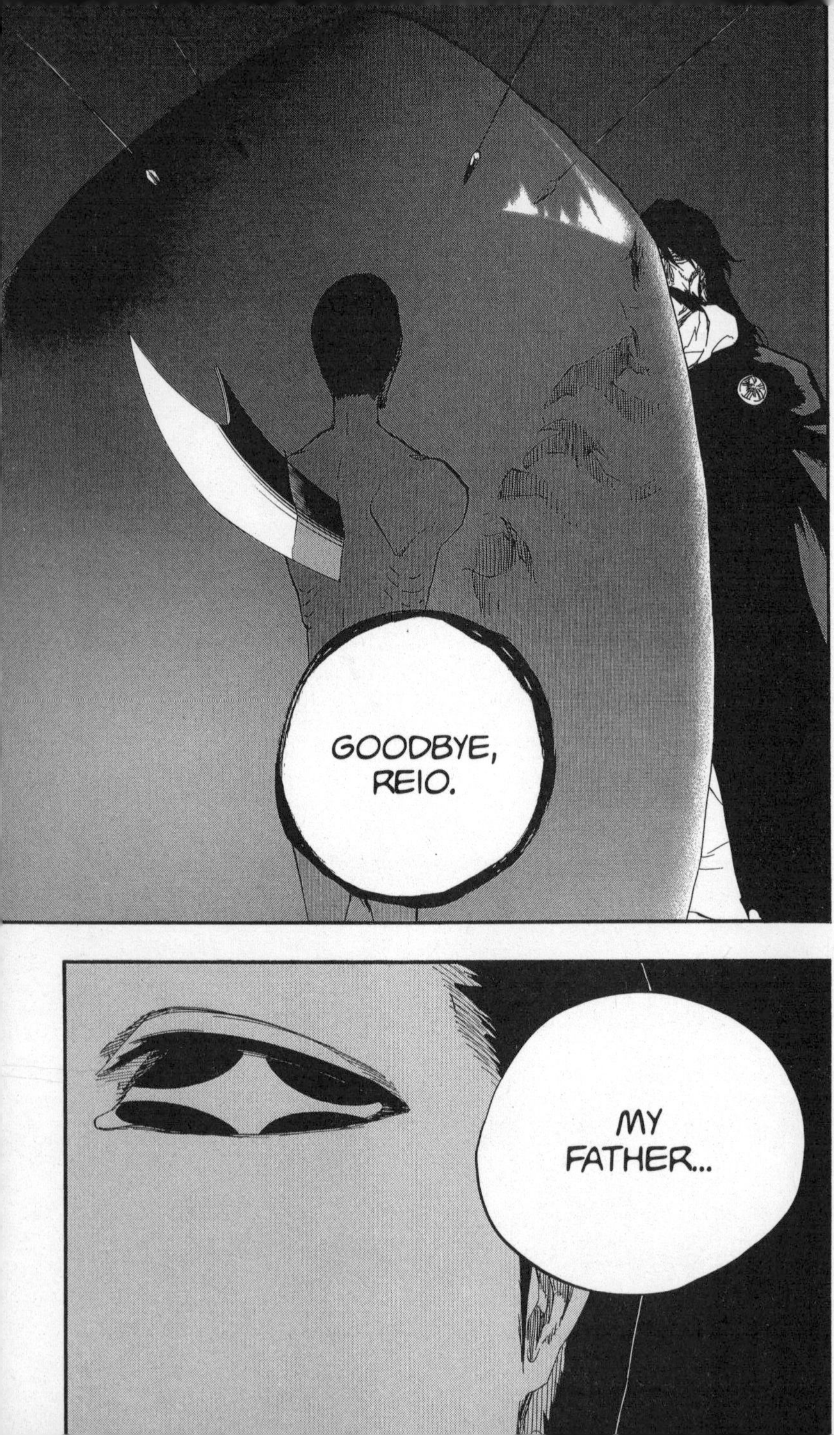
GOODBYE, REIO.
MY FATHER...

...WHO HAS SEEN THE FUTURE.

BLEACH 612.

DIRTY

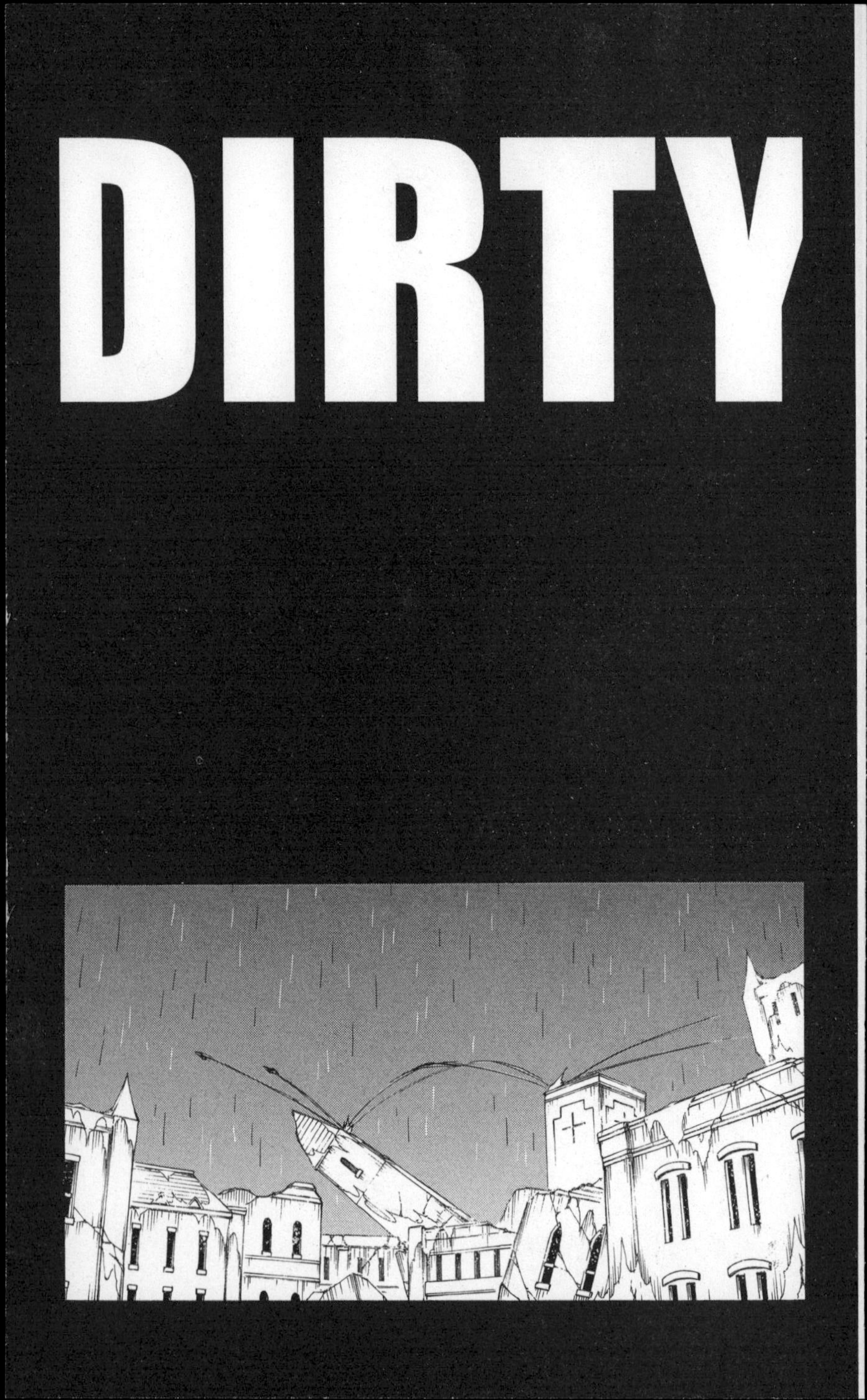

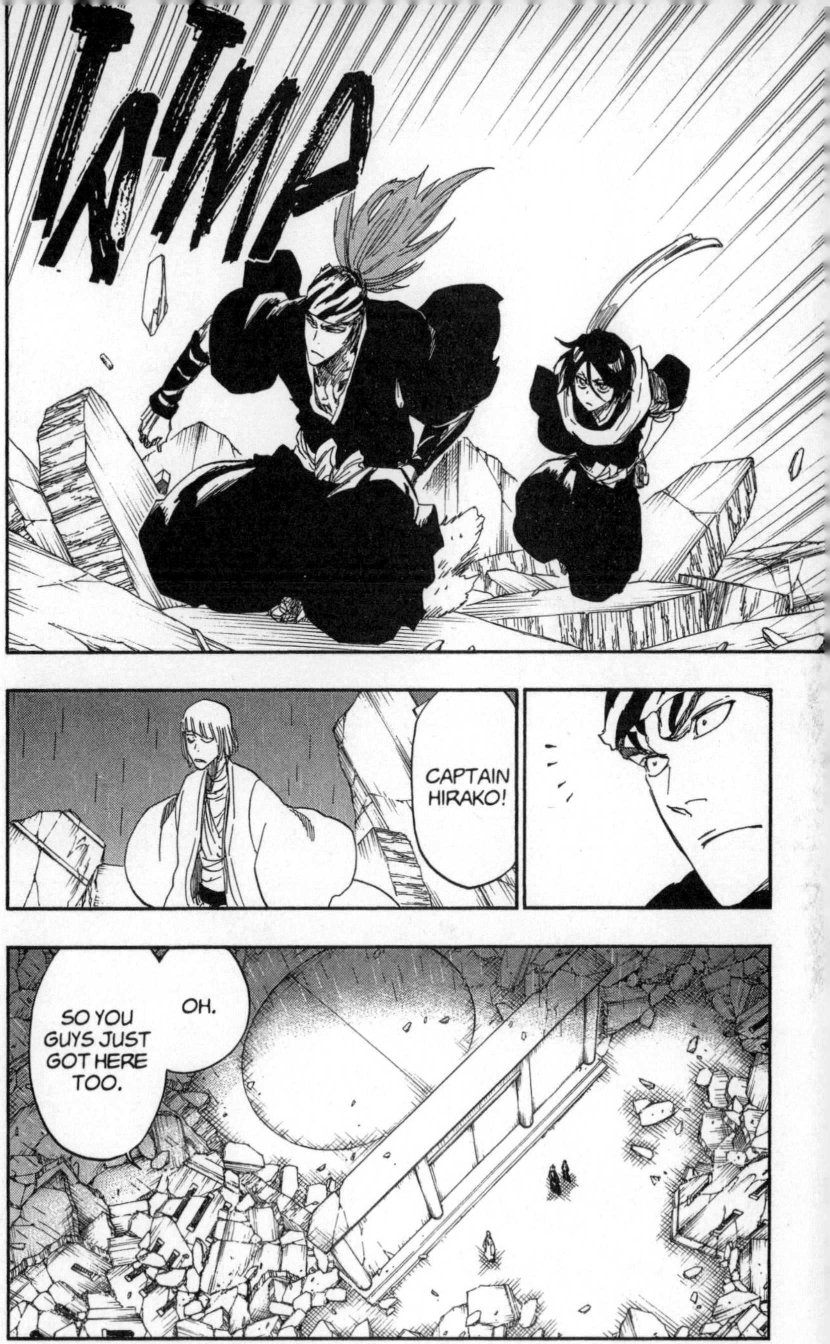
TAMP
CAPTAIN HIRAKO!
OH.
SO YOU GUYS JUST GOT HERE TOO.

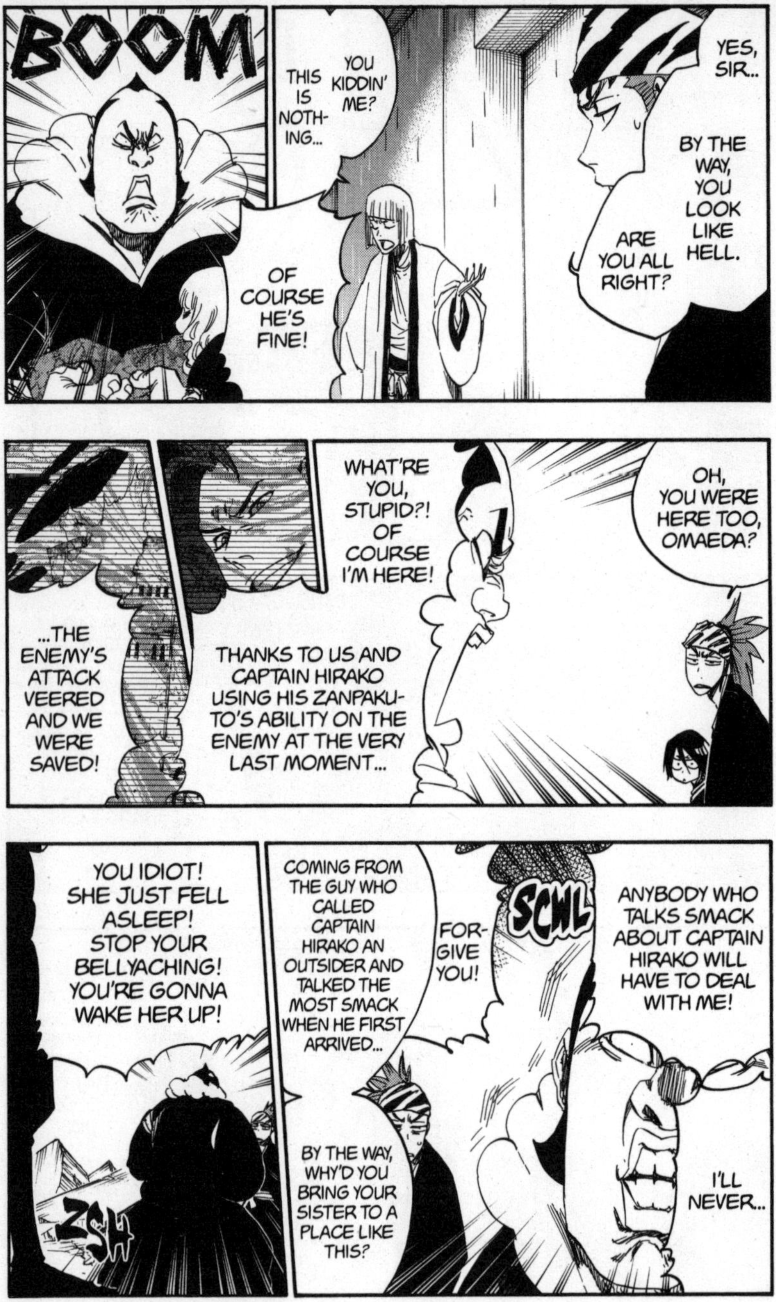
YES, SIR...
BY THE WAY, YOU LOOK LIKE HELL.
ARE YOU ALL RIGHT?
YOU KIDDIN' ME?
THIS IS NOTHING...
OF COURSE HE'S FINE!
BOOM
OH, YOU WERE HERE TOO, OMAEDA?
WHAT'RE YOU, STUPID?! OF COURSE I'M HERE!
THANKS TO US AND CAPTAIN HIRAKO USING HIS ZANPAKU-TO'S ABILITY ON THE ENEMY AT THE VERY LAST MOMENT...
...THE ENEMY'S ATTACK VEERED AND WE WERE SAVED!
ANYBODY WHO TALKS SMACK ABOUT CAPTAIN HIRAKO WILL HAVE TO DEAL WITH ME!
SCWL
I'LL NEVER...
FOR-GIVE YOU!
COMING FROM THE GUY WHO CALLED CAPTAIN HIRAKO AN OUTSIDER AND TALKED THE MOST SMACK WHEN HE FIRST ARRIVED...
BY THE WAY, WHY'D YOU BRING YOUR SISTER TO A PLACE LIKE THIS?
YOU IDIOT! SHE JUST FELL ASLEEP! STOP YOUR BELLYACHING! YOU'RE GONNA WAKE HER UP!
ZSH

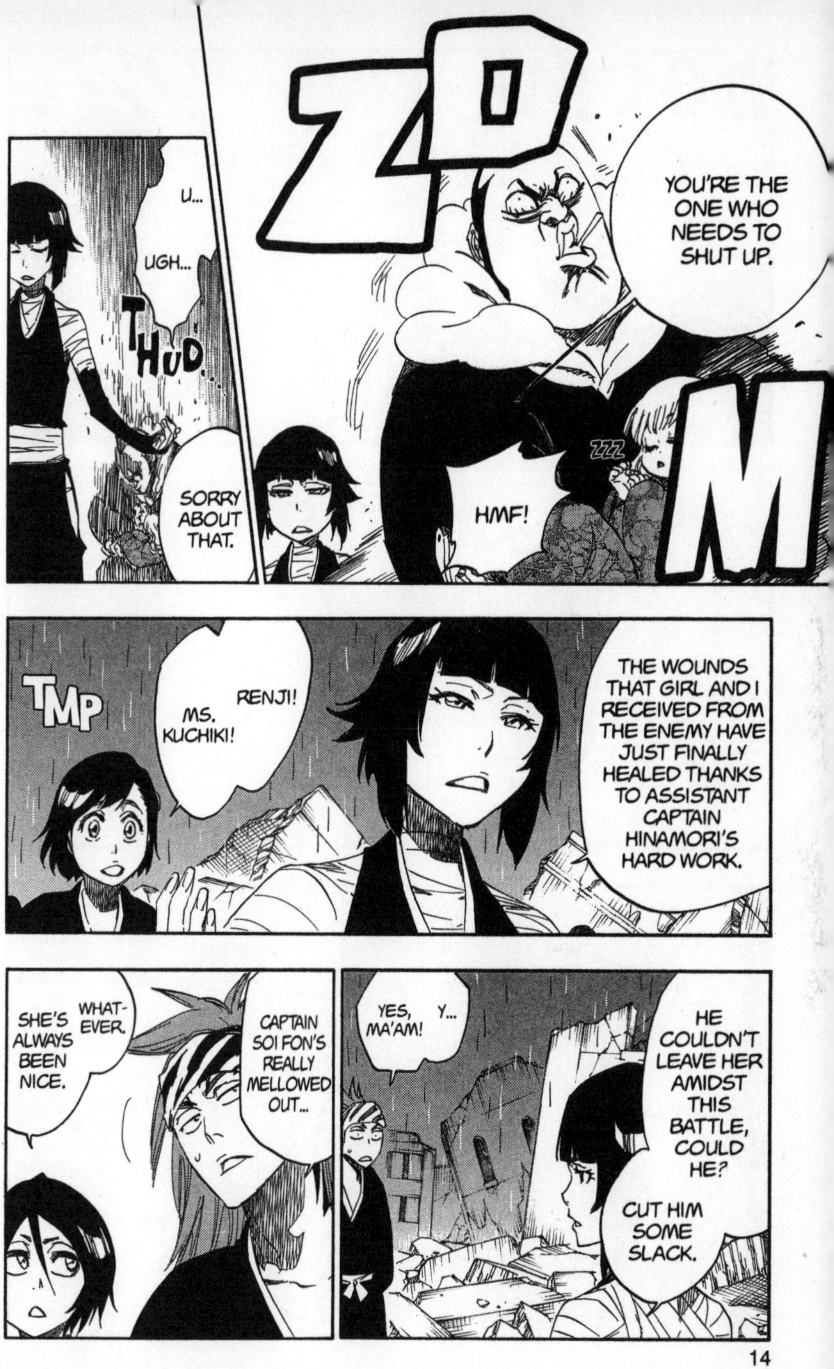
ZOM
YOU'RE THE ONE WHO NEEDS TO SHUT UP.
ZZZ
HMF!
U...
UGH...
THUD...
SORRY ABOUT THAT.
THE WOUNDS THAT GIRL AND I RECEIVED FROM THE ENEMY HAVE JUST FINALLY HEALED THANKS TO ASSISTANT CAPTAIN HINAMORI'S HARD WORK.
RENJI!
MS. KUCHIKI!
TMP
HE COULDN'T LEAVE HER AMIDST THIS BATTLE, COULD HE?
CUT HIM SOME SLACK.
Y...
YES, MA'AM!
CAPTAIN SOI FON'S REALLY MELLOWED OUT...
WHATEVER.
SHE'S ALWAYS BEEN NICE.

READ THIS WAY

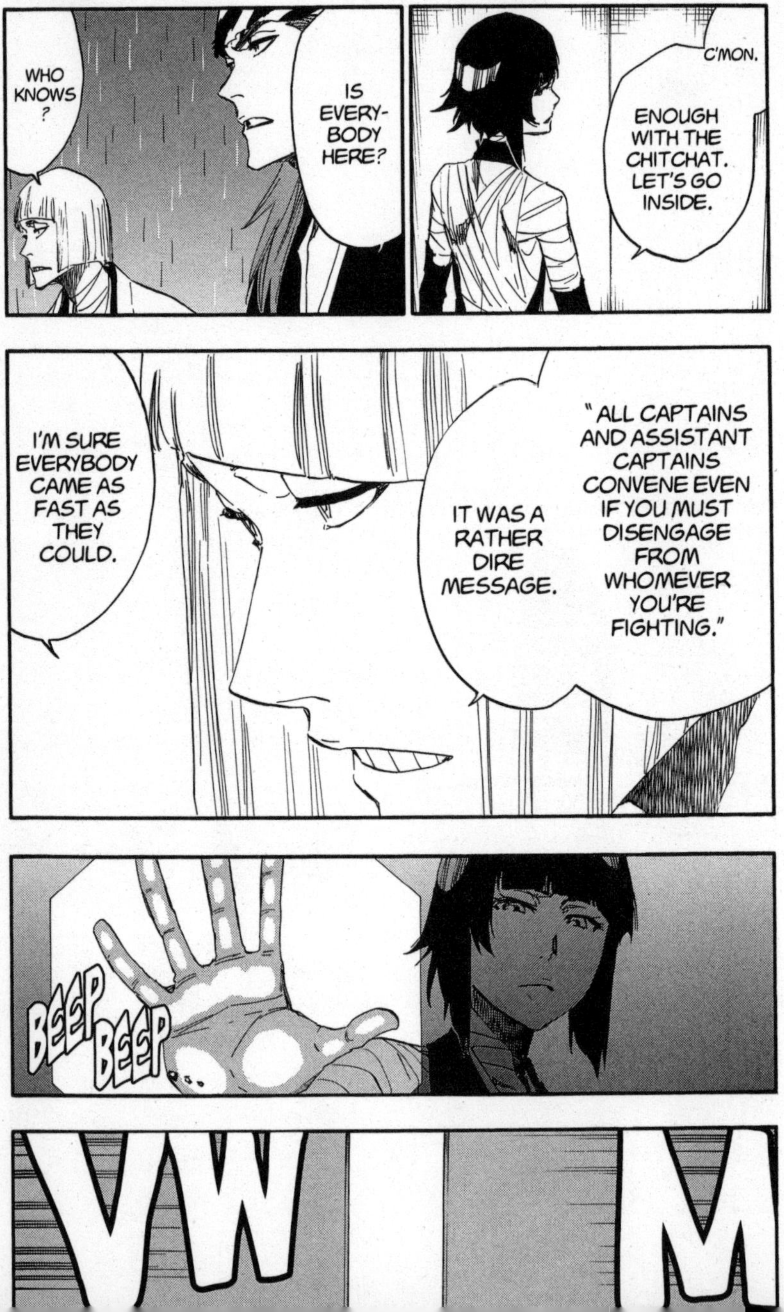
C'MON.
ENOUGH WITH THE CHITCHAT. LET'S GO INSIDE.
IS EVERYBODY HERE?
WHO KNOWS?
"ALL CAPTAINS AND ASSISTANT CAPTAINS CONVENE EVEN IF YOU MUST DISENGAGE FROM WHOMEVER YOU'RE FIGHTING."
IT WAS A RATHER DIRE MESSAGE.
I'M SURE EVERYBODY CAME AS FAST AS THEY COULD.
BEEP BEEP
VWM

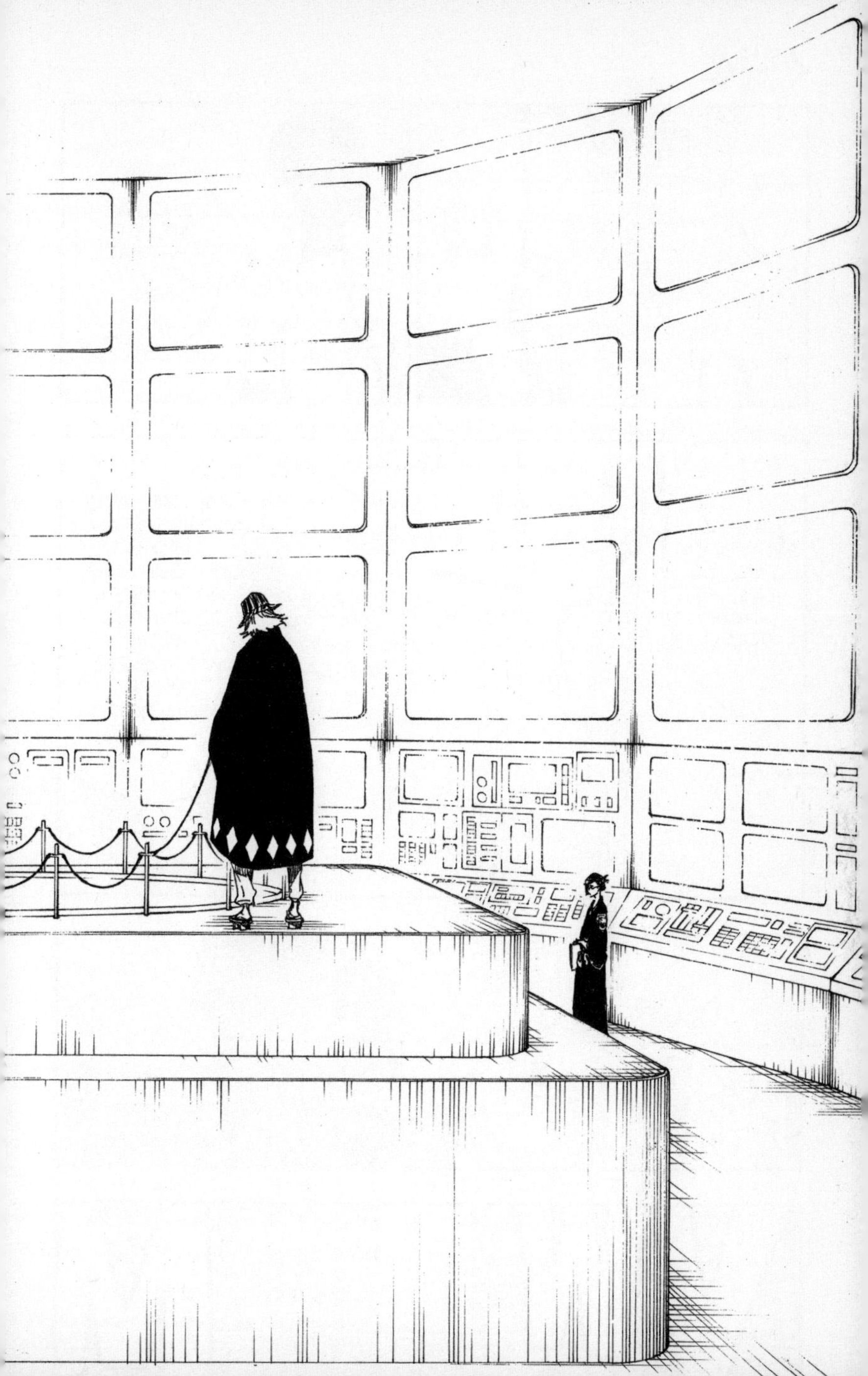

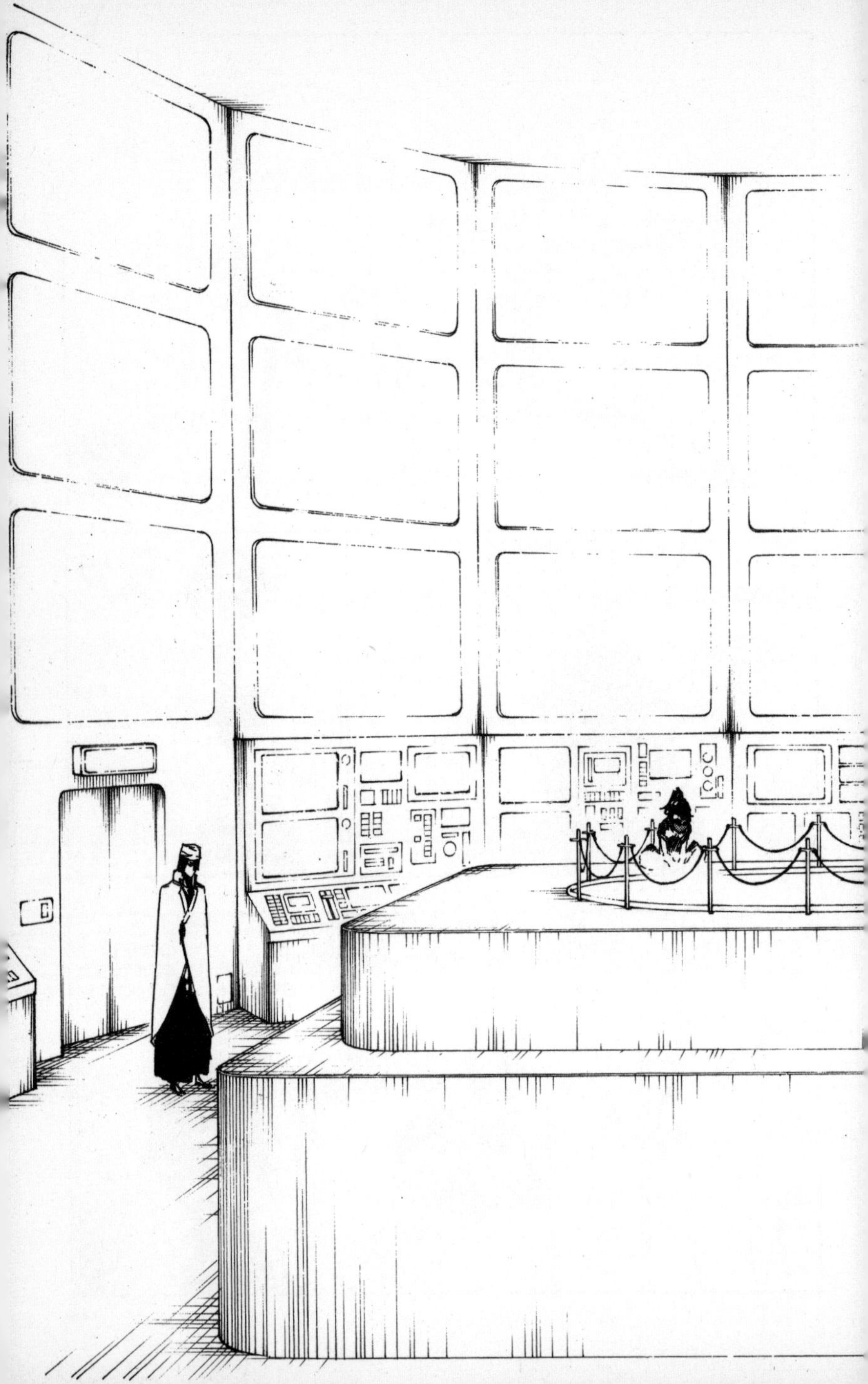

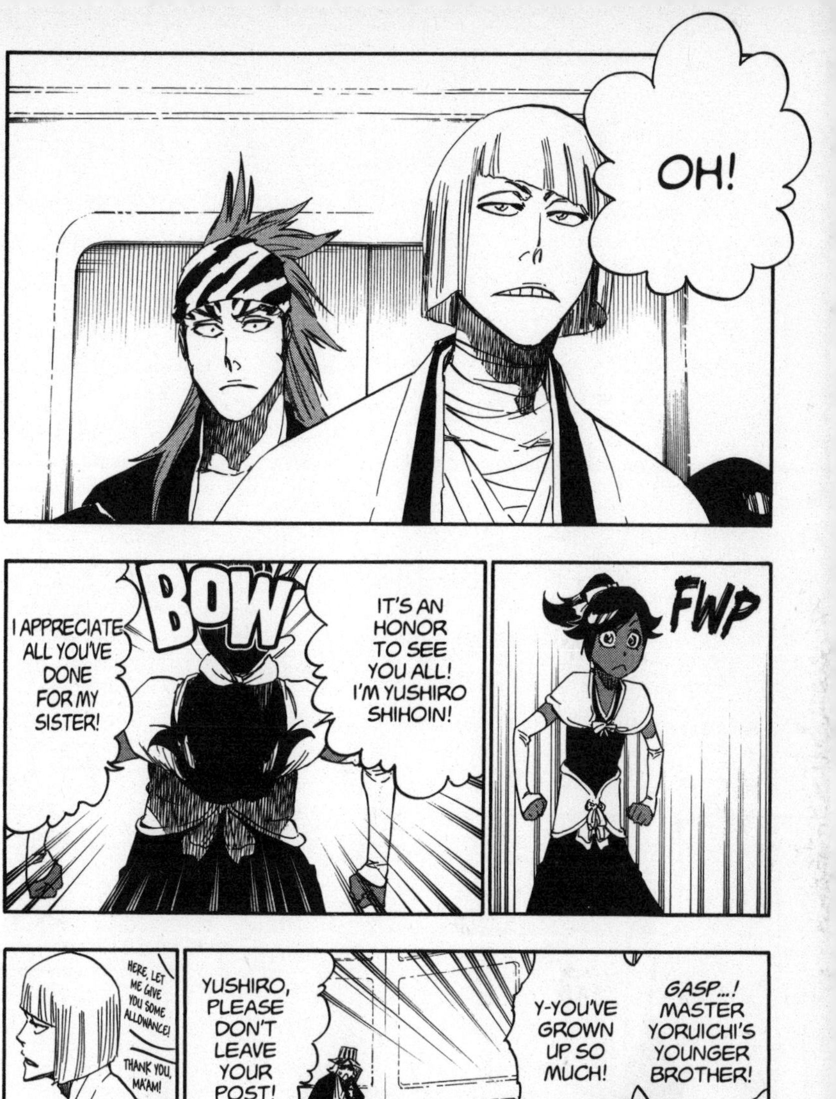
OH!
FWP
BOW
IT'S AN HONOR TO SEE YOU ALL! I'M YUSHIRO SHIHOIN!
I APPRECIATE ALL YOU'VE DONE FOR MY SISTER!
GASP...! MASTER YORUICHI'S YOUNGER BROTHER!
Y-YOU'VE GROWN UP SO MUCH!
SNFF
YUSHIRO, PLEASE DON'T LEAVE YOUR POST!
YES, SIR!
HERE, LET ME GIVE YOU SOME ALLOWANCE!
THANK YOU, MA'AM!
WHAT THE ...?

READ THIS WAY

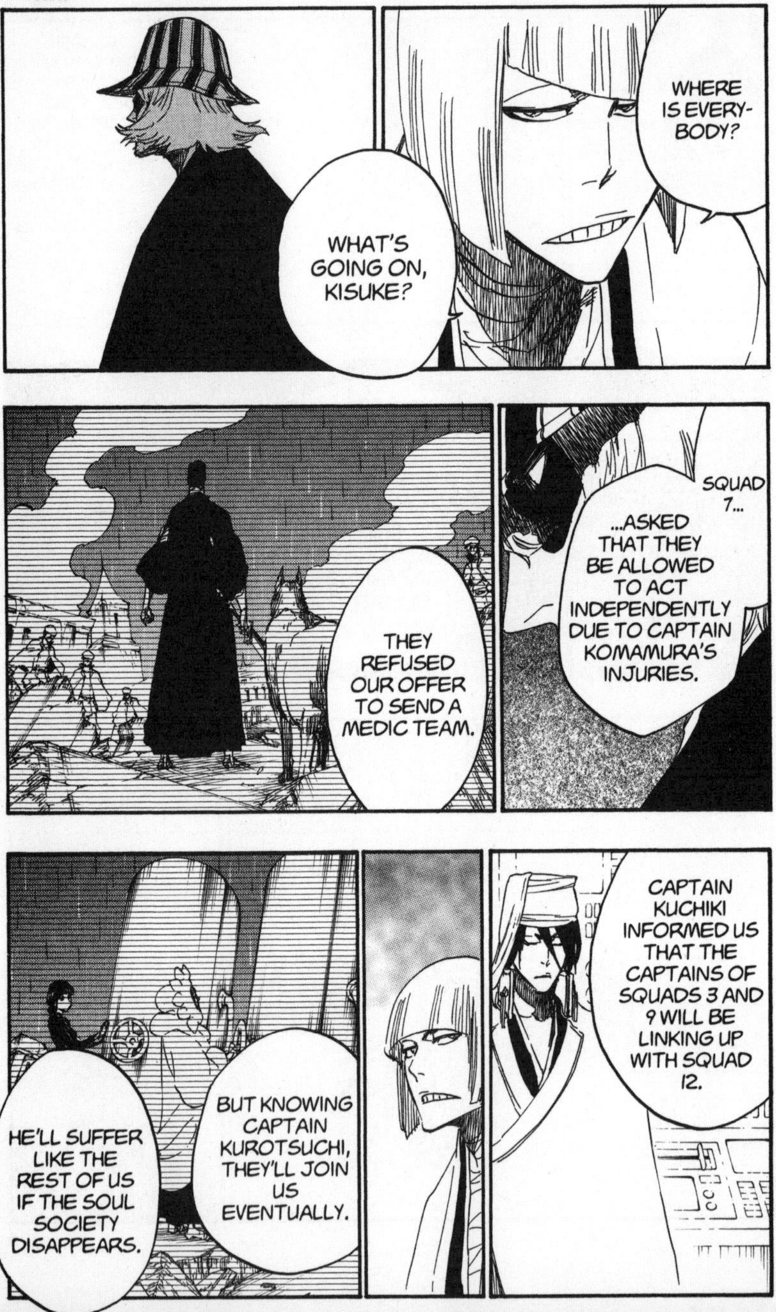

WHERE IS EVERYBODY?
WHAT'S GOING ON, KISUKE?
SQUAD 7...
...ASKED THAT THEY BE ALLOWED TO ACT INDEPENDENTLY DUE TO CAPTAIN KOMAMURA'S INJURIES.
THEY REFUSED OUR OFFER TO SEND A MEDIC TEAM.
CAPTAIN KUCHIKI INFORMED US THAT THE CAPTAINS OF SQUADS 3 AND 9 WILL BE LINKING UP WITH SQUAD 12.
BUT KNOWING CAPTAIN KUROTSUCHI, THEY'LL JOIN US EVENTUALLY.
HE'LL SUFFER LIKE THE REST OF US IF THE SOUL SOCIETY DISAPPEARS.

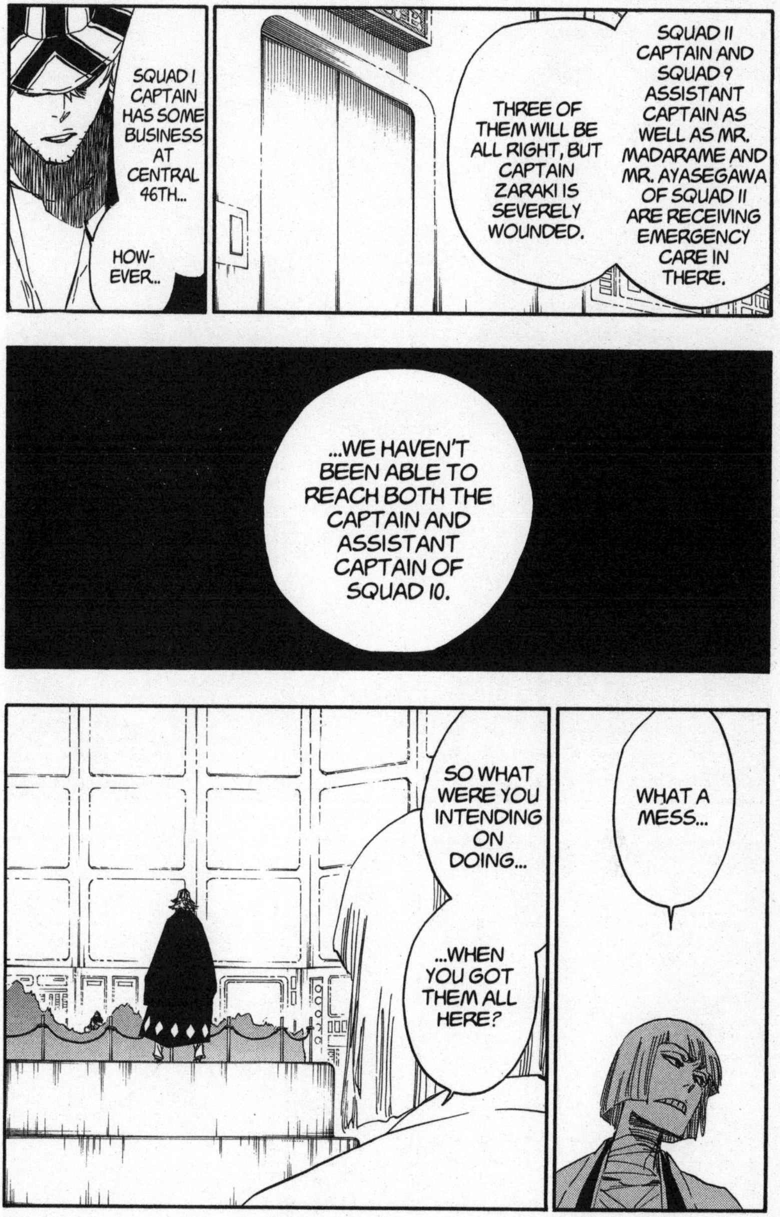
SQUAD II CAPTAIN AND SQUAD 9 ASSISTANT CAPTAIN AS WELL AS MR. MADARAME AND MR. AYASEGAWA OF SQUAD II ARE RECEIVING EMERGENCY CARE IN THERE.
THREE OF THEM WILL BE ALL RIGHT, BUT CAPTAIN ZARAKI IS SEVERELY WOUNDED.
SQUAD I CAPTAIN HAS SOME BUSINESS AT CENTRAL 46TH...
HOW-EVER..
...WE HAVEN'T BEEN ABLE TO REACH BOTH THE CAPTAIN AND ASSISTANT CAPTAIN OF SQUAD 10.
WHAT A MESS...
SO WHAT WERE YOU INTENDING ON DOING...
...WHEN YOU GOT THEM ALL HERE?

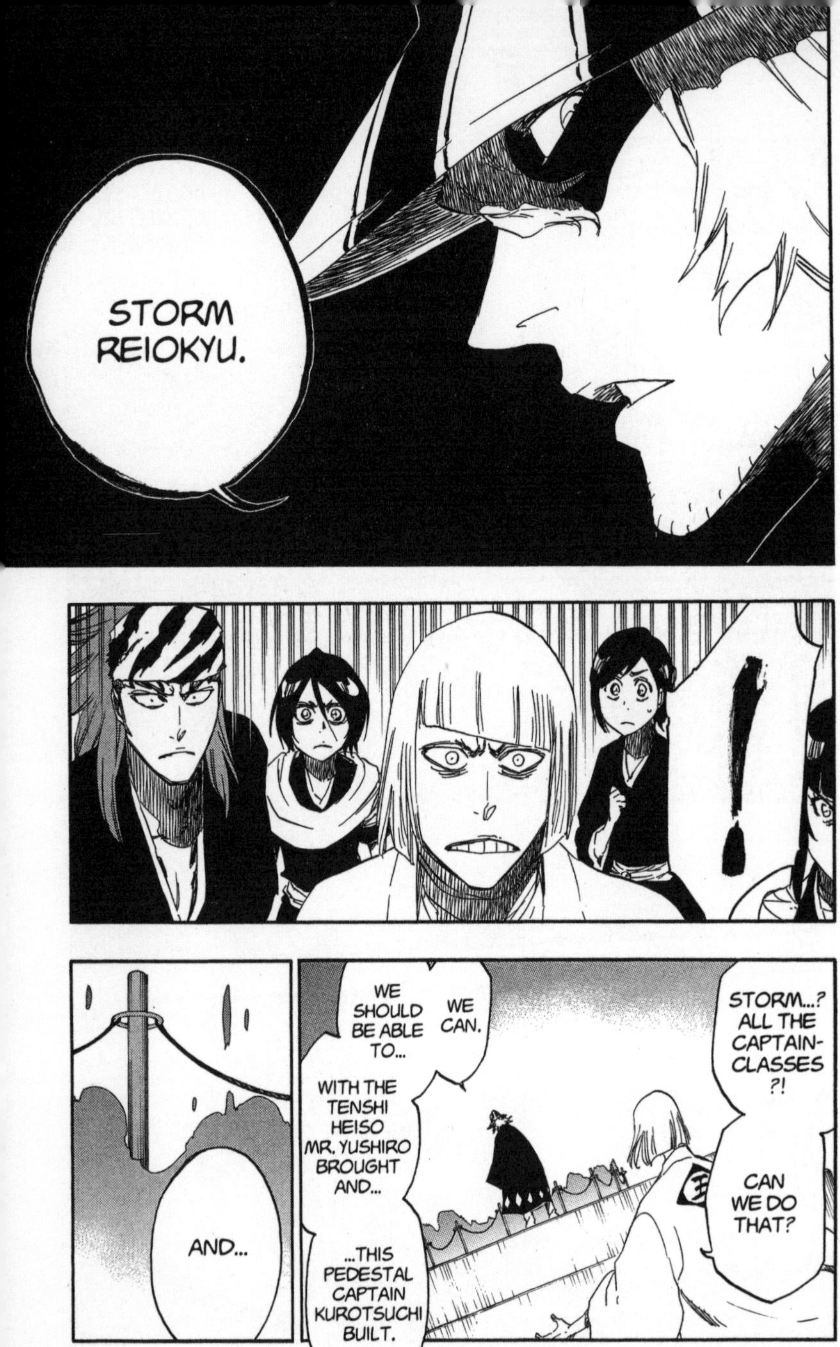
STORM REIOKYU.
STORM...? ALL THE CAPTAIN-CLASSES?!
CAN WE DO THAT?
WE CAN.
WE SHOULD BE ABLE TO...
WITH THE TENSHI HEISO MR. YUSHIRO BROUGHT AND...
...THIS PEDESTAL CAPTAIN KUROTSUCHI BUILT.
AND...

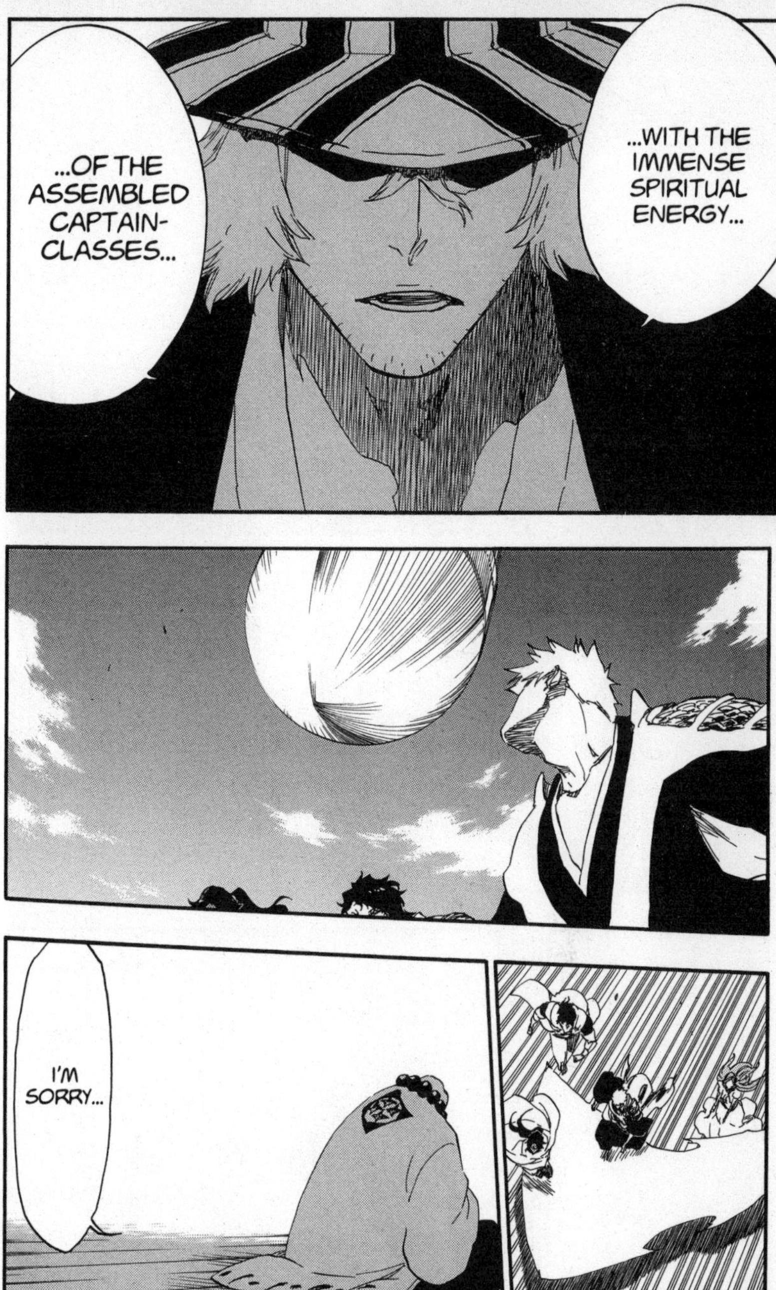
...WITH THE IMMENSE SPIRITUAL ENERGY...
...OF THE ASSEMBLED CAPTAIN-CLASSES...
I'M SORRY...

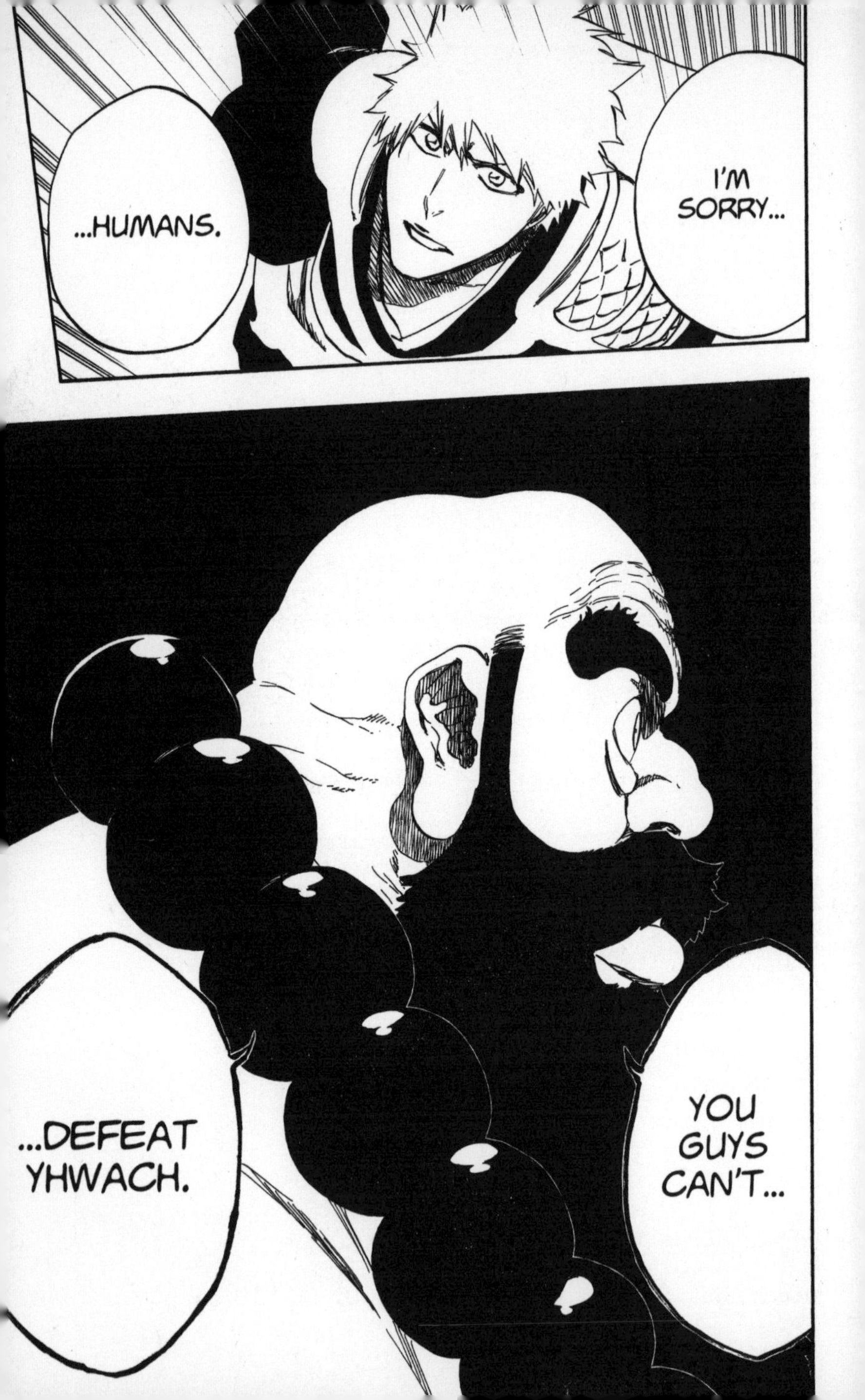
I'M SORRY...
...HUMANS.
YOU GUYS CAN'T...
...DEFEAT YHWACH.

WHAT'S THE DEAL, CAPTAIN?
YOU SAW YUSHIRO JUST LAST MONTH.

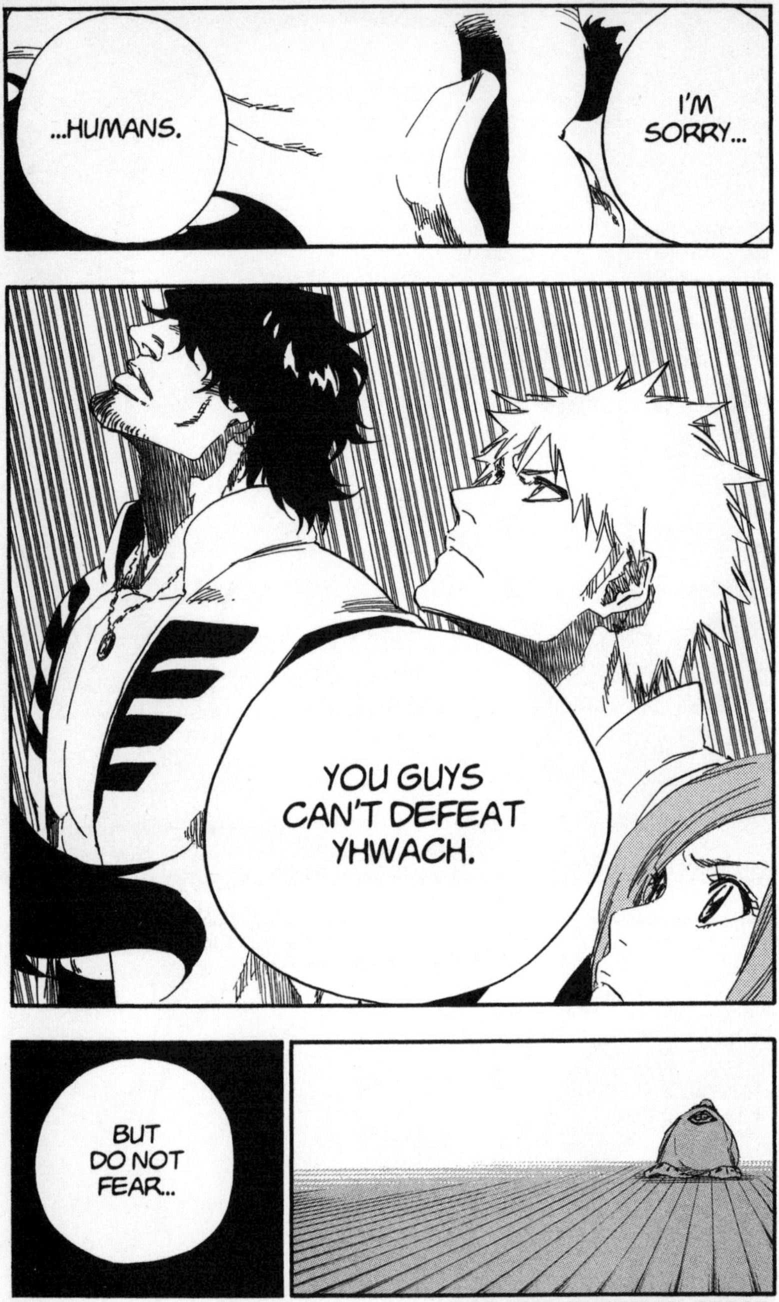
I'M SORRY...
...HUMANS.
YOU GUYS CAN'T DEFEAT YHWACH.
BUT DO NOT FEAR...

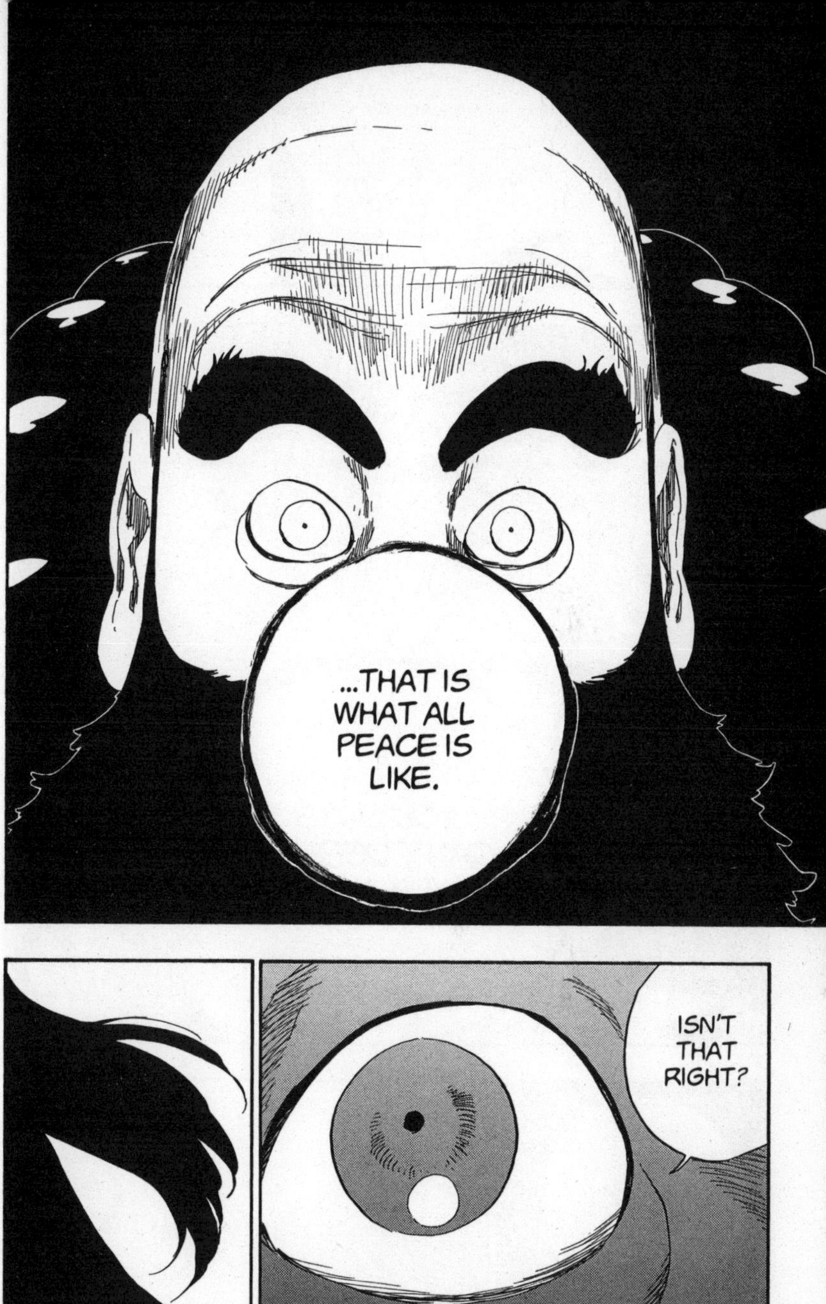
...THAT IS WHAT ALL PEACE IS LIKE.
ISN'T THAT RIGHT?

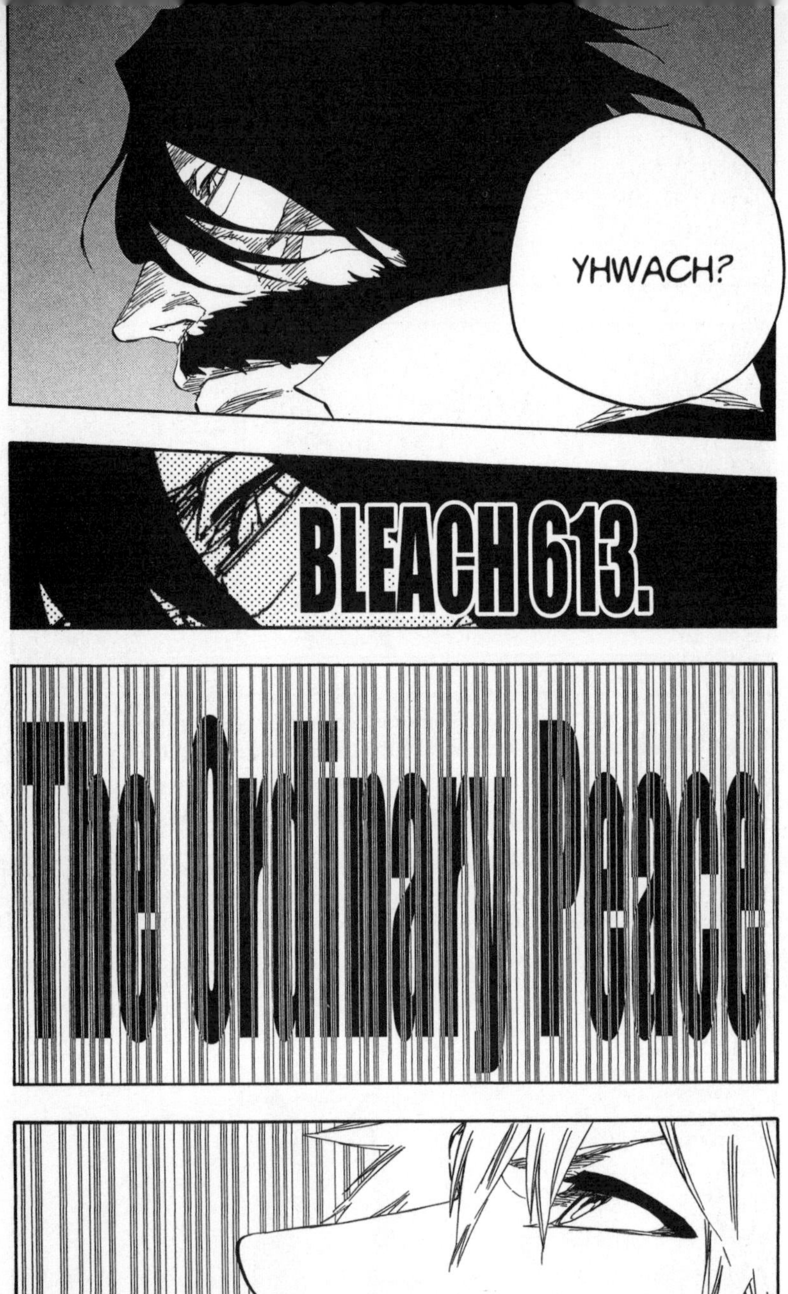
YHWACH?
BLEACH 613.
The Ordinary Peace

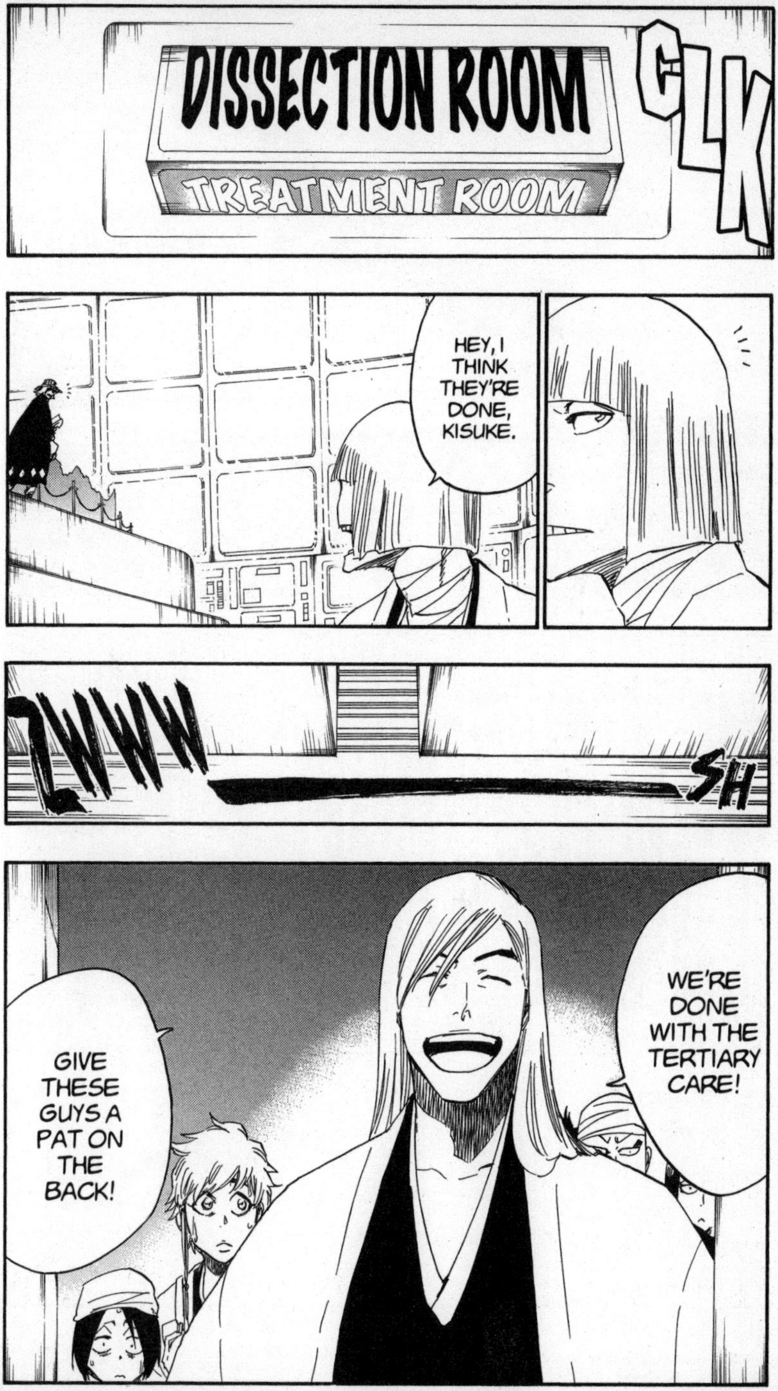
CLK
DISSECTION ROOM
TREATMENT ROOM
HEY, I THINK THEY'RE DONE, KISUKE.
SH
ZWWW
WE'RE DONE WITH THE TERTIARY CARE!
GIVE THESE GUYS A PAT ON THE BACK!

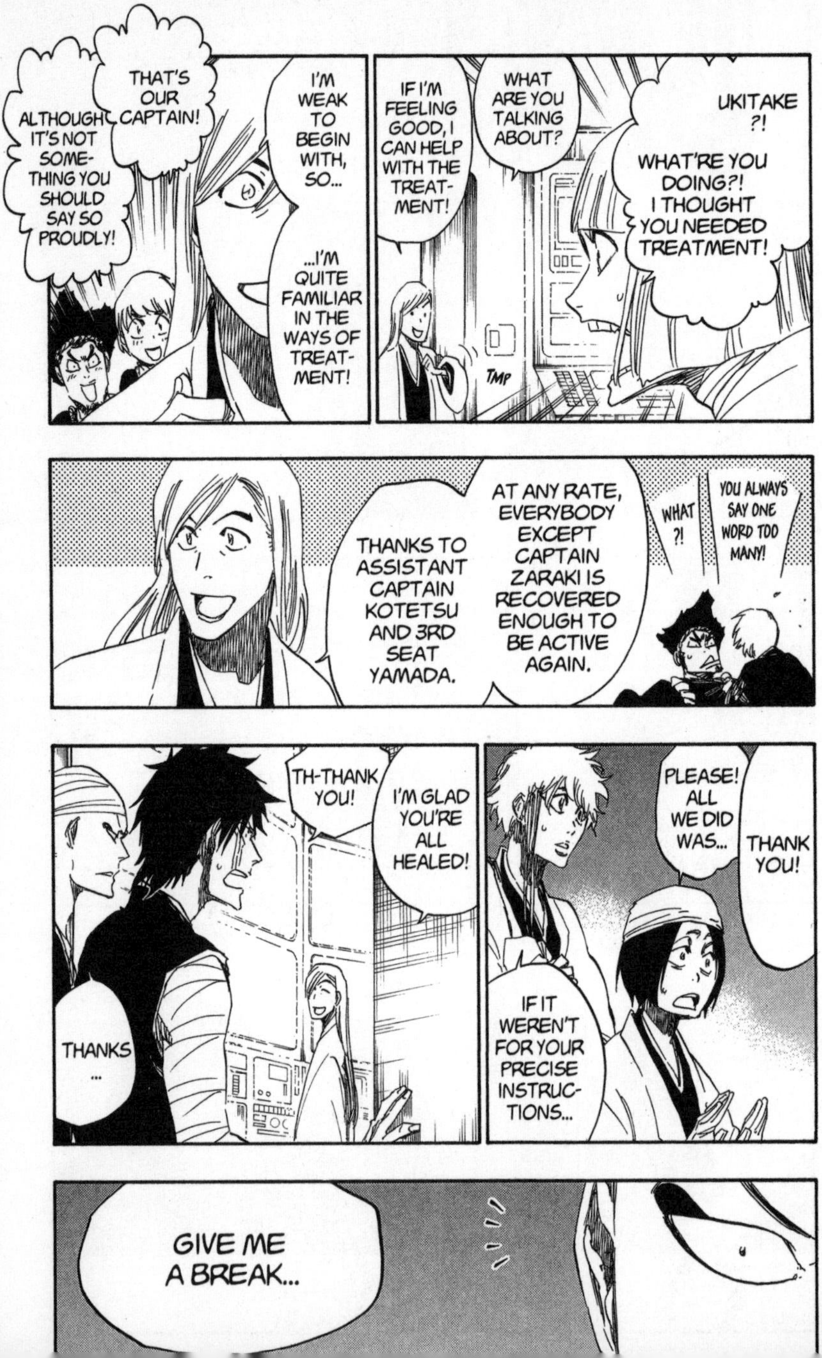
UKITAKE ?!
WHAT'RE YOU DOING?! I THOUGHT YOU NEEDED TREATMENT!
WHAT ARE YOU TALKING ABOUT?
TMP
IF I'M FEELING GOOD, I CAN HELP WITH THE TREATMENT!
I'M WEAK TO BEGIN WITH, SO...
...I'M QUITE FAMILIAR IN THE WAYS OF TREATMENT!
THAT'S OUR CAPTAIN!
ALTHOUGH IT'S NOT SOMETHING YOU SHOULD SAY SO PROUDLY!
YOU ALWAYS SAY ONE WORD TOO MANY!
WHAT ?!
AT ANY RATE, EVERYBODY EXCEPT CAPTAIN ZARAKI IS RECOVERED ENOUGH TO BE ACTIVE AGAIN.
THANKS TO ASSISTANT CAPTAIN KOTETSU AND 3RD SEAT YAMADA.
THANK YOU!
PLEASE! ALL WE DID WAS...
IF IT WEREN'T FOR YOUR PRECISE INSTRUCTIONS...
I'M GLAD YOU'RE ALL HEALED!
TH-THANK YOU!
THANKS ...
GIVE ME A BREAK...

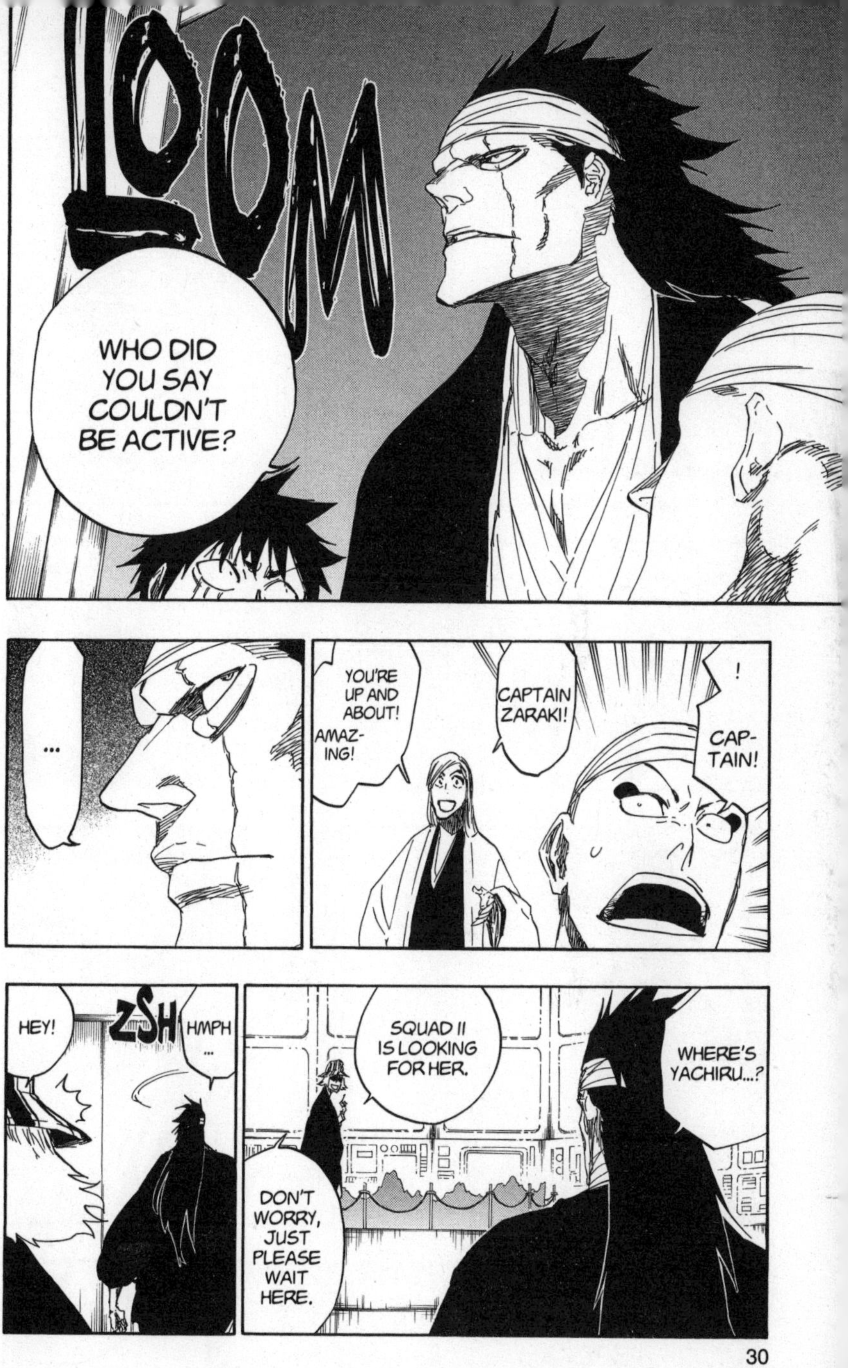
WHO DID YOU SAY COULDN'T BE ACTIVE?
!
CAP-TAIN!
CAPTAIN ZARAKI!
YOU'RE UP AND ABOUT! AMAZ-ING!
...
WHERE'S YACHIRU...?
SQUAD 11 IS LOOKING FOR HER.
DON'T WORRY, JUST PLEASE WAIT HERE.
HMPH ...
ZSH
HEY!

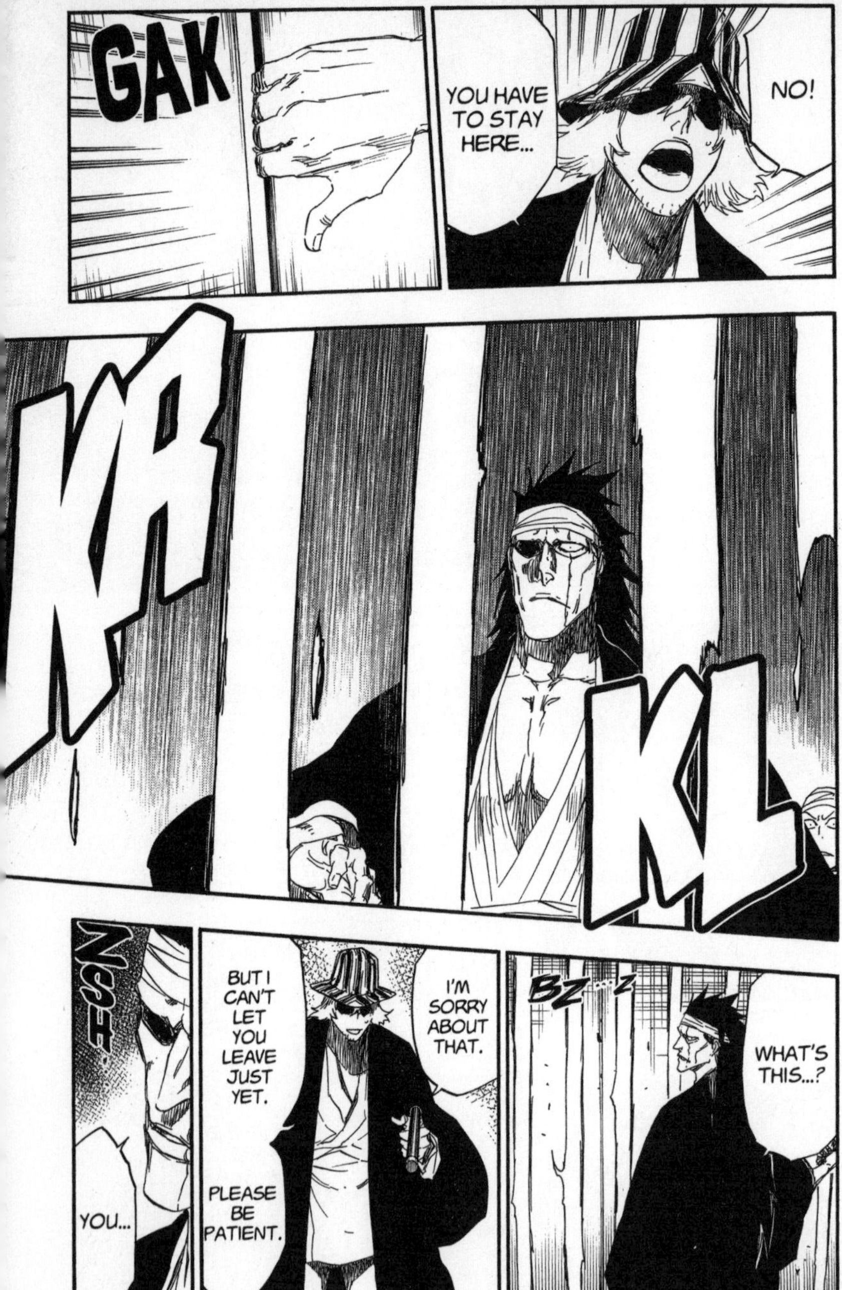
NO!
YOU HAVE TO STAY HERE...
GAK
KA
KL
WHAT'S THIS...?
BZ...Z
I'M SORRY ABOUT THAT.
BUT I CAN'T LET YOU LEAVE JUST YET.
PLEASE BE PATIENT.
ZSH
YOU...

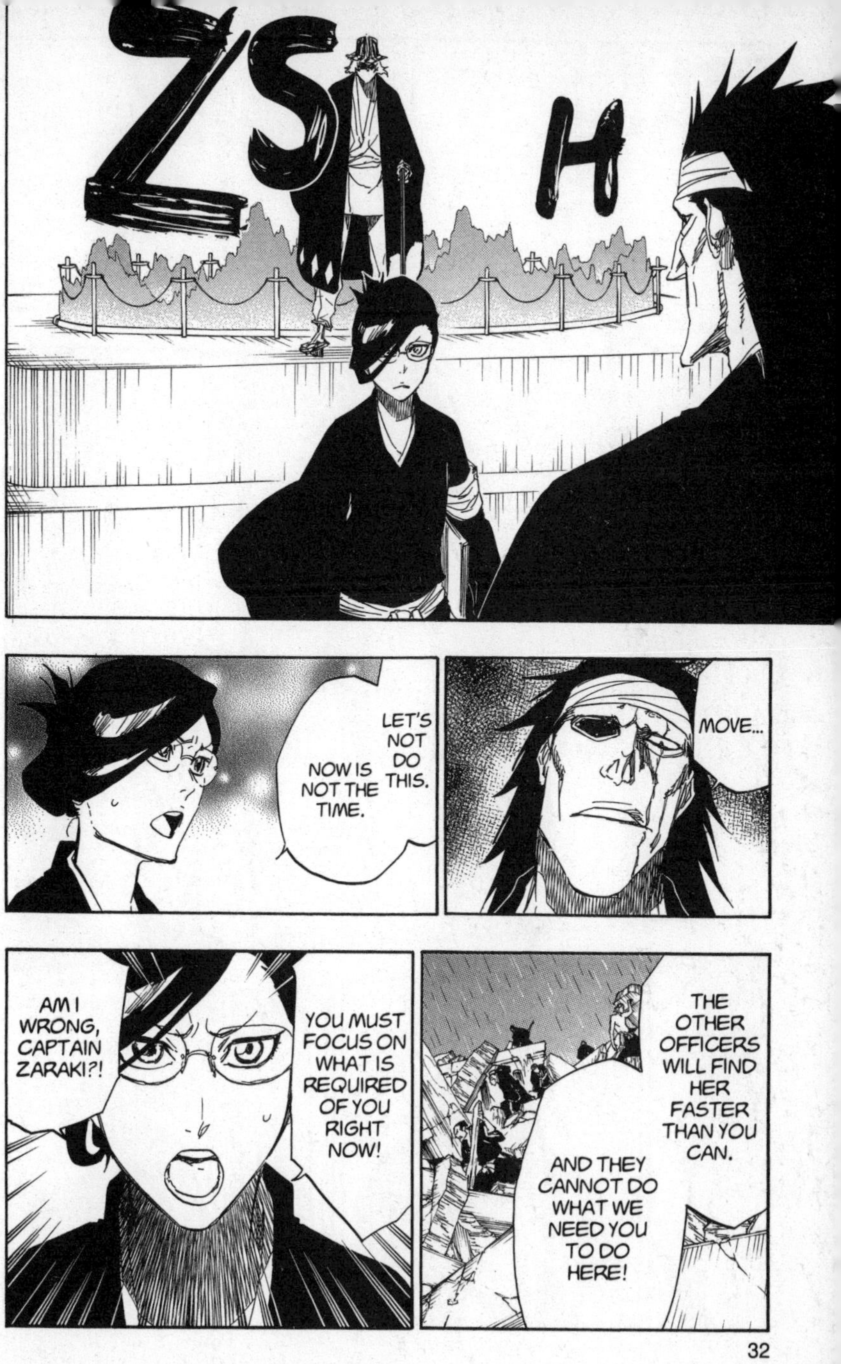
ZSH
MOVE...
LET'S NOT DO THIS.
NOW IS NOT THE TIME.
THE OTHER OFFICERS WILL FIND HER FASTER THAN YOU CAN.
AND THEY CANNOT DO WHAT WE NEED YOU TO DO HERE!
YOU MUST FOCUS ON WHAT IS REQUIRED OF YOU RIGHT NOW!
AM I WRONG, CAPTAIN ZARAKI?!

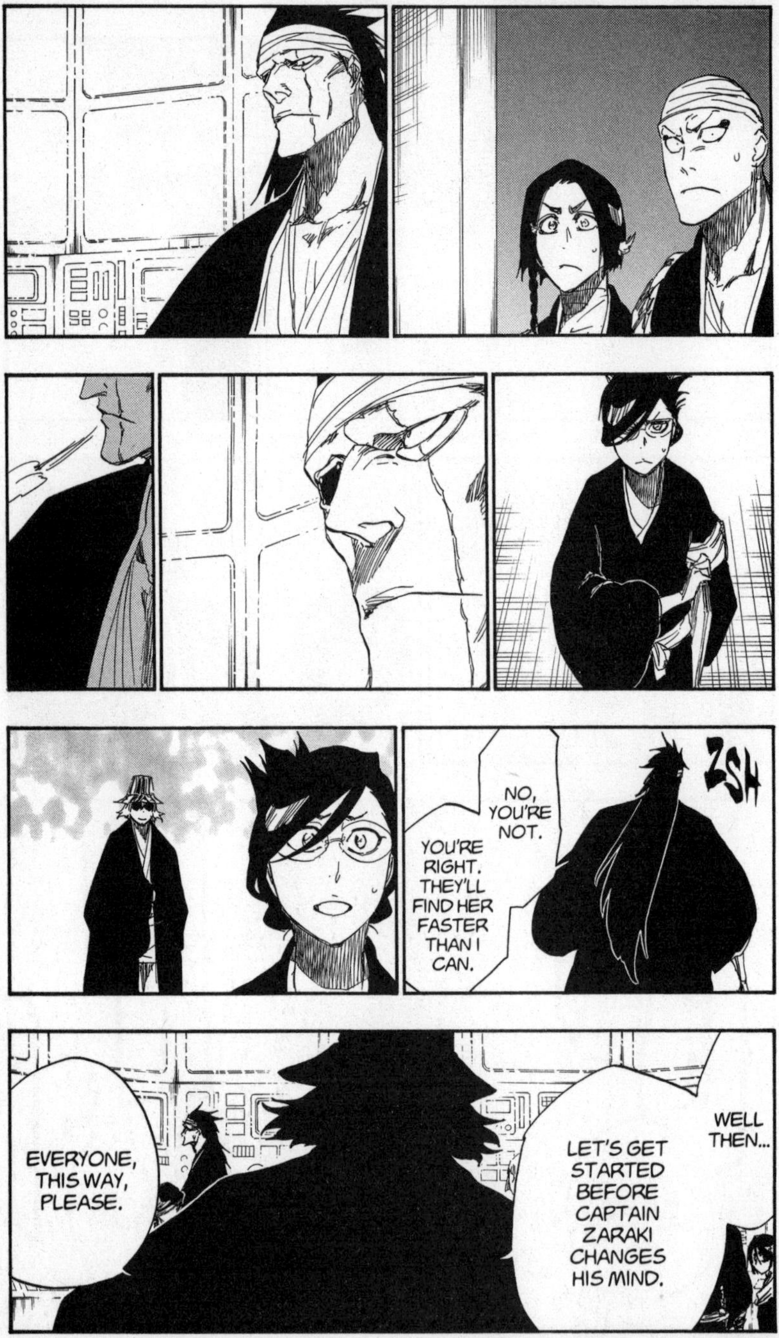
ZSH
NO, YOU'RE NOT.
YOU'RE RIGHT. THEY'LL FIND HER FASTER THAN I CAN.
WELL THEN...
LET'S GET STARTED BEFORE CAPTAIN ZARAKI CHANGES HIS MIND.
EVERYONE, THIS WAY, PLEASE.

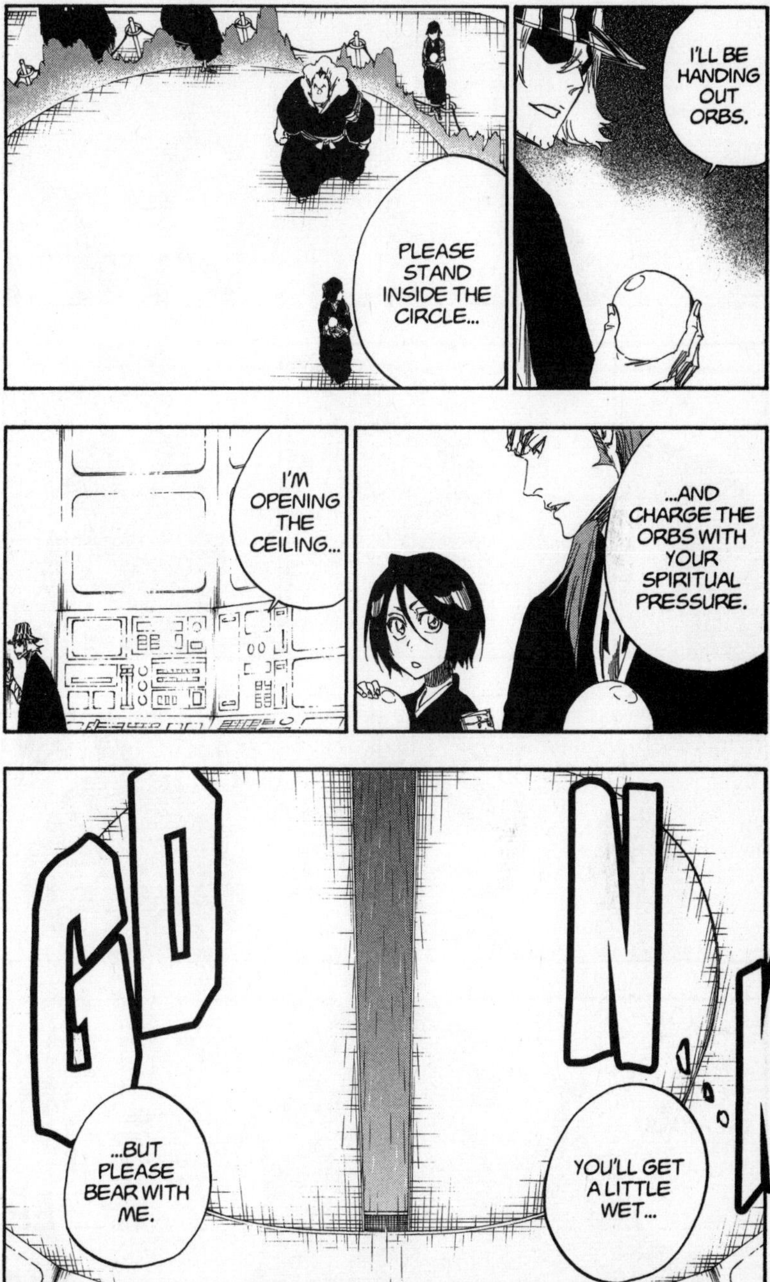
I'LL BE HANDING OUT ORBS.
PLEASE STAND INSIDE THE CIRCLE...
...AND CHARGE THE ORBS WITH YOUR SPIRITUAL PRESSURE.
I'M OPENING THE CEILING...
GO N..K
YOU'LL GET A LITTLE WET...
...BUT PLEASE BEAR WITH ME.

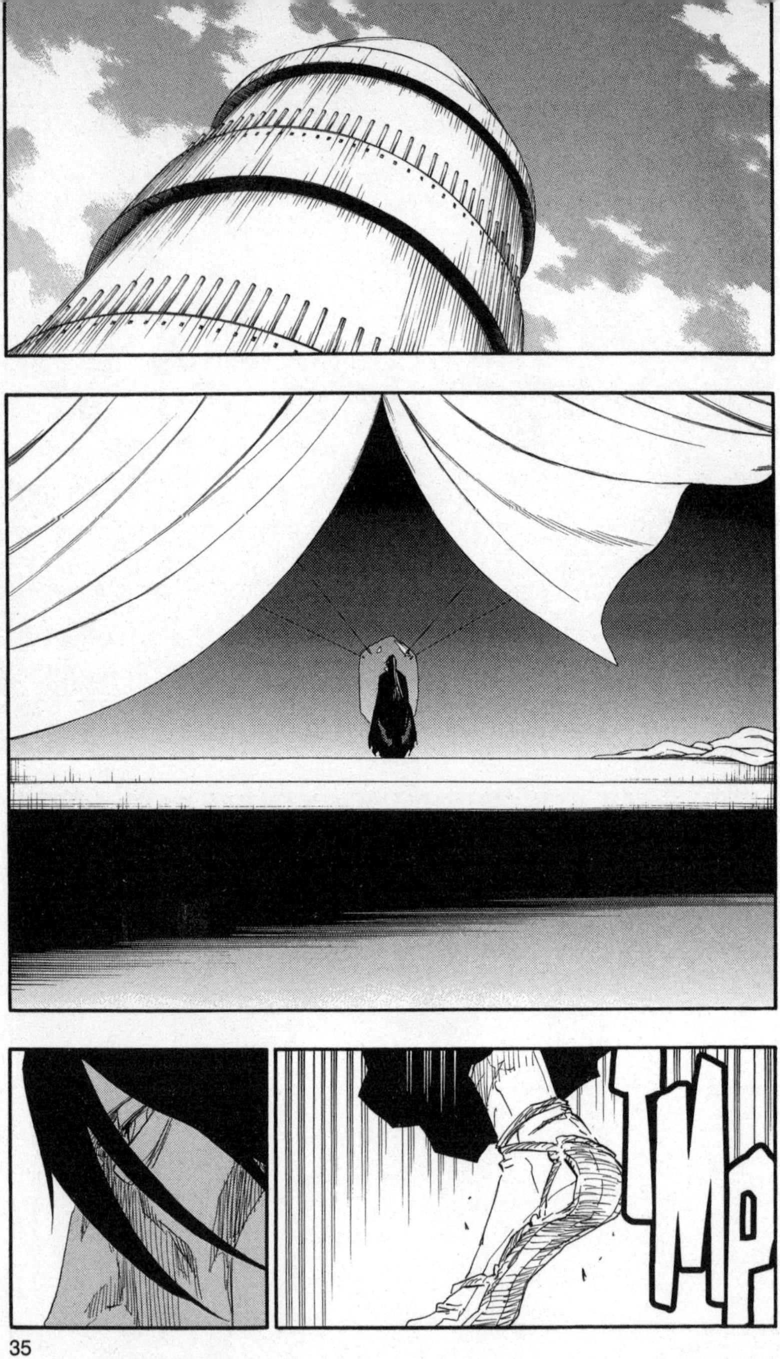
TMP

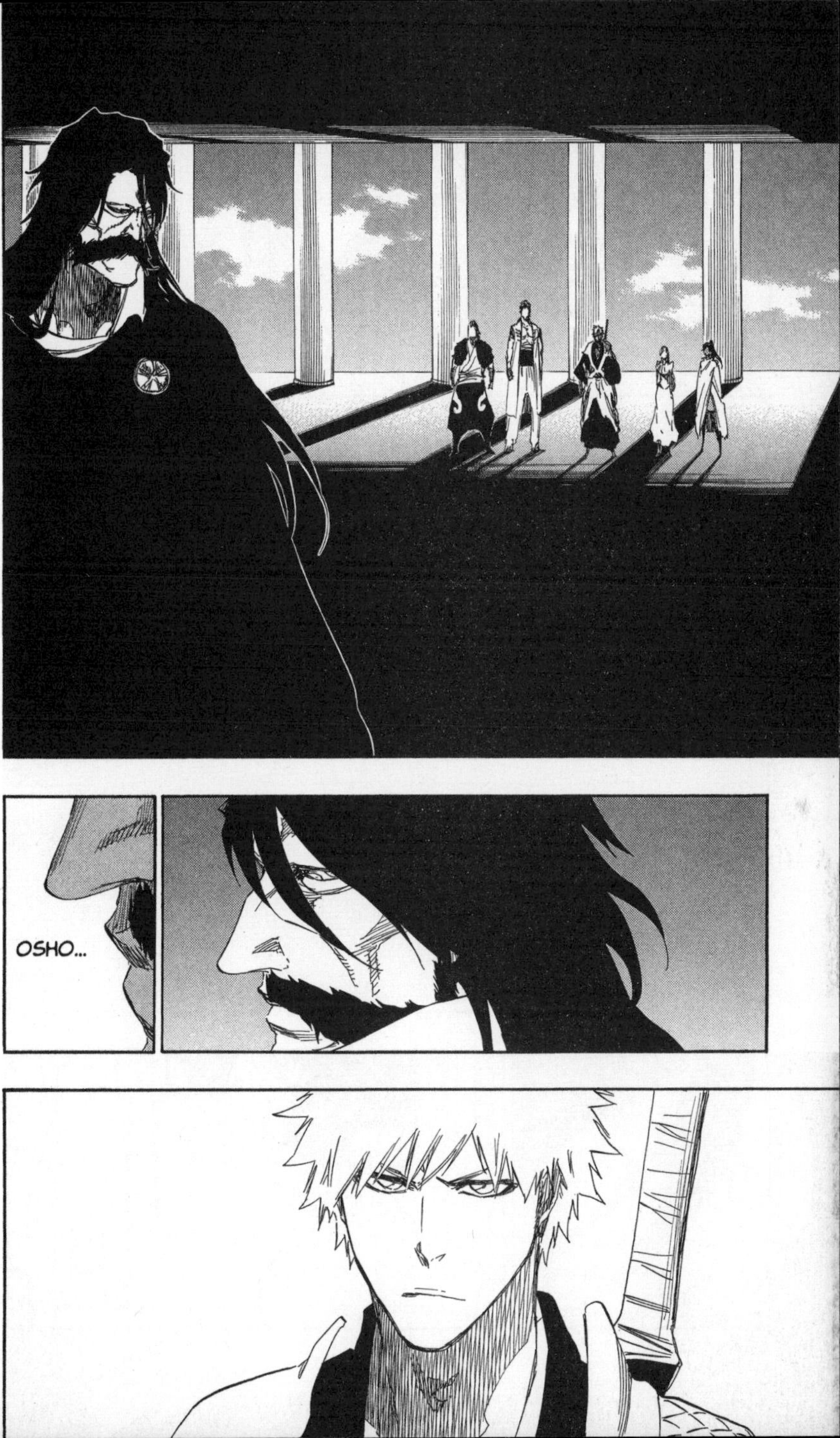
OSHO...

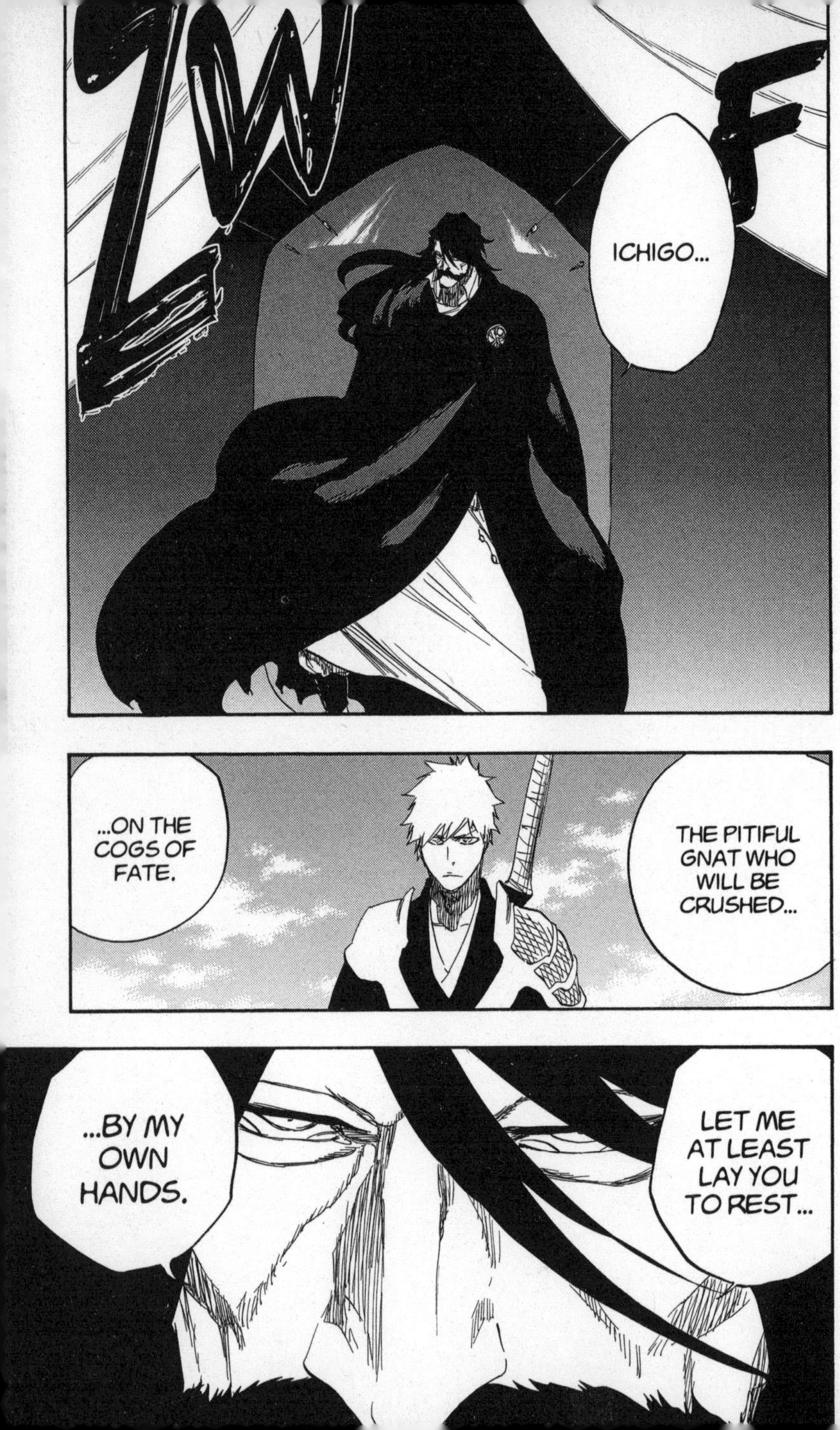
ZOWF
ICHIGO...
THE PITIFUL GNAT WHO WILL BE CRUSHED...
...ON THE COGS OF FATE.
LET ME AT LEAST LAY YOU TO REST...
...BY MY OWN HANDS.

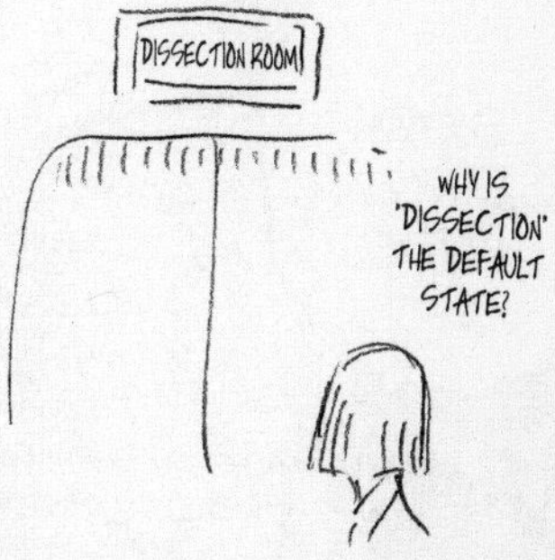
DISSECTION ROOM
WHY IS 'DISSECTION' THE DEFAULT STATE?

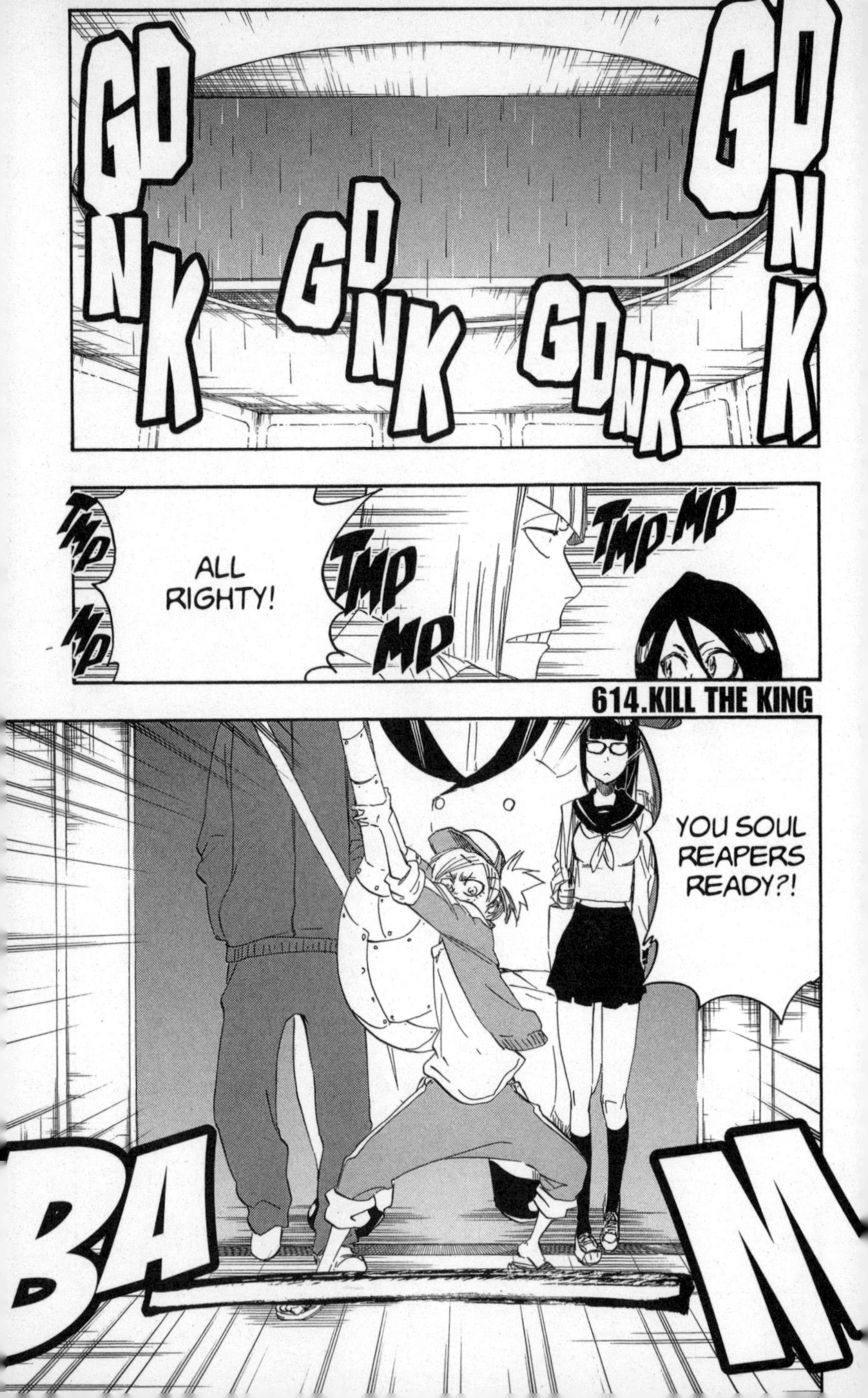
GONK
GONK
GONK
GONK
TMP MP
TMP MP
ALL RIGHTY!
TMP MP
614. KILL THE KING
YOU SOUL REAPERS READY?!
BAM

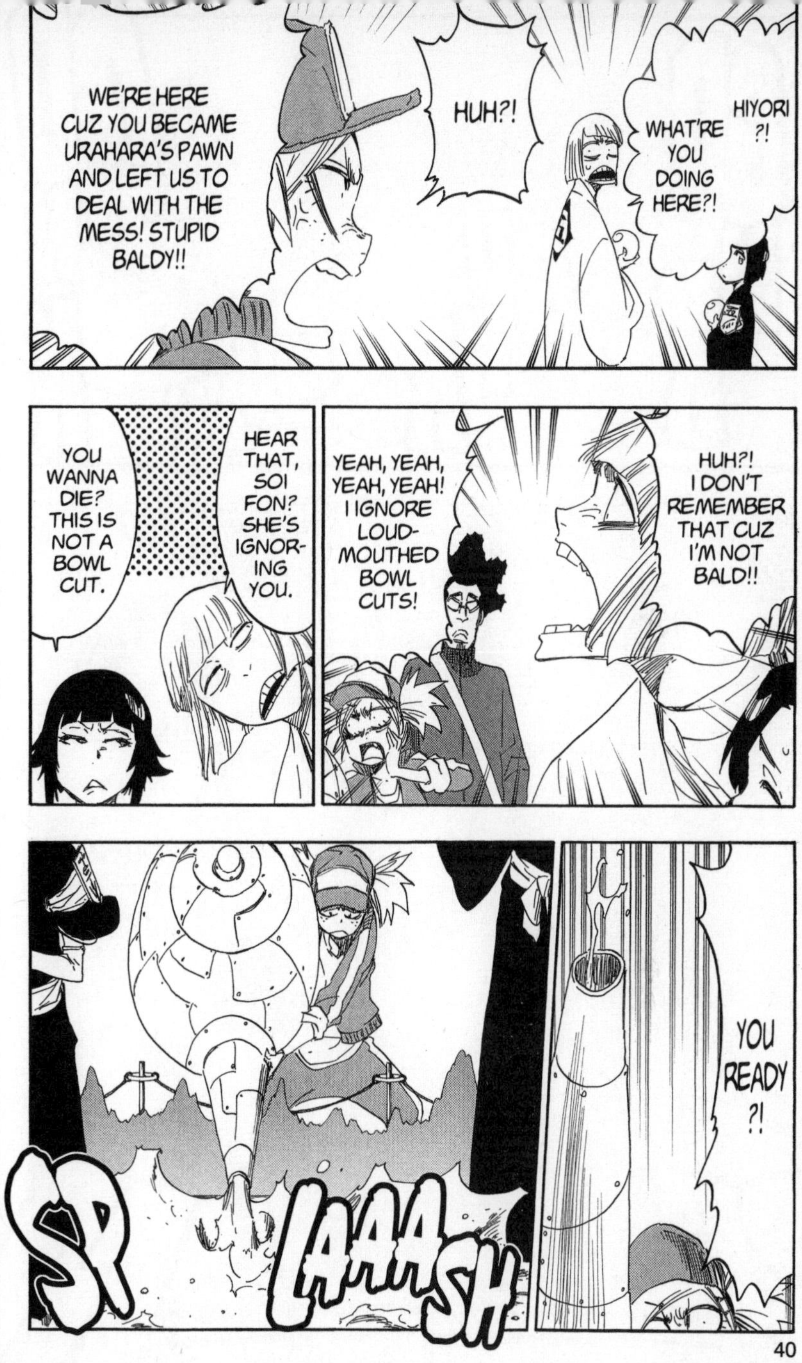
HIYORI ?!
WHAT'RE YOU DOING HERE?!
HUH?!
WE'RE HERE CUZ YOU BECAME URAHARA'S PAWN AND LEFT US TO DEAL WITH THE MESS! STUPID BALDY!!
HUH?! I DON'T REMEMBER THAT CUZ I'M NOT BALD!!
YEAH, YEAH, YEAH, YEAH! I IGNORE LOUD-MOUTHED BOWL CUTS!
HEAR THAT, SOI FON? SHE'S IGNOR-ING YOU.
YOU WANNA DIE? THIS IS NOT A BOWL CUT.
YOU READY ?!
SPLAAASH

READ THIS WAY

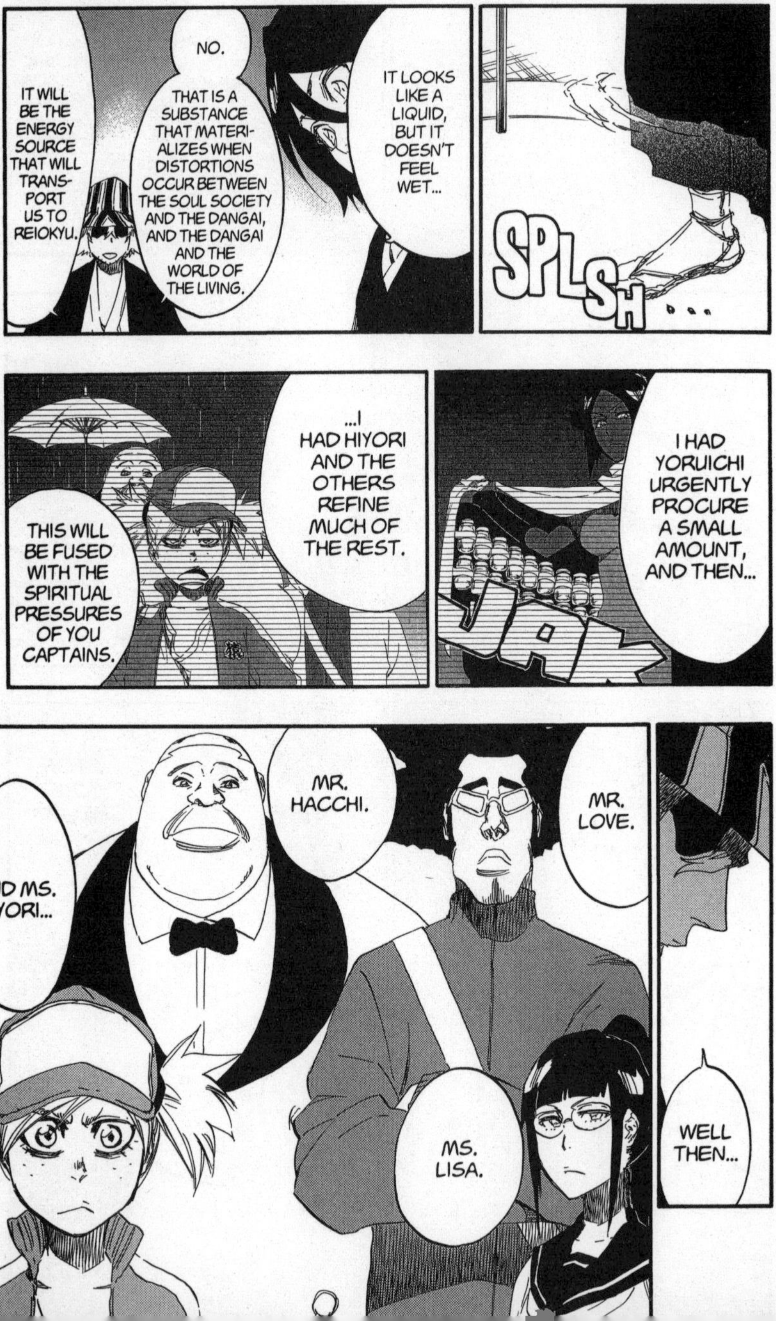
SPLSH...
IT LOOKS LIKE A LIQUID, BUT IT DOESN'T FEEL WET...
NO.
THAT IS A SUBSTANCE THAT MATERIALIZES WHEN DISTORTIONS OCCUR BETWEEN THE SOUL SOCIETY AND THE DANGAI, AND THE DANGAI AND THE WORLD OF THE LIVING.
IT WILL BE THE ENERGY SOURCE THAT WILL TRANSPORT US TO REIOKYU.
I HAD YORUICHI URGENTLY PROCURE A SMALL AMOUNT, AND THEN...
...I HAD HIYORI AND THE OTHERS REFINE MUCH OF THE REST.
THIS WILL BE FUSED WITH THE SPIRITUAL PRESSURES OF YOU CAPTAINS.
WELL THEN...
MR. LOVE.
MR. HACCHI.
MS. LISA.
AND MS. HIYORI...

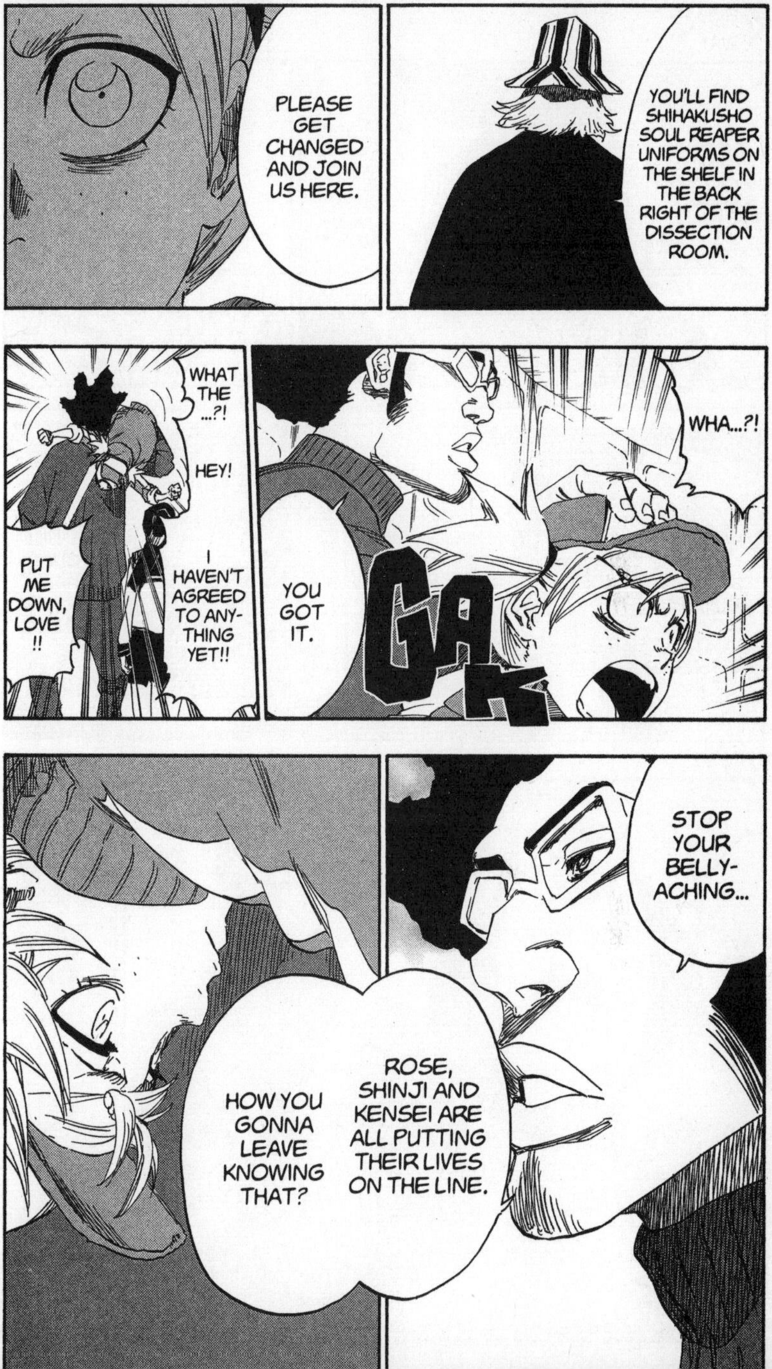
YOU'LL FIND SHIHAKUSHO SOUL REAPER UNIFORMS ON THE SHELF IN THE BACK RIGHT OF THE DISSECTION ROOM.
PLEASE GET CHANGED AND JOIN US HERE.
WHA...?!
GAK
YOU GOT IT.
WHAT THE ...?!
HEY!
I HAVEN'T AGREED TO ANY-THING YET!!
PUT ME DOWN, LOVE !!
STOP YOUR BELLY-ACHING...
ROSE, SHINJI AND KENSEI ARE ALL PUTTING THEIR LIVES ON THE LINE.
HOW YOU GONNA LEAVE KNOWING THAT?

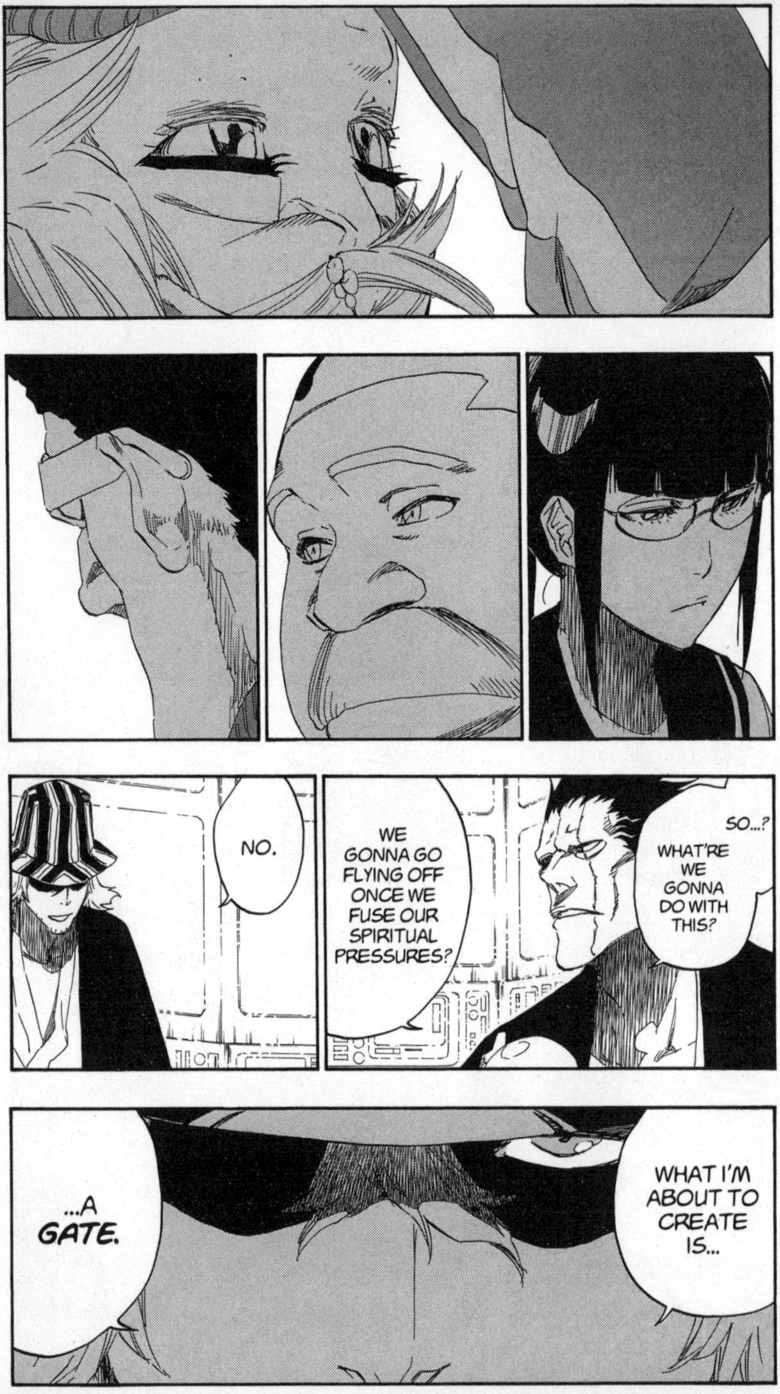
SO...?
WHAT'RE WE GONNA DO WITH THIS?
WE GONNA GO FLYING OFF ONCE WE FUSE OUR SPIRITUAL PRESSURES?
NO.
WHAT I'M ABOUT TO CREATE IS...
...A GATE.

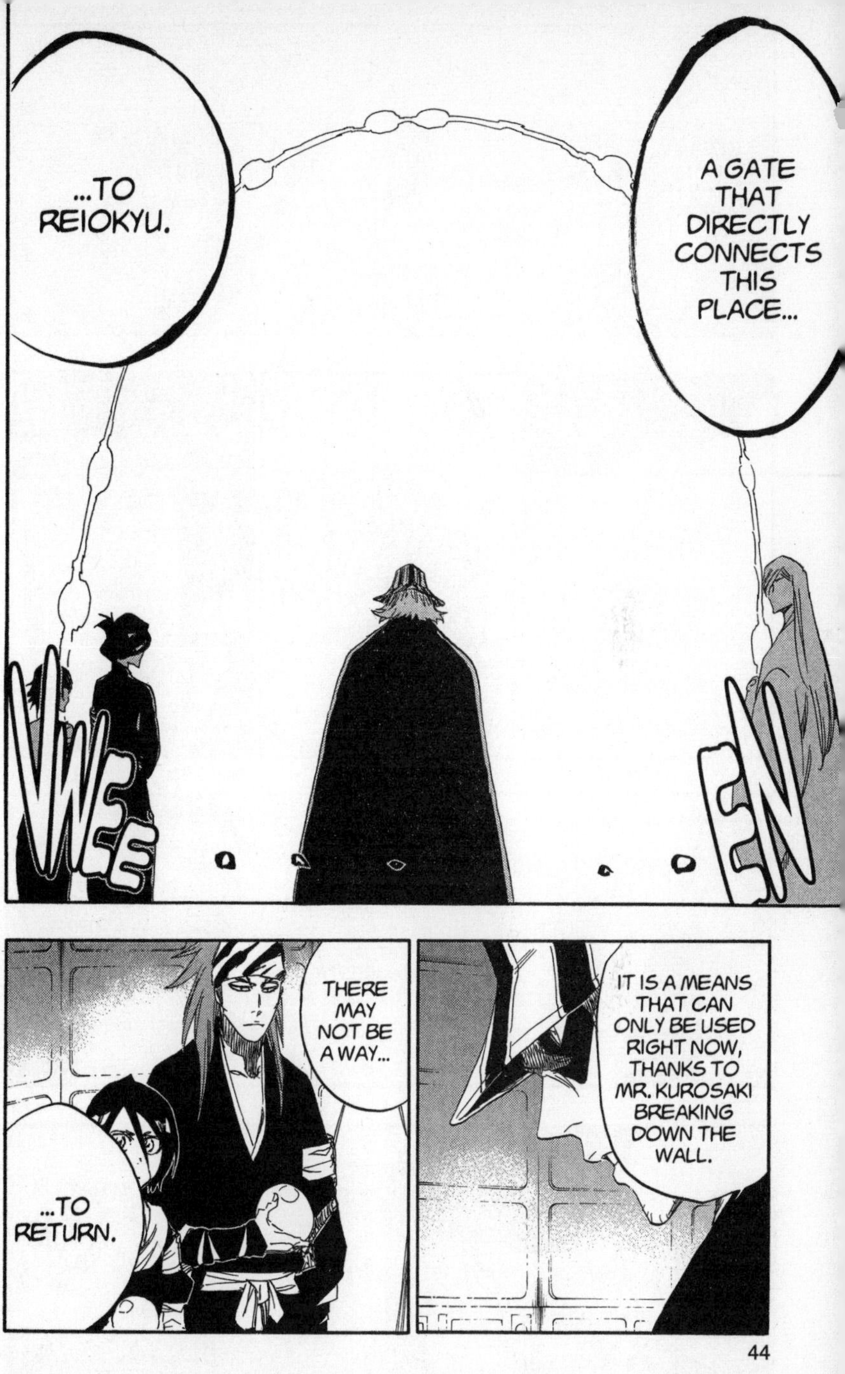
A GATE THAT DIRECTLY CONNECTS THIS PLACE...
...TO REIOKYU.
WEE
EN
IT IS A MEANS THAT CAN ONLY BE USED RIGHT NOW, THANKS TO MR. KUROSAKI BREAKING DOWN THE WALL.
THERE MAY NOT BE A WAY...
...TO RETURN.

READ THIS WAY

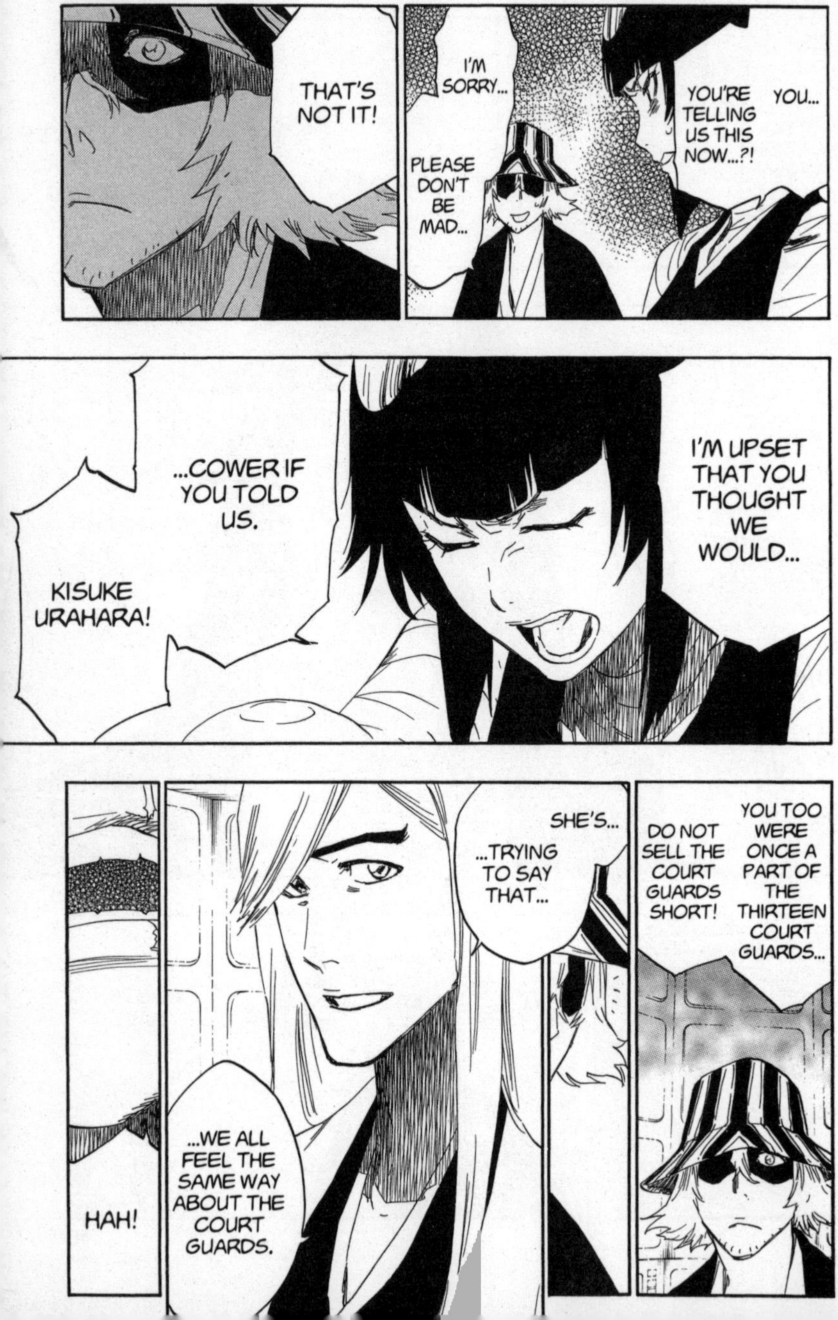
YOU...
YOU'RE TELLING US THIS NOW...?!
I'M SORRY...
PLEASE DON'T BE MAD...
THAT'S NOT IT!
I'M UPSET THAT YOU THOUGHT WE WOULD...
...COWER IF YOU TOLD US.
KISUKE URAHARA!
YOU TOO WERE ONCE A PART OF THE THIRTEEN COURT GUARDS...
DO NOT SELL THE COURT GUARDS SHORT!
SHE'S...
...TRYING TO SAY THAT...
...WE ALL FEEL THE SAME WAY ABOUT THE COURT GUARDS.
HAH!

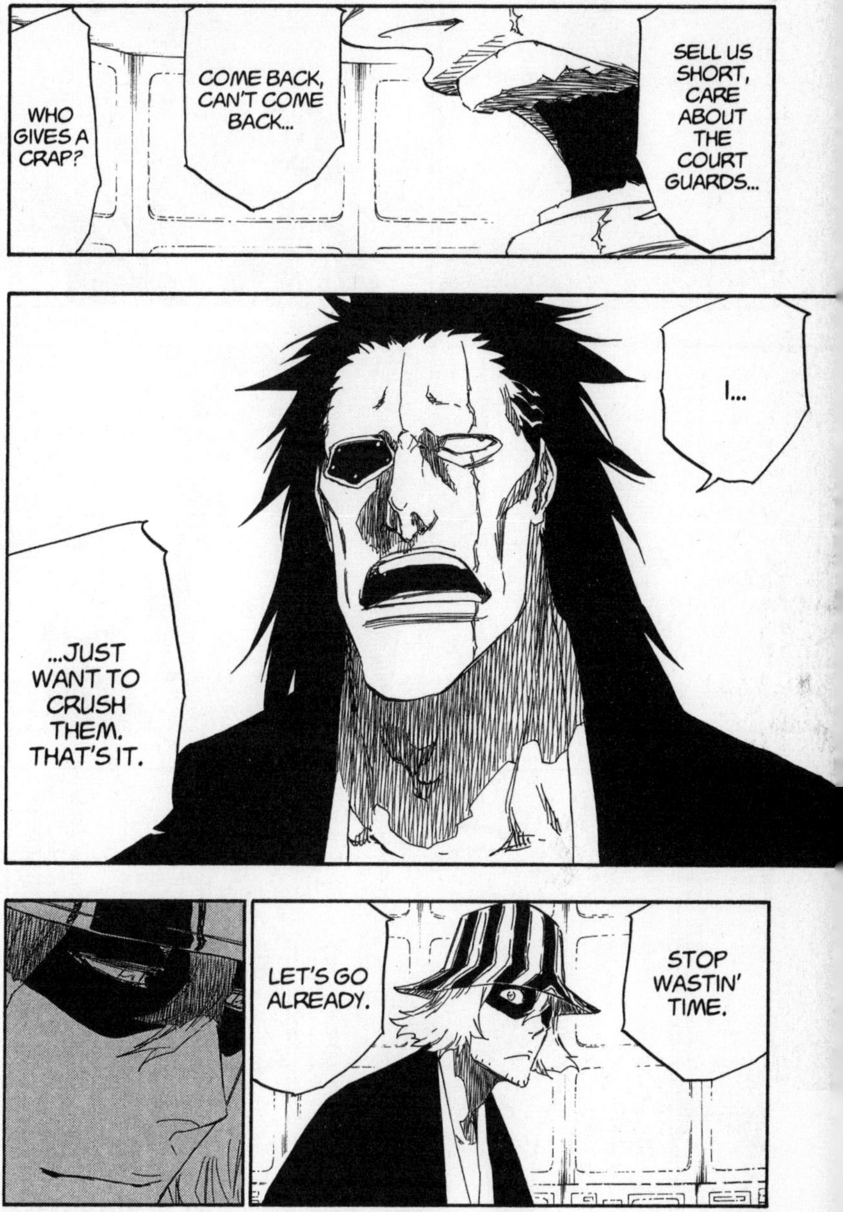
SELL US SHORT, CARE ABOUT THE COURT GUARDS...
COME BACK, CAN'T COME BACK...
WHO GIVES A CRAP?
I...
...JUST WANT TO CRUSH THEM. THAT'S IT.
STOP WASTIN' TIME.
LET'S GO ALREADY.

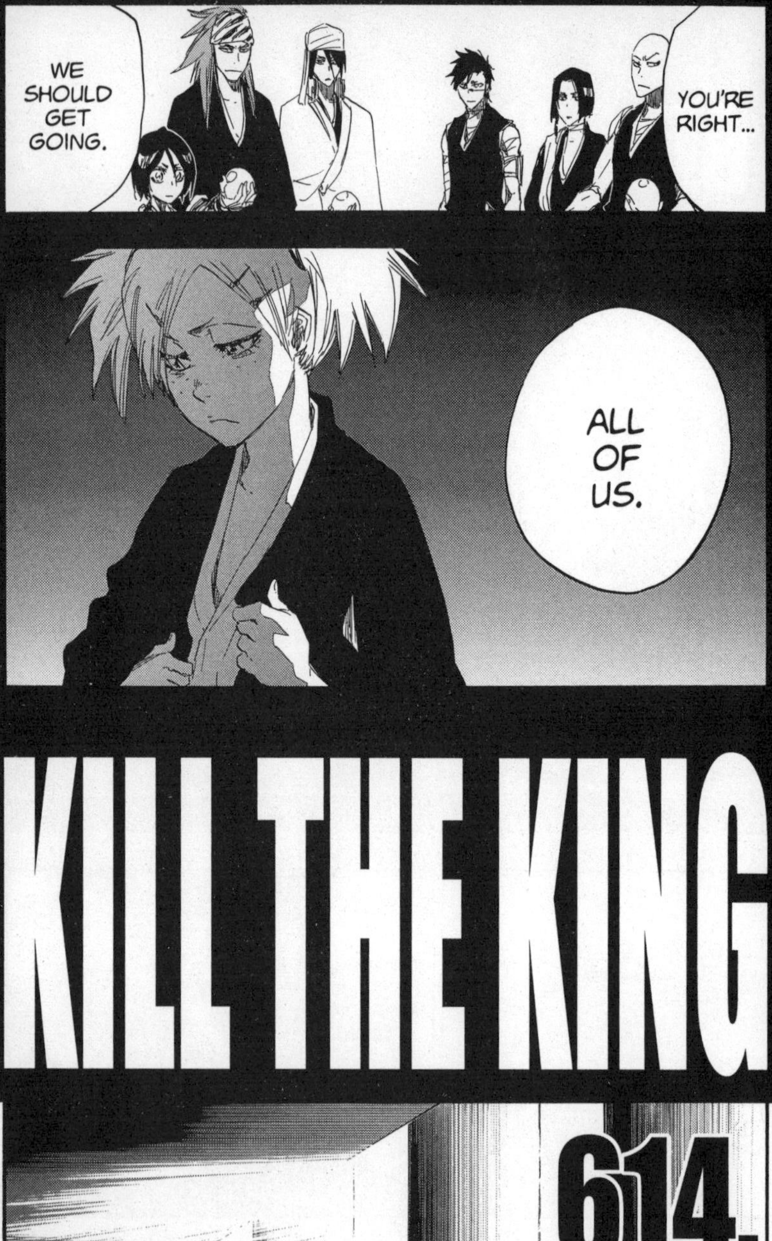
YOU'RE RIGHT...
WE SHOULD GET GOING.
ALL OF US.
KILL THE KING
614.

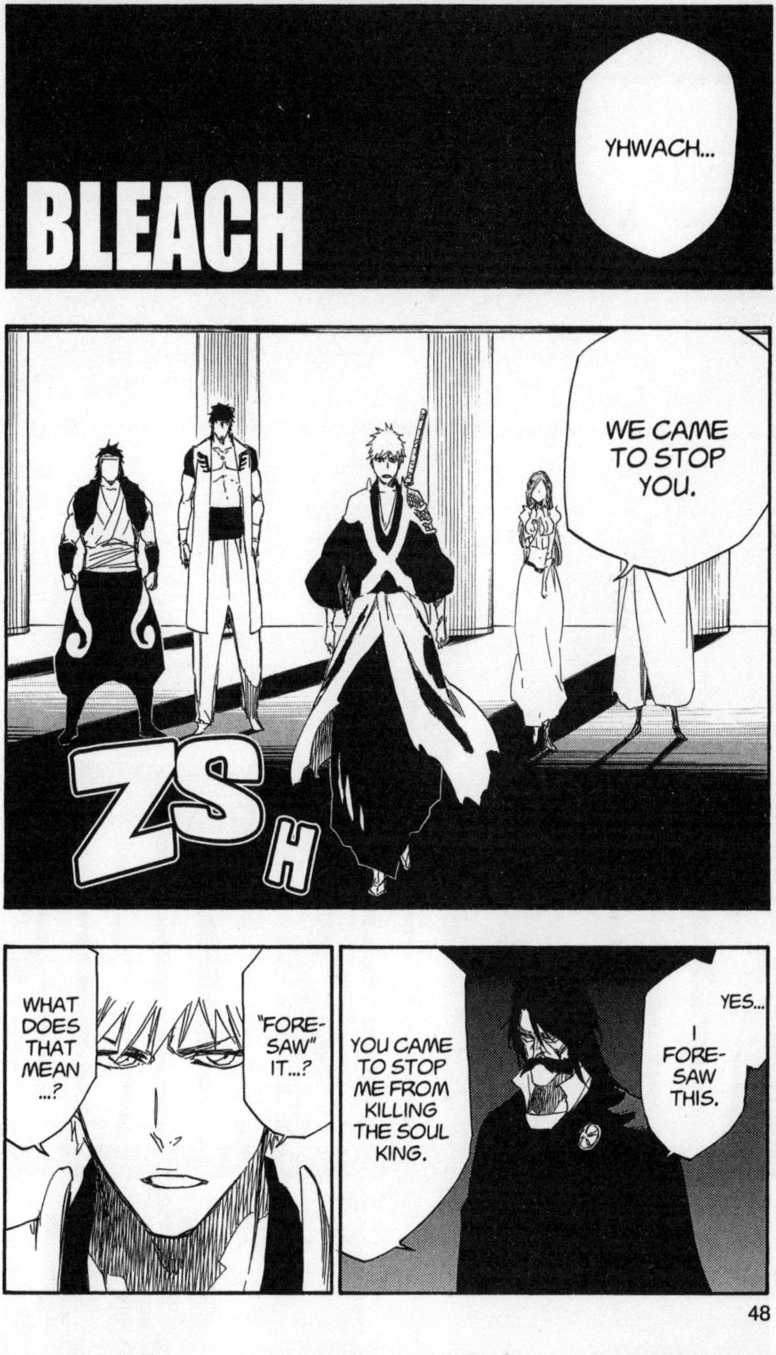

BLEACH
YHWACH...
WE CAME TO STOP YOU.
ZSH
YES...
I FORESAW THIS.
YOU CAME TO STOP ME FROM KILLING THE SOUL KING.
"FORESAW" IT...?
WHAT DOES THAT MEAN...?

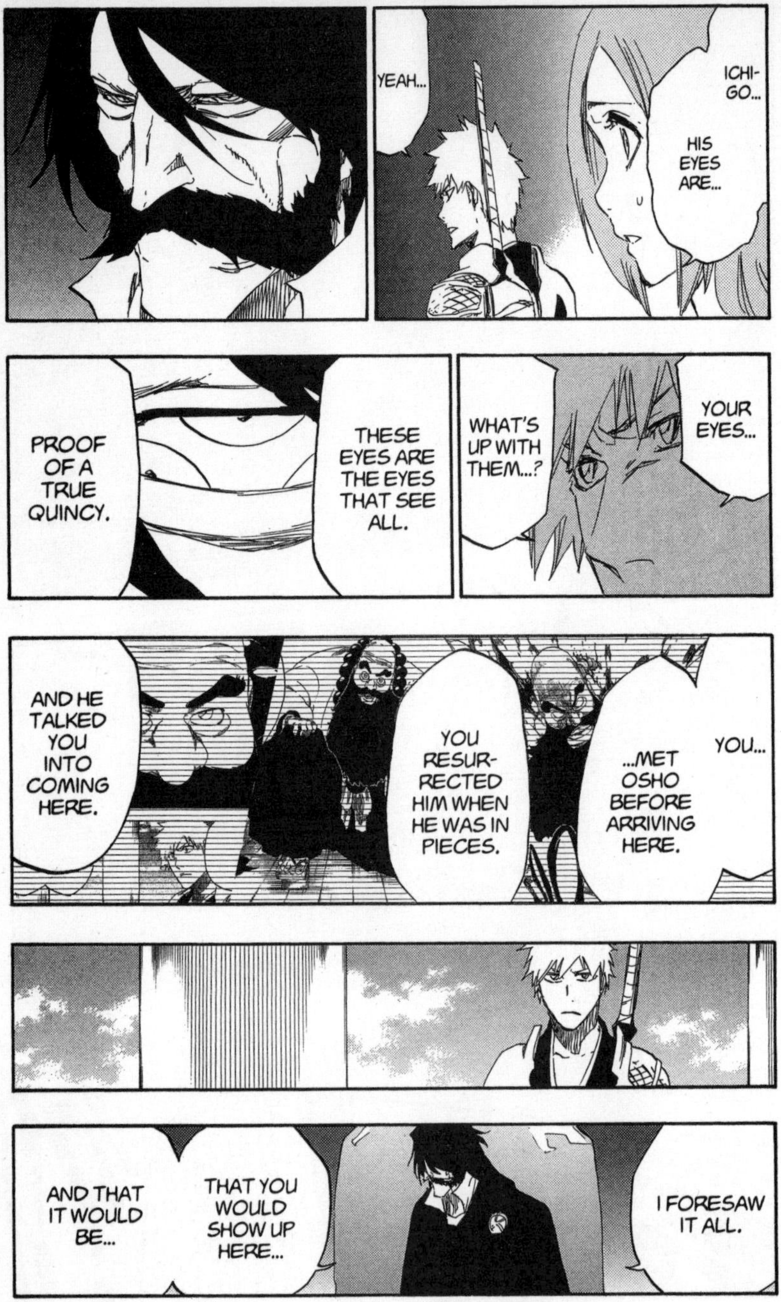
ICHI-GO...
HIS EYES ARE...
YEAH...
YOUR EYES...
WHAT'S UP WITH THEM...?
THESE EYES ARE THE EYES THAT SEE ALL.
PROOF OF A TRUE QUINCY.
YOU...
...MET OSHO BEFORE ARRIVING HERE.
YOU RESUR-RECTED HIM WHEN HE WAS IN PIECES.
AND HE TALKED YOU INTO COMING HERE.
I FORESAW IT ALL.
THAT YOU WOULD SHOW UP HERE...
AND THAT IT WOULD BE...

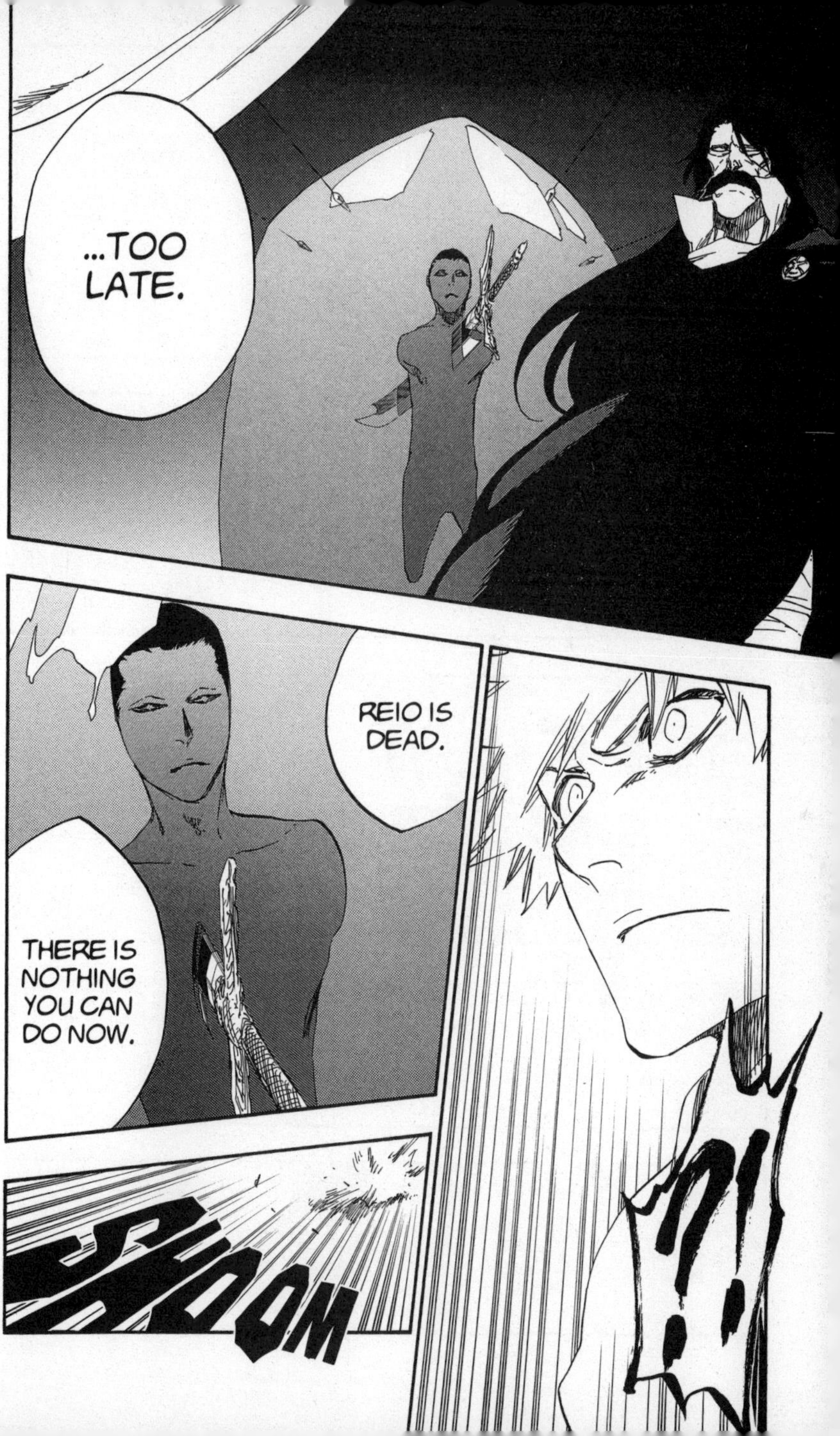
...TOO LATE.
?!
REIO IS DEAD.
THERE IS NOTHING YOU CAN DO NOW.
SHOOM

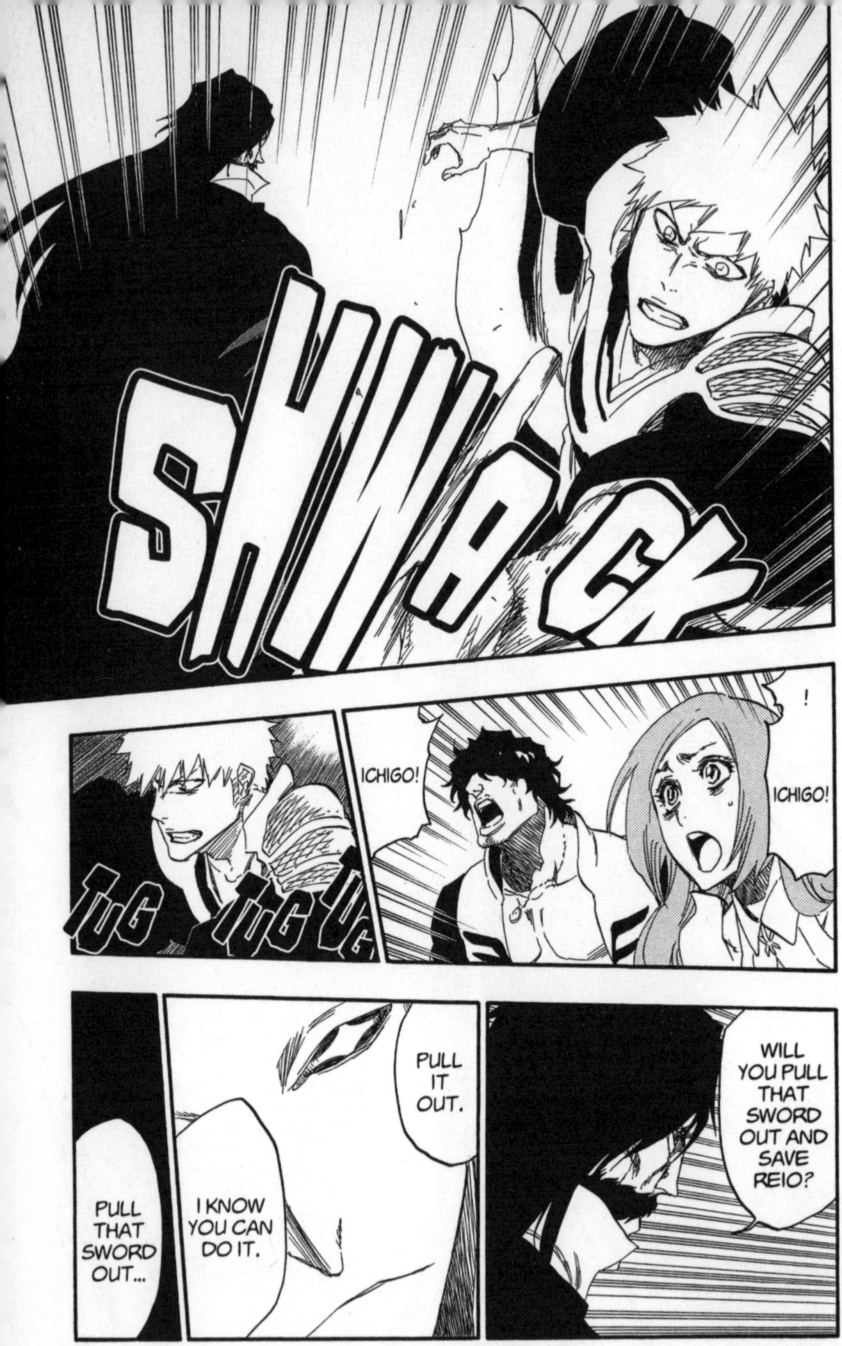
SHWACK
!
ICHIGO!
ICHIGO!
TUG
TUG
WILL YOU PULL THAT SWORD OUT AND SAVE REIO?
PULL IT OUT.
I KNOW YOU CAN DO IT.
PULL THAT SWORD OUT...

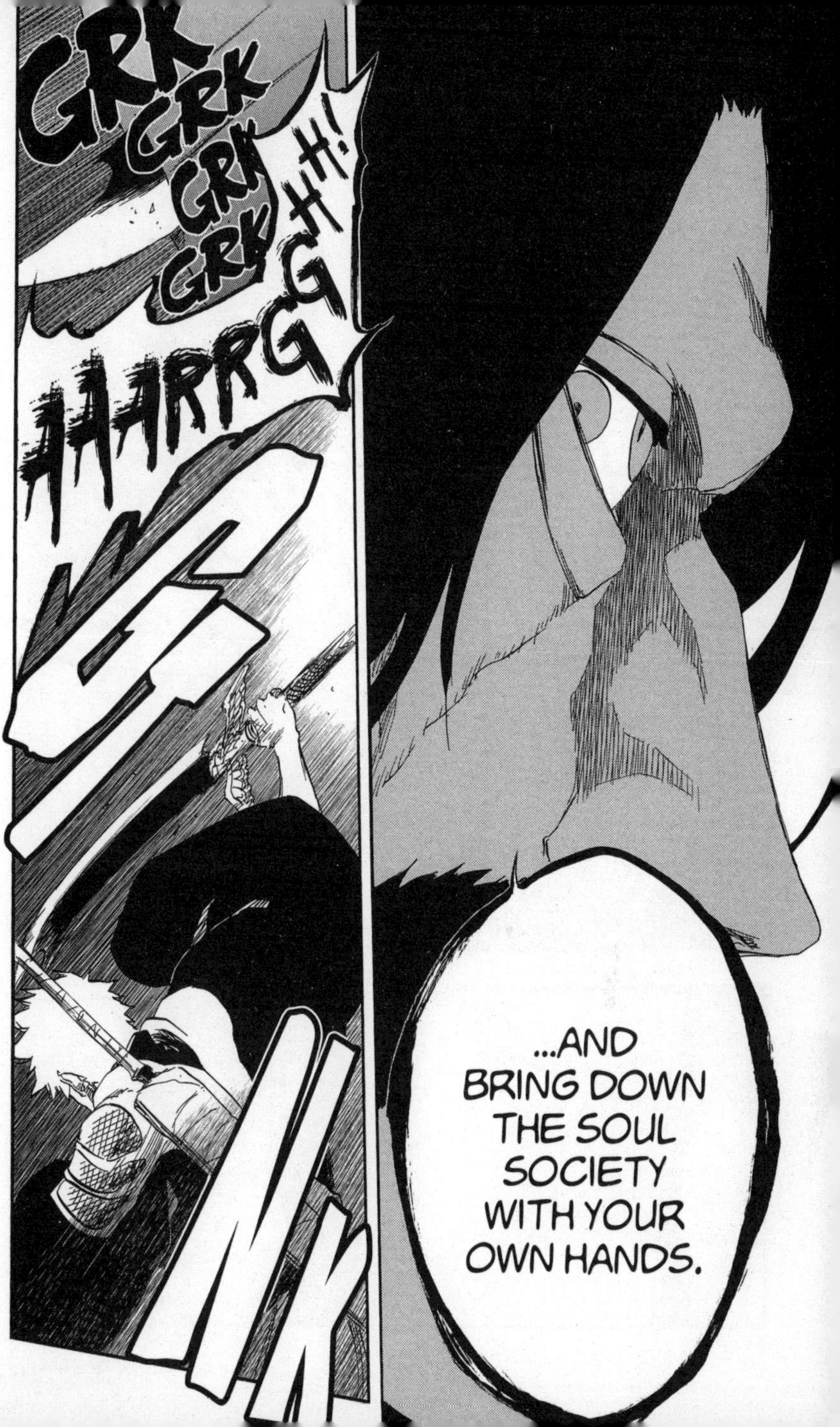
...AND BRING DOWN THE SOUL SOCIETY WITH YOUR OWN HANDS.
GRK GRK GRK GRK
AAARRGGHH!

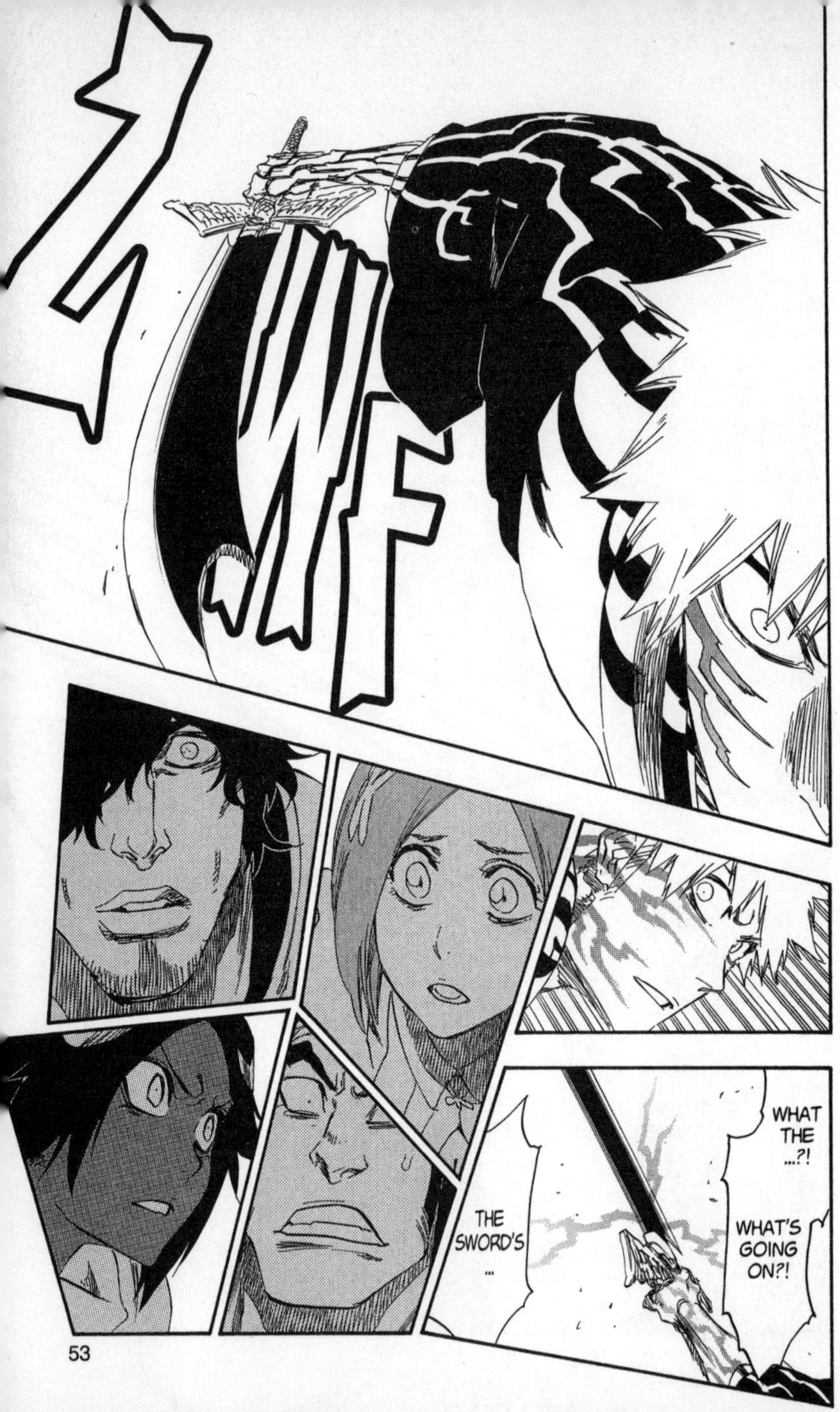
WHAT THE ...?!
WHAT'S GOING ON?!
THE SWORD'S ...

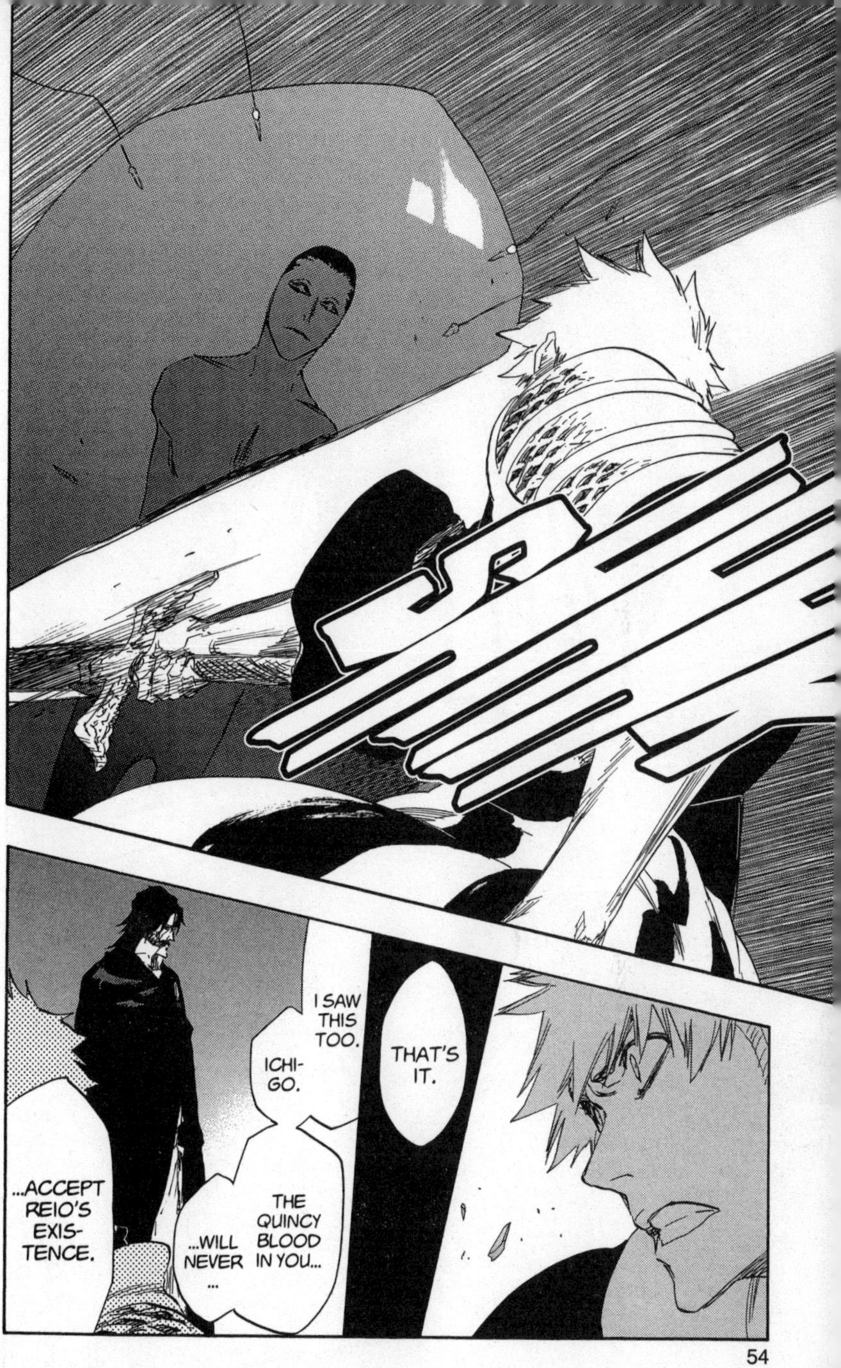
THAT'S IT.
I SAW THIS TOO.
ICHI-GO.
THE QUINCY BLOOD IN YOU...
...WILL NEVER ...
...ACCEPT REIO'S EXIS-TENCE.

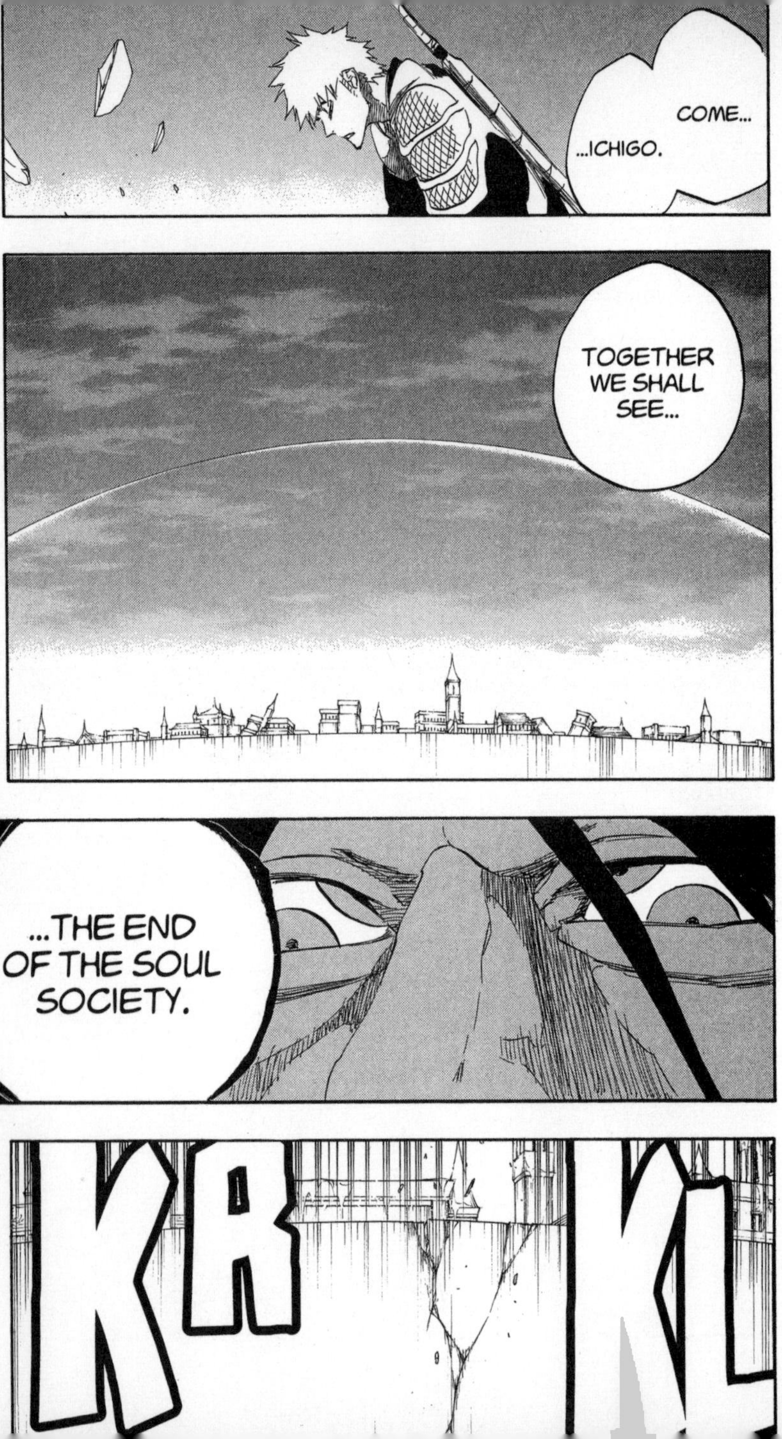
COME... ...ICHIGO.
TOGETHER WE SHALL SEE...
...THE END OF THE SOUL SOCIETY.
KR KL

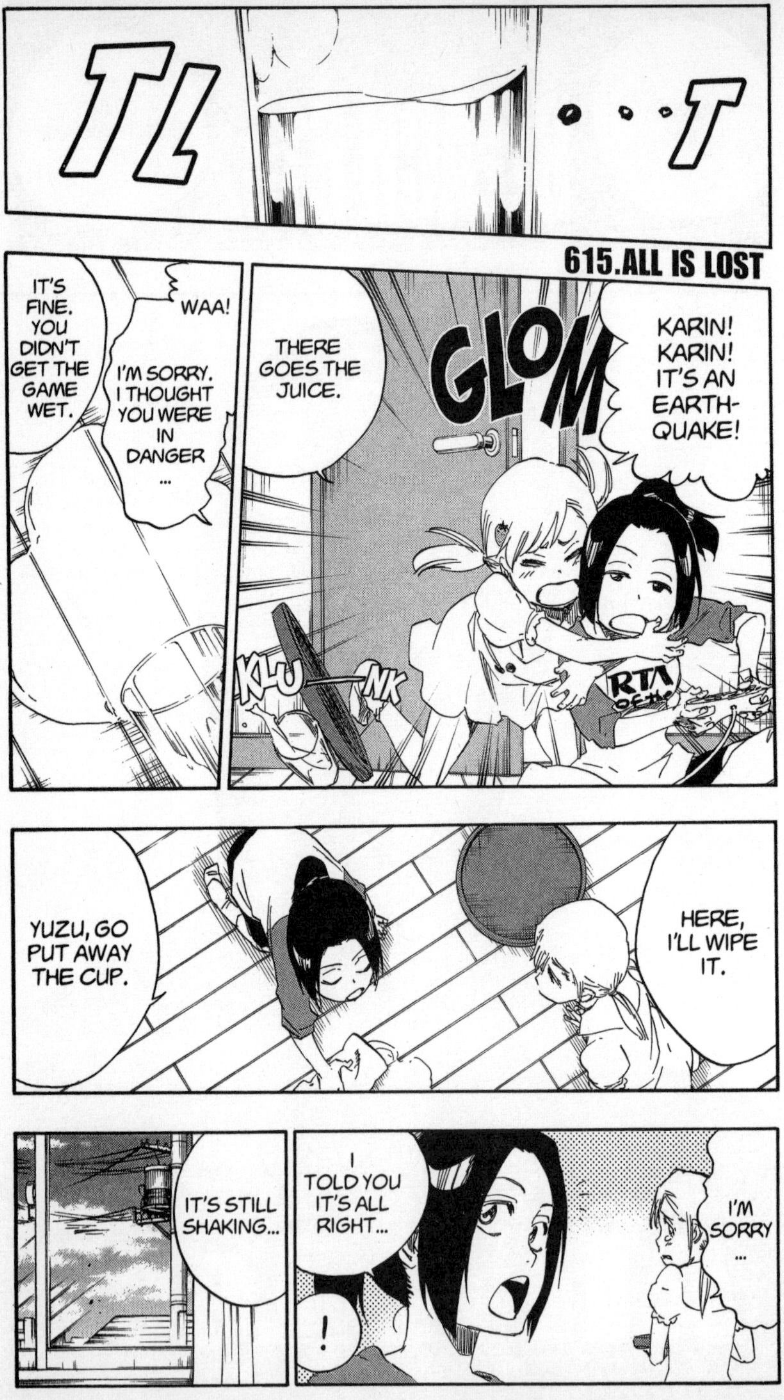
TL...T
615.ALL IS LOST
KARIN! KARIN! IT'S AN EARTH-QUAKE!
GLOM
THERE GOES THE JUICE.
KLU—NK
WAA!
I'M SORRY. I THOUGHT YOU WERE IN DANGER ...
IT'S FINE. YOU DIDN'T GET THE GAME WET.
HERE, I'LL WIPE IT.
YUZU, GO PUT AWAY THE CUP.
I'M SORRY ...
I TOLD YOU IT'S ALL RIGHT...
!
IT'S STILL SHAKING...

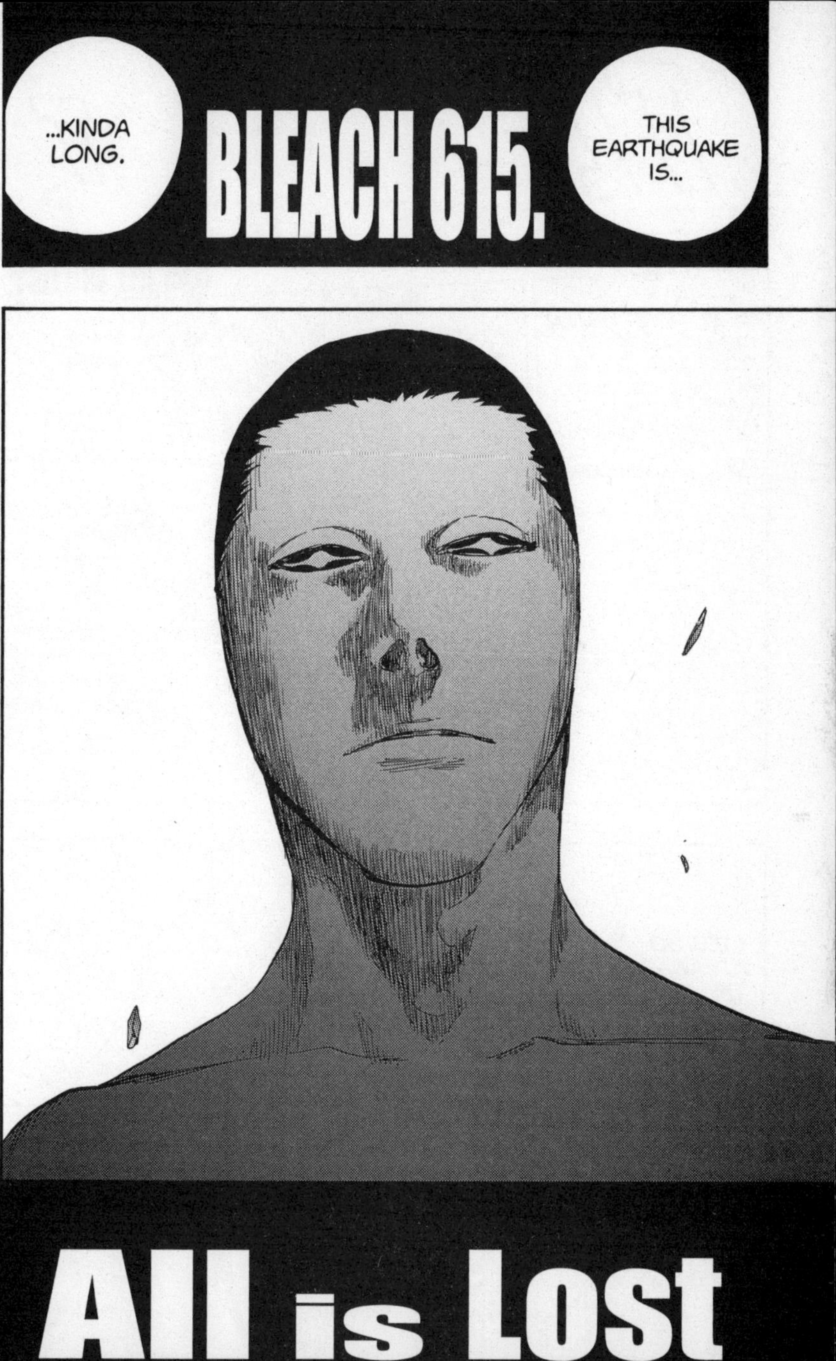
THIS EARTHQUAKE IS...
...KINDA LONG.
BLEACH 615.
All is Lost

READ THIS WAY

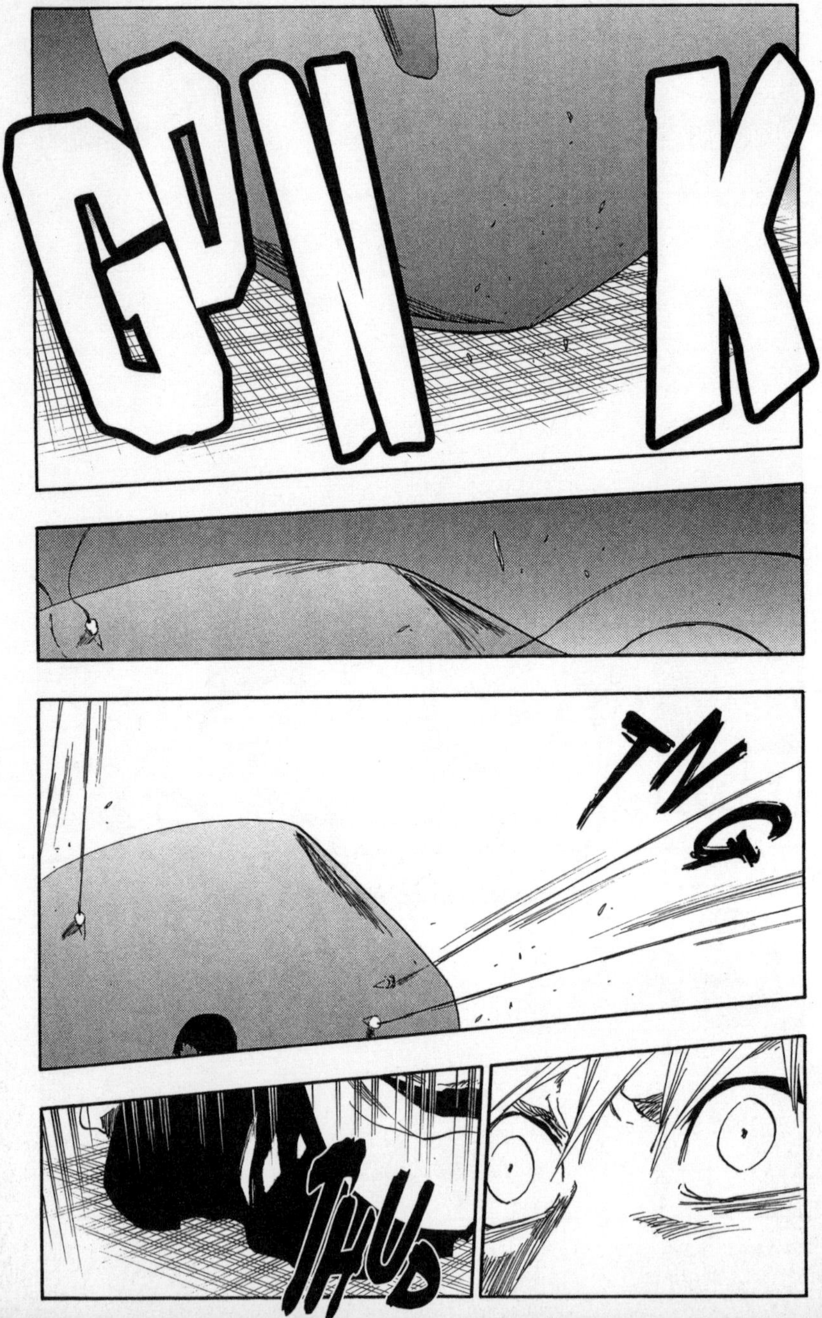
GDINK
TNG
THUD

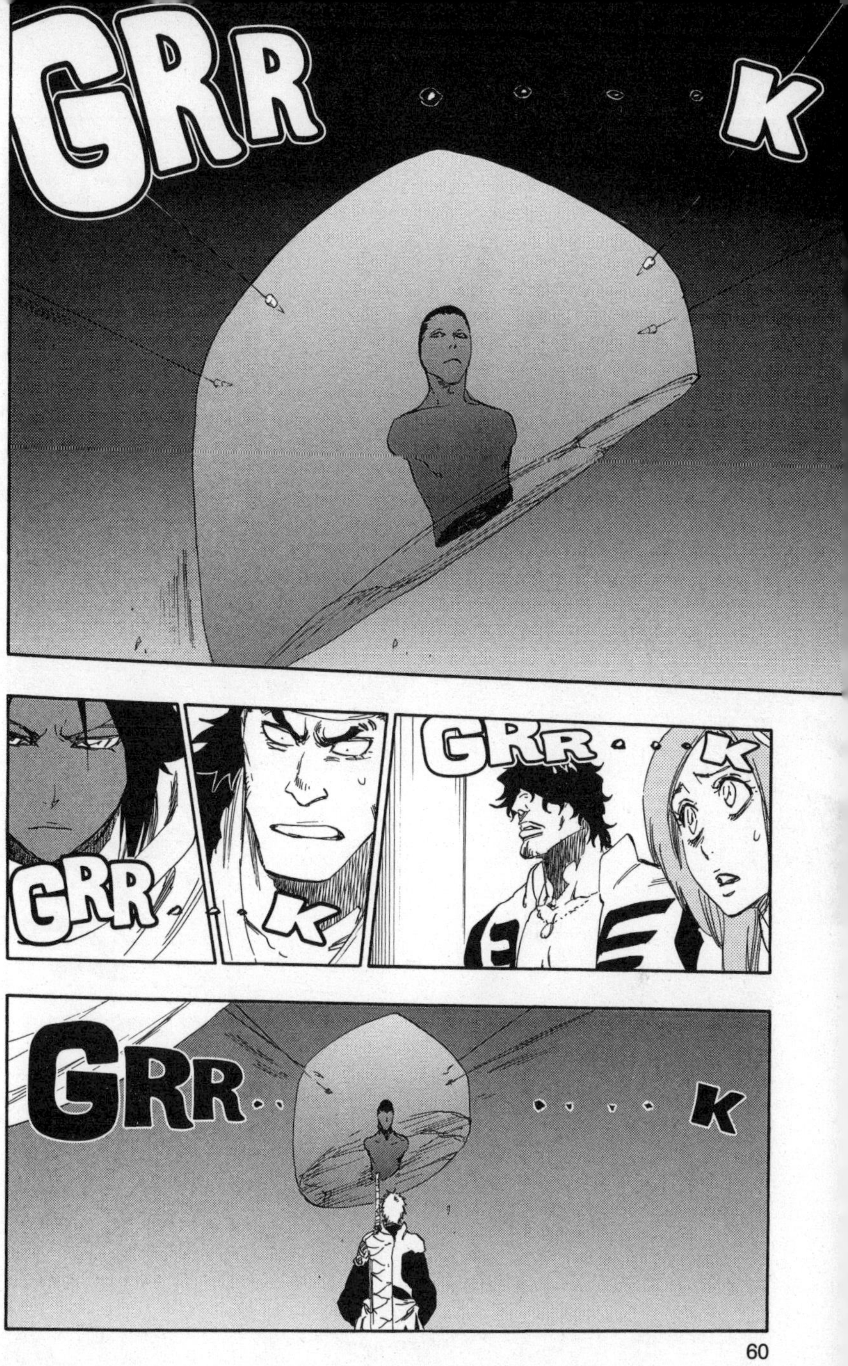
GRR...K
GRR...K
GRR...K
GRR...K

READ THIS WAY

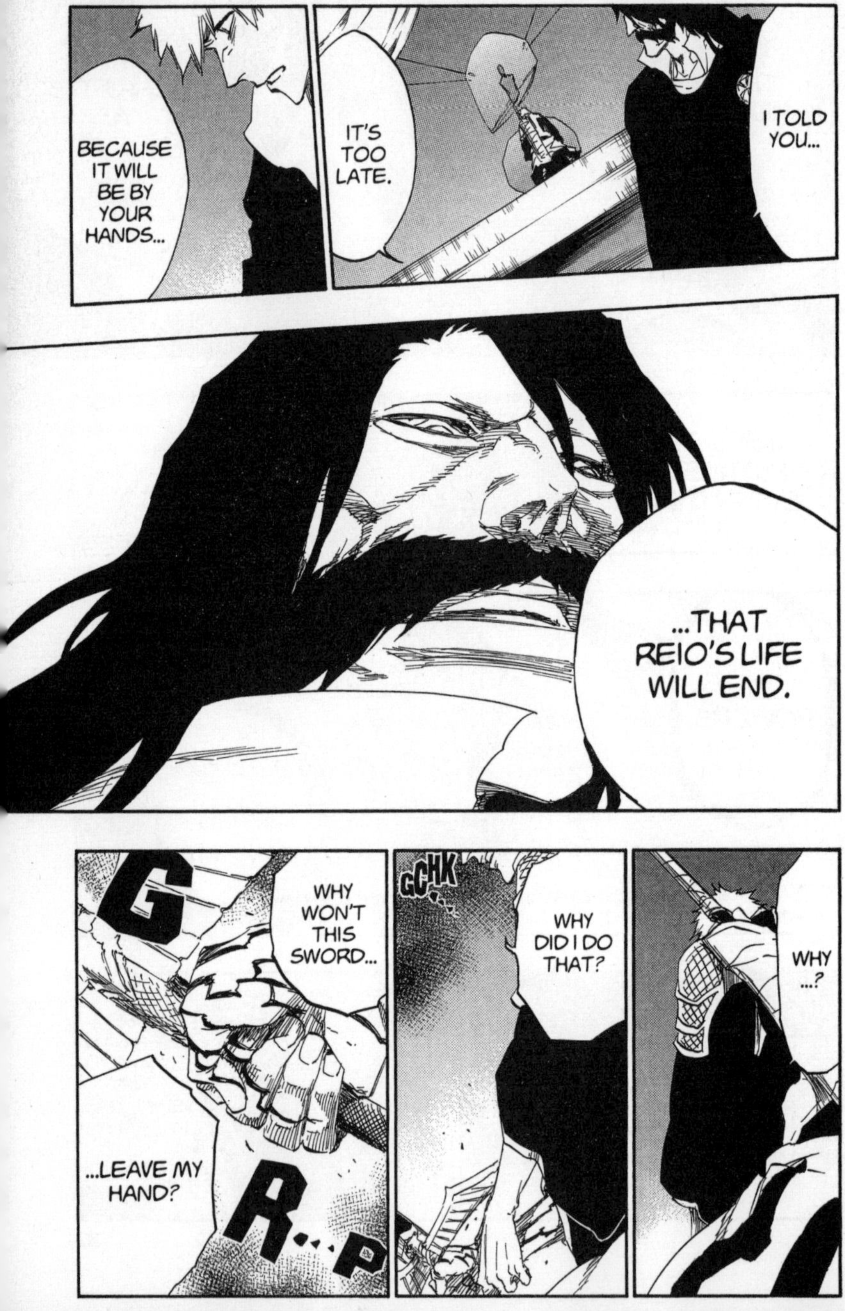
I TOLD YOU...
IT'S TOO LATE.
BECAUSE IT WILL BE BY YOUR HANDS...
...THAT REIO'S LIFE WILL END.
WHY ...?
GCHK
WHY DID I DO THAT?
G
WHY WON'T THIS SWORD...
...LEAVE MY HAND?
R...P

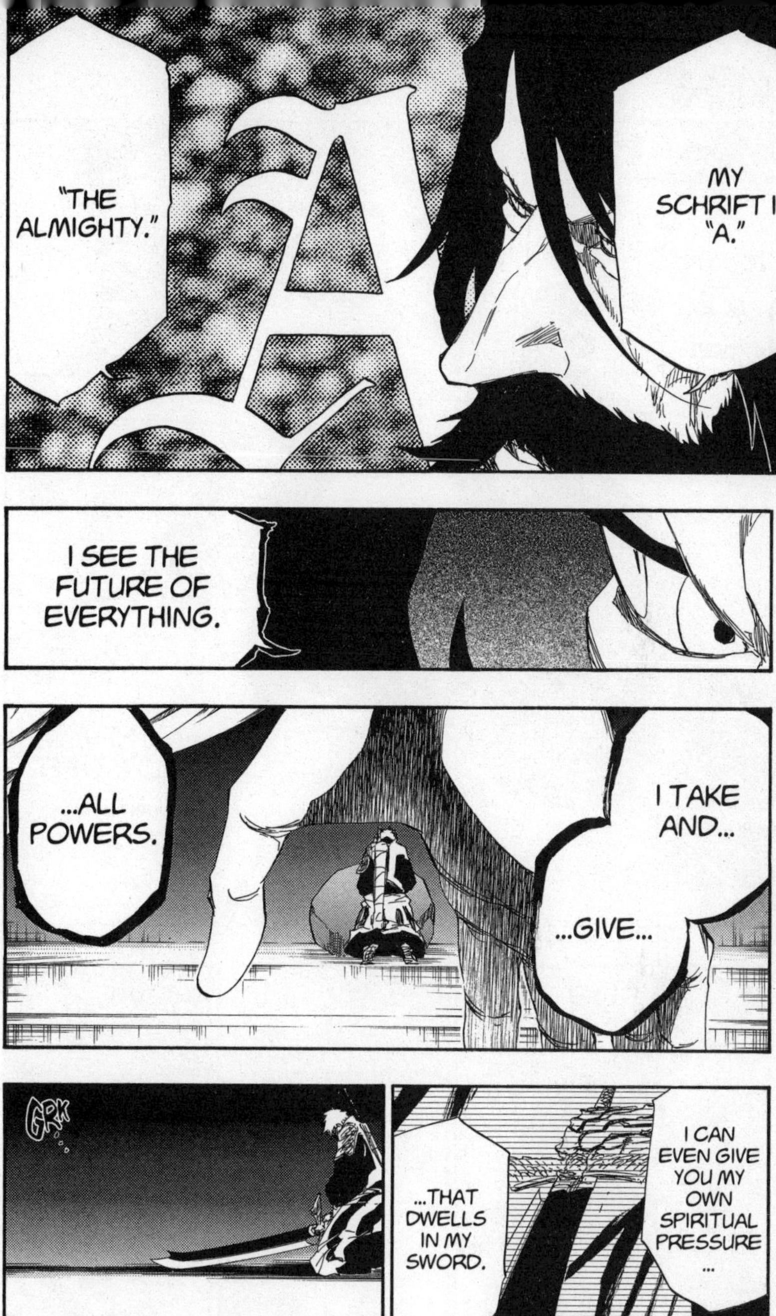
MY SCHRIFT IS "A."
"THE ALMIGHTY."
I SEE THE FUTURE OF EVERYTHING.
I TAKE AND...
...GIVE...
...ALL POWERS.
I CAN EVEN GIVE YOU MY OWN SPIRITUAL PRESSURE ...
...THAT DWELLS IN MY SWORD.
GRK

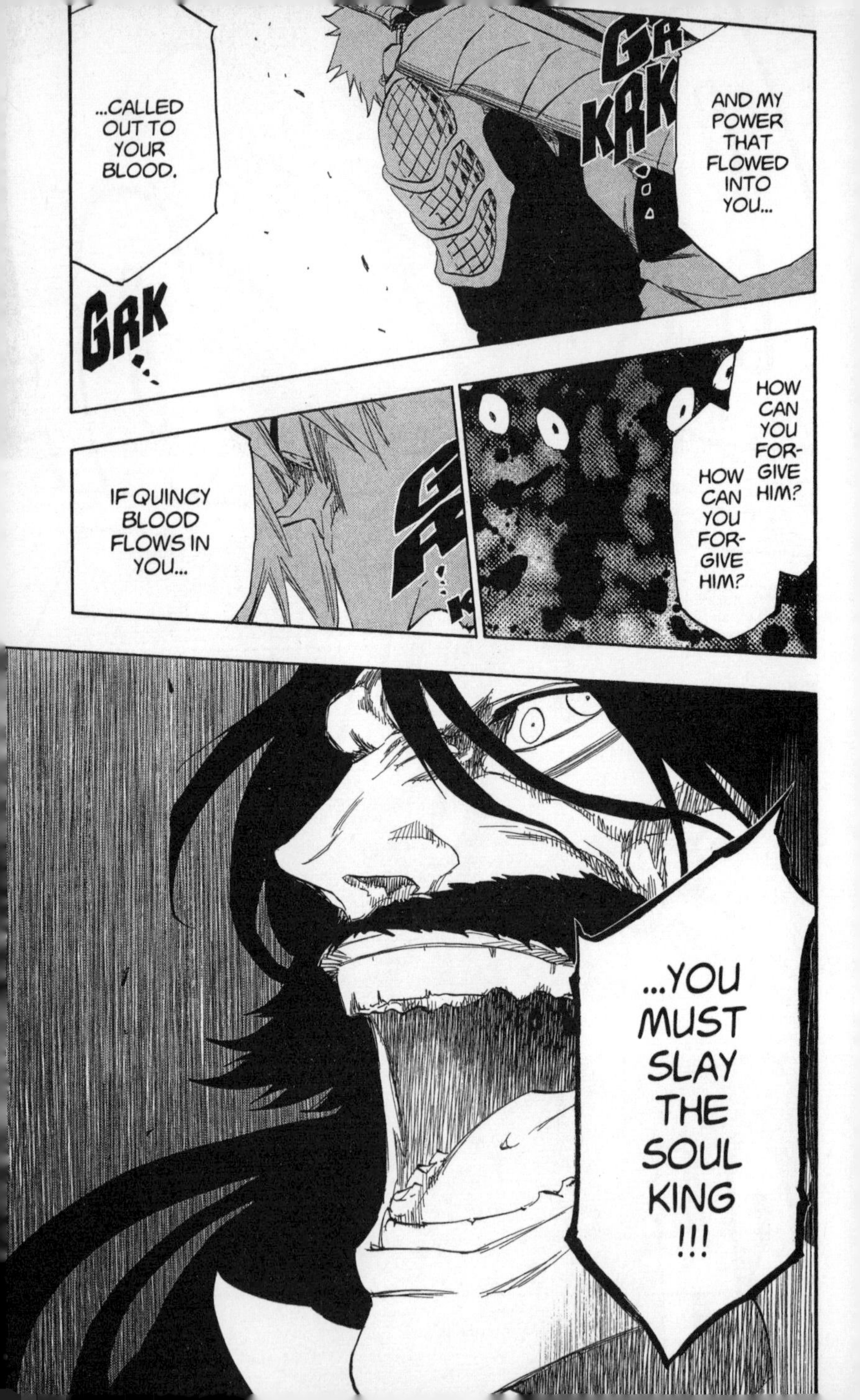
AND MY POWER THAT FLOWED INTO YOU...
GRKAK
...CALLED OUT TO YOUR BLOOD.
GRK
HOW CAN YOU FORGIVE HIM?
HOW CAN YOU FORGIVE HIM?
IF QUINCY BLOOD FLOWS IN YOU...
...YOU MUST SLAY THE SOUL KING!!!

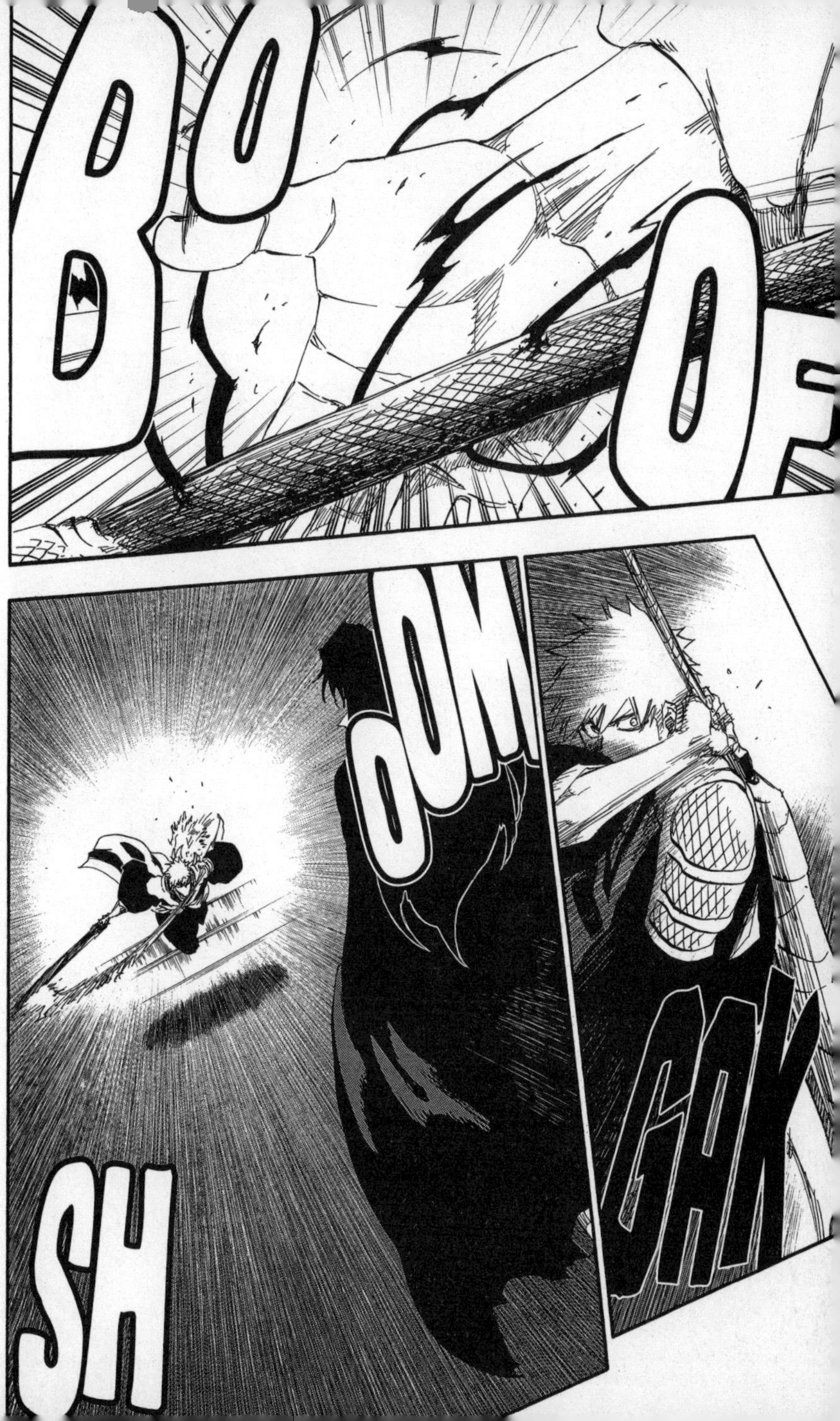
BO
OF
SHK
OOM
SH

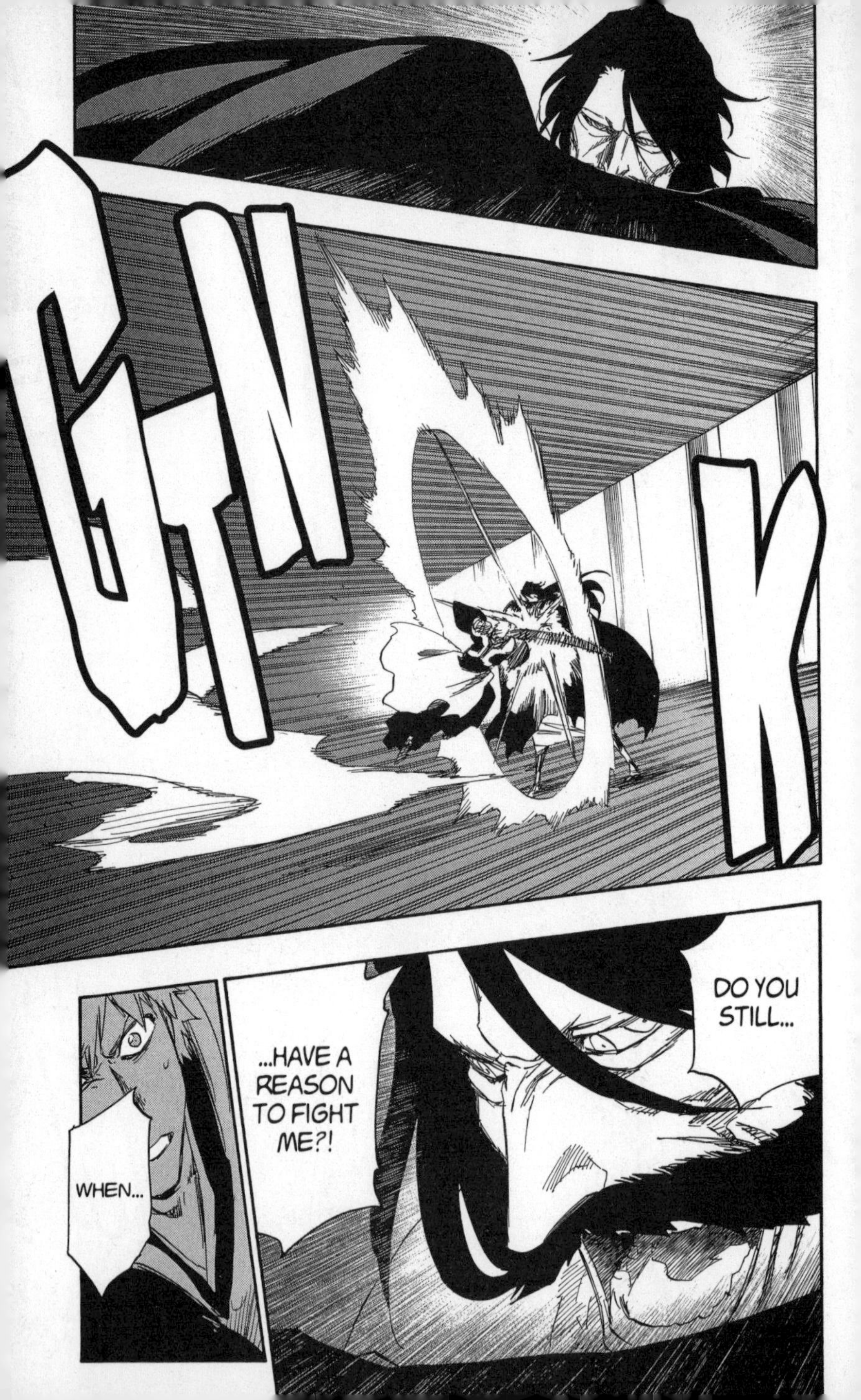
GTNK
DO YOU STILL...
...HAVE A REASON TO FIGHT ME?!
WHEN...

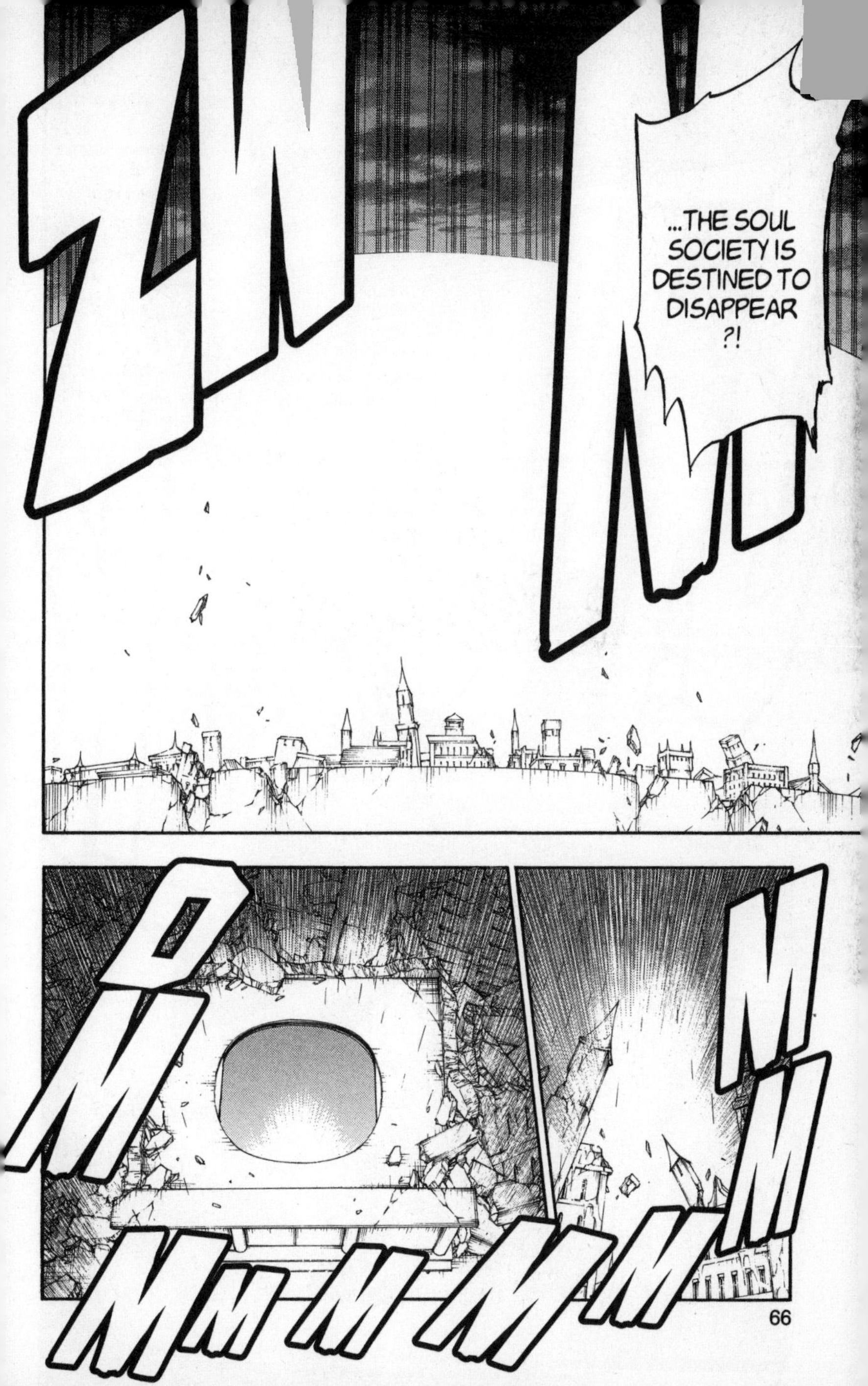
...THE SOUL SOCIETY IS DESTINED TO DISAPPEAR ?!

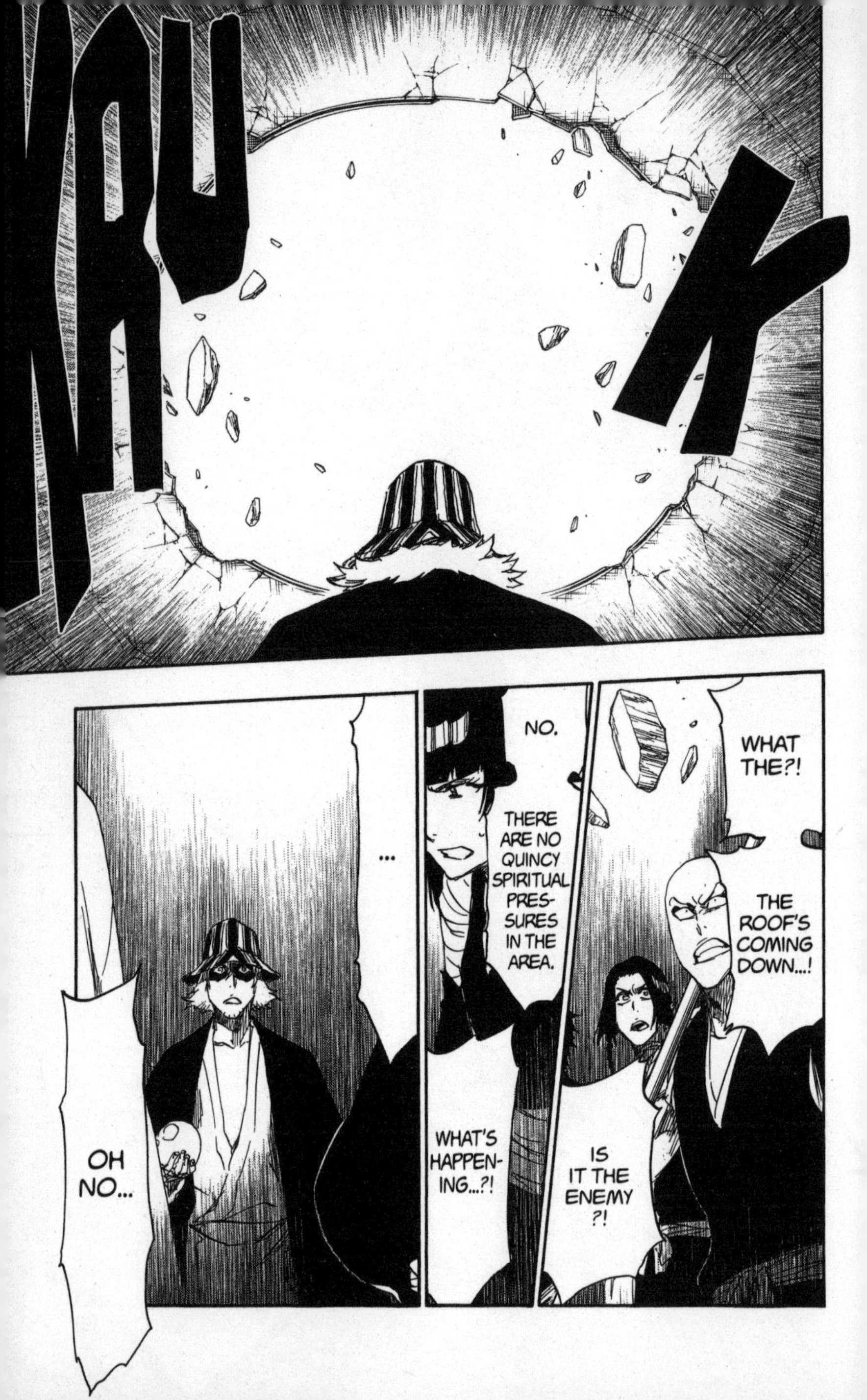
WHAT THE?!
THE ROOF'S COMING DOWN...!
IS IT THE ENEMY ?!
NO.
THERE ARE NO QUINCY SPIRITUAL PRES-SURES IN THE AREA.
WHAT'S HAPPEN-ING...?!
...
OH NO...

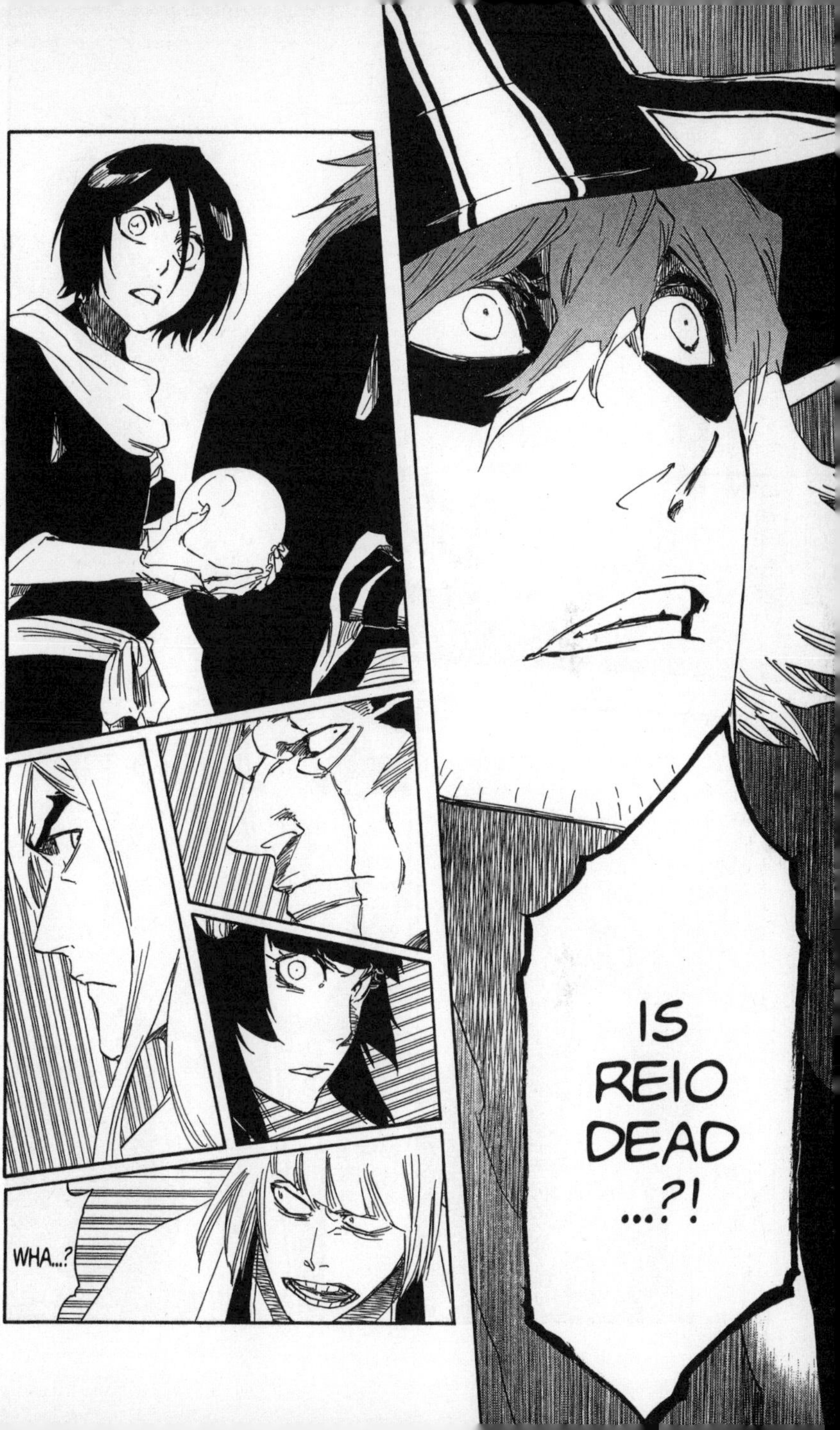
IS REIO DEAD ...?!
WHA...?

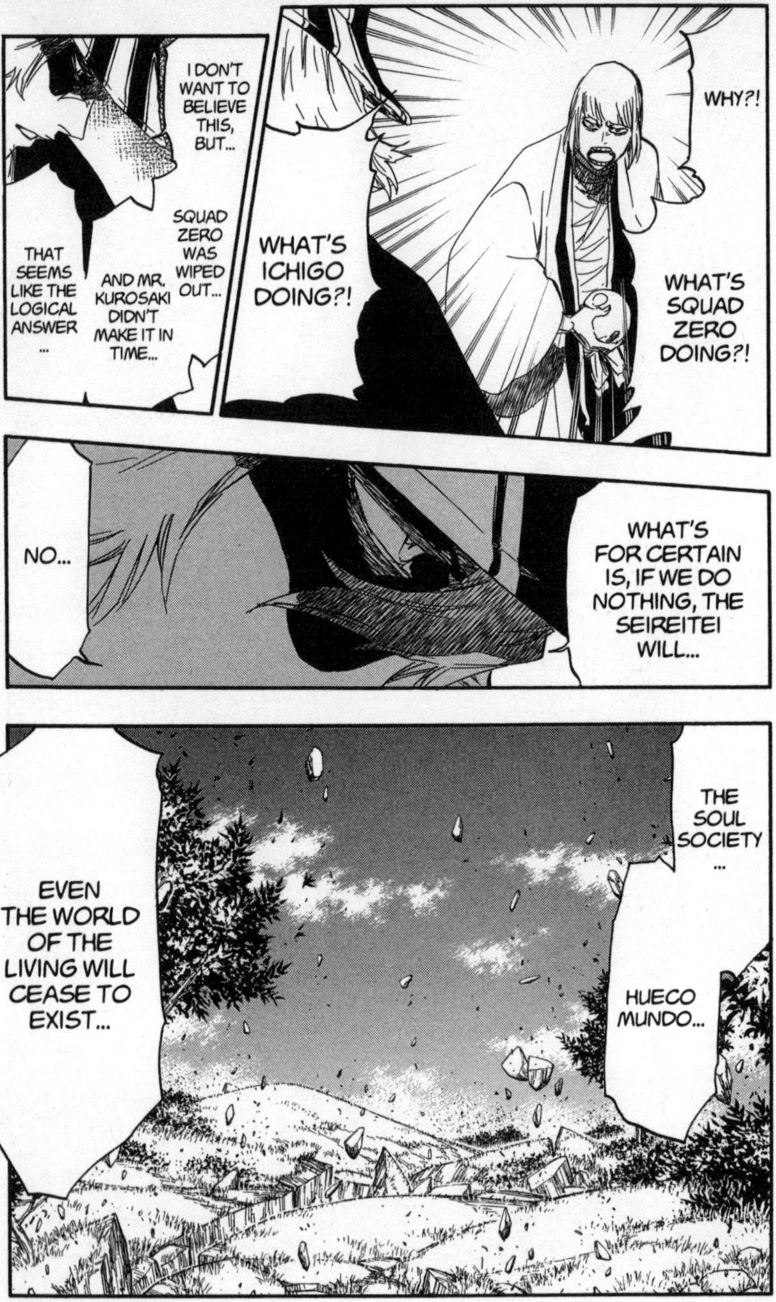
WHY?!
WHAT'S SQUAD ZERO DOING?!
WHAT'S ICHIGO DOING?!
I DON'T WANT TO BELIEVE THIS, BUT...
SQUAD ZERO WAS WIPED OUT...
AND MR. KUROSAKI DIDN'T MAKE IT IN TIME...
THAT SEEMS LIKE THE LOGICAL ANSWER ...
WHAT'S FOR CERTAIN IS, IF WE DO NOTHING, THE SEIREITEI WILL...
NO...
THE SOUL SOCIETY ...
HUECO MUNDO...
EVEN THE WORLD OF THE LIVING WILL CEASE TO EXIST...

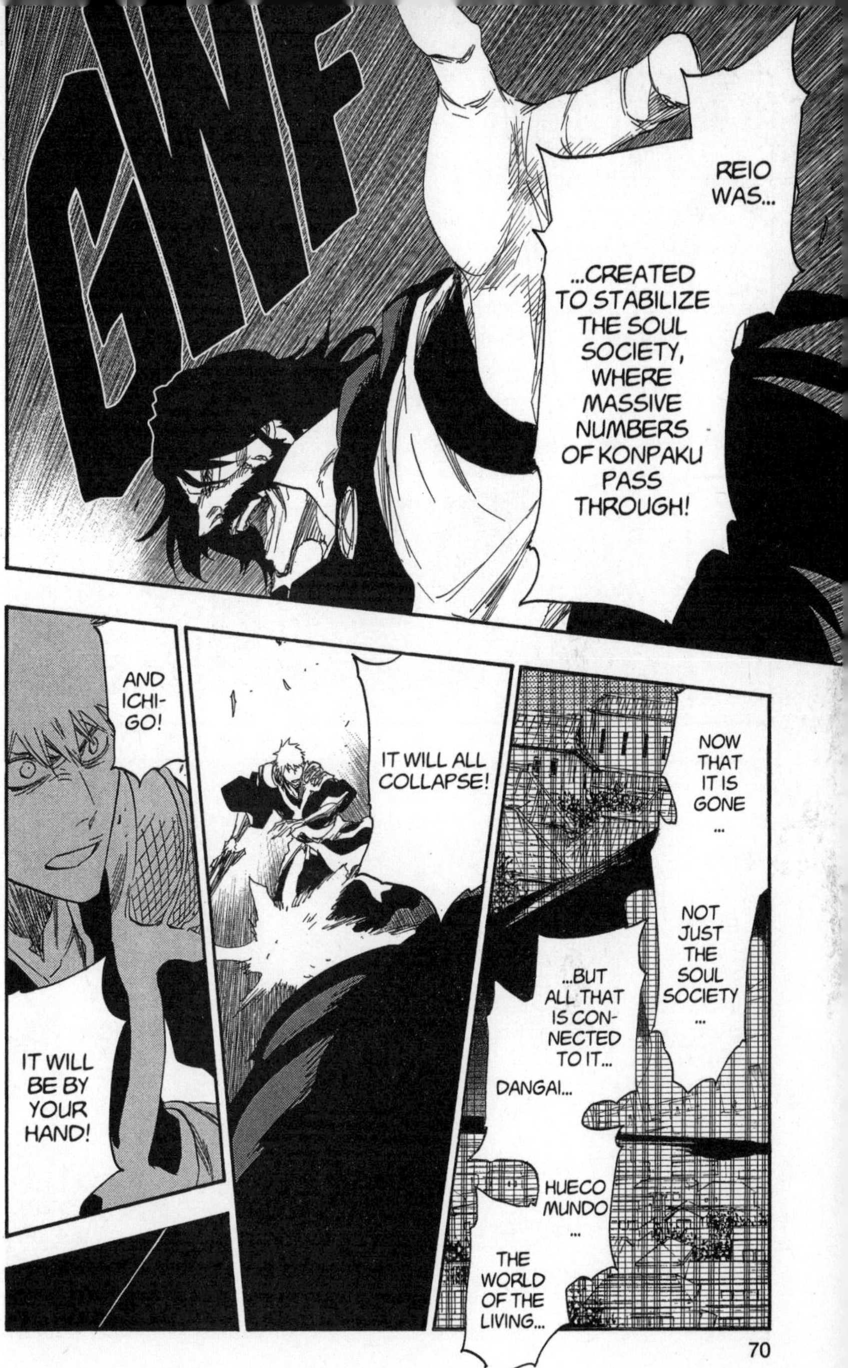
REIO WAS...
...CREATED TO STABILIZE THE SOUL SOCIETY, WHERE MASSIVE NUMBERS OF KONPAKU PASS THROUGH!
NOW THAT IT IS GONE ...
NOT JUST THE SOUL SOCIETY ...
...BUT ALL THAT IS CONNECTED TO IT...
DANGAI...
HUECO MUNDO ...
THE WORLD OF THE LIVING...
IT WILL ALL COLLAPSE!
AND ICHIGO!
IT WILL BE BY YOUR HAND!

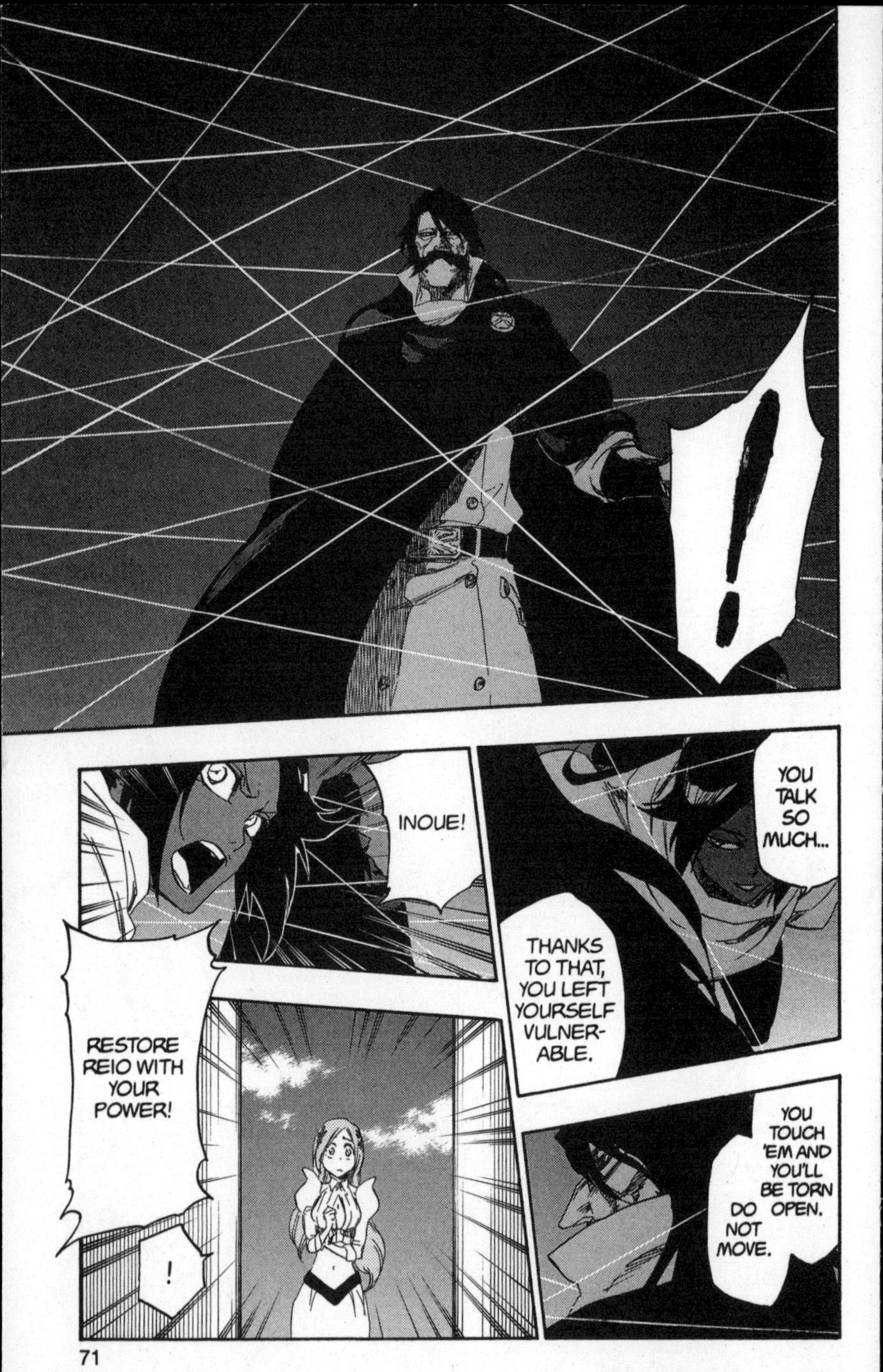
!
YOU TALK SO MUCH...
THANKS TO THAT, YOU LEFT YOURSELF VULNER-ABLE.
INOUE!
YOU TOUCH 'EM AND YOU'LL BE TORN OPEN.
DO NOT MOVE.
RESTORE REIO WITH YOUR POWER!
!

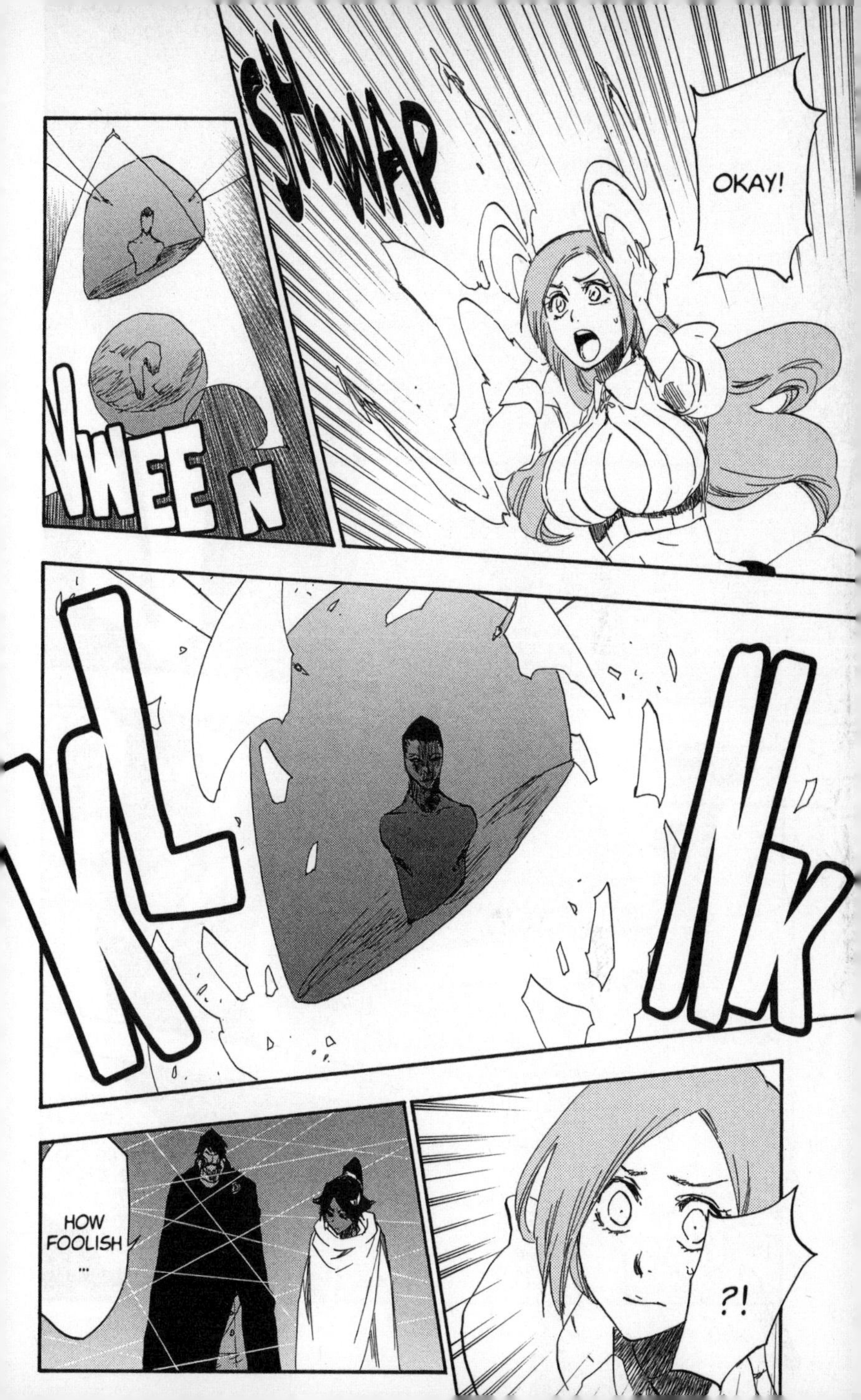
OKAY!
SHWAP
VWEEN
KLINK
?!
HOW FOOLISH ...

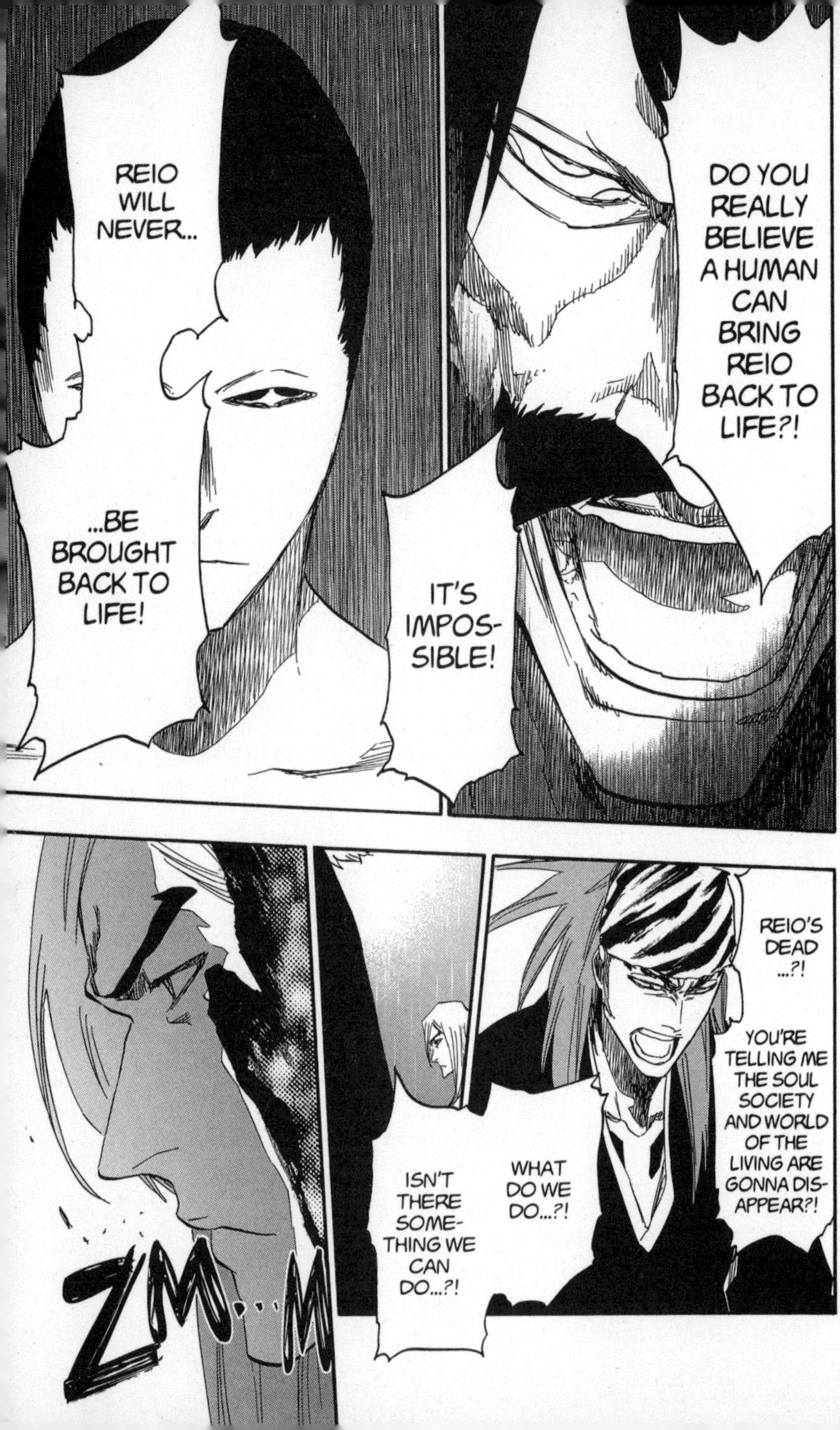
DO YOU REALLY BELIEVE A HUMAN CAN BRING REIO BACK TO LIFE?!
IT'S IMPOSSIBLE!
REIO WILL NEVER...
...BE BROUGHT BACK TO LIFE!
REIO'S DEAD ...?!
YOU'RE TELLING ME THE SOUL SOCIETY AND WORLD OF THE LIVING ARE GONNA DISAPPEAR?!
WHAT DO WE DO...?!
ISN'T THERE SOMETHING WE CAN DO...?!
ZM...M

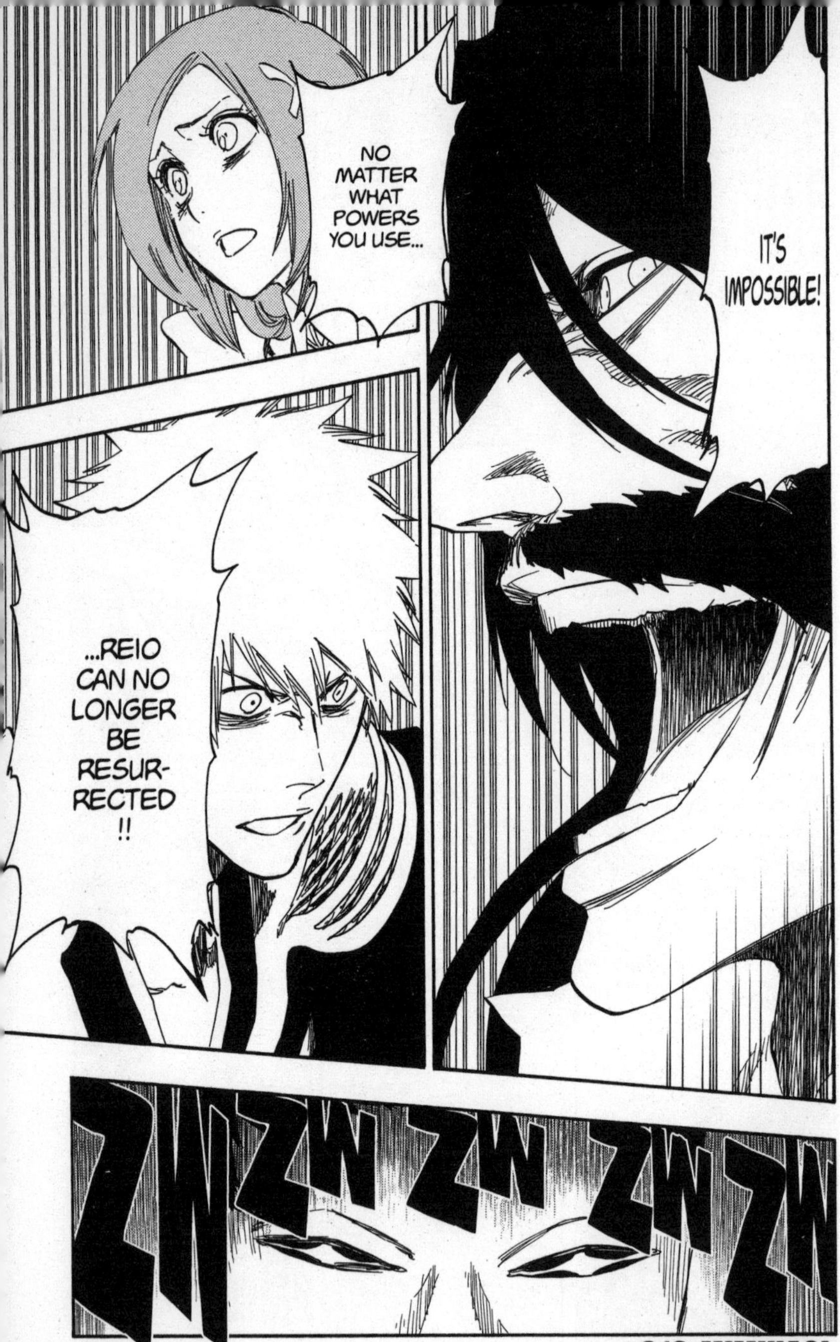
IT'S IMPOSSIBLE!
NO MATTER WHAT POWERS YOU USE...
...REIO CAN NO LONGER BE RESURREC-TED!!
ZWN ZWN ZWN ZWN ZWN ZWN

616. MIMIHAGI

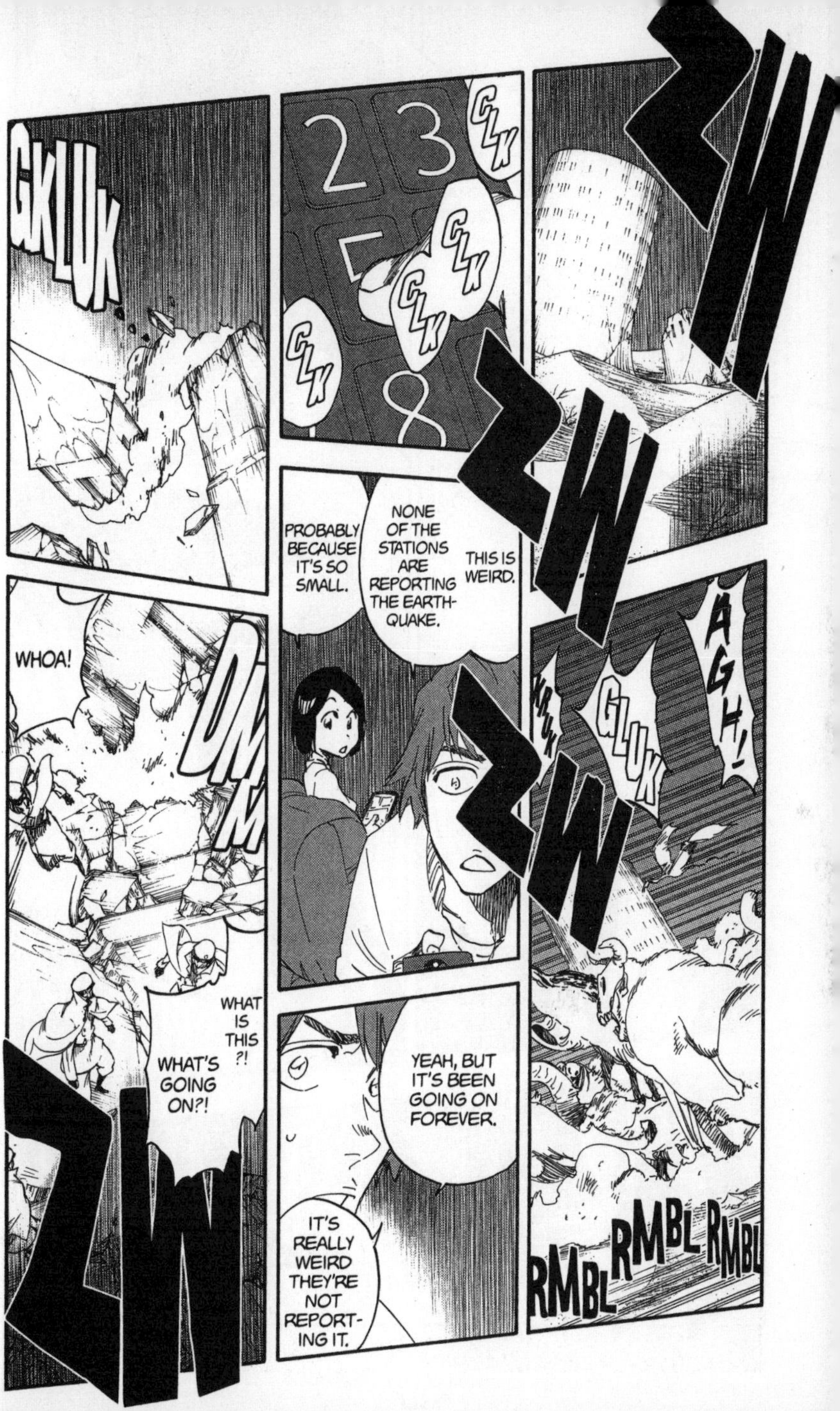
ZWW
CLK
CLK
CLK
CLK
GKLUK
ZWW
ZWW
AGH!
GLUK
KRUK
RMBL RMBL RMBL
THIS IS WEIRD.
NONE OF THE STATIONS ARE REPORTING THE EARTHQUAKE.
PROBABLY BECAUSE IT'S SO SMALL.
YEAH, BUT IT'S BEEN GOING ON FOREVER.
IT'S REALLY WEIRD THEY'RE NOT REPORTING IT.
WHOA!
DMM
WHAT IS THIS?!
WHAT'S GOING ON?!
ZWW

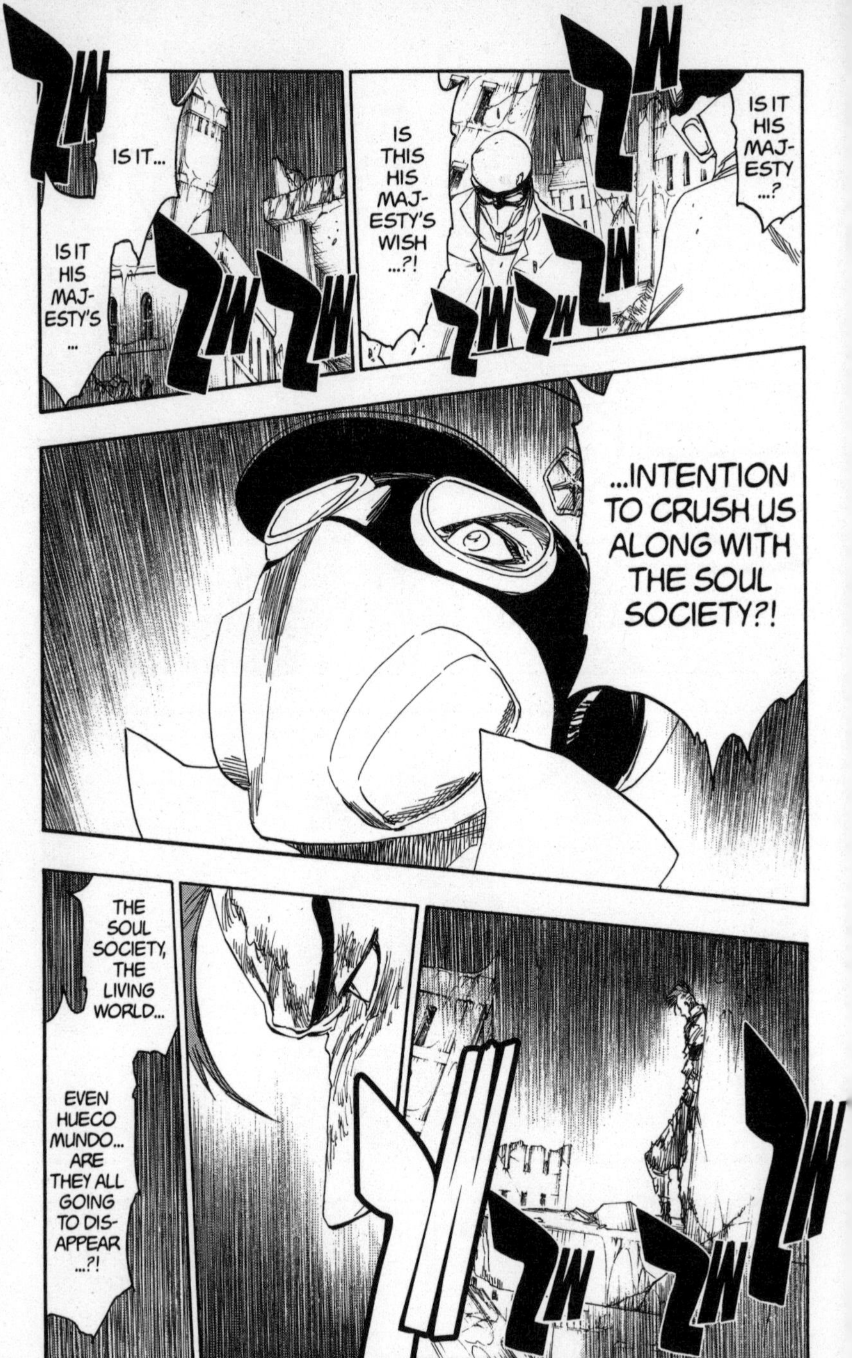
IS IT HIS MAJESTY...?
IS THIS HIS MAJESTY'S WISH...?!
IS IT...
IS IT HIS MAJESTY'S...
...INTENTION TO CRUSH US ALONG WITH THE SOUL SOCIETY?!
THE SOUL SOCIETY, THE LIVING WORLD...
EVEN HUECO MUNDO... ARE THEY ALL GOING TO DISAPPEAR...?!

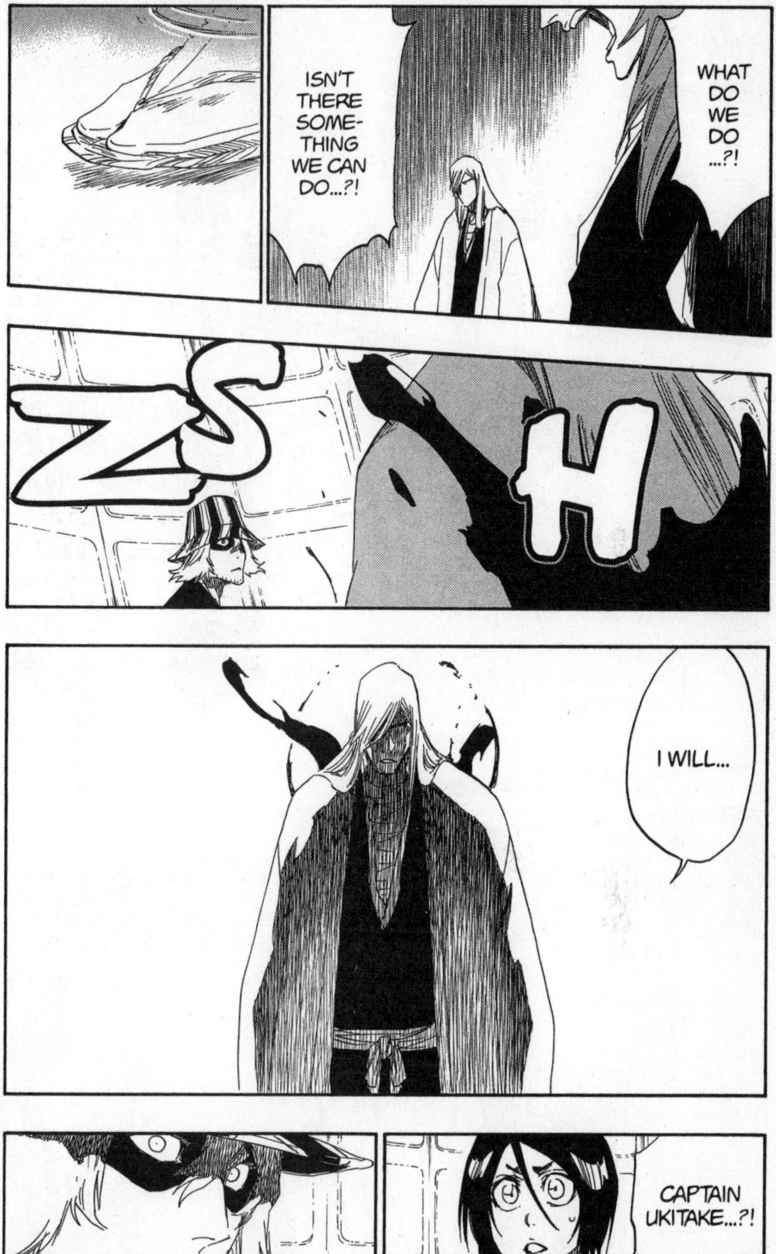
WHAT DO WE DO...?!
ISN'T THERE SOME-THING WE CAN DO...?!
ZSH
I WILL...
CAPTAIN UKITAKE...?!

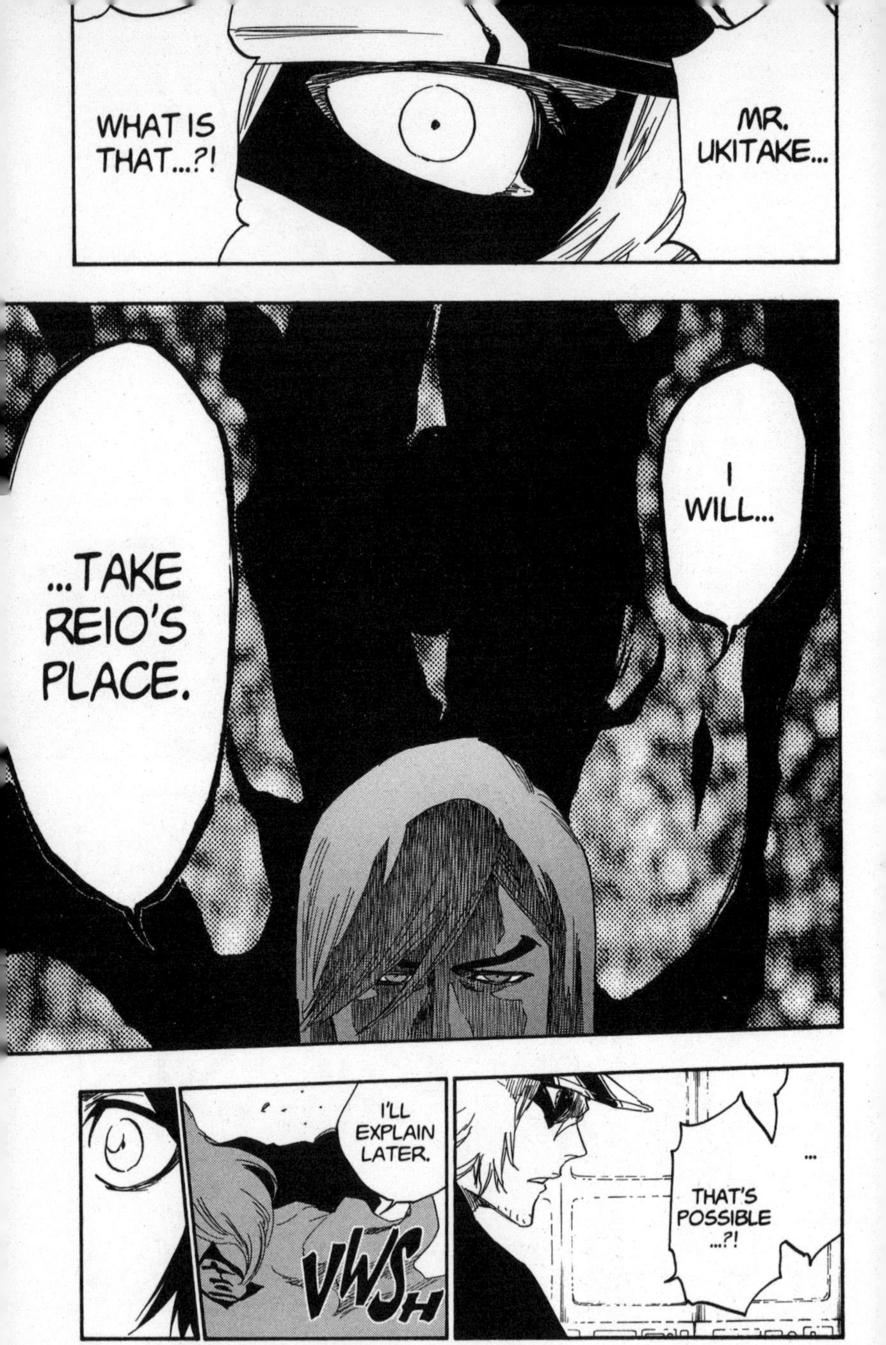
MR. UKITAKE...
WHAT IS THAT...?!
I WILL...
...TAKE REIO'S PLACE.
...
THAT'S POSSIBLE ...?!
I'LL EXPLAIN LATER.
VWSH

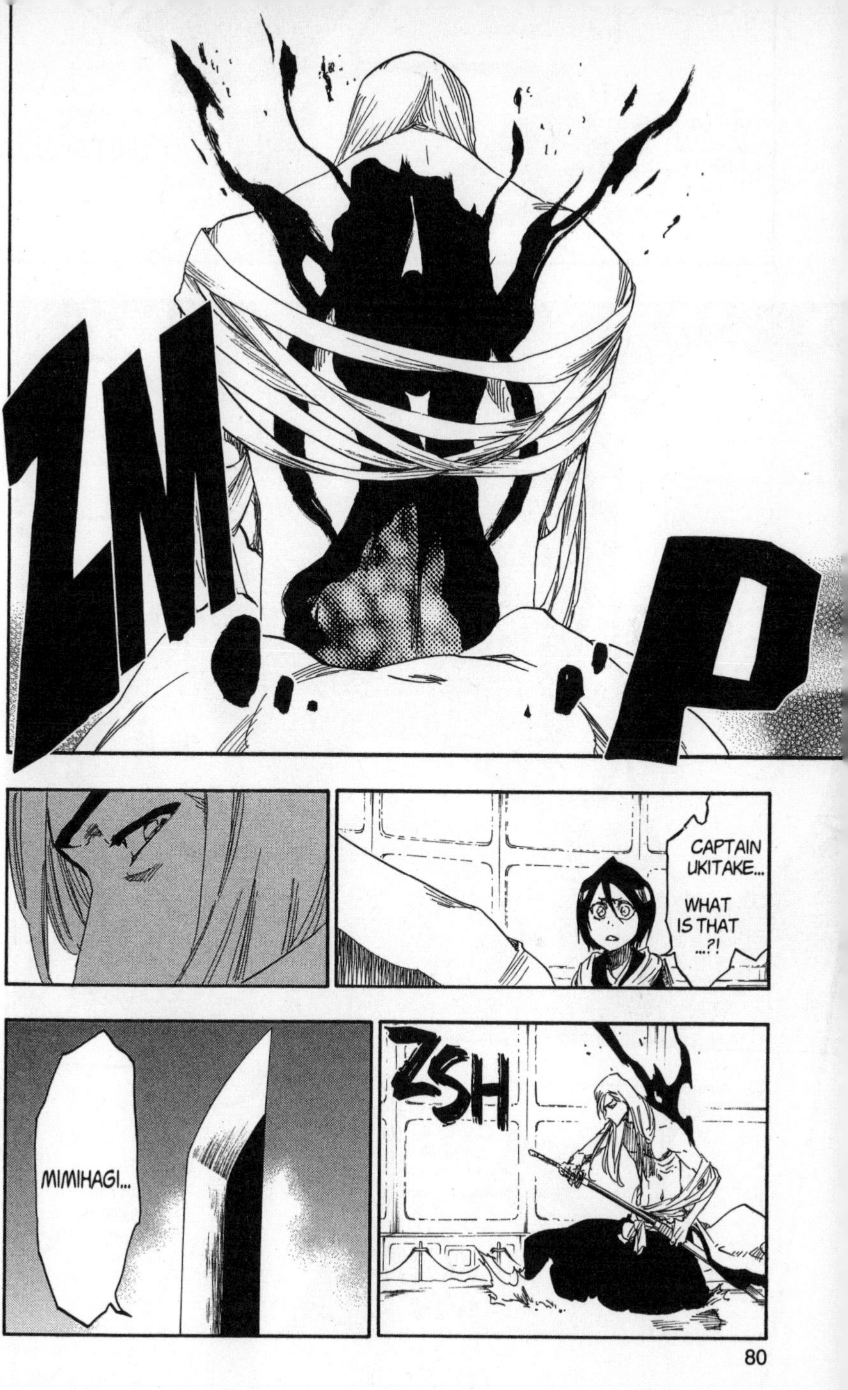
ZM...P
CAPTAIN UKITAKE...
WHAT IS THAT ...?!
ZSH
MIMIHAGI...

READ THIS WAY

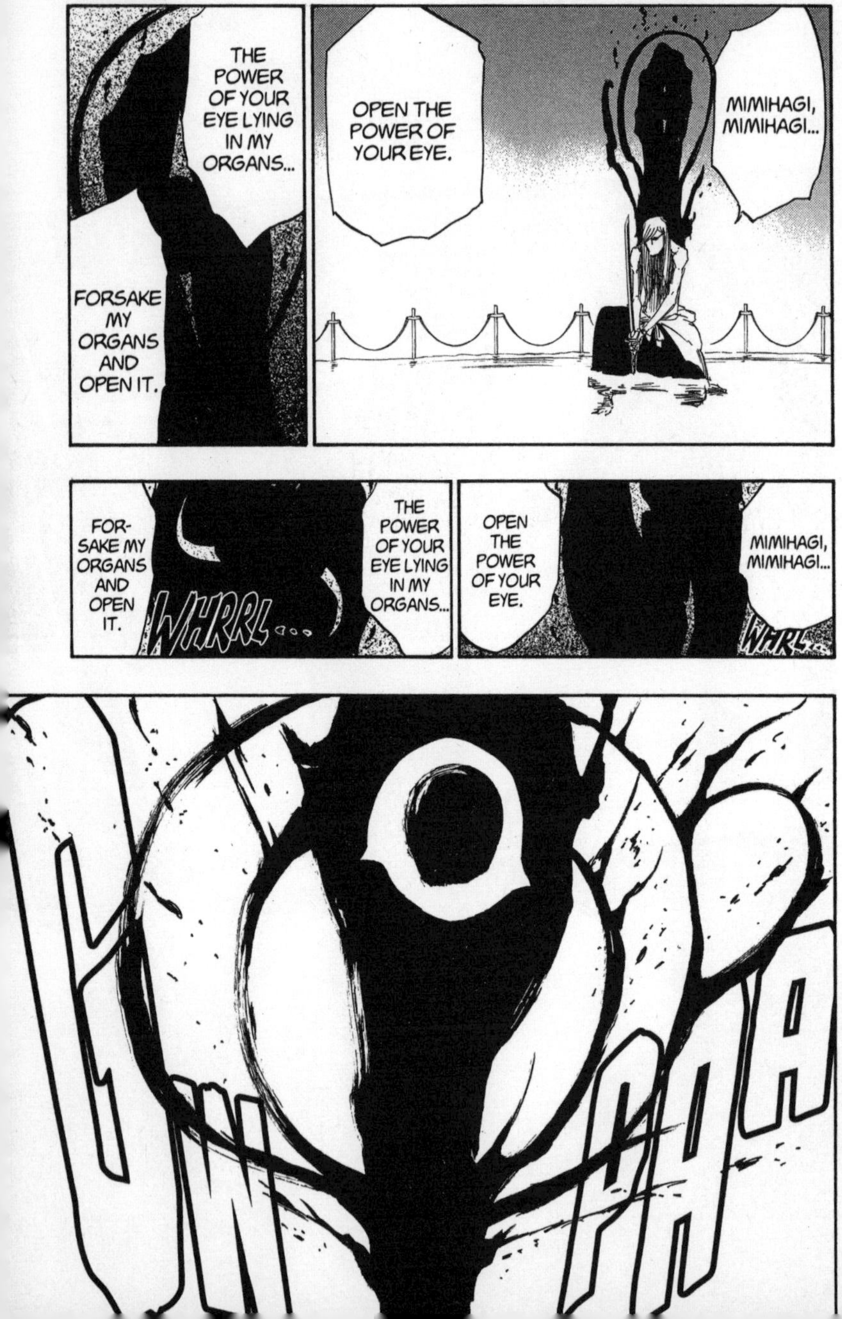

MIMIHAGI, MIMIHAGI...
OPEN THE POWER OF YOUR EYE.
THE POWER OF YOUR EYE LYING IN MY ORGANS...
FORSAKE MY ORGANS AND OPEN IT.
MIMIHAGI, MIMIHAGI...
OPEN THE POWER OF YOUR EYE.
WHRL...
THE POWER OF YOUR EYE LYING IN MY ORGANS...
FORSAKE MY ORGANS AND OPEN IT.
WHRRL...

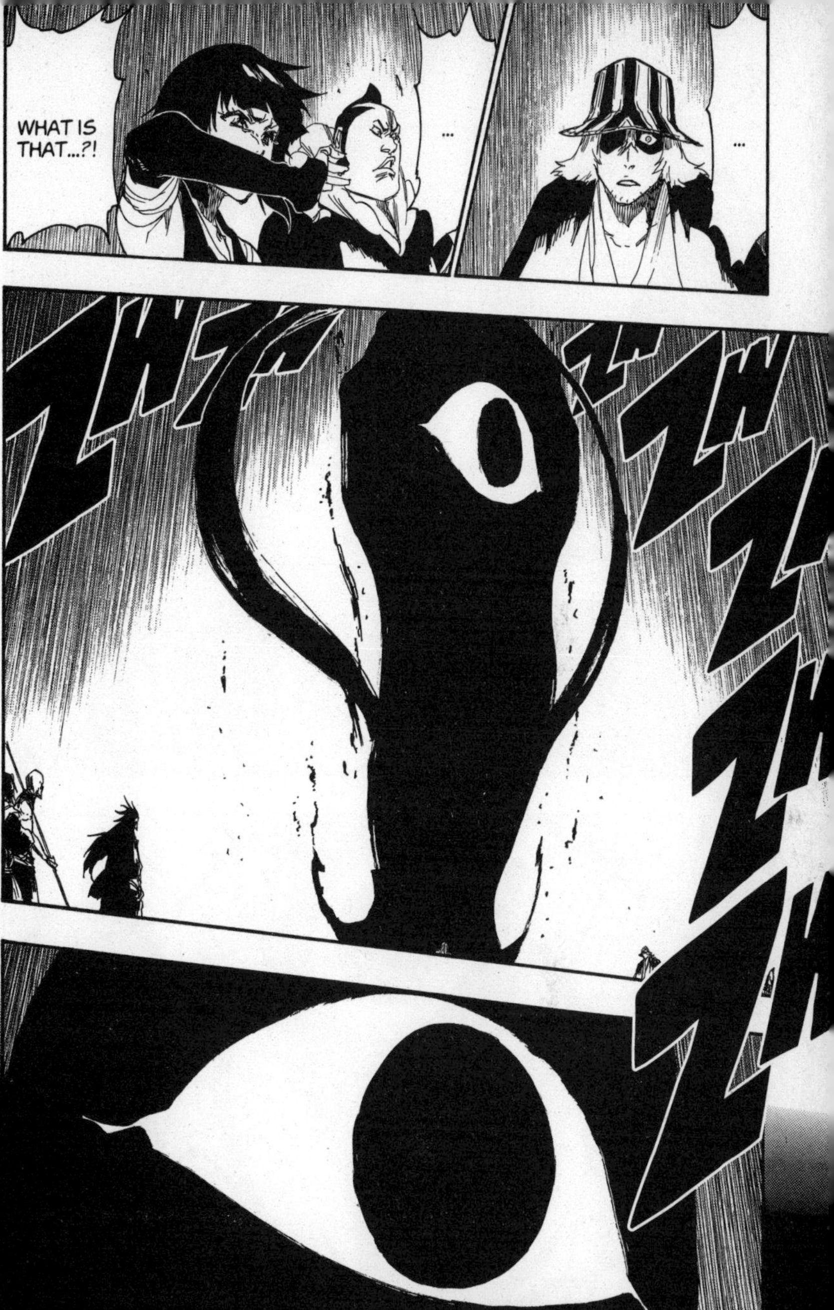
...
...
WHAT IS THAT...?!

616. MIMIHAGI

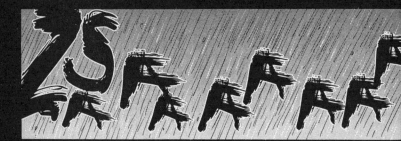

BLEACH

MIMIHAGI, MIMIHAGI!
PLEASE SAVE THIS CHILD!

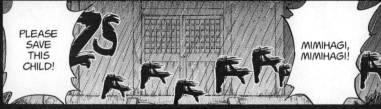

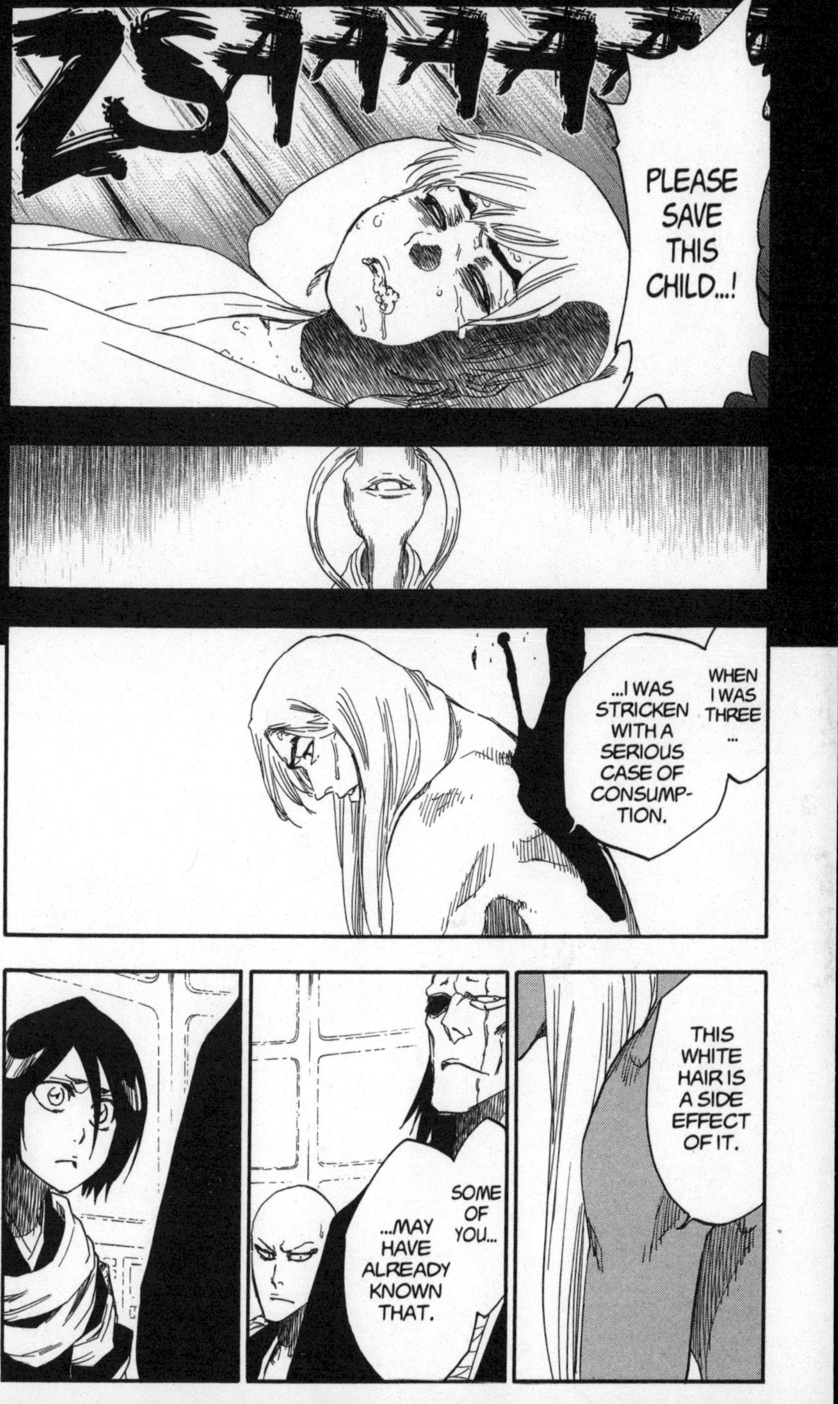
ZSHHHH
PLEASE SAVE THIS CHILD...!
WHEN I WAS THREE...
...I WAS STRICKEN WITH A SERIOUS CASE OF CONSUMPTION.
THIS WHITE HAIR IS A SIDE EFFECT OF IT.
SOME OF YOU...
...MAY HAVE ALREADY KNOWN THAT.

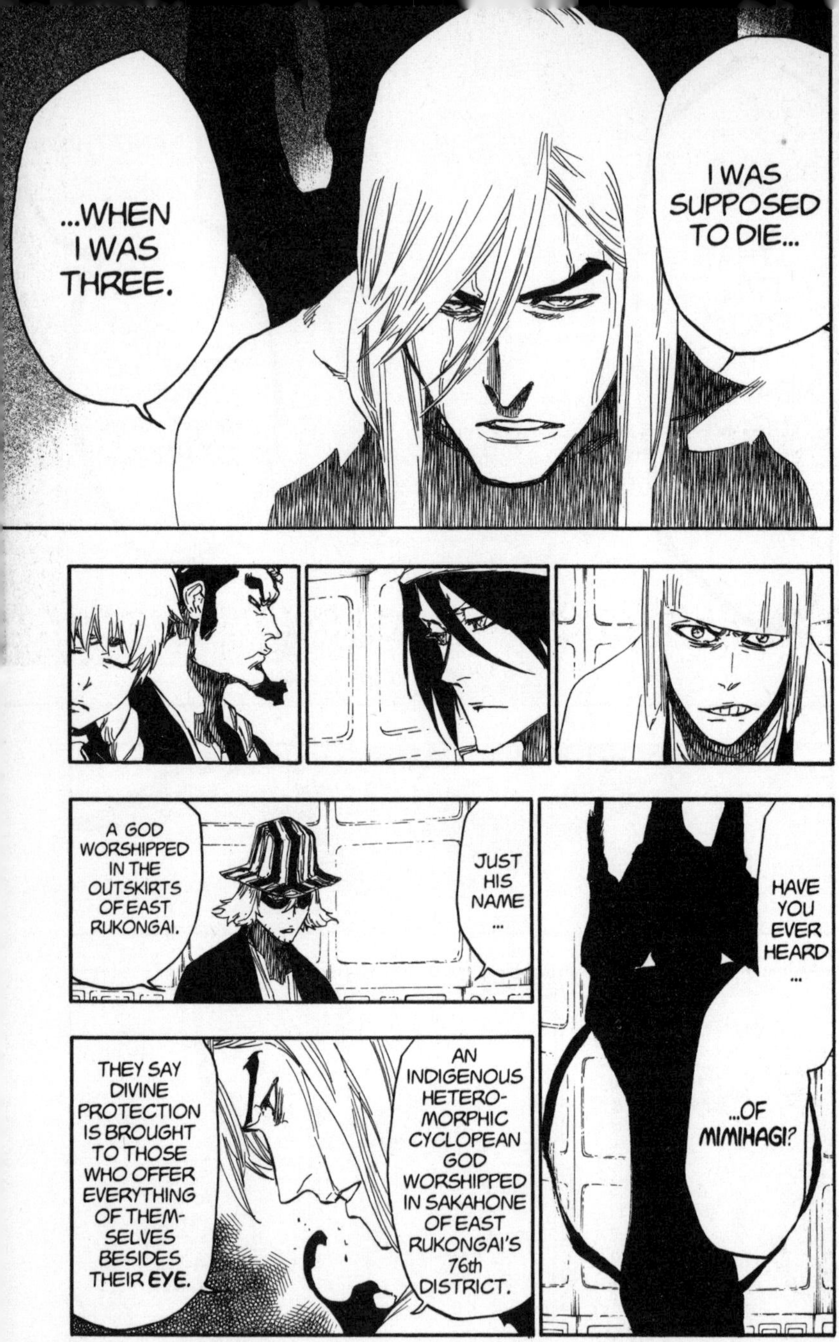
I WAS SUPPOSED TO DIE...
...WHEN I WAS THREE.
HAVE YOU EVER HEARD ...
...OF MIMIHAGI?
JUST HIS NAME ...
A GOD WORSHIPPED IN THE OUTSKIRTS OF EAST RUKONGAI.
AN INDIGENOUS HETERO-MORPHIC CYCLOPEAN GOD WORSHIPPED IN SAKAHONE OF EAST RUKONGAI'S 76th DISTRICT.
THEY SAY DIVINE PROTECTION IS BROUGHT TO THOSE WHO OFFER EVERYTHING OF THEM-SELVES BESIDES THEIR EYE.

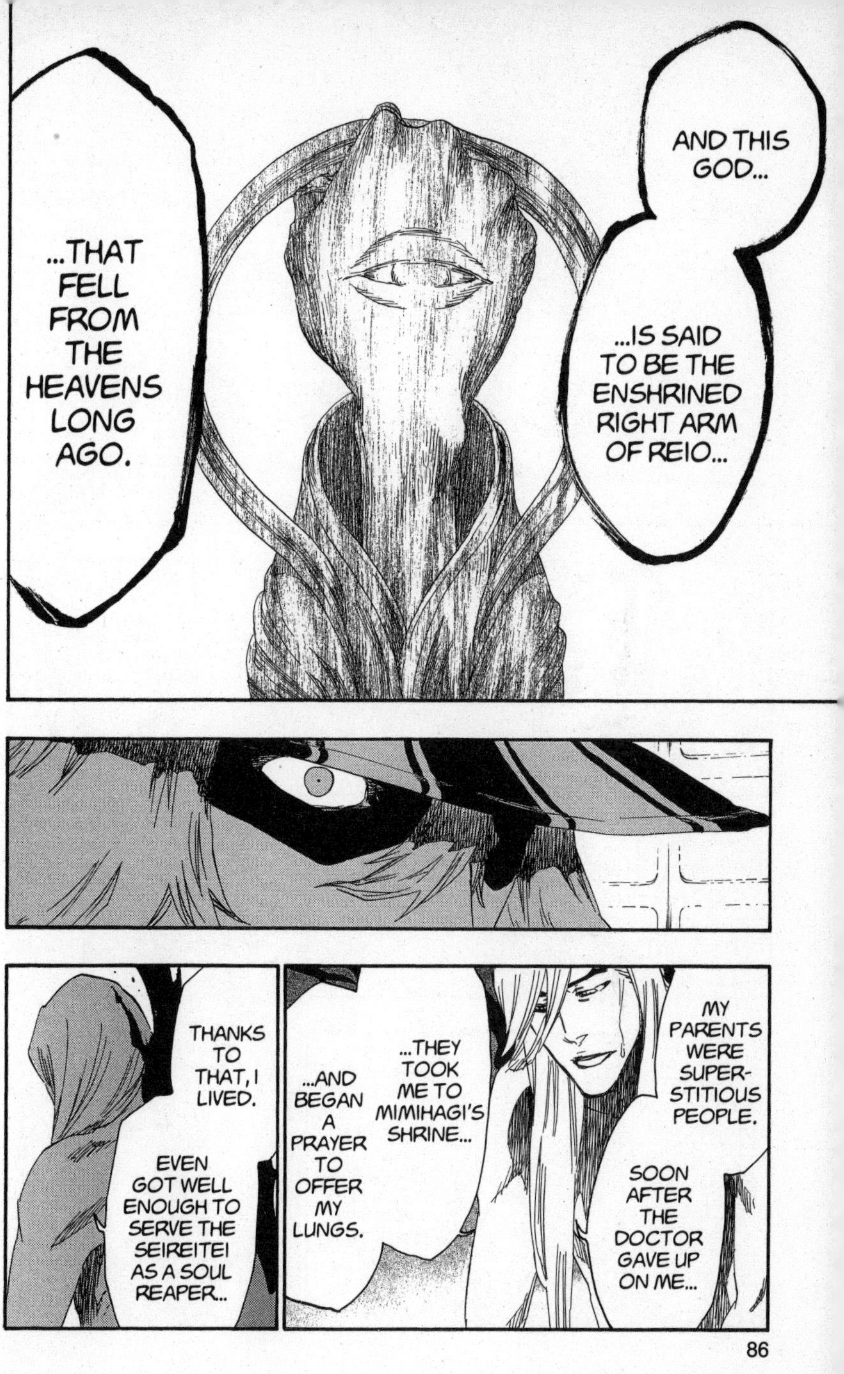
AND THIS GOD...
...IS SAID TO BE THE ENSHRINED RIGHT ARM OF REIO...
...THAT FELL FROM THE HEAVENS LONG AGO.
MY PARENTS WERE SUPER-STITIOUS PEOPLE.
SOON AFTER THE DOCTOR GAVE UP ON ME...
...THEY TOOK ME TO MIMIHAGI'S SHRINE...
...AND BEGAN A PRAYER TO OFFER MY LUNGS.
THANKS TO THAT, I LIVED.
EVEN GOT WELL ENOUGH TO SERVE THE SEIREITEI AS A SOUL REAPER...

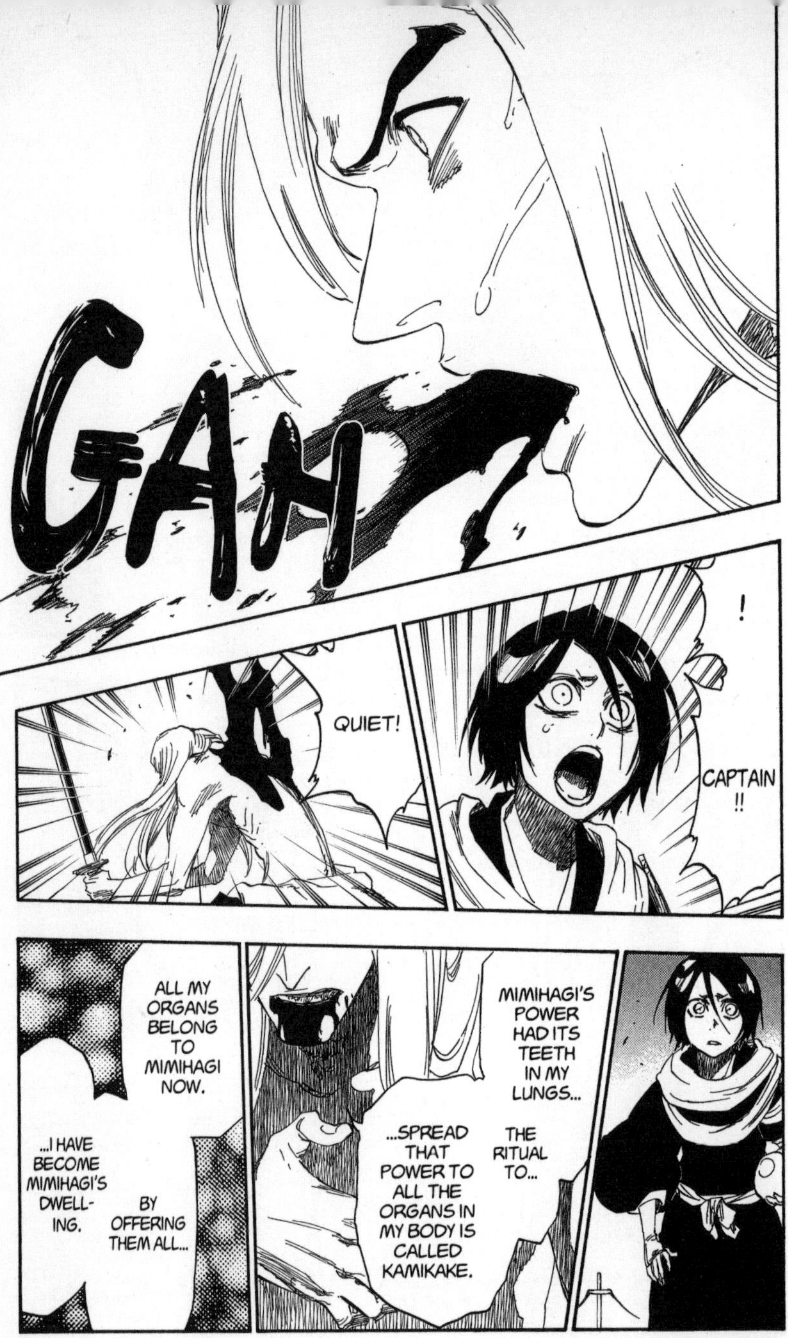
GAH
!
CAPTAIN !!
QUIET!
MIMIHAGI'S POWER HAD ITS TEETH IN MY LUNGS...
THE RITUAL TO...
...SPREAD THAT POWER TO ALL THE ORGANS IN MY BODY IS CALLED KAMIKAKE.
ALL MY ORGANS BELONG TO MIMIHAGI NOW.
BY OFFERING THEM ALL...
...I HAVE BECOME MIMIHAGI'S DWELL-ING.

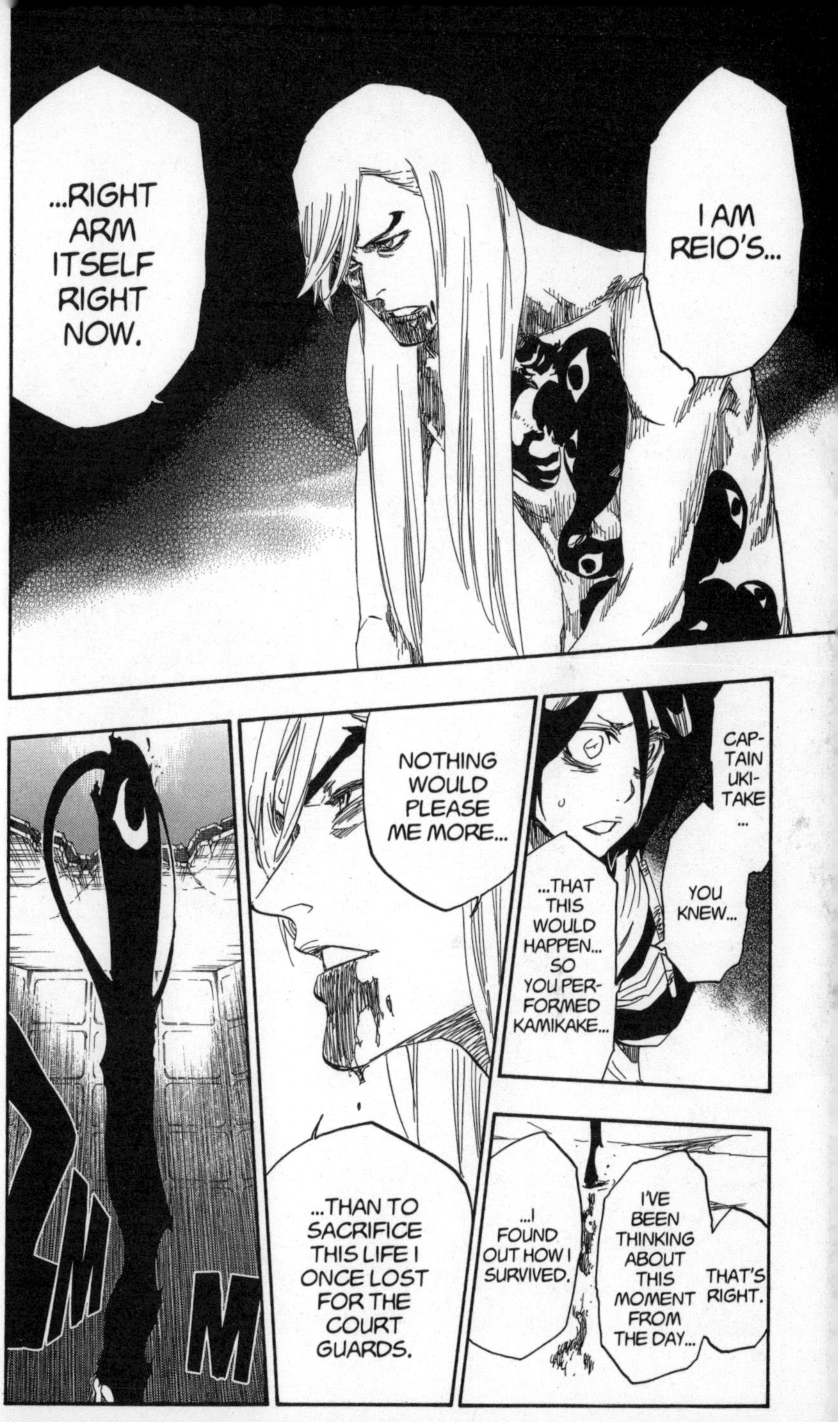
I AM REIO'S...
...RIGHT ARM ITSELF RIGHT NOW.
CAPTAIN UKITAKE...
YOU KNEW...
...THAT THIS WOULD HAPPEN... SO YOU PERFORMED KAMIKAKE...
THAT'S RIGHT.
I'VE BEEN THINKING ABOUT THIS MOMENT FROM THE DAY...
...I FOUND OUT HOW I SURVIVED.
NOTHING WOULD PLEASE ME MORE...
...THAN TO SACRIFICE THIS LIFE I ONCE LOST FOR THE COURT GUARDS.
MMM

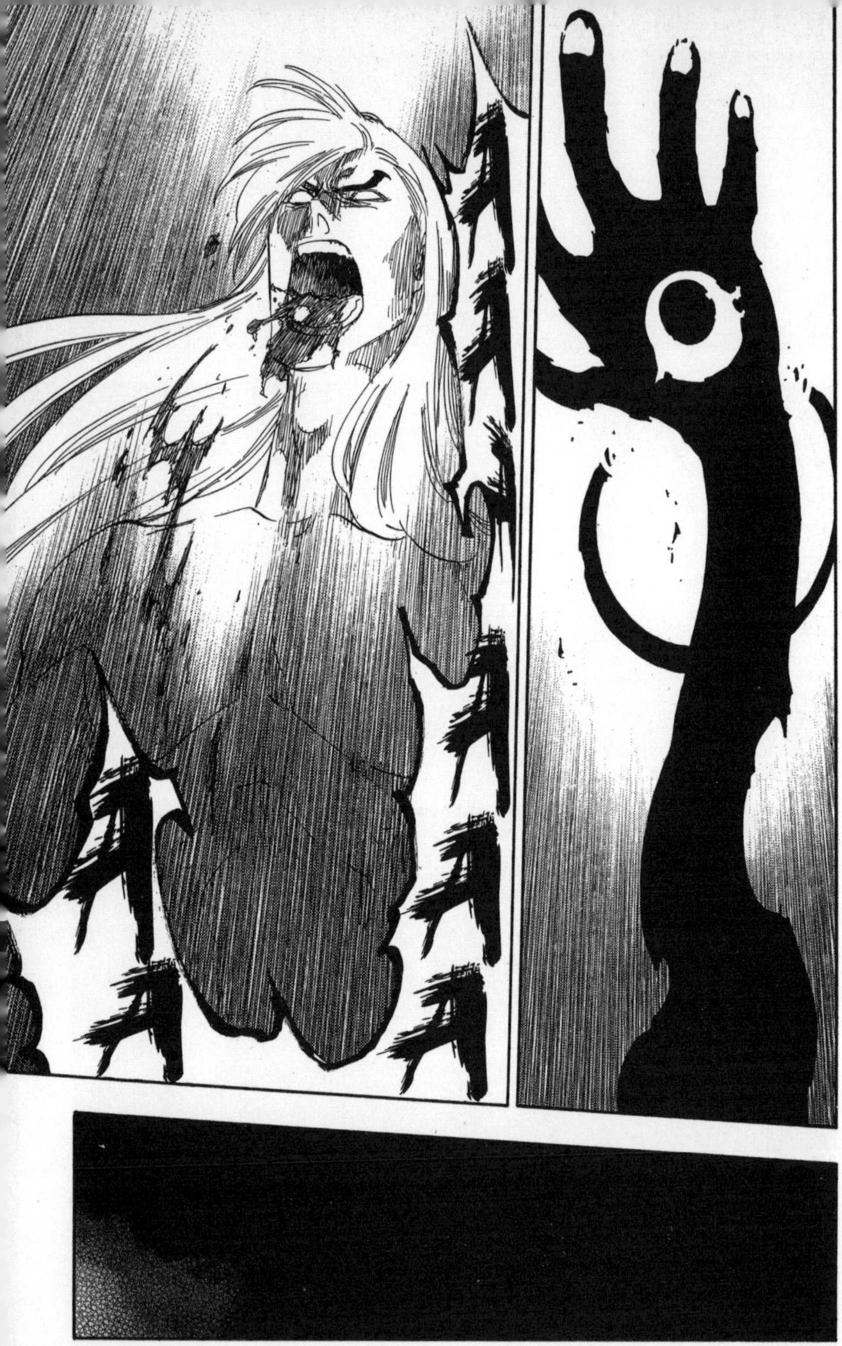

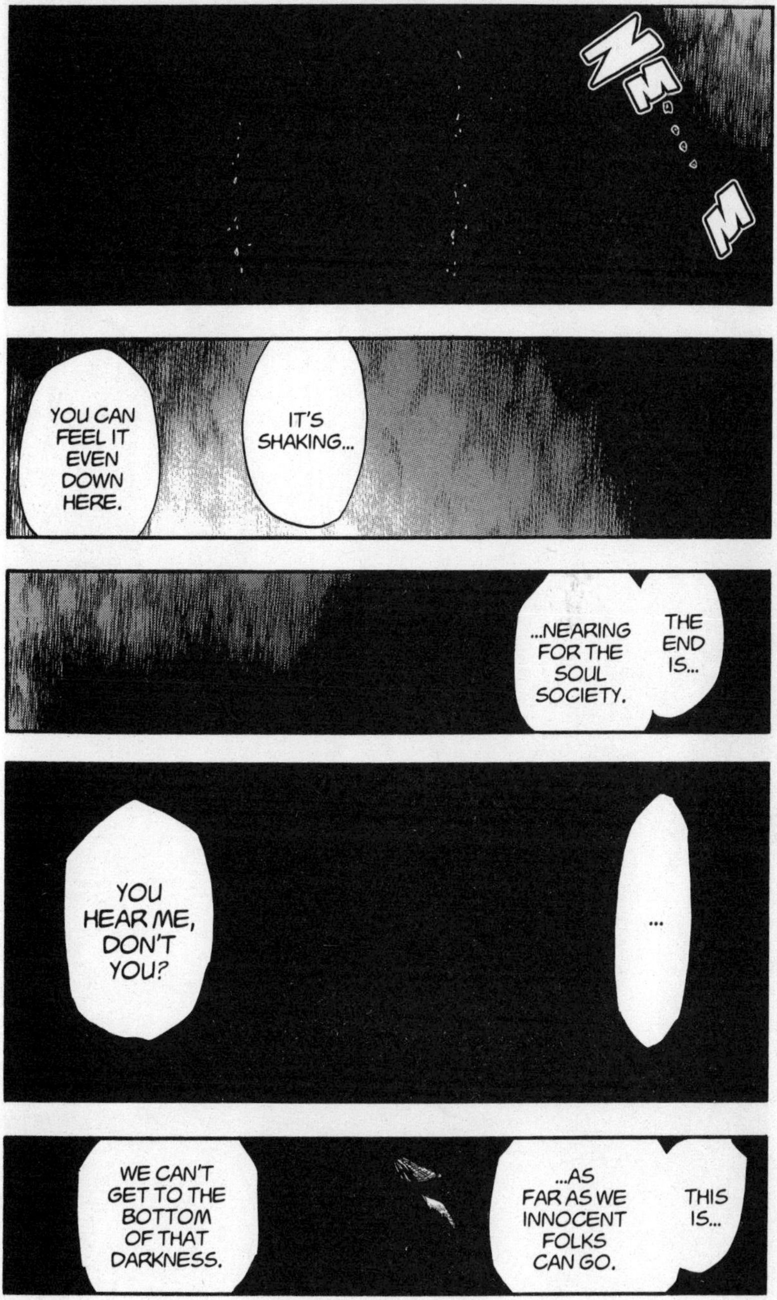
ZM....M
IT'S SHAKING...
YOU CAN FEEL IT EVEN DOWN HERE.
THE END IS...
...NEARING FOR THE SOUL SOCIETY.
...
YOU HEAR ME, DON'T YOU?
THIS IS...
...AS FAR AS WE INNOCENT FOLKS CAN GO.
WE CAN'T GET TO THE BOTTOM OF THAT DARKNESS.

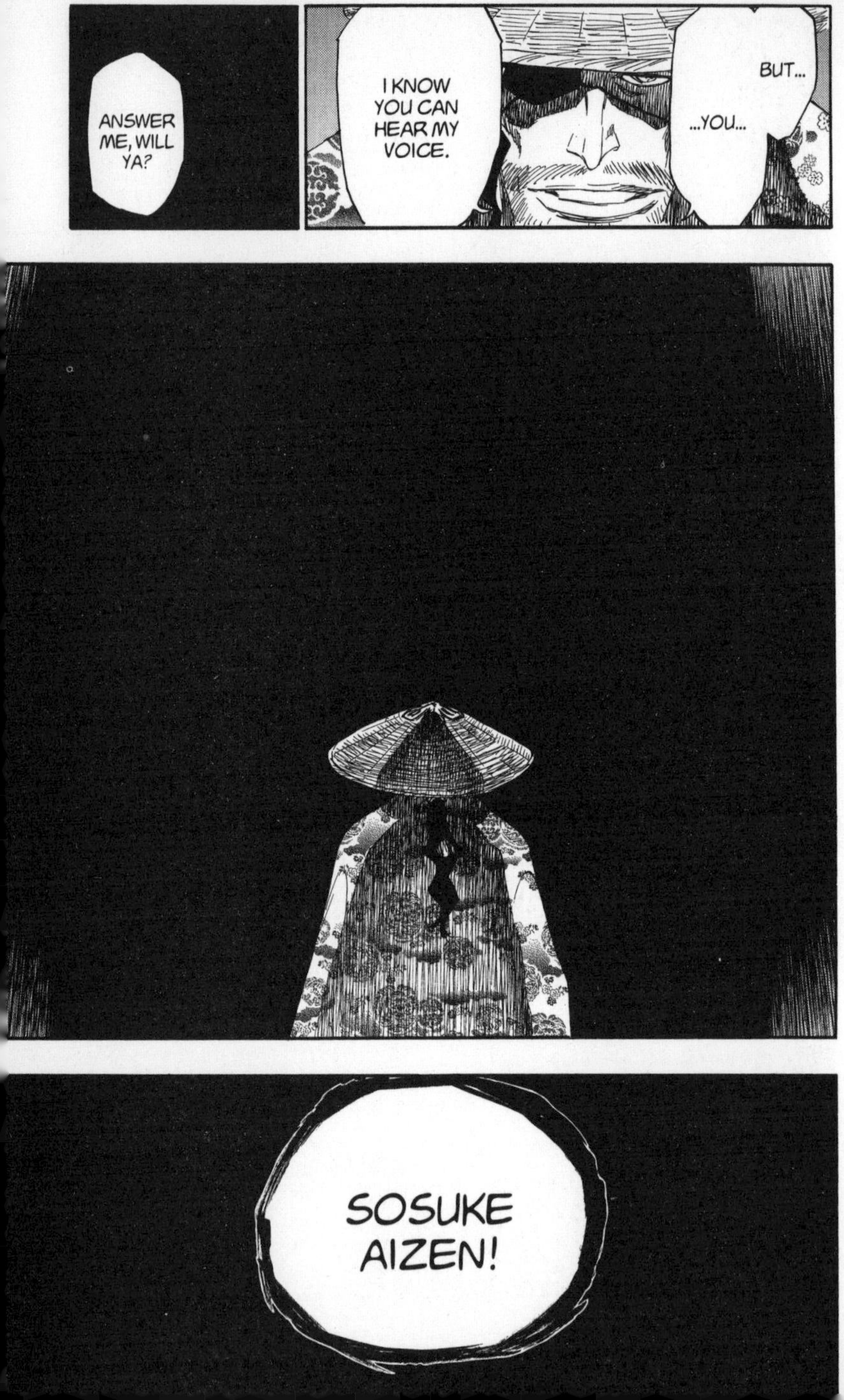
BUT...
...YOU...
I KNOW YOU CAN HEAR MY VOICE.
ANSWER ME, WILL YA?
SOSUKE AIZEN!

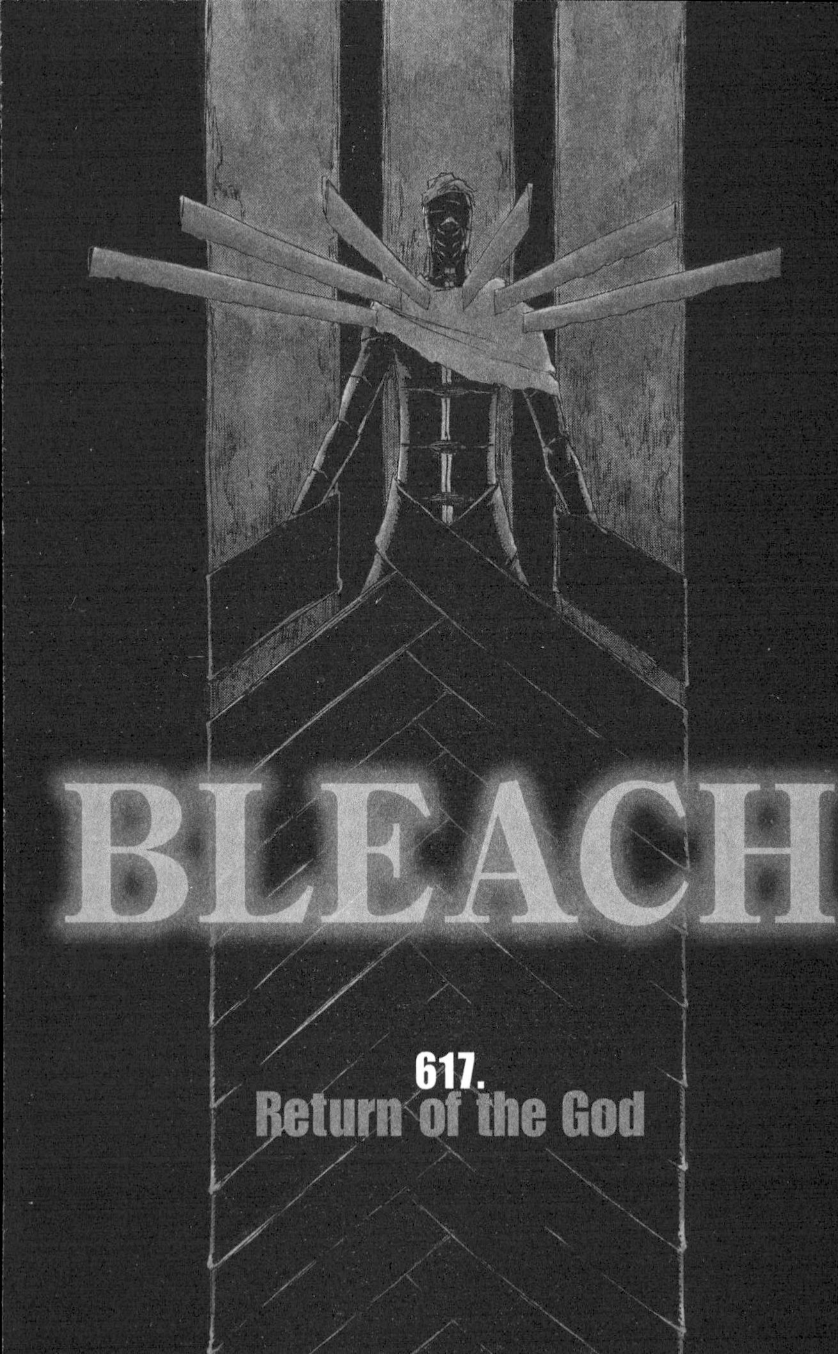
BLEACH
617.
Return of the God

BLEACH
ブリーチ

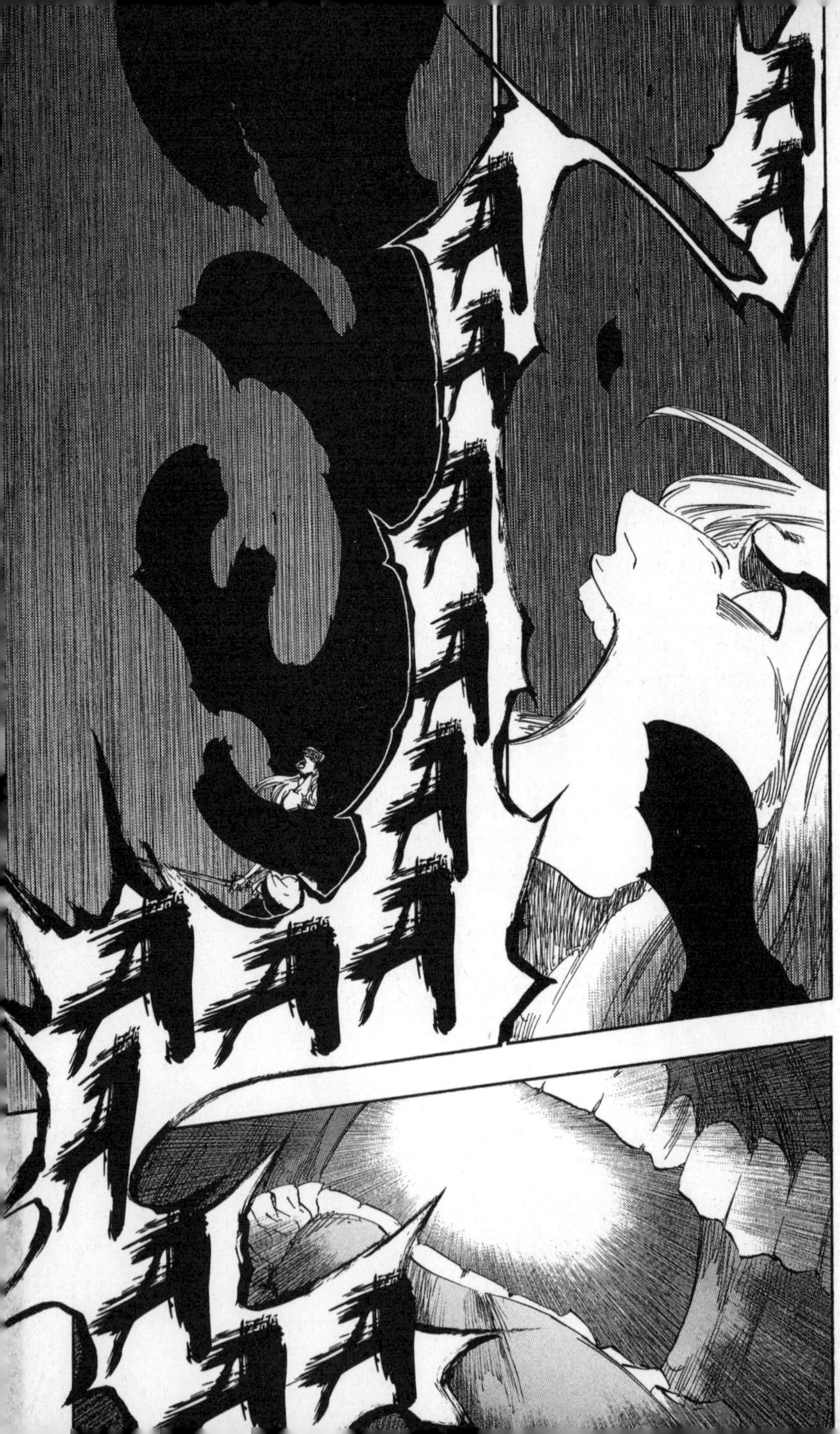

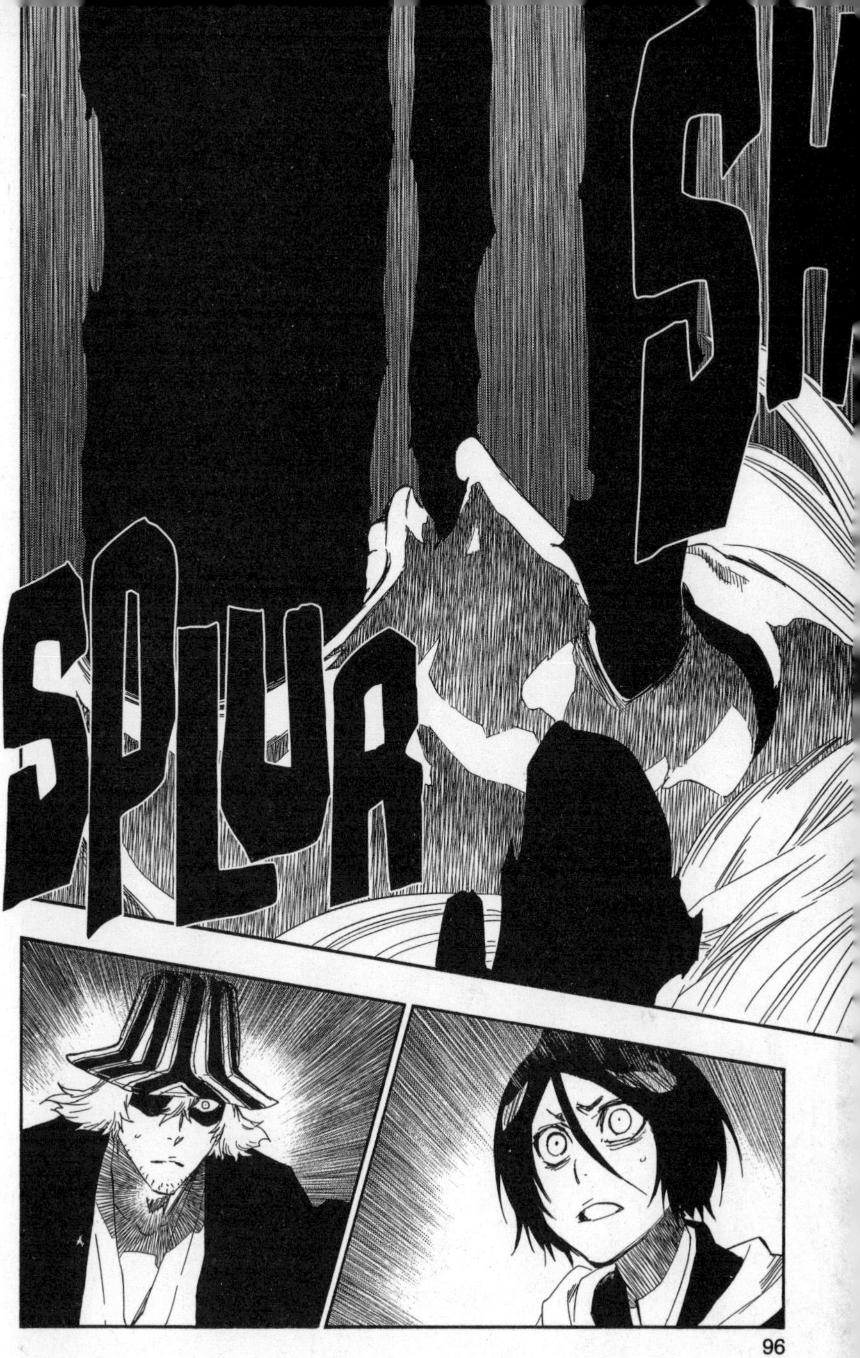
SPLUR

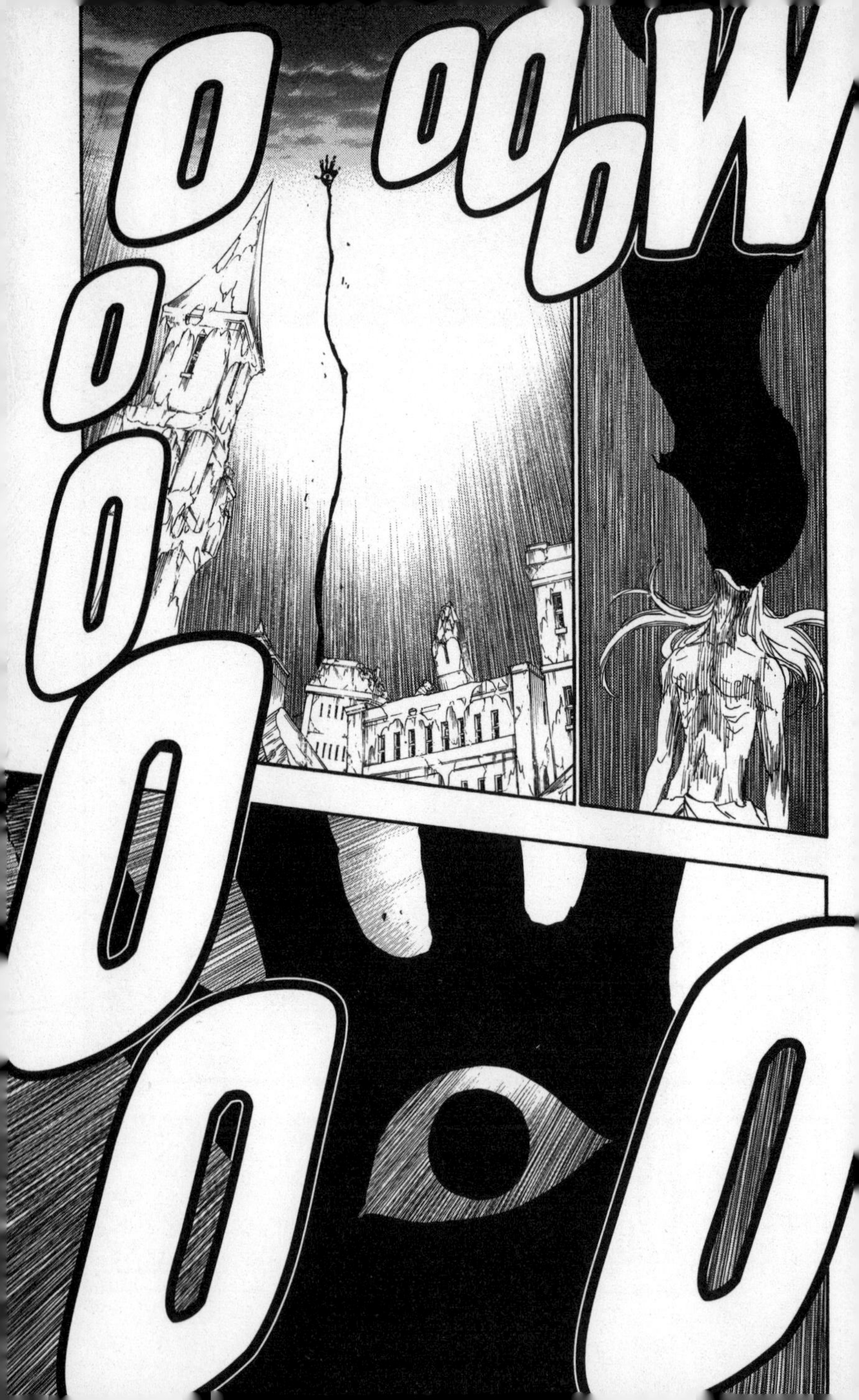
OOOOOOOOOW

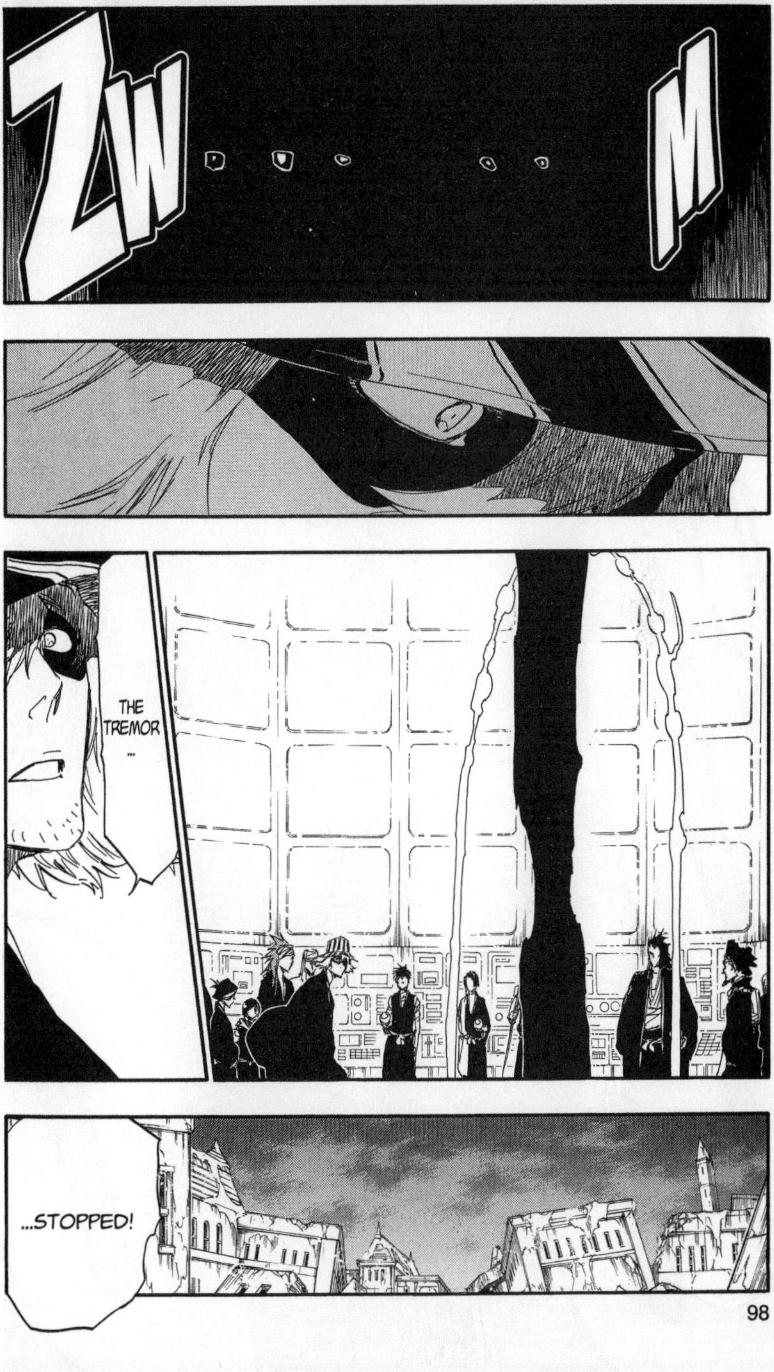
ZWMM
THE TREMOR ...
...STOPPED!

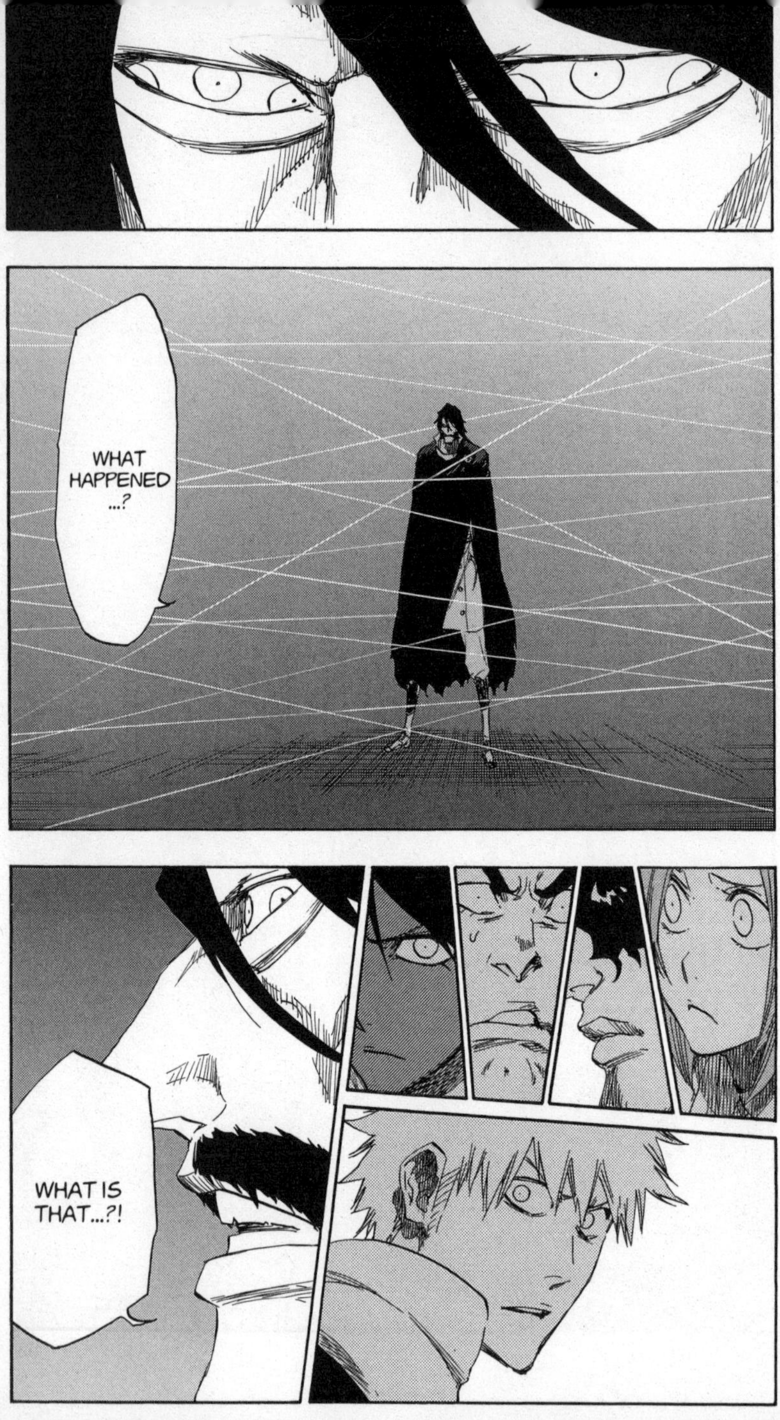
WHAT HAPPENED ...?
WHAT IS THAT...?!

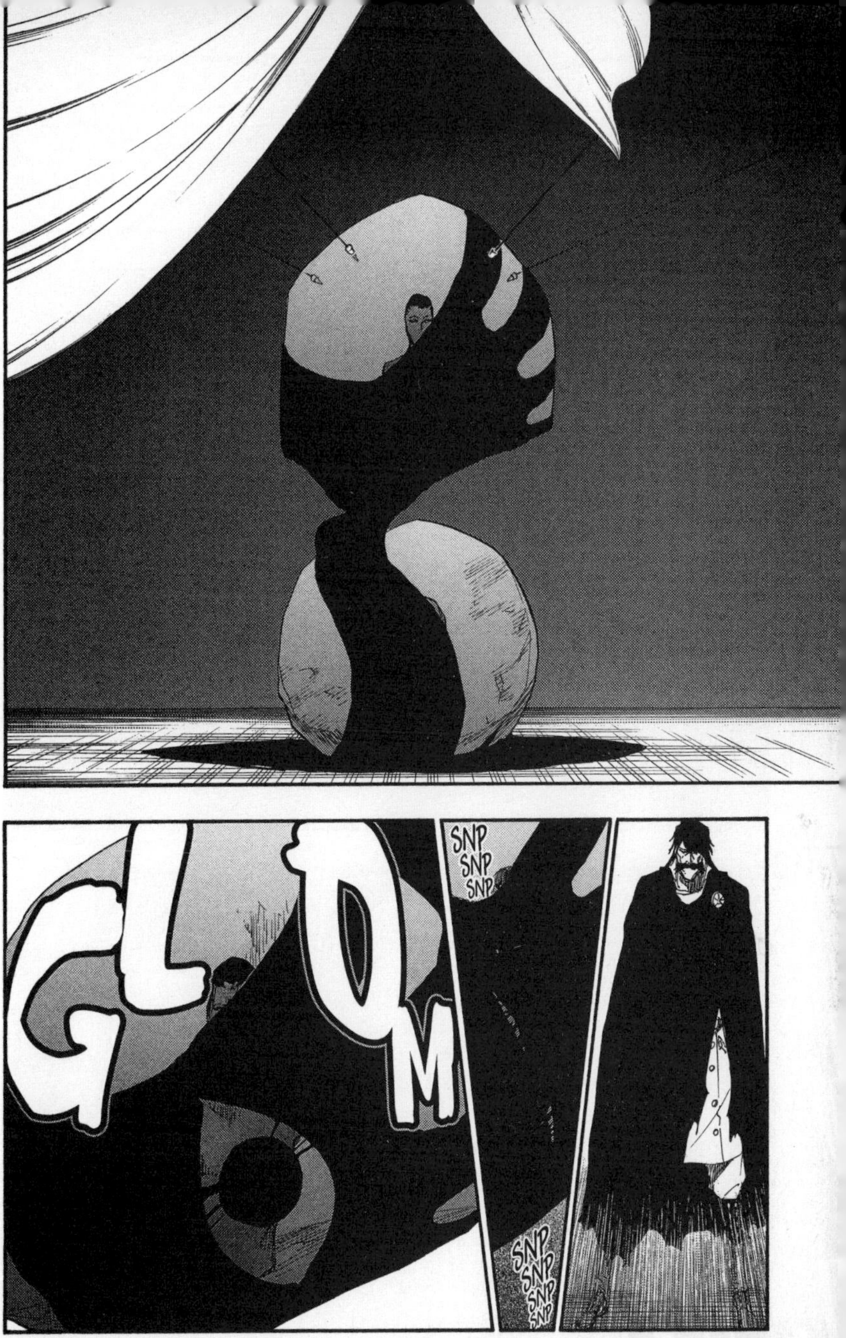
SNP SNP SNP
SNP SNP SNP SNP SNP
GLOM

READ THIS WAY

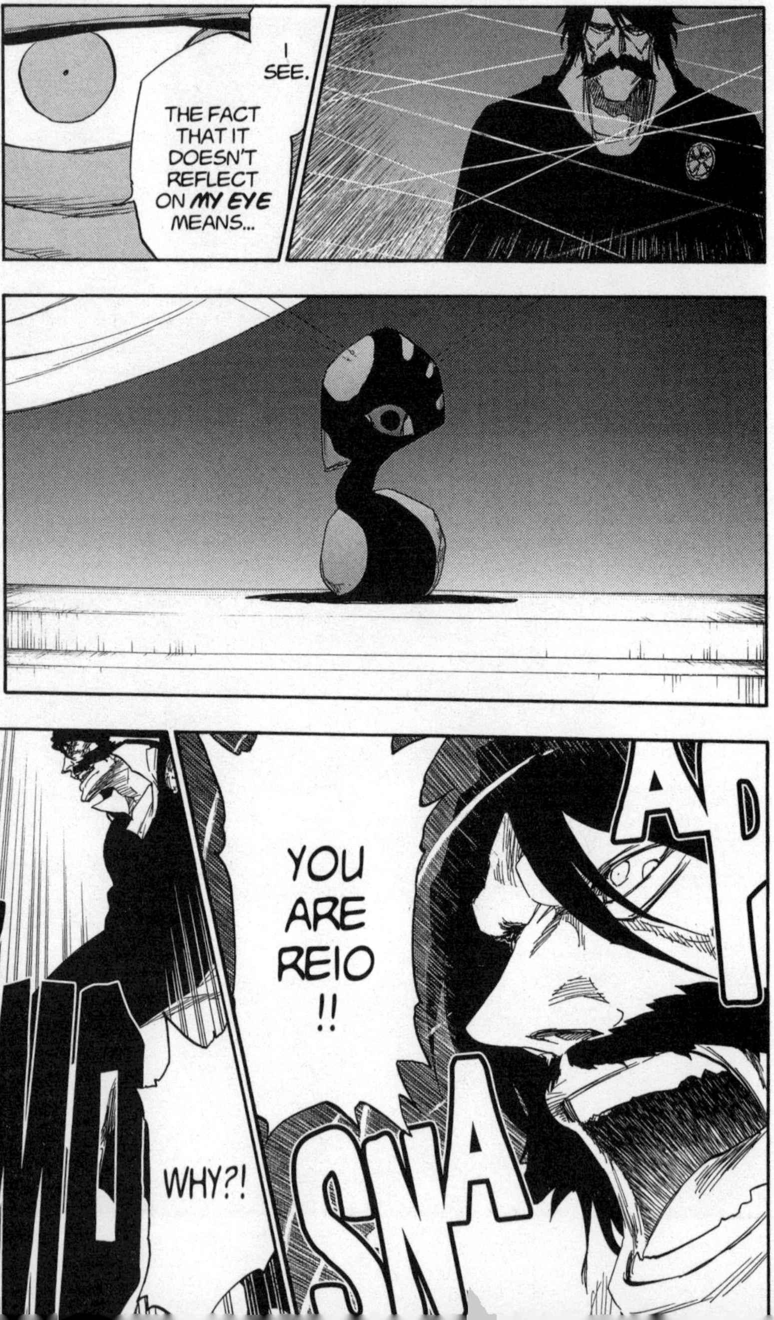
I SEE.
THE FACT THAT IT DOESN'T REFLECT ON ***MY EYE*** MEANS...
YOU ARE REIO!!
WHY?!

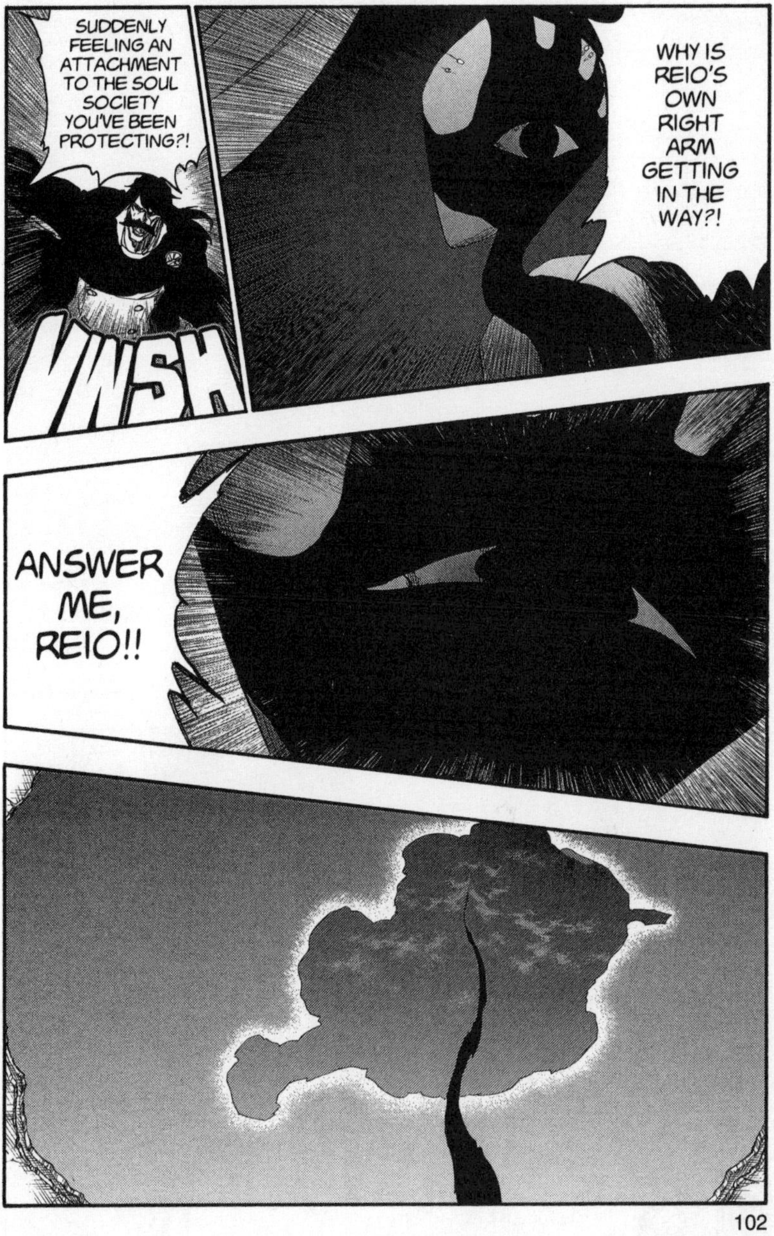
WHY IS REIO'S OWN RIGHT ARM GETTING IN THE WAY?!
SUDDENLY FEELING AN ATTACHMENT TO THE SOUL SOCIETY YOU'VE BEEN PROTECTING?!
VNSH
ANSWER ME, REIO!!

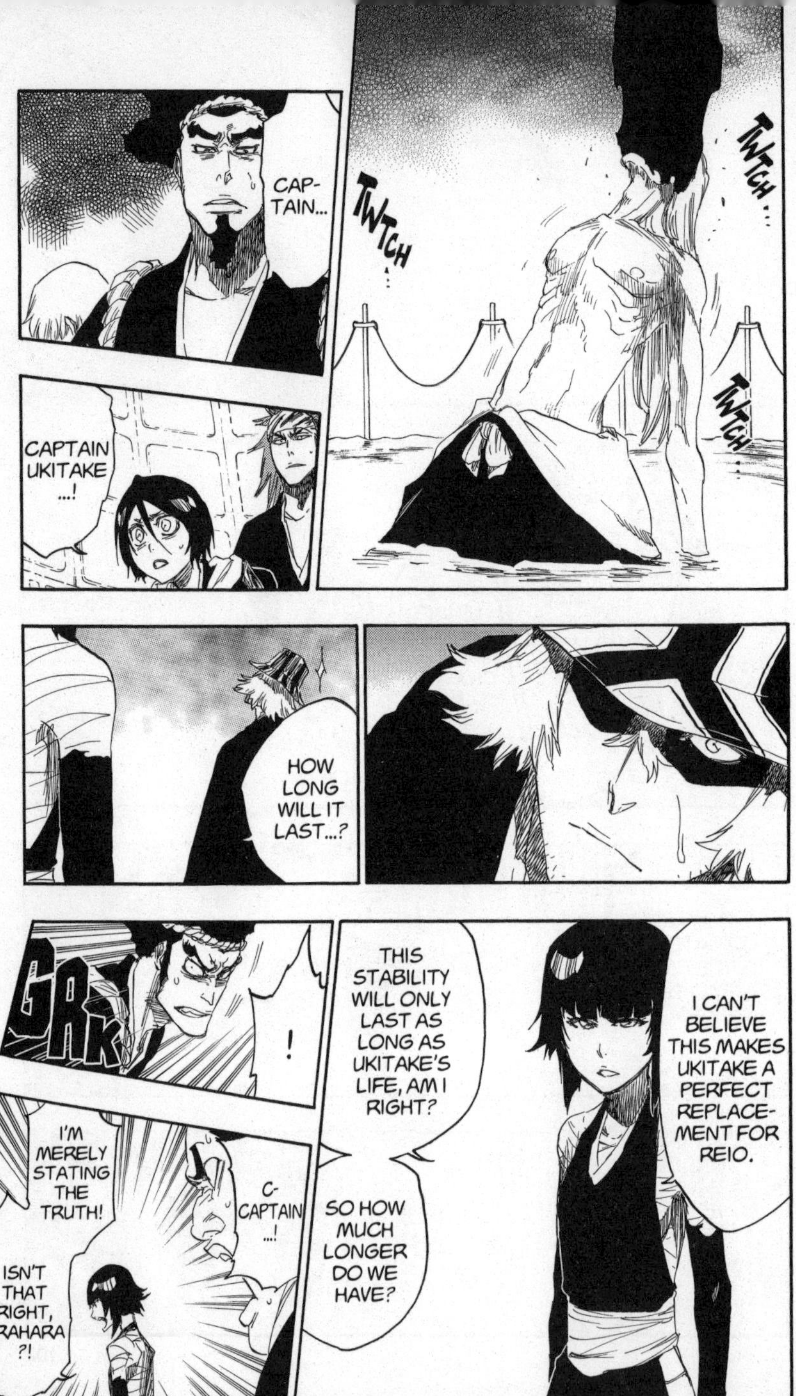
TWITCH...
TWITCH...
TWITCH
CAPTAIN...
CAPTAIN UKITAKE...!
HOW LONG WILL IT LAST...?
I CAN'T BELIEVE THIS MAKES UKITAKE A PERFECT REPLACEMENT FOR REIO.
THIS STABILITY WILL ONLY LAST AS LONG AS UKITAKE'S LIFE, AM I RIGHT?
SO HOW MUCH LONGER DO WE HAVE?
!
GRK
C-CAPTAIN...!
I'M MERELY STATING THE TRUTH!
ISN'T THAT RIGHT, URAHARA?!

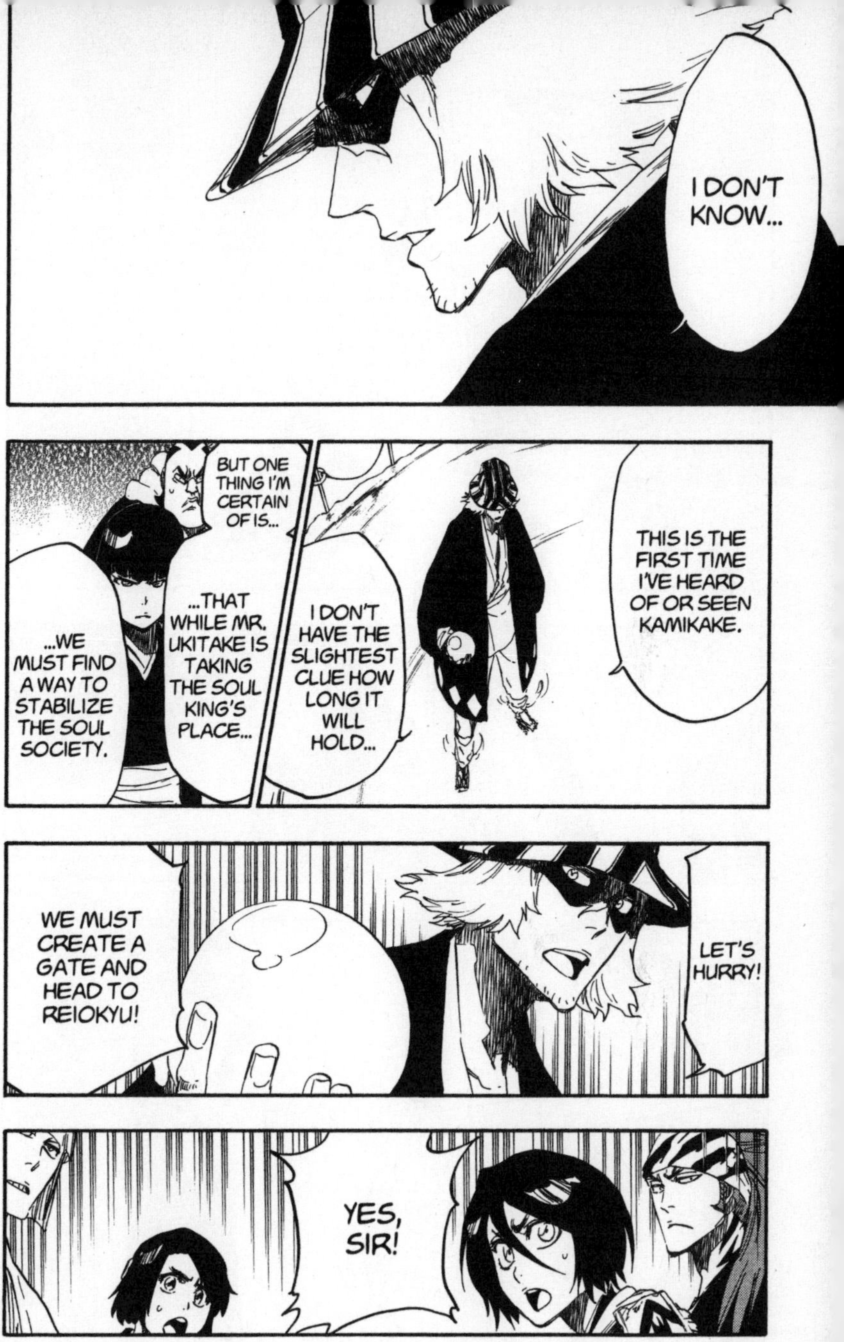
I DON'T KNOW...
THIS IS THE FIRST TIME I'VE HEARD OF OR SEEN KAMIKAKE.
I DON'T HAVE THE SLIGHTEST CLUE HOW LONG IT WILL HOLD...
BUT ONE THING I'M CERTAIN OF IS...
...THAT WHILE MR. UKITAKE IS TAKING THE SOUL KING'S PLACE...
...WE MUST FIND A WAY TO STABILIZE THE SOUL SOCIETY.
LET'S HURRY!
WE MUST CREATE A GATE AND HEAD TO REIOKYU!
YES, SIR!

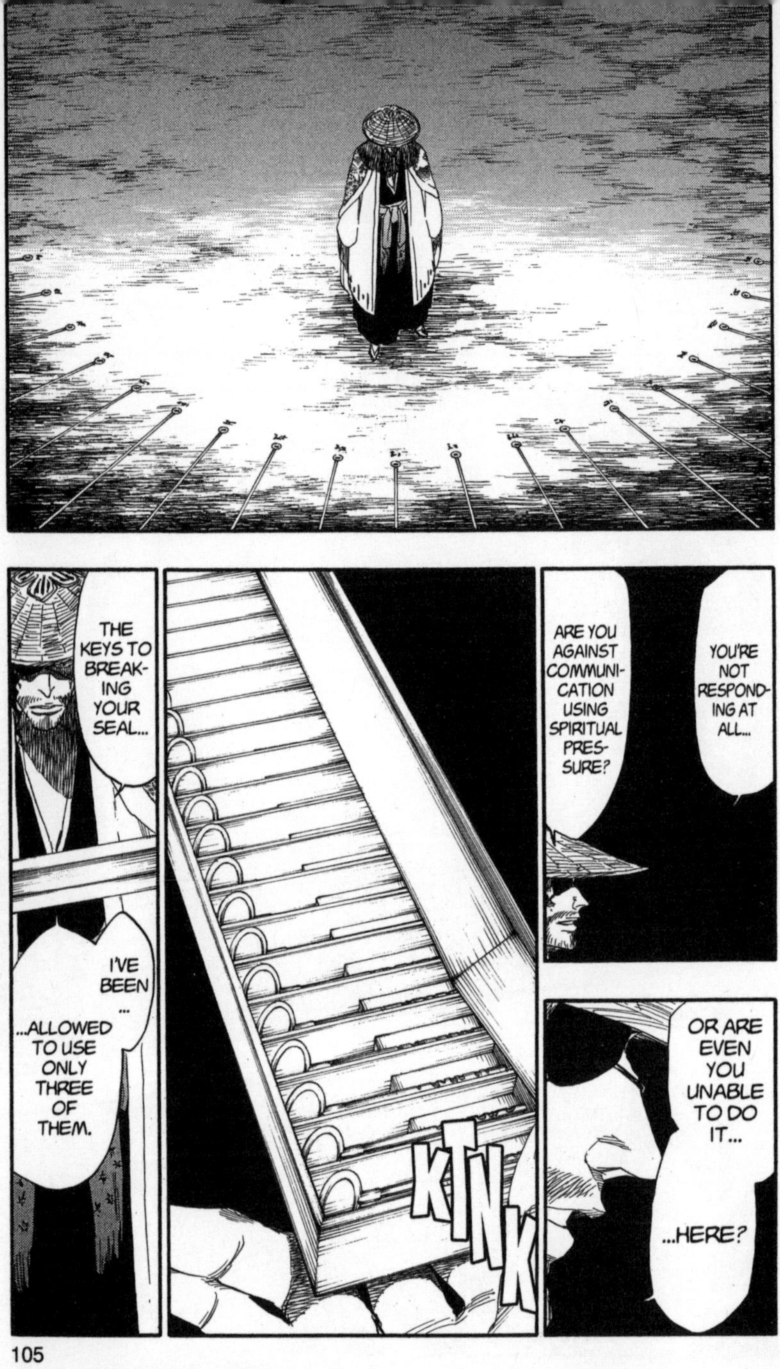
YOU'RE NOT RESPONDING AT ALL...
ARE YOU AGAINST COMMUNICATION USING SPIRITUAL PRESSURE?
OR ARE EVEN YOU UNABLE TO DO IT...
...HERE?
KTNK
THE KEYS TO BREAKING YOUR SEAL...
I'VE BEEN...
...ALLOWED TO USE ONLY THREE OF THEM.

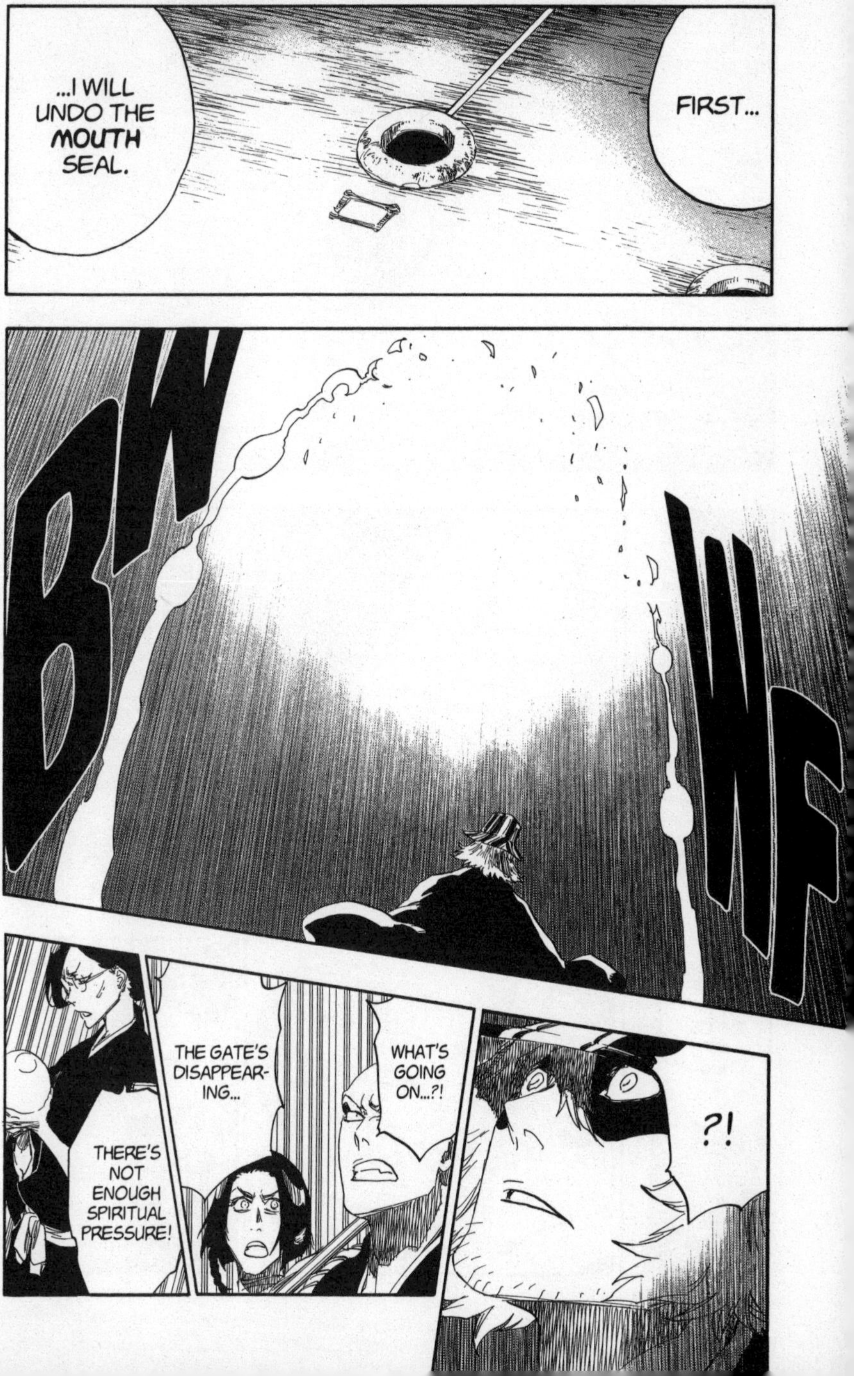
FIRST...
...I WILL UNDO THE MOUTH SEAL.
BW
WF
?!
WHAT'S GOING ON...?!
THE GATE'S DISAPPEAR-ING...
THERE'S NOT ENOUGH SPIRITUAL PRESSURE!

READ THIS WAY

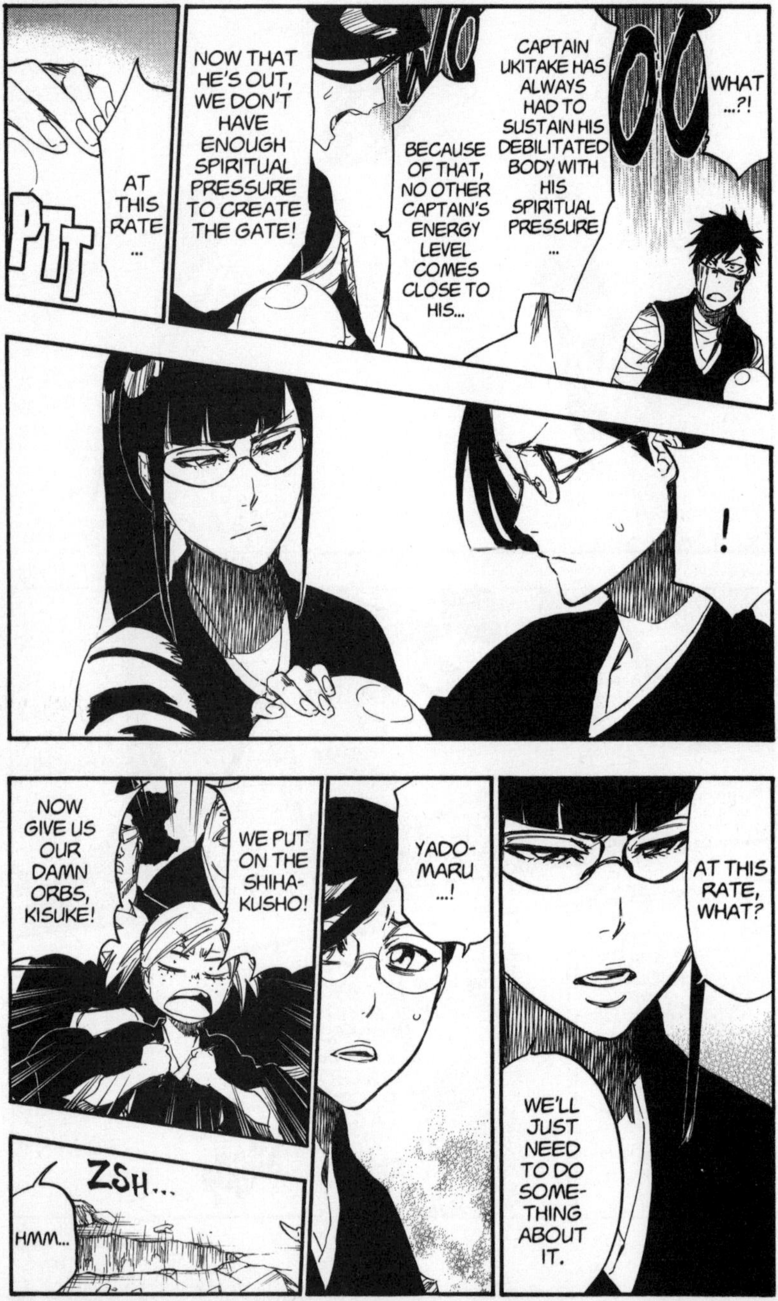
WHAT ...?!
WOOO
CAPTAIN UKITAKE HAS ALWAYS HAD TO SUSTAIN HIS DEBILITATED BODY WITH HIS SPIRITUAL PRESSURE ...
BECAUSE OF THAT, NO OTHER CAPTAIN'S ENERGY LEVEL COMES CLOSE TO HIS...
NOW THAT HE'S OUT, WE DON'T HAVE ENOUGH SPIRITUAL PRESSURE TO CREATE THE GATE!
AT THIS RATE ...
PTT
!
AT THIS RATE, WHAT?
WE'LL JUST NEED TO DO SOME-THING ABOUT IT.
YADO-MARU ...!
WE PUT ON THE SHIHA-KUSHO!
NOW GIVE US OUR DAMN ORBS, KISUKE!
ZSH...
HMM...

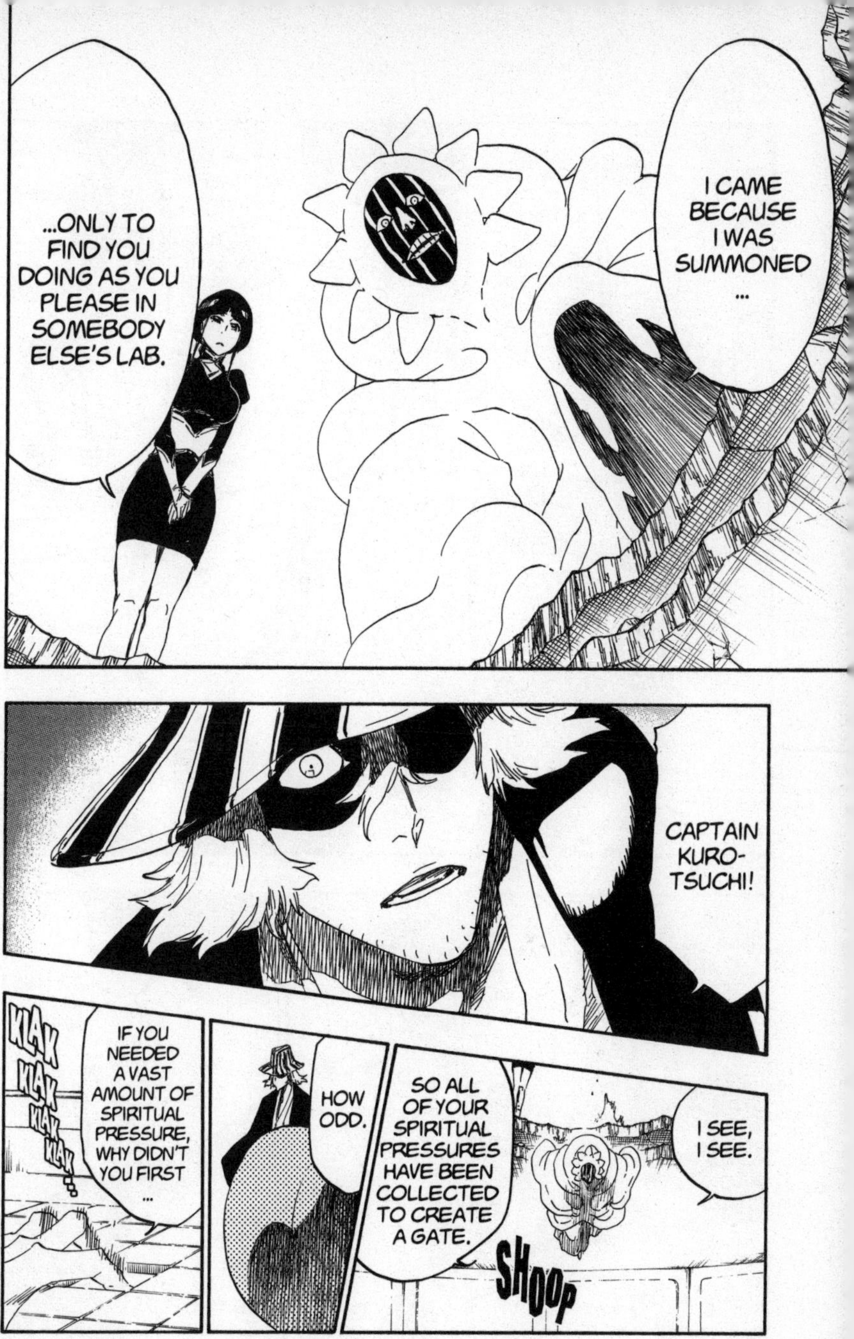
I CAME BECAUSE I WAS SUMMONED ...
...ONLY TO FIND YOU DOING AS YOU PLEASE IN SOMEBODY ELSE'S LAB.
CAPTAIN KURO-TSUCHI!
I SEE, I SEE.
SHOOP
SO ALL OF YOUR SPIRITUAL PRESSURES HAVE BEEN COLLECTED TO CREATE A GATE.
HOW ODD.
IF YOU NEEDED A VAST AMOUNT OF SPIRITUAL PRESSURE, WHY DIDN'T YOU FIRST ...
KLAK KLAK KLAK KLAK

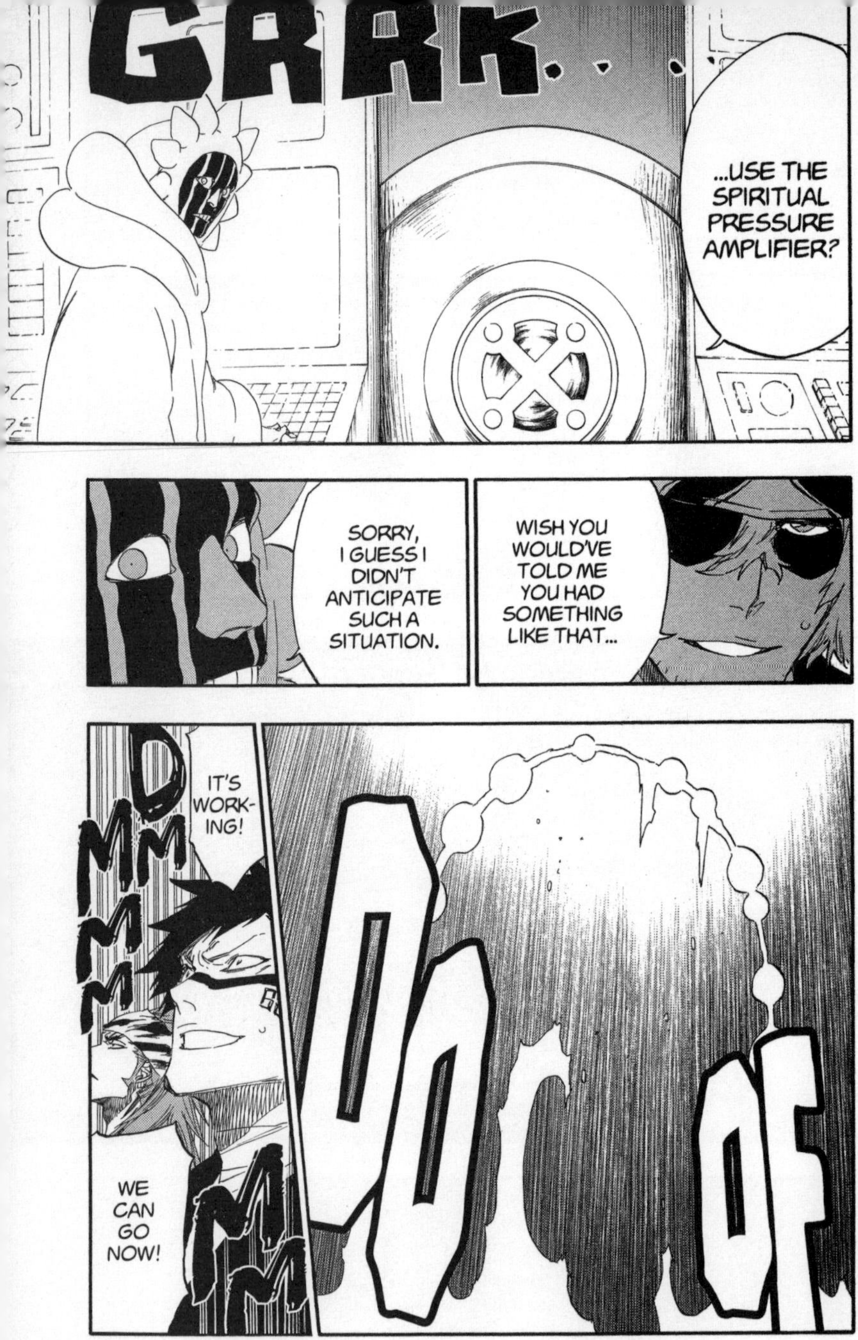
...USE THE SPIRITUAL PRESSURE AMPLIFIER?
GRRR...
WISH YOU WOULD'VE TOLD ME YOU HAD SOMETHING LIKE THAT...
SORRY, I GUESS I DIDN'T ANTICIPATE SUCH A SITUATION.
DOOF
IT'S WORKING!
DMMMM
WE CAN GO NOW!

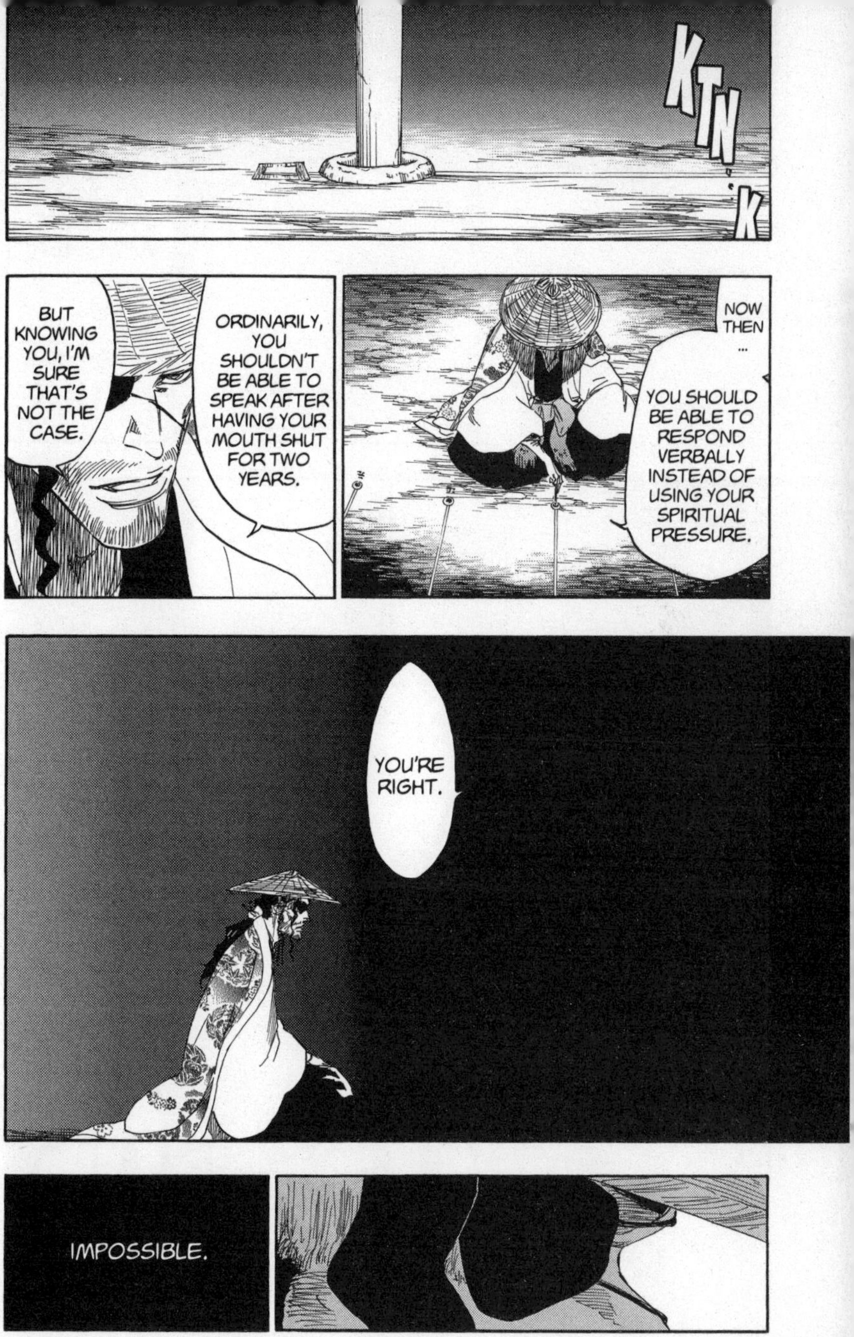

KTNK
NOW THEN ...
YOU SHOULD BE ABLE TO RESPOND VERBALLY INSTEAD OF USING YOUR SPIRITUAL PRESSURE.
ORDINARILY, YOU SHOULDN'T BE ABLE TO SPEAK AFTER HAVING YOUR MOUTH SHUT FOR TWO YEARS.
BUT KNOWING YOU, I'M SURE THAT'S NOT THE CASE.
YOU'RE RIGHT.
IMPOSSIBLE.

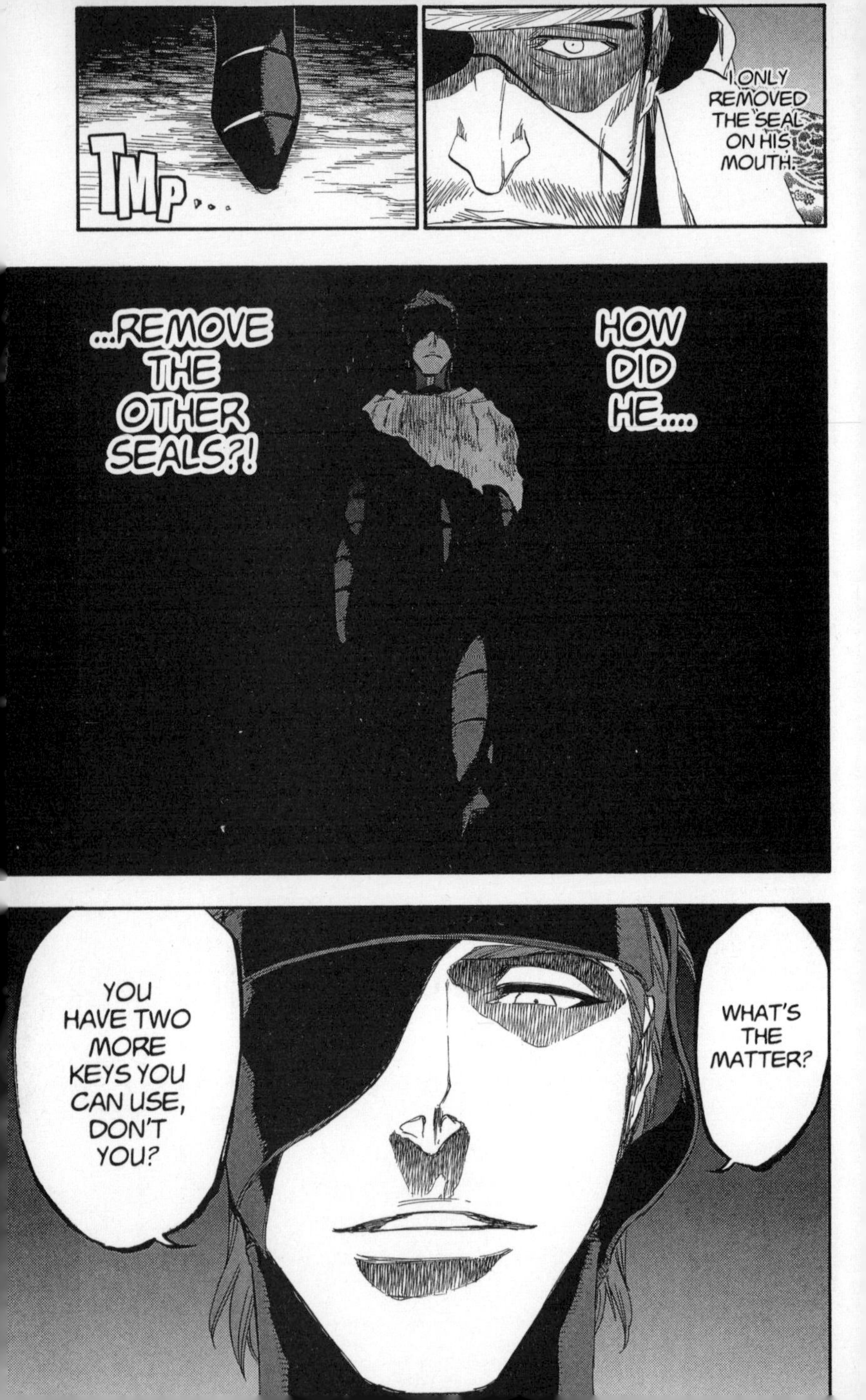
I ONLY REMOVED THE SEAL ON HIS MOUTH.
TMP...
HOW DID HE....
...REMOVE THE OTHER SEALS?!
WHAT'S THE MATTER?
YOU HAVE TWO MORE KEYS YOU CAN USE, DON'T YOU?

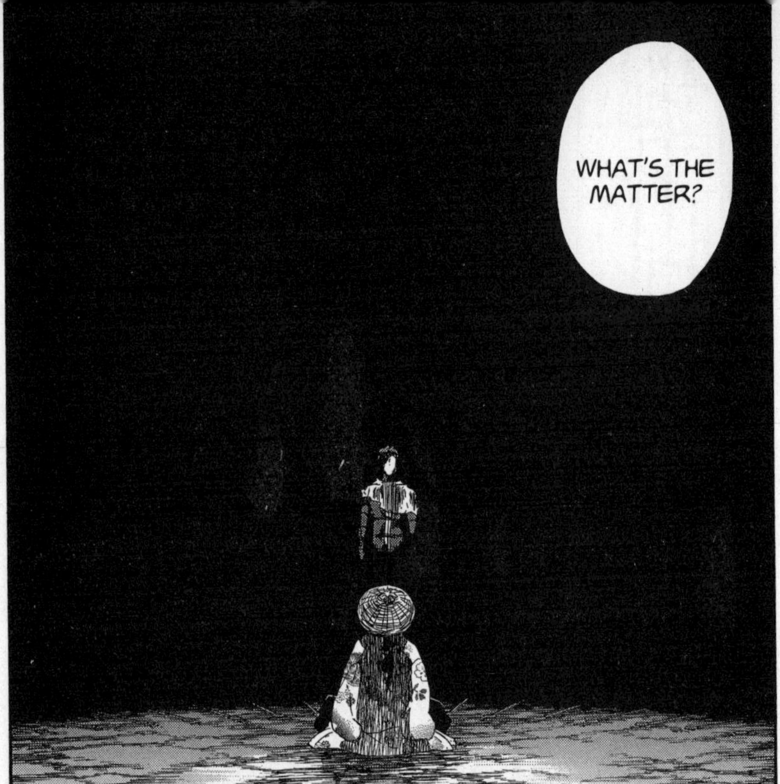
WHAT'S THE MATTER?

618. THE DARK ARM

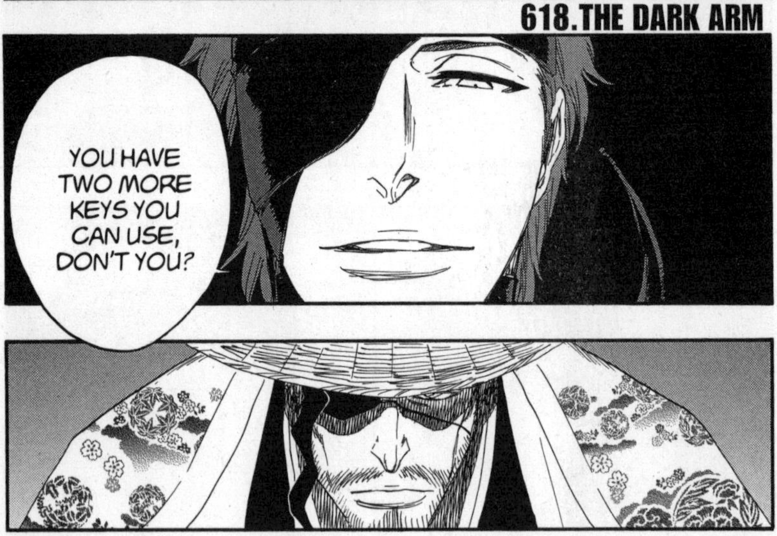
YOU HAVE TWO MORE KEYS YOU CAN USE, DON'T YOU?

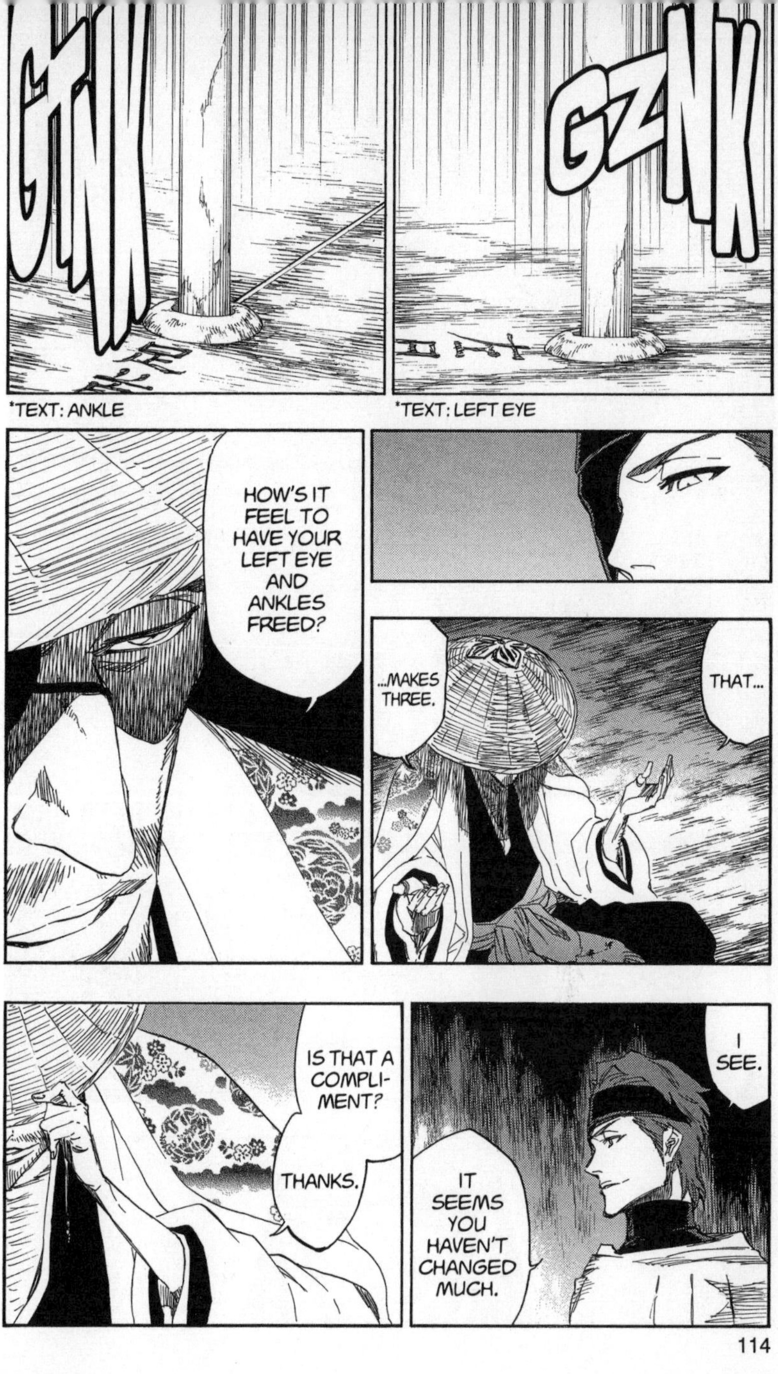
GZNK
*TEXT: LEFT EYE
GTNK
*TEXT: ANKLE
THAT...
...MAKES THREE.
HOW'S IT FEEL TO HAVE YOUR LEFT EYE AND ANKLES FREED?
I SEE.
IT SEEMS YOU HAVEN'T CHANGED MUCH.
IS THAT A COMPLIMENT?
THANKS.

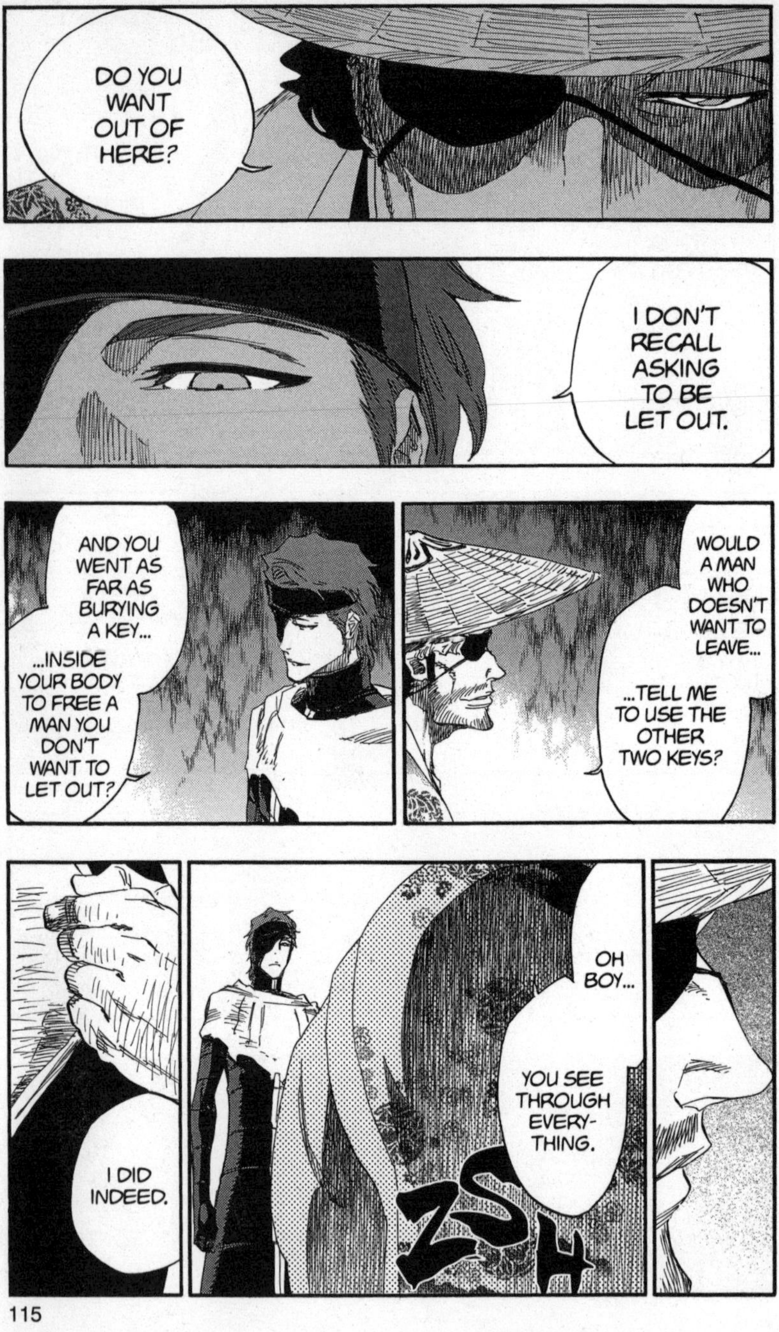
DO YOU WANT OUT OF HERE?
I DON'T RECALL ASKING TO BE LET OUT.
WOULD A MAN WHO DOESN'T WANT TO LEAVE...
...TELL ME TO USE THE OTHER TWO KEYS?
AND YOU WENT AS FAR AS BURYING A KEY...
...INSIDE YOUR BODY TO FREE A MAN YOU DON'T WANT TO LET OUT?
OH BOY...
YOU SEE THROUGH EVERY-THING.
ZSH
I DID INDEED.

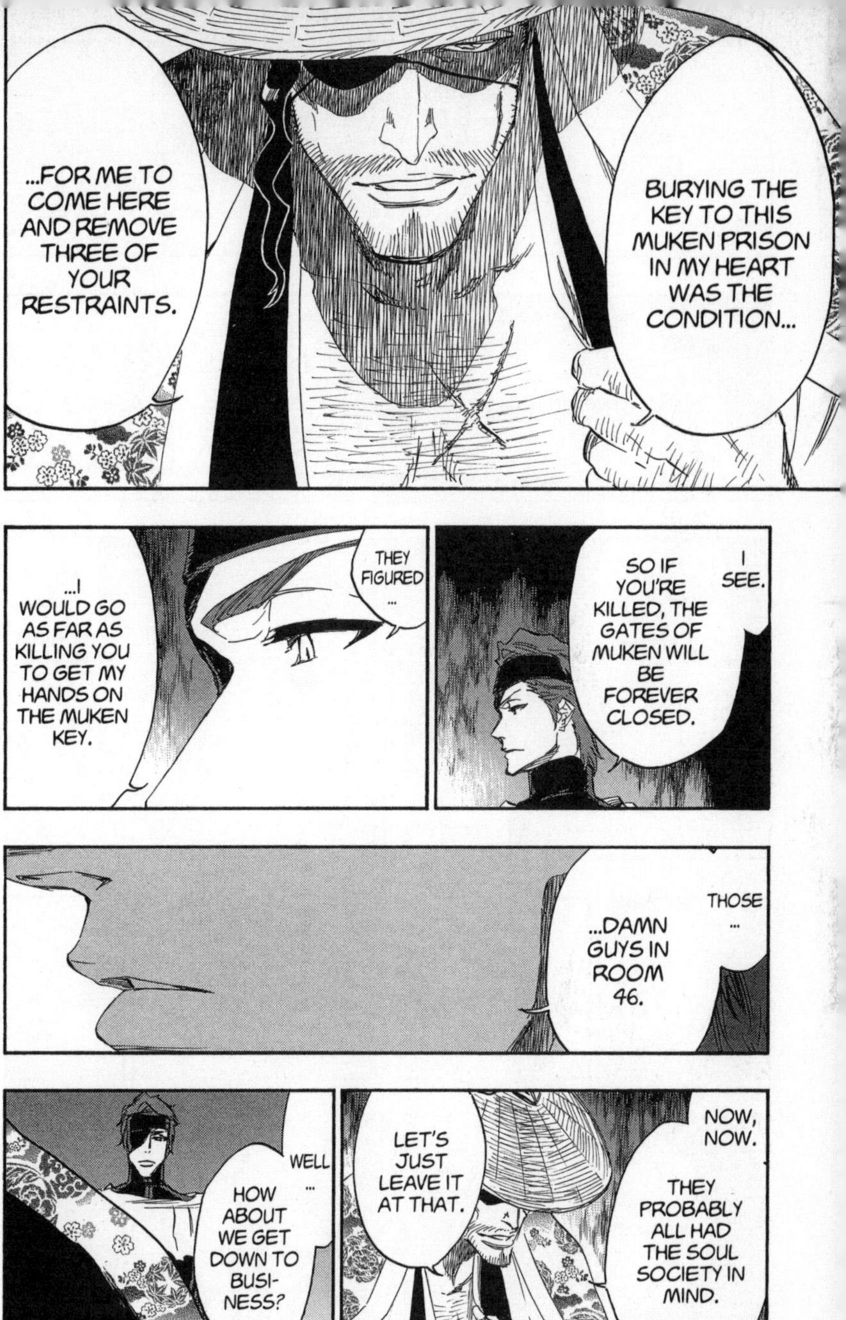
BURYING THE KEY TO THIS MUKEN PRISON IN MY HEART WAS THE CONDITION...
...FOR ME TO COME HERE AND REMOVE THREE OF YOUR RESTRAINTS.
I SEE.
SO IF YOU'RE KILLED, THE GATES OF MUKEN WILL BE FOREVER CLOSED.
THEY FIGURED...
...I WOULD GO AS FAR AS KILLING YOU TO GET MY HANDS ON THE MUKEN KEY.
THOSE...
...DAMN GUYS IN ROOM 46.
NOW, NOW.
THEY PROBABLY ALL HAD THE SOUL SOCIETY IN MIND.
LET'S JUST LEAVE IT AT THAT.
WELL...
HOW ABOUT WE GET DOWN TO BUSI-NESS?

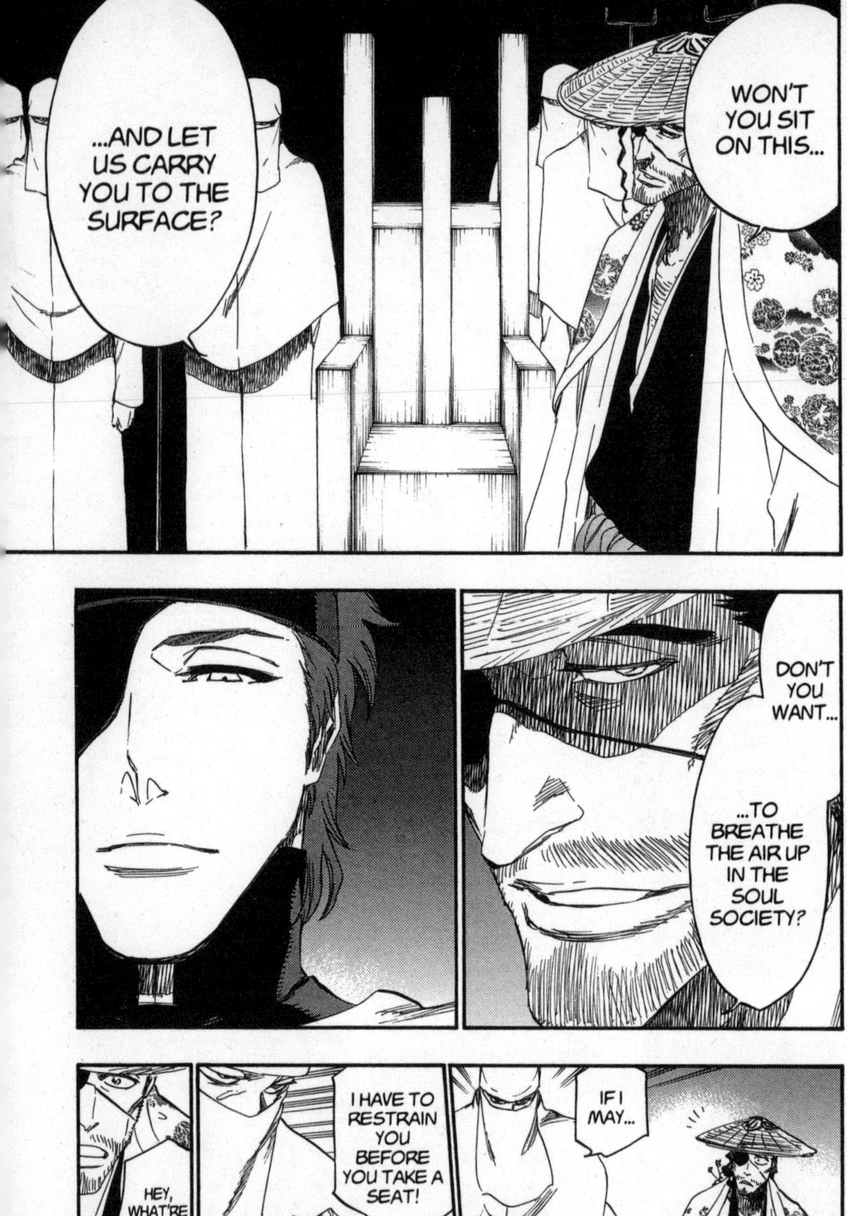
WON'T YOU SIT ON THIS...
...AND LET US CARRY YOU TO THE SURFACE?
DON'T YOU WANT...
...TO BREATHE THE AIR UP IN THE SOUL SOCIETY?
IF I MAY...
TMP
I HAVE TO RESTRAIN YOU BEFORE YOU TAKE A SEAT!
HEY, WHAT'RE YOU–

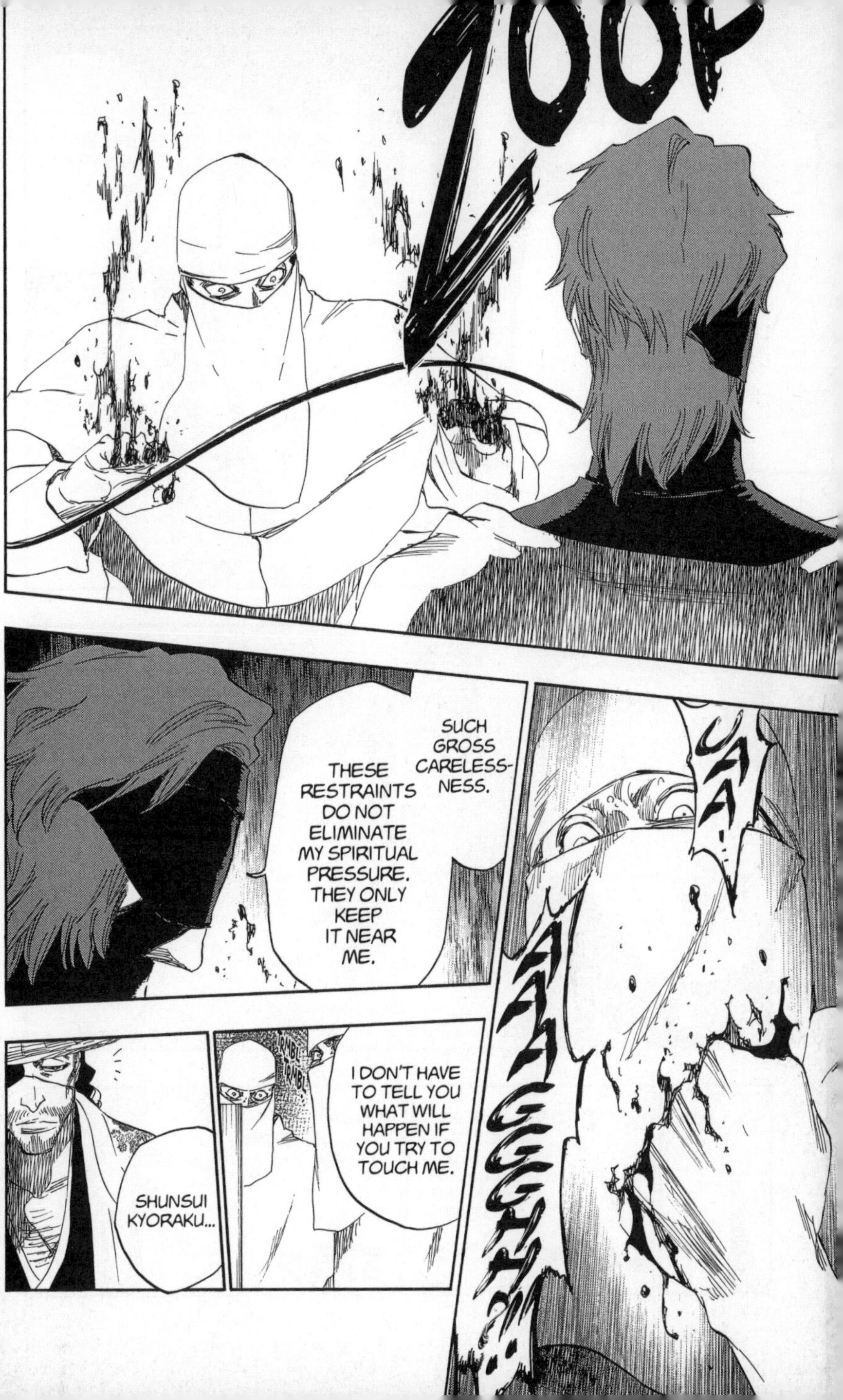
ZOOP
UAA!
AAAGGGGHH!!?
SUCH GROSS CARELESS-NESS.
THESE RESTRAINTS DO NOT ELIMINATE MY SPIRITUAL PRESSURE. THEY ONLY KEEP IT NEAR ME.
TRMBL TRMBL
I DON'T HAVE TO TELL YOU WHAT WILL HAPPEN IF YOU TRY TO TOUCH ME.
SHUNSUI KYORAKU...

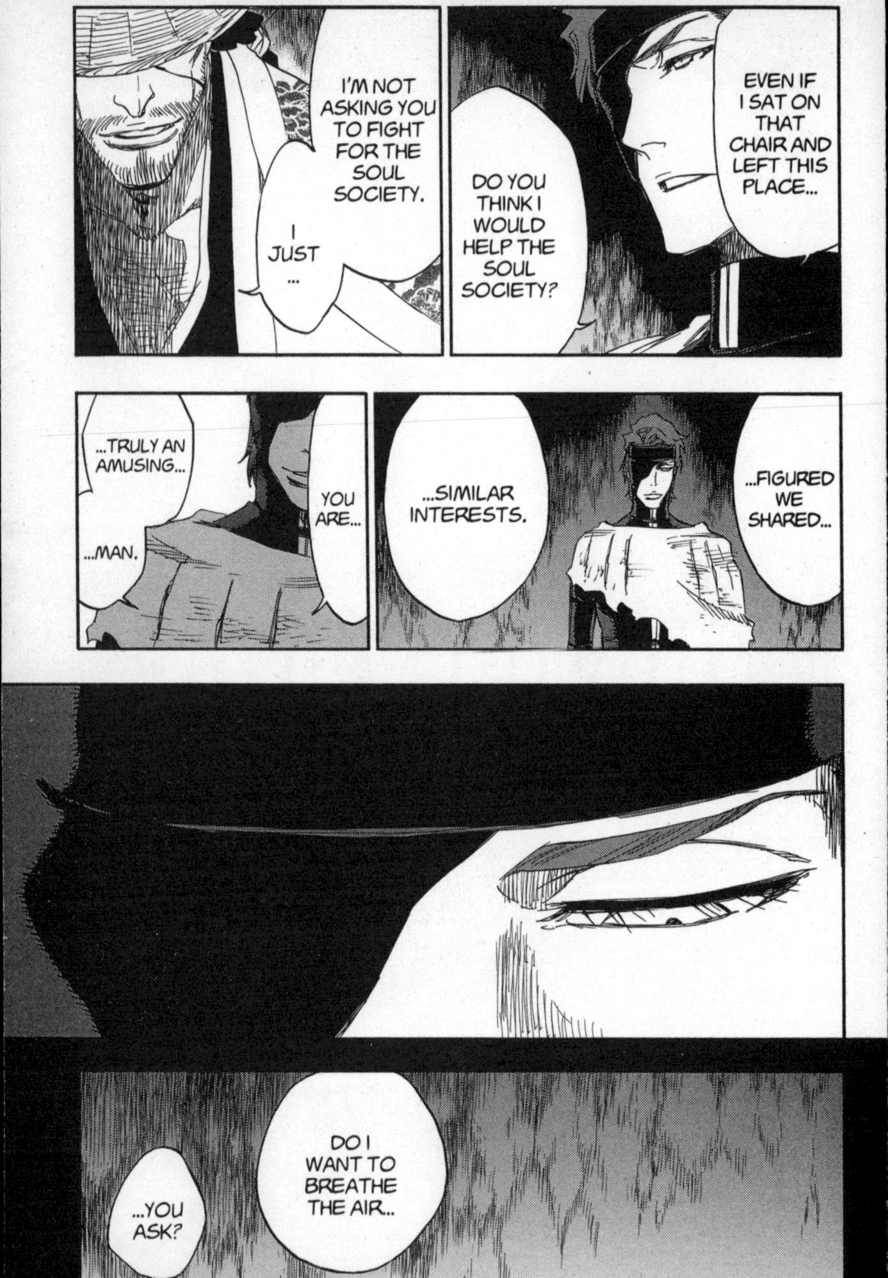
EVEN IF I SAT ON THAT CHAIR AND LEFT THIS PLACE...
DO YOU THINK I WOULD HELP THE SOUL SOCIETY?
I'M NOT ASKING YOU TO FIGHT FOR THE SOUL SOCIETY.
I JUST ...
...FIGURED WE SHARED...
...SIMILAR INTERESTS.
YOU ARE...
...TRULY AN AMUSING...
...MAN.
DO I WANT TO BREATHE THE AIR...
...YOU ASK?

BLEACH 618.

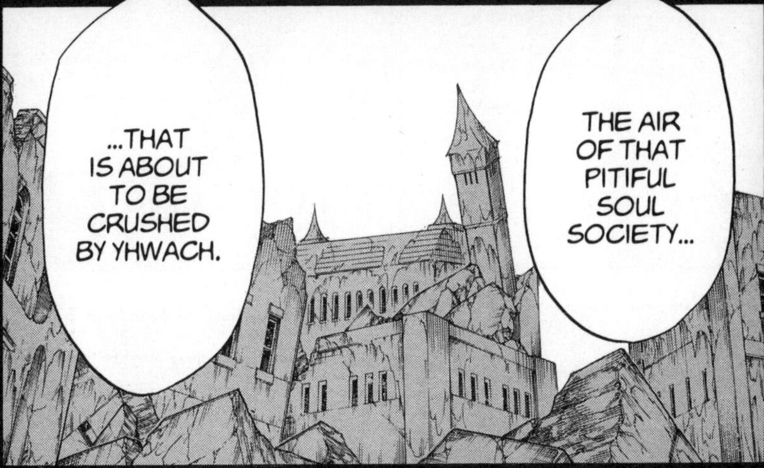
THE AIR OF THAT PITIFUL SOUL SOCIETY...
...THAT IS ABOUT TO BE CRUSHED BY YHWACH.

The Dark Arm

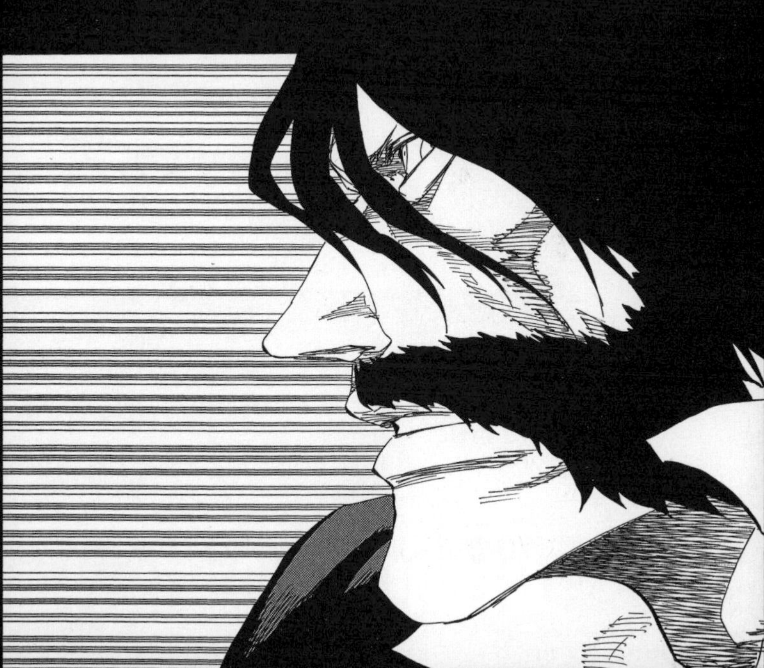

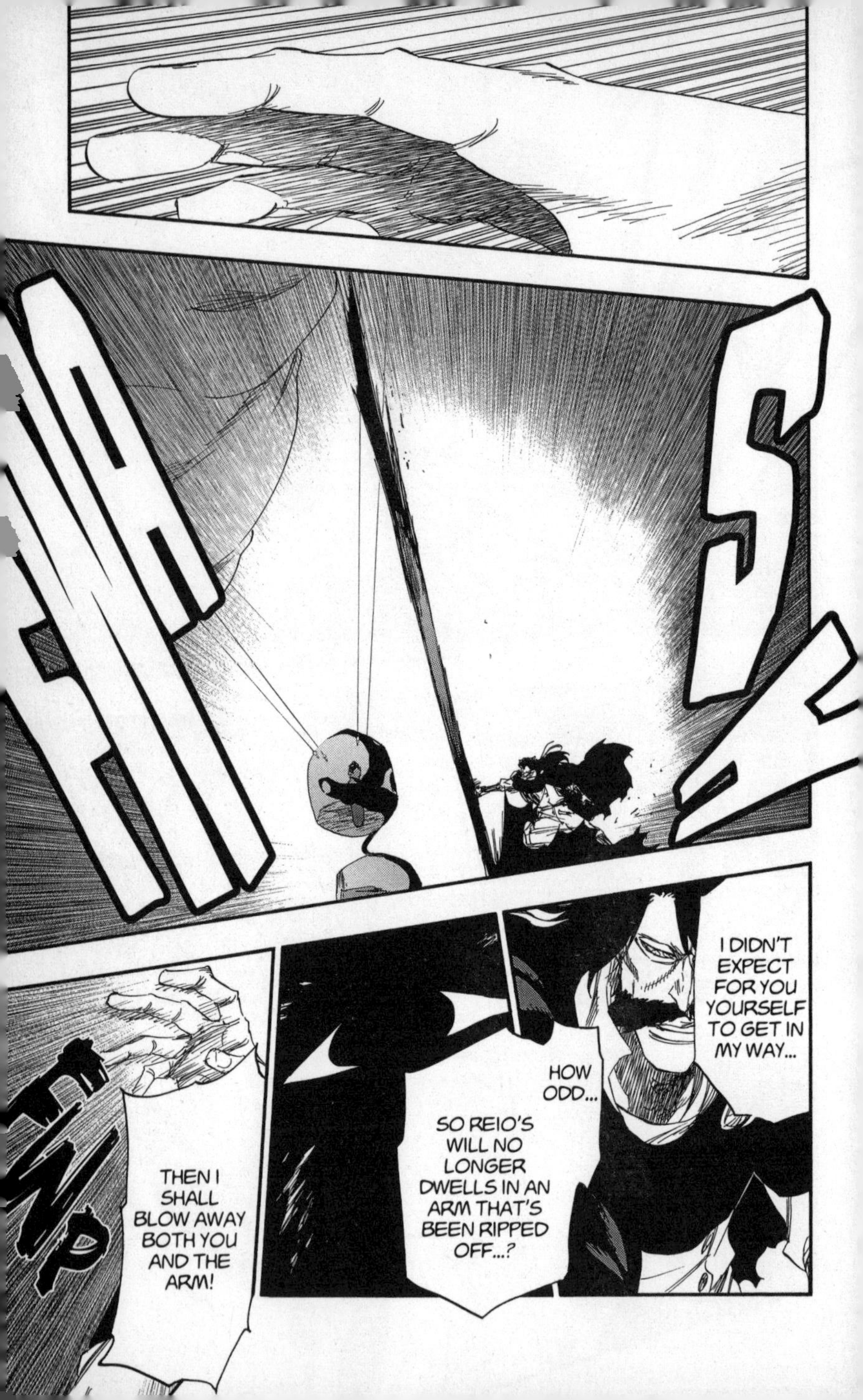
I DIDN'T EXPECT FOR YOU YOURSELF TO GET IN MY WAY...
HOW ODD...
SO REIO'S WILL NO LONGER DWELLS IN AN ARM THAT'S BEEN RIPPED OFF...?
THEN I SHALL BLOW AWAY BOTH YOU AND THE ARM!

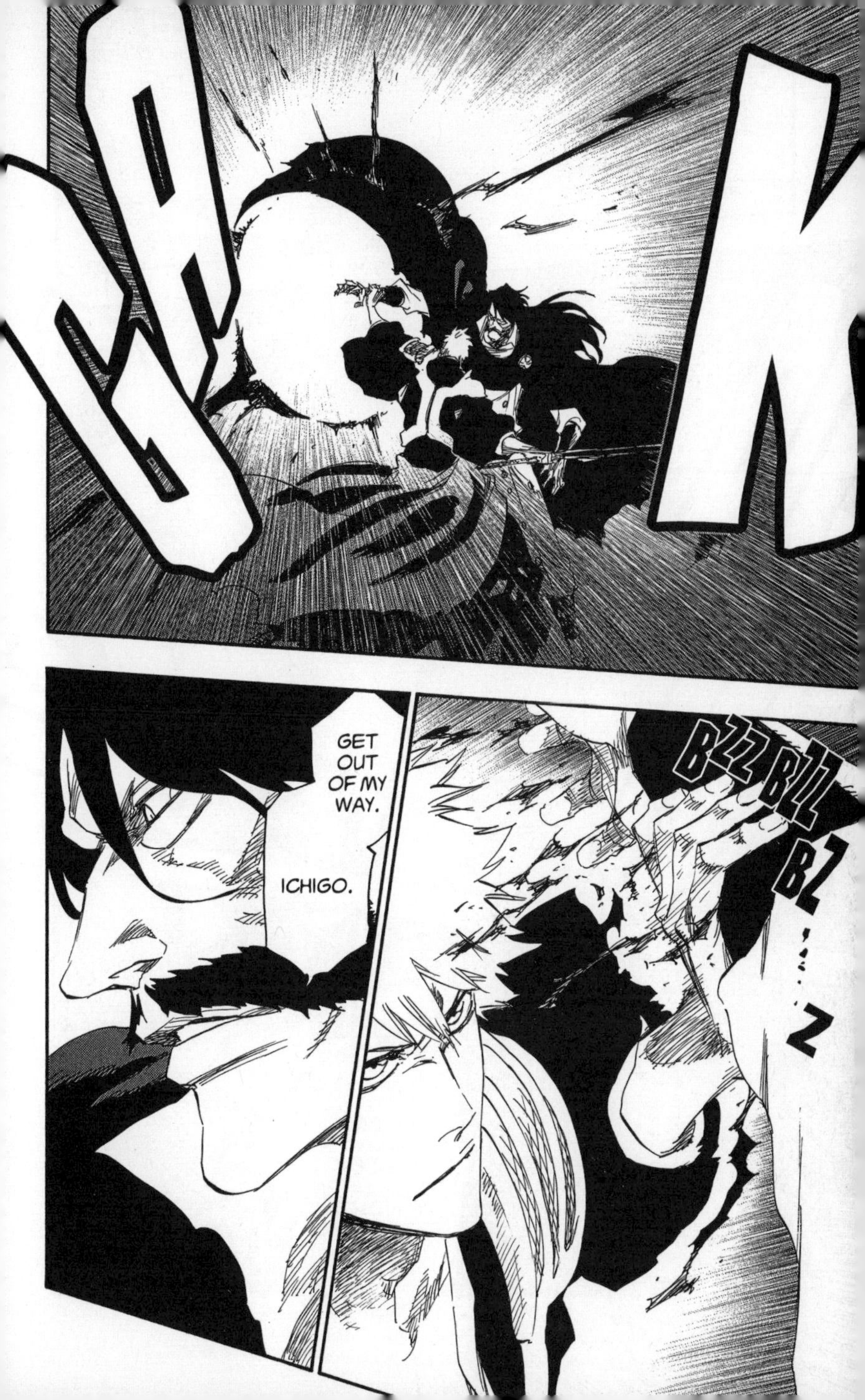
BZZ BZZ
BZ
Z
GET OUT OF MY WAY.
ICHIGO.

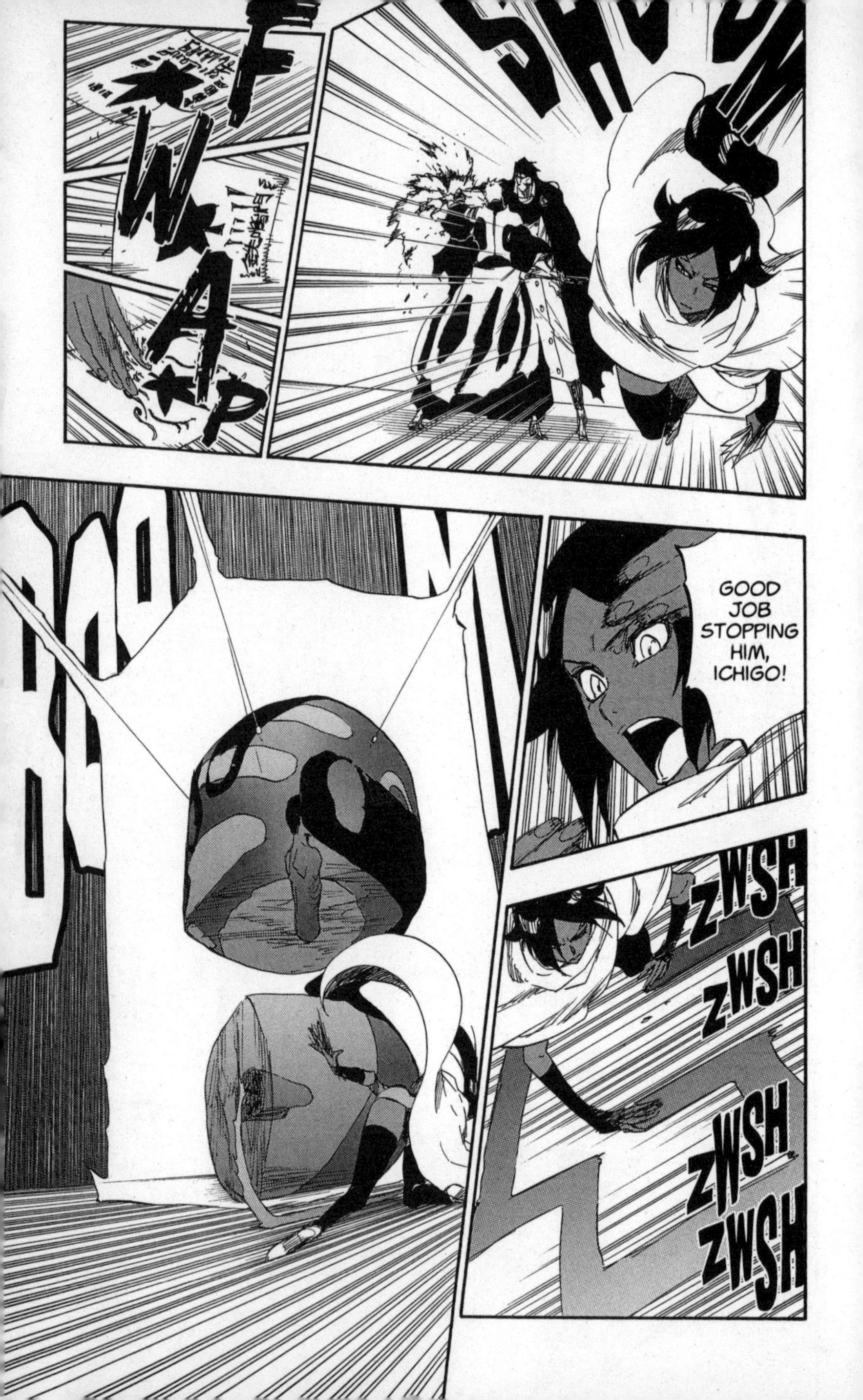
FWAP
GOOD JOB STOPPING HIM, ICHIGO!
ZWSH
ZWSH
ZWSH
ZWSH

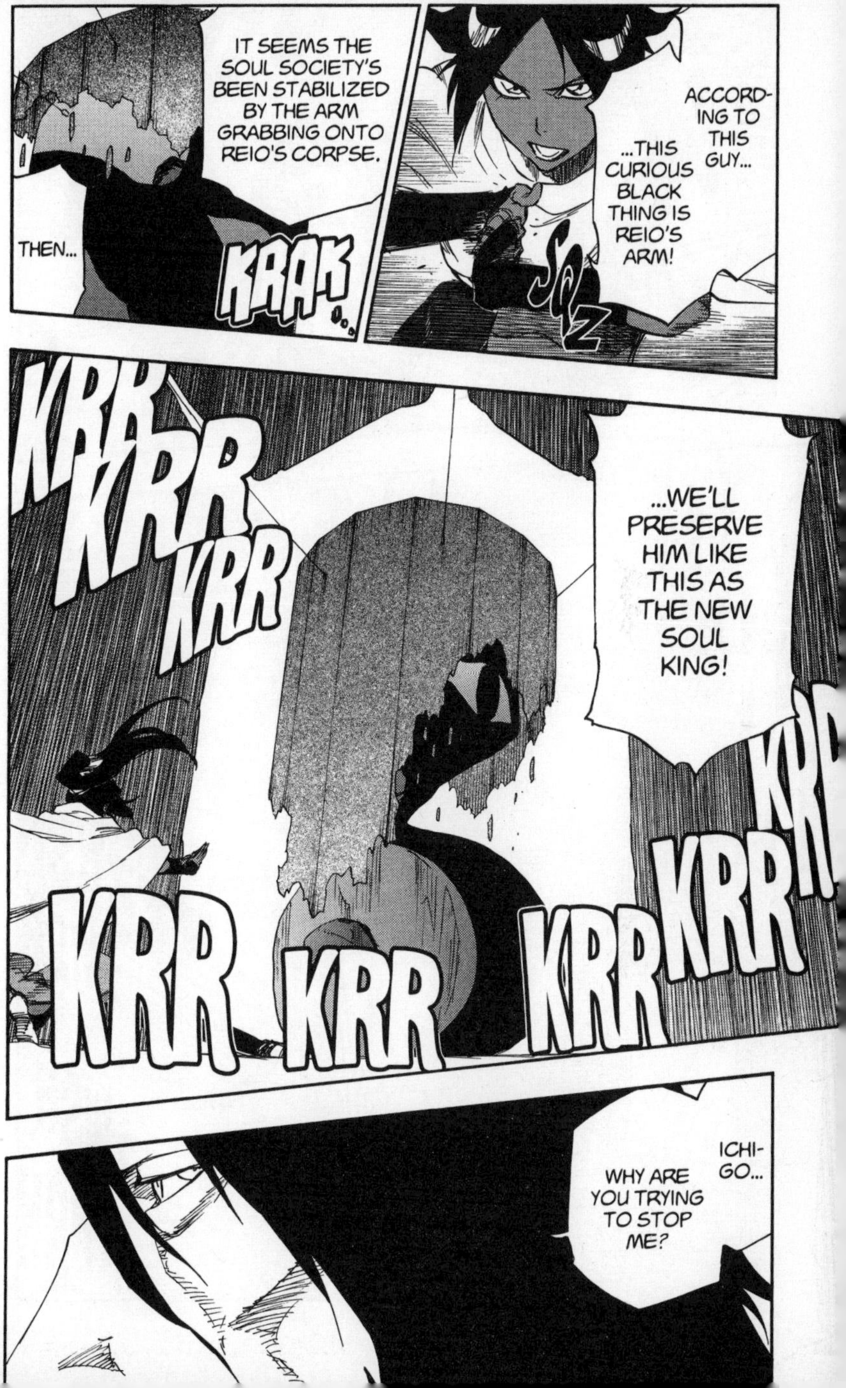
ACCORDING TO THIS GUY...
...THIS CURIOUS BLACK THING IS REIO'S ARM!
SQZ
IT SEEMS THE SOUL SOCIETY'S BEEN STABILIZED BY THE ARM GRABBING ONTO REIO'S CORPSE.
THEN...
KRAK
...WE'LL PRESERVE HIM LIKE THIS AS THE NEW SOUL KING!
KRR KRR KRR
KRR KRR KRR KRR KRR
ICHIGO...
WHY ARE YOU TRYING TO STOP ME?

READ THIS WAY

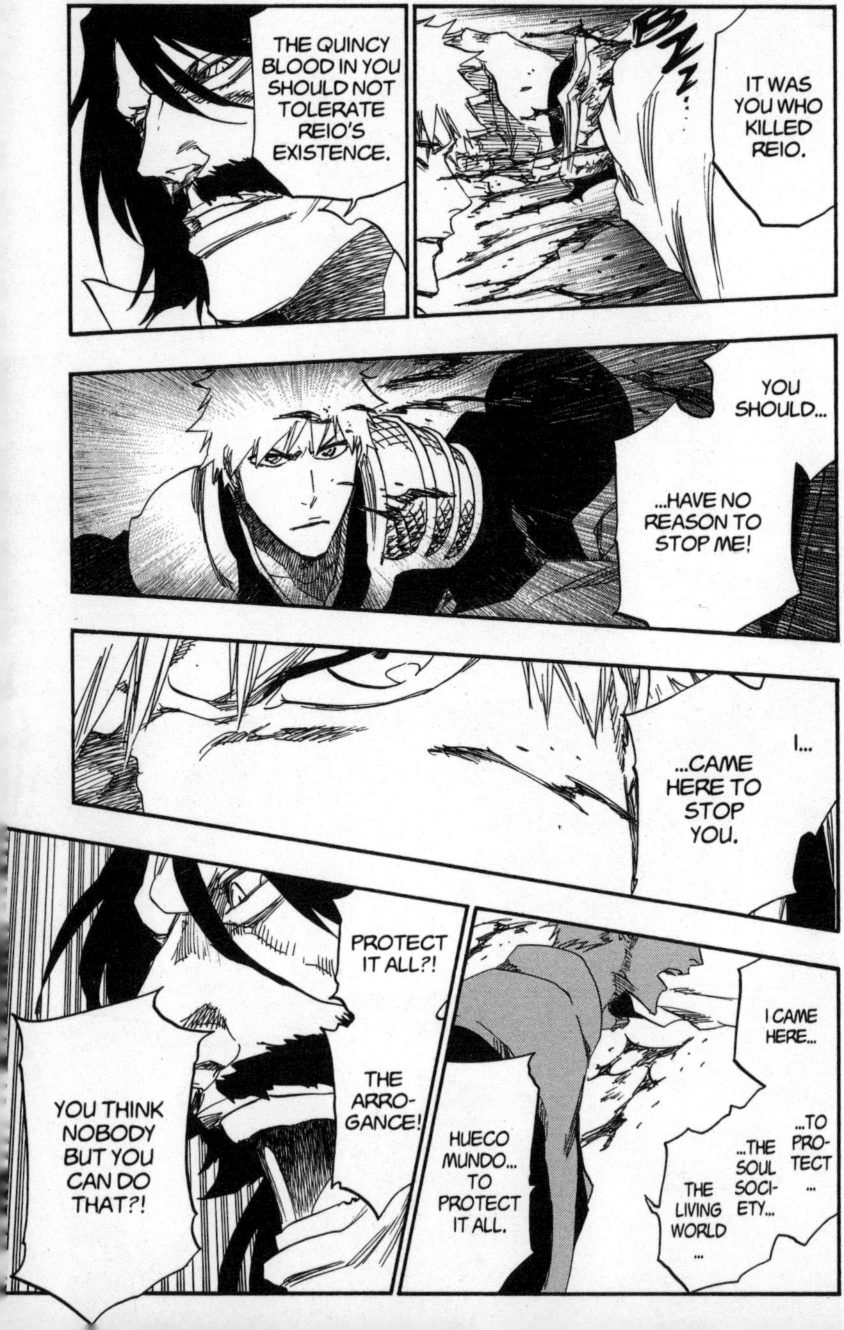

BZZ
IT WAS YOU WHO KILLED REIO.
THE QUINCY BLOOD IN YOU SHOULD NOT TOLERATE REIO'S EXISTENCE.
YOU SHOULD...
...HAVE NO REASON TO STOP ME!
I...
...CAME HERE TO STOP YOU.
I CAME HERE...
...TO PROTECT...
...THE SOUL SOCIETY...
THE LIVING WORLD...
HUECO MUNDO... TO PROTECT IT ALL.
PROTECT IT ALL?!
THE ARRO-GANCE!
YOU THINK NOBODY BUT YOU CAN DO THAT?!

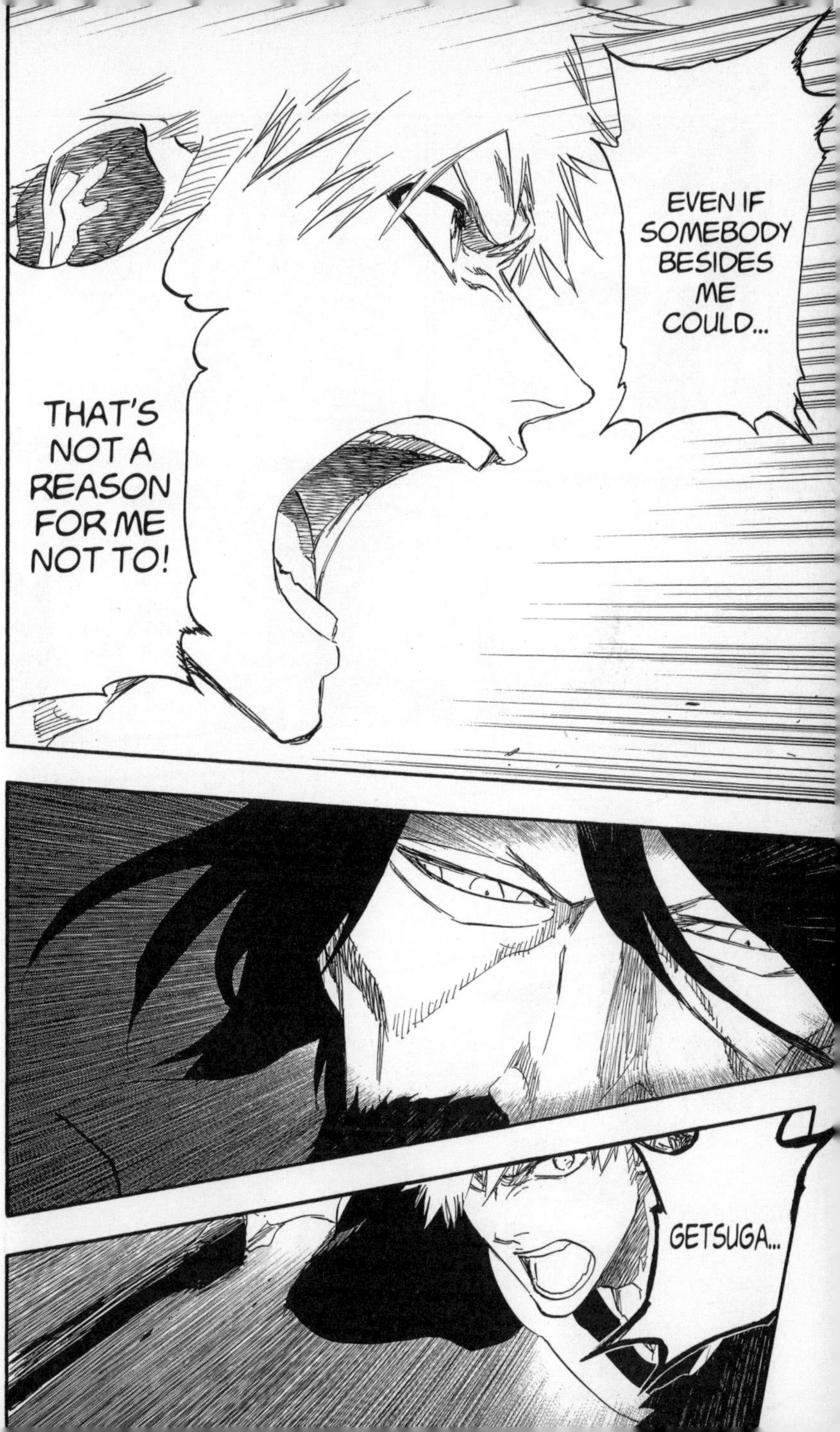
EVEN IF SOMEBODY BESIDES ME COULD...
THAT'S NOT A REASON FOR ME NOT TO!
GETSUGA...

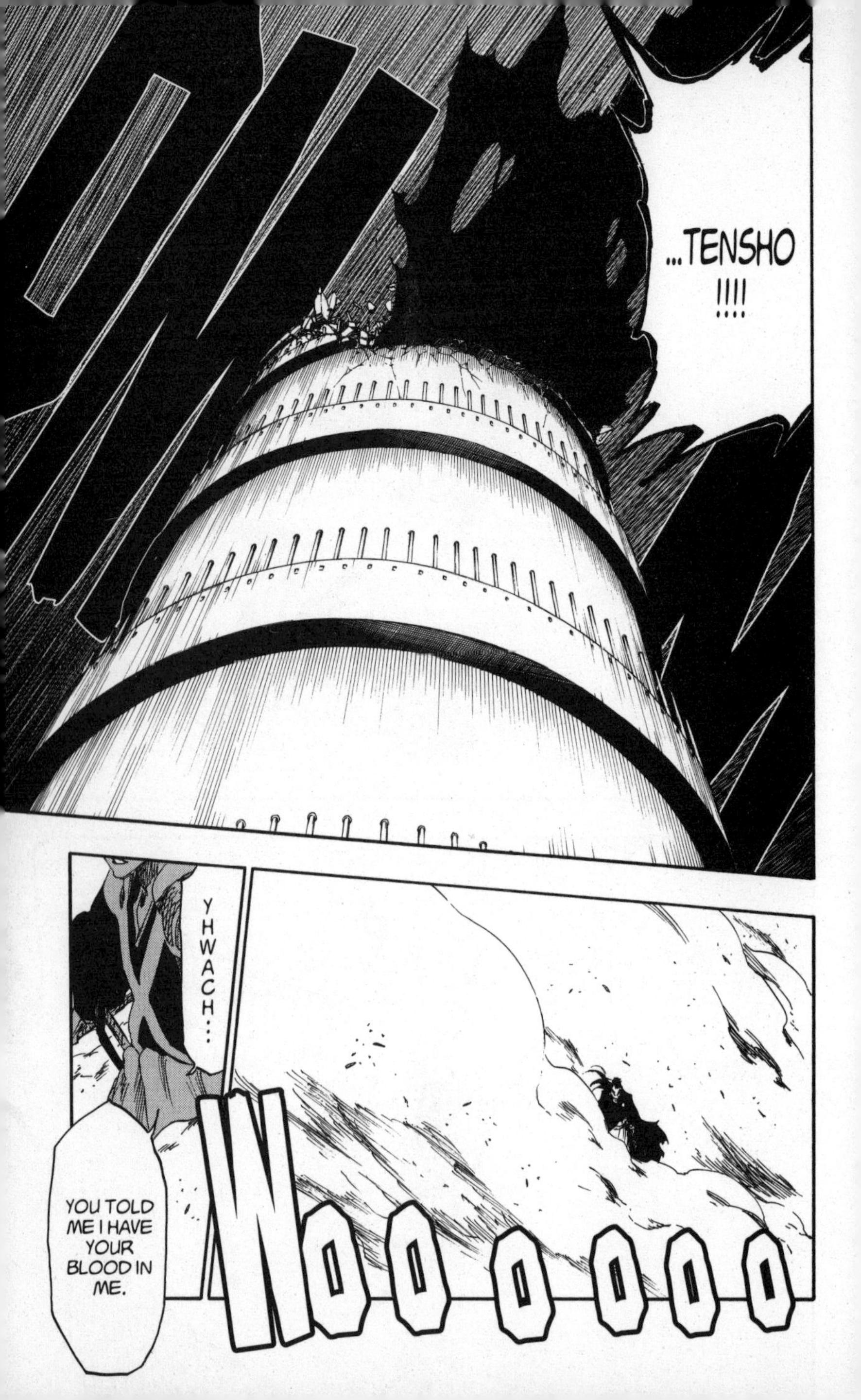
...TENSHO !!!!
WOOOOOOO
YHWACH...
YOU TOLD ME I HAVE YOUR BLOOD IN ME.

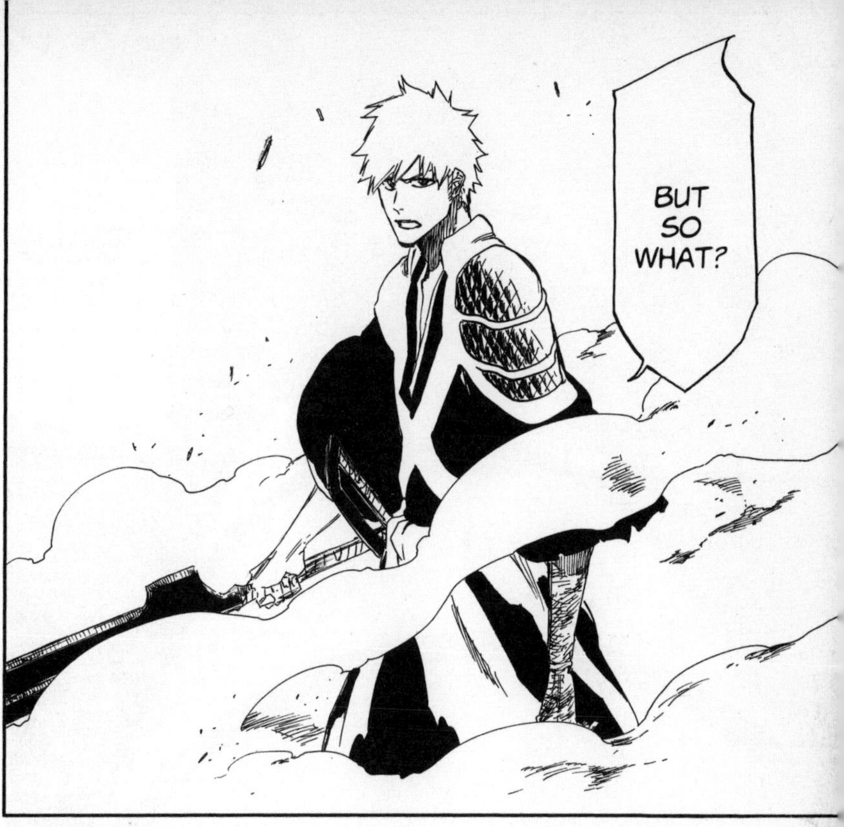
BUT SO WHAT?
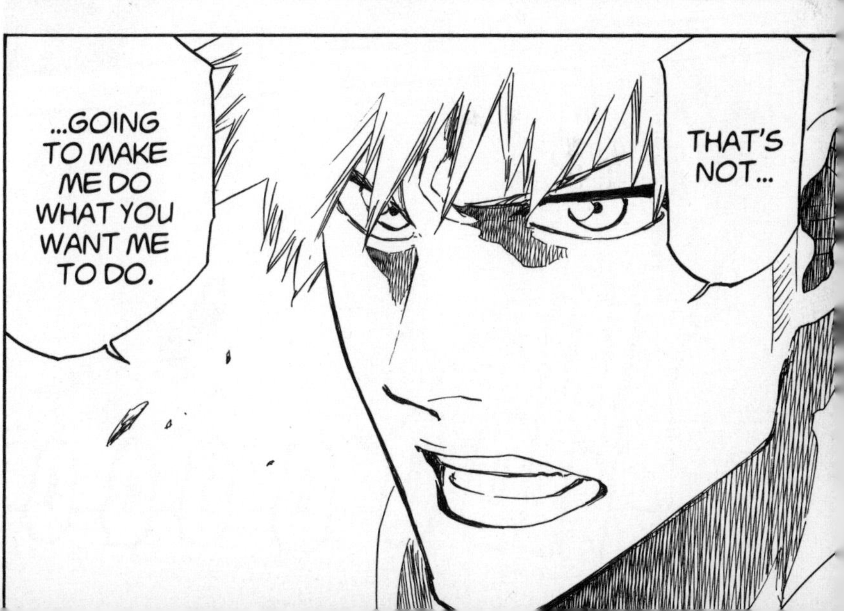
THAT'S NOT...
...GOING TO MAKE ME DO WHAT YOU WANT ME TO DO.

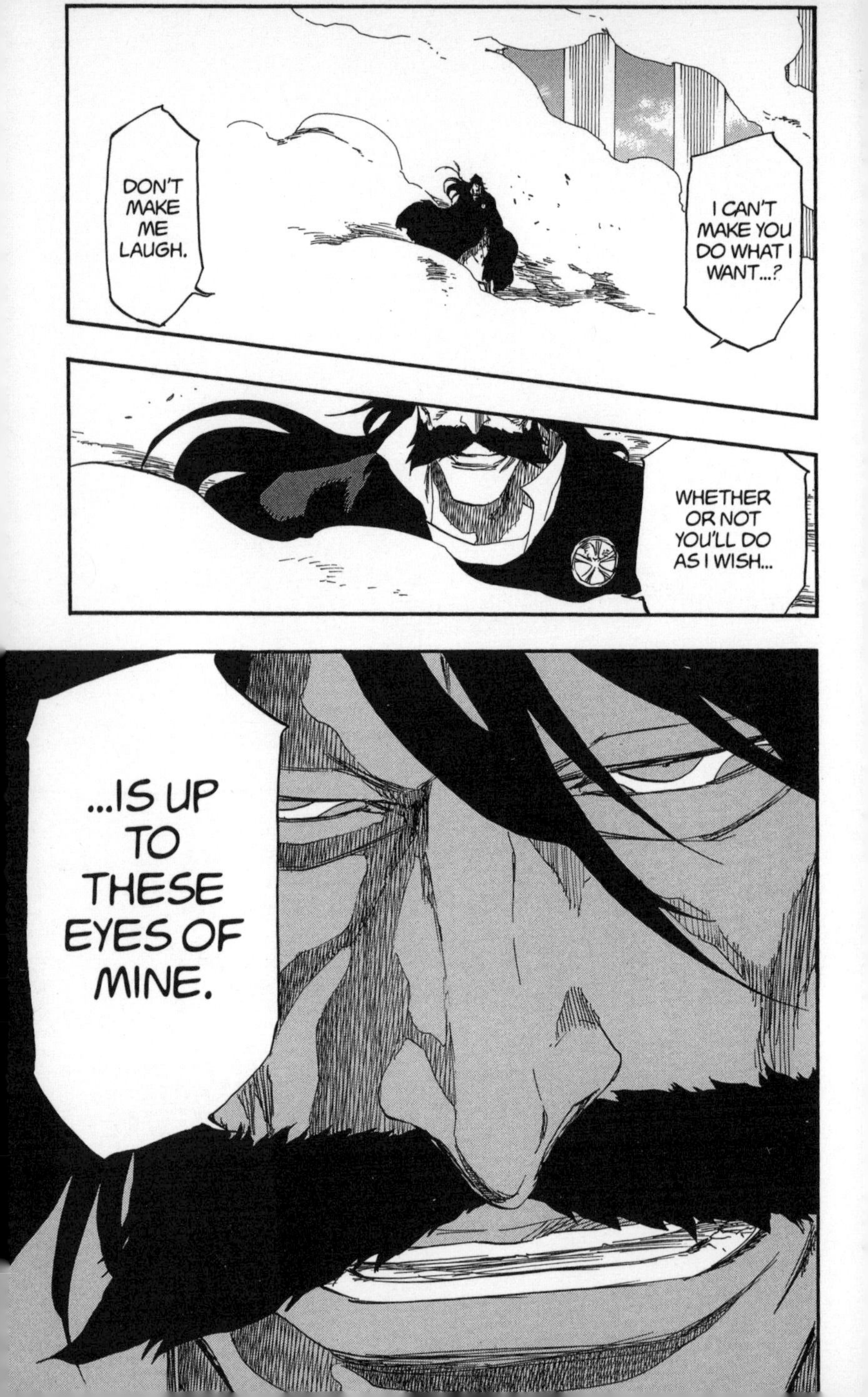
I CAN'T MAKE YOU DO WHAT I WANT...?
DON'T MAKE ME LAUGH.
WHETHER OR NOT YOU'LL DO AS I WISH...
...IS UP TO THESE EYES OF MINE.

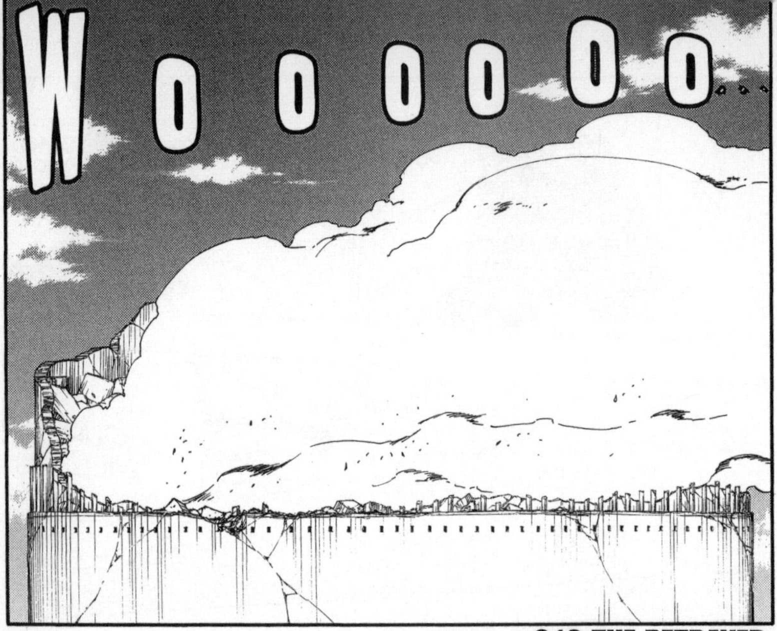
WOOOOOO...

619. THE BETRAYER

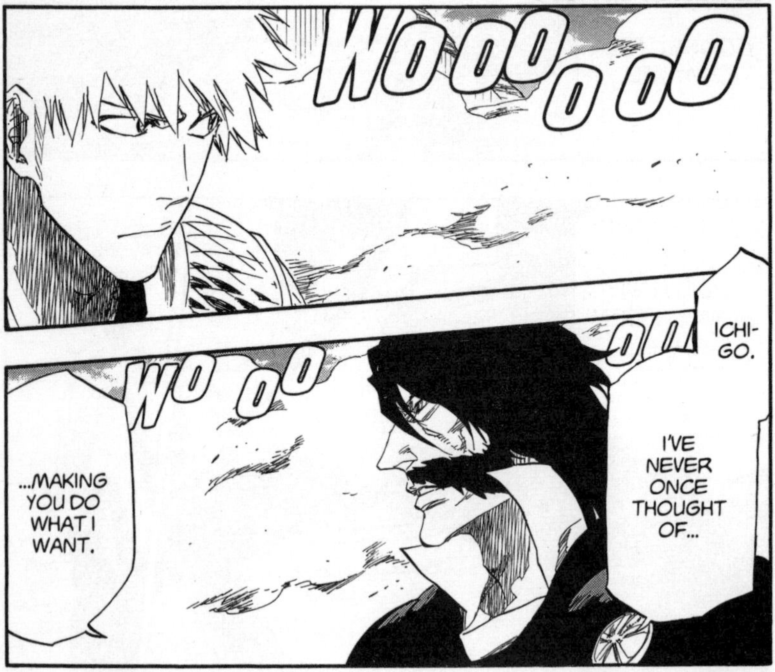
WOOOOOO
WOOOOO
ICHI-GO.
I'VE NEVER ONCE THOUGHT OF...
...MAKING YOU DO WHAT I WANT.

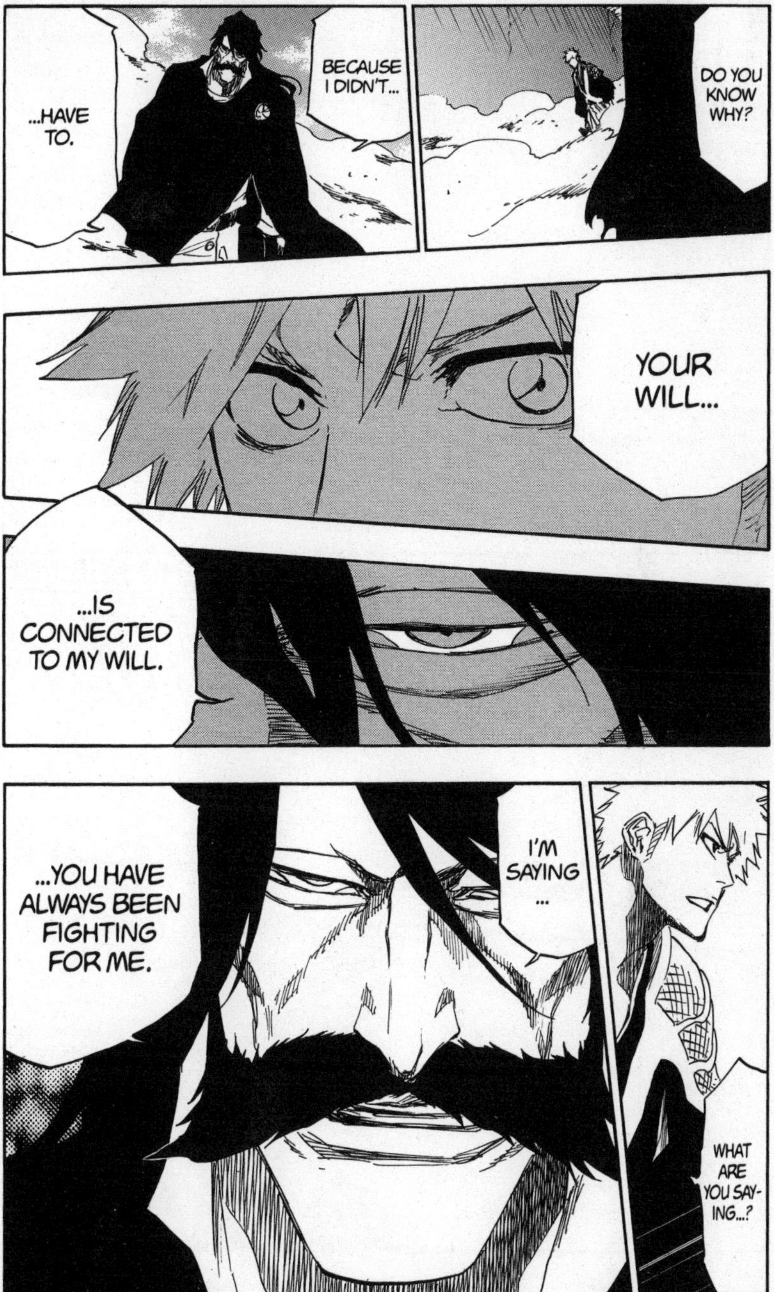
DO YOU KNOW WHY?
BECAUSE I DIDN'T...
...HAVE TO.
YOUR WILL...
...IS CONNECTED TO MY WILL.
WHAT ARE YOU SAYING...?
I'M SAYING ...
...YOU HAVE ALWAYS BEEN FIGHTING FOR ME.

READ THIS WAY

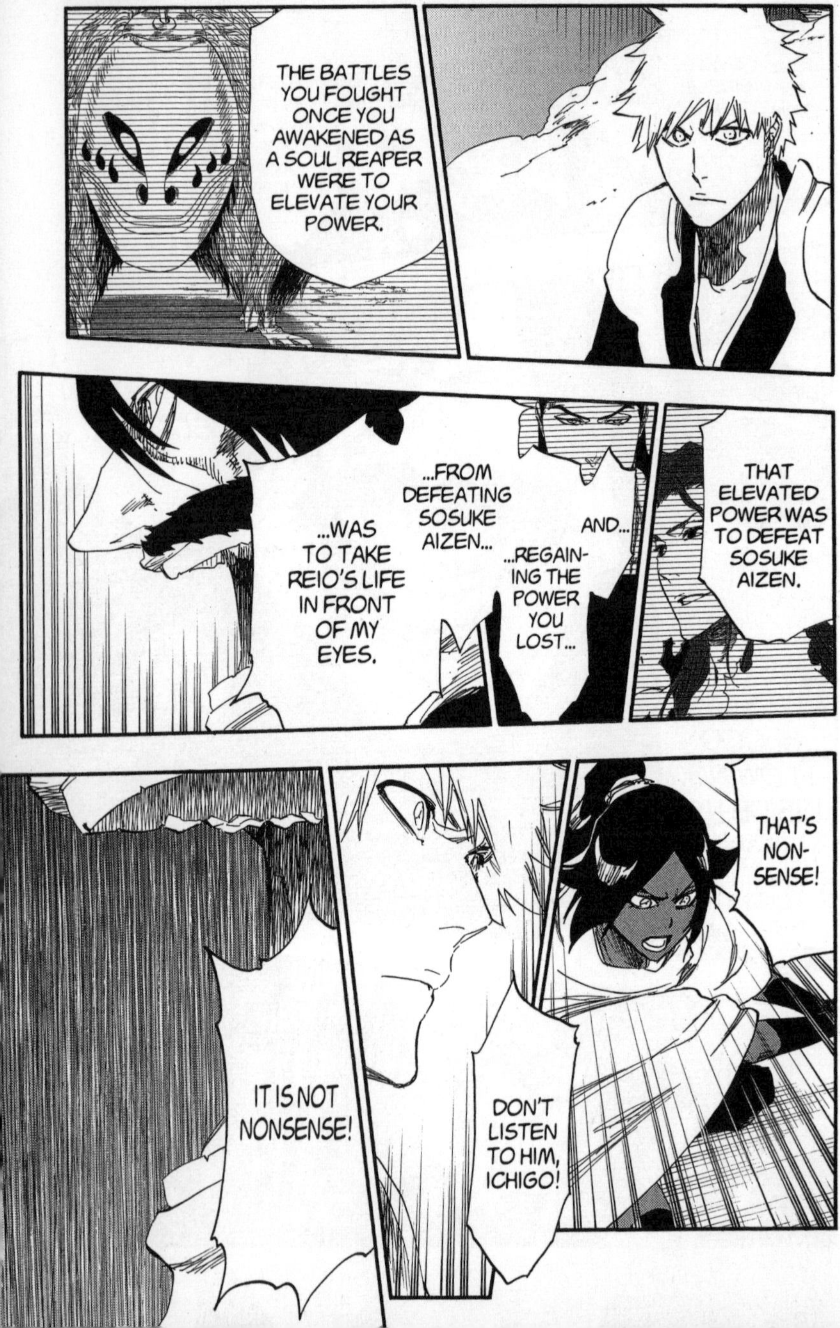
THE BATTLES YOU FOUGHT ONCE YOU AWAKENED AS A SOUL REAPER WERE TO ELEVATE YOUR POWER.
THAT ELEVATED POWER WAS TO DEFEAT SOSUKE AIZEN.
AND...
...REGAIN-ING THE POWER YOU LOST...
...FROM DEFEATING SOSUKE AIZEN...
...WAS TO TAKE REIO'S LIFE IN FRONT OF MY EYES.
THAT'S NON-SENSE!
DON'T LISTEN TO HIM, ICHIGO!
IT IS NOT NONSENSE!

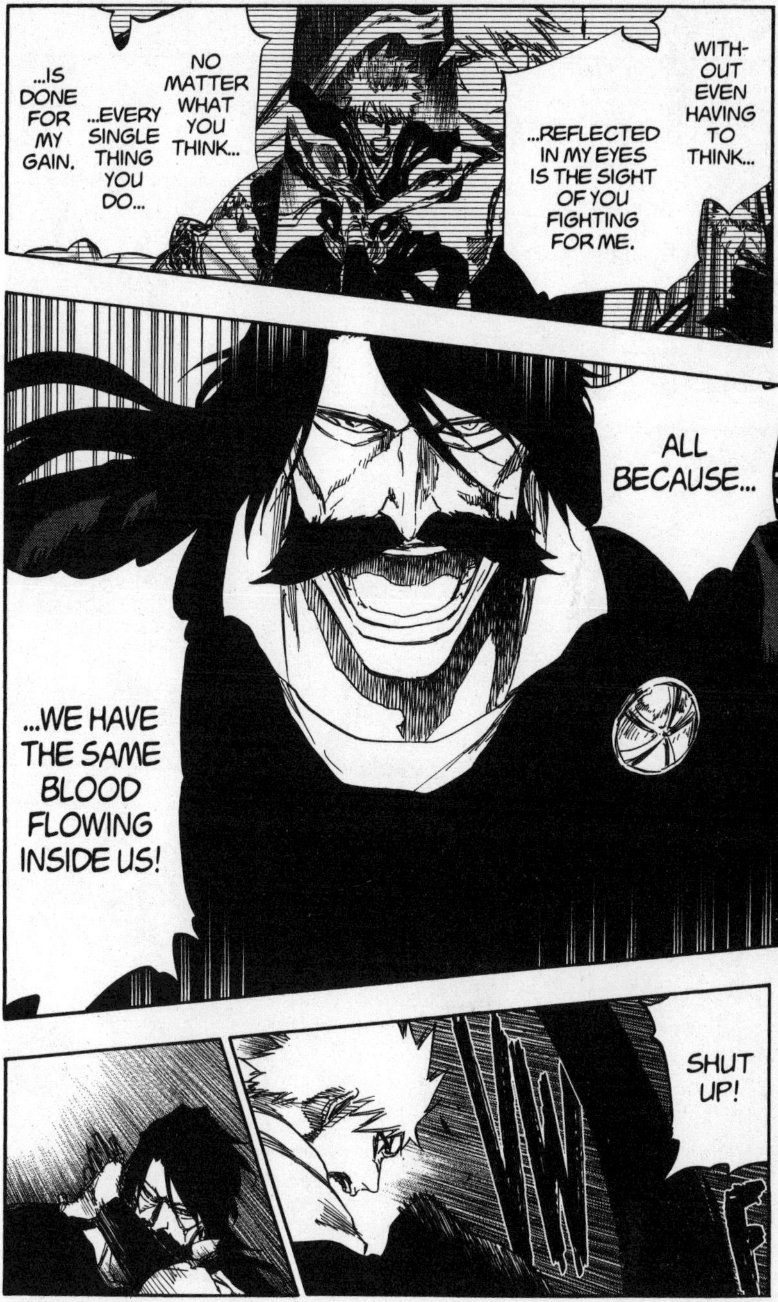
WITH-OUT EVEN HAVING TO THINK...
...REFLECTED IN MY EYES IS THE SIGHT OF YOU FIGHTING FOR ME.
NO MATTER WHAT YOU THINK...
...EVERY SINGLE THING YOU DO...
...IS DONE FOR MY GAIN.
ALL BECAUSE...
...WE HAVE THE SAME BLOOD FLOWING INSIDE US!
SHUT UP!

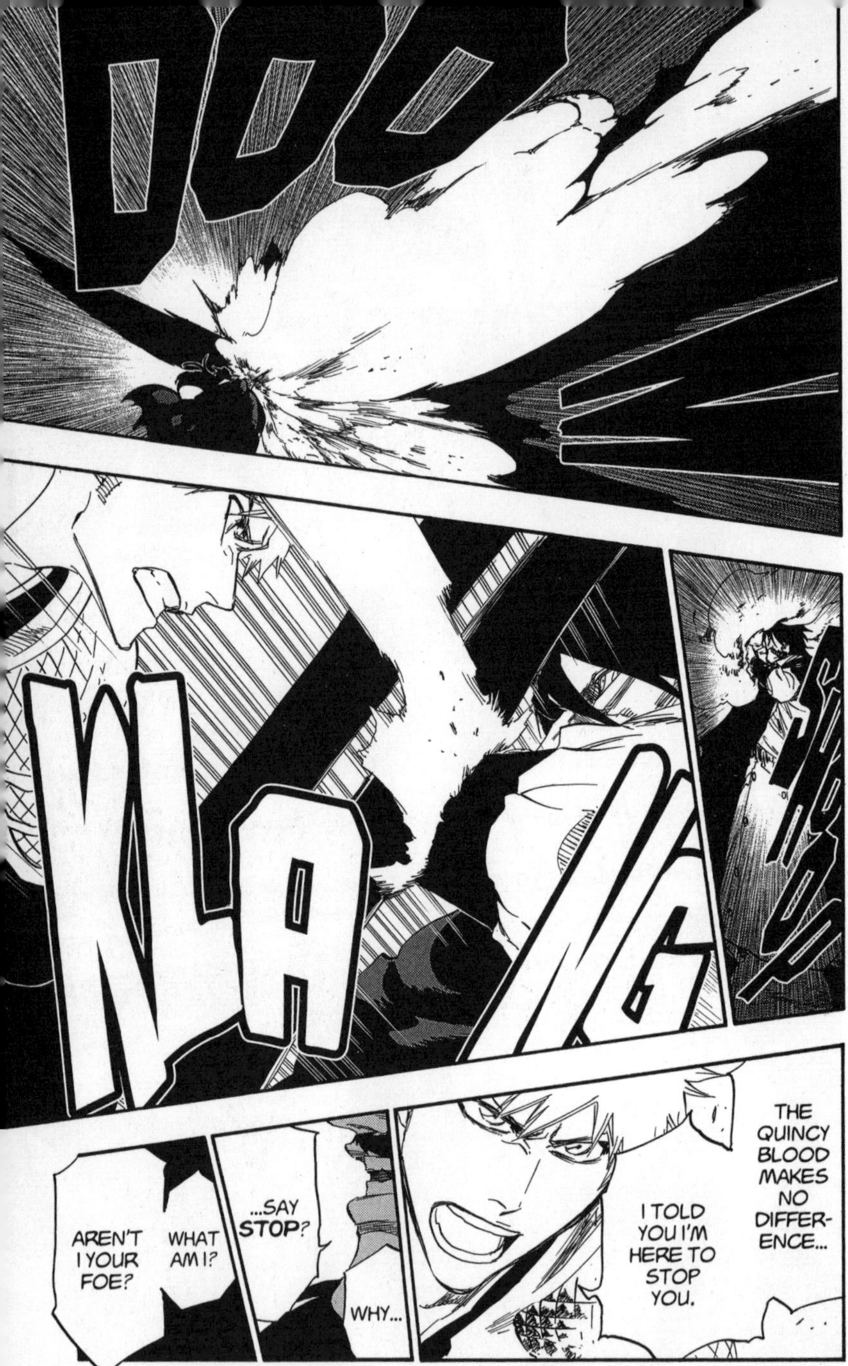
KLANG
THE QUINCY BLOOD MAKES NO DIFFERENCE...
I TOLD YOU I'M HERE TO STOP YOU.
WHY...
...SAY STOP?
WHAT AM I?
AREN'T I YOUR FOE?

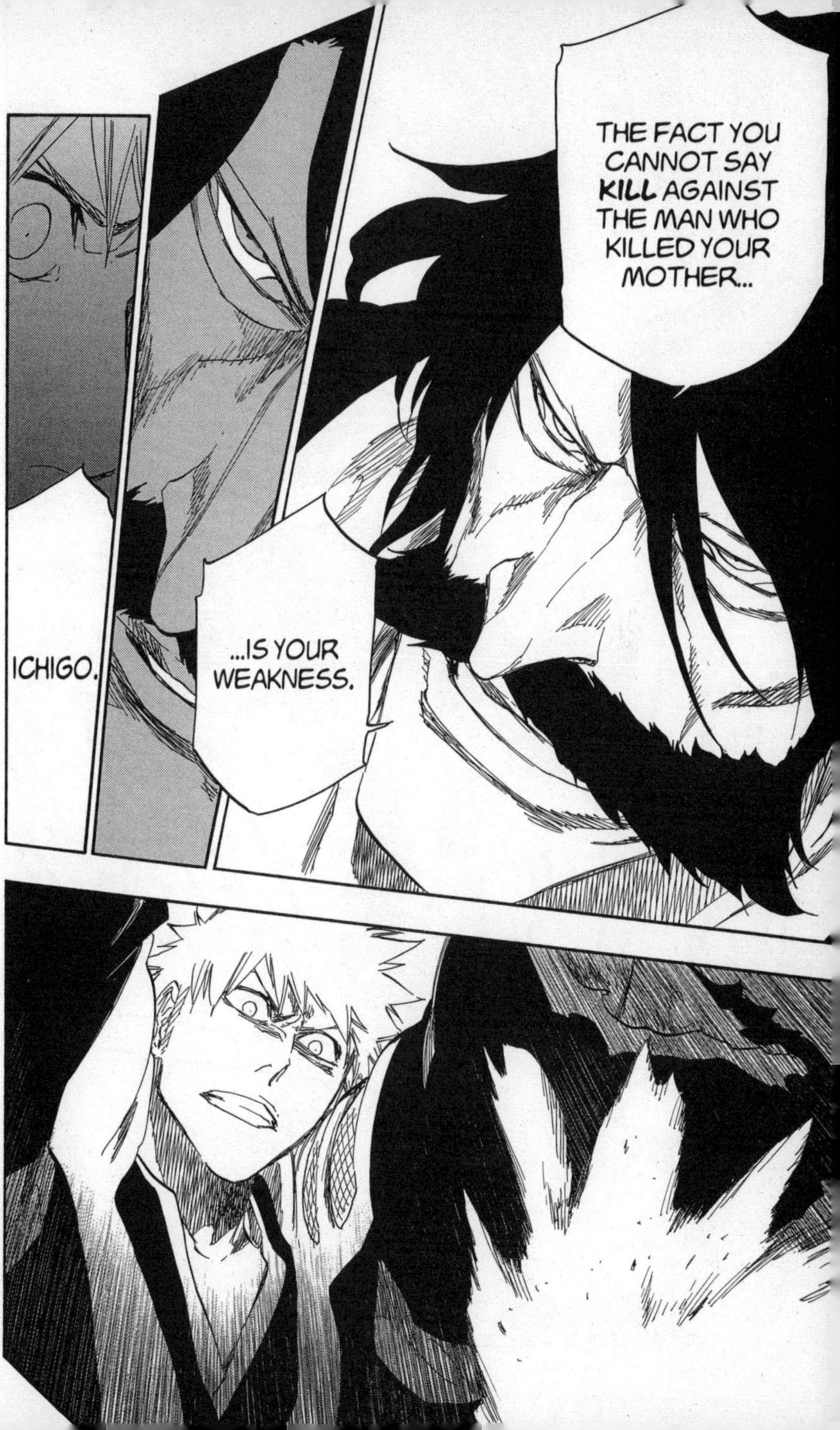
THE FACT YOU CANNOT SAY **KILL** AGAINST THE MAN WHO KILLED YOUR MOTHER...
...IS YOUR WEAKNESS.
ICHIGO.

READ THIS WAY

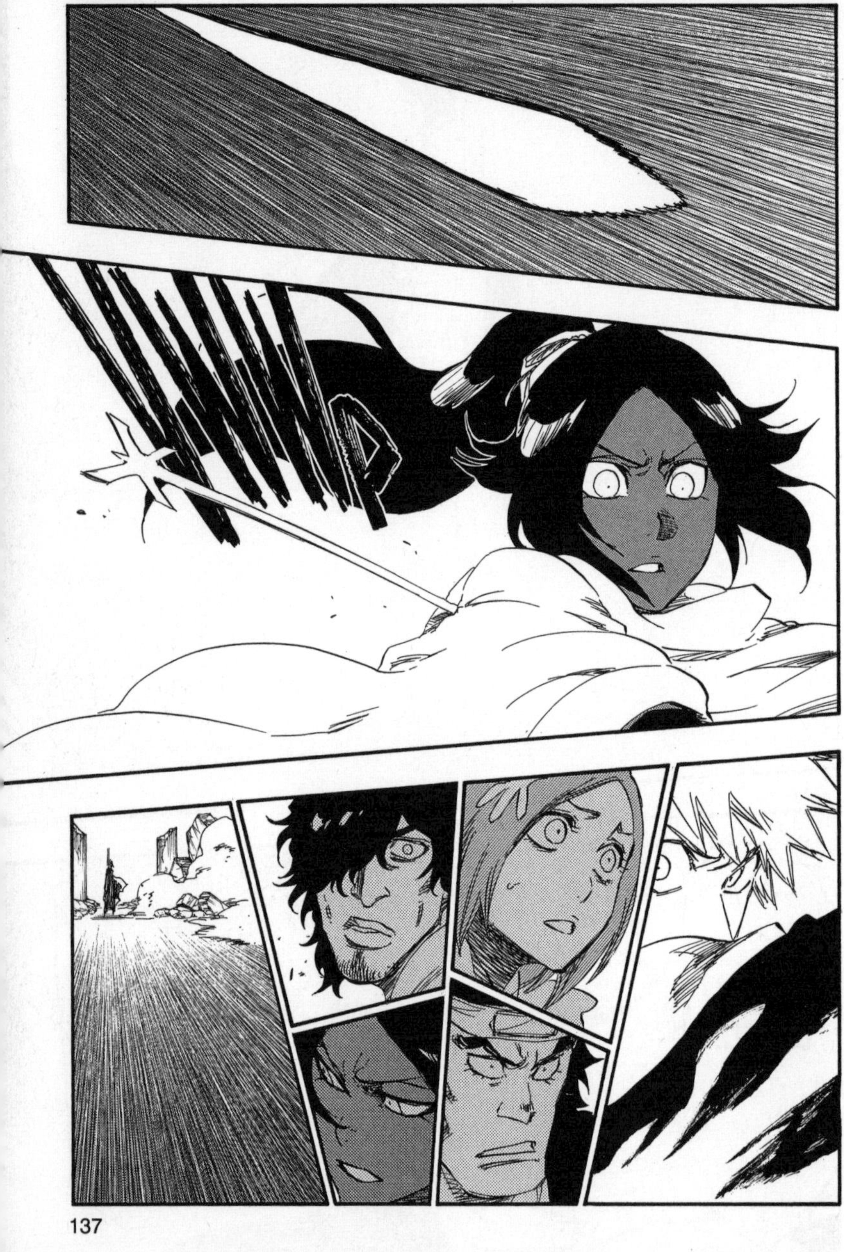
WHAP

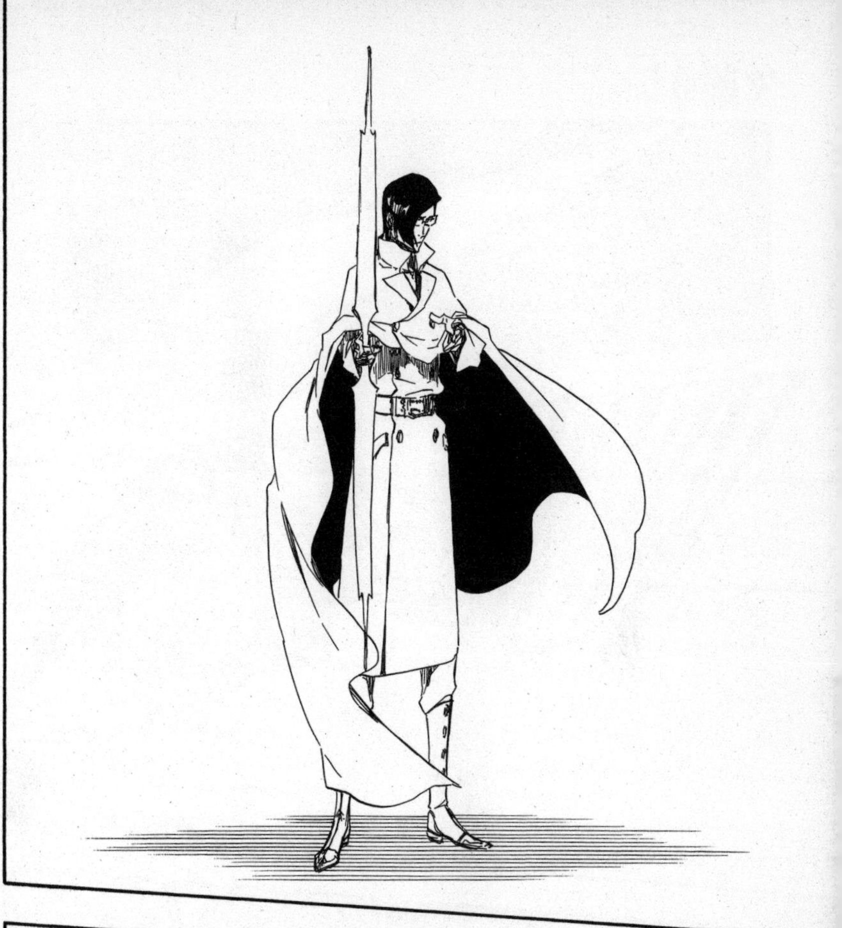

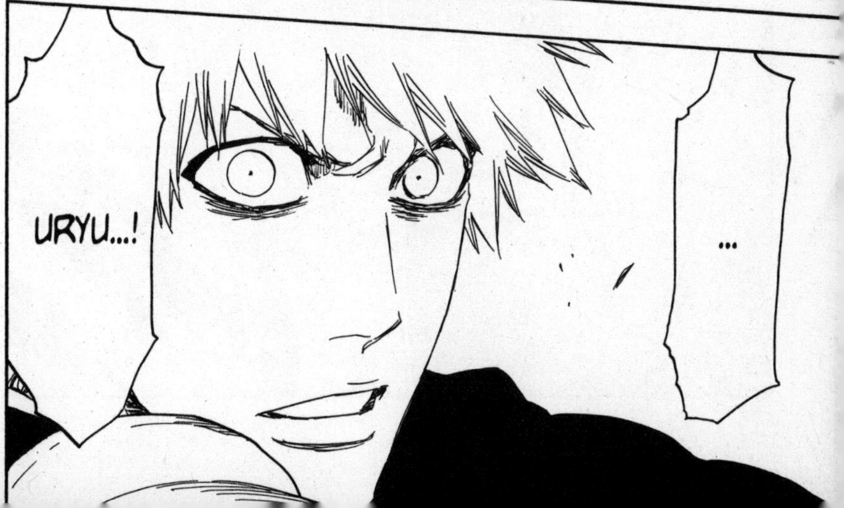
...
URYU...!

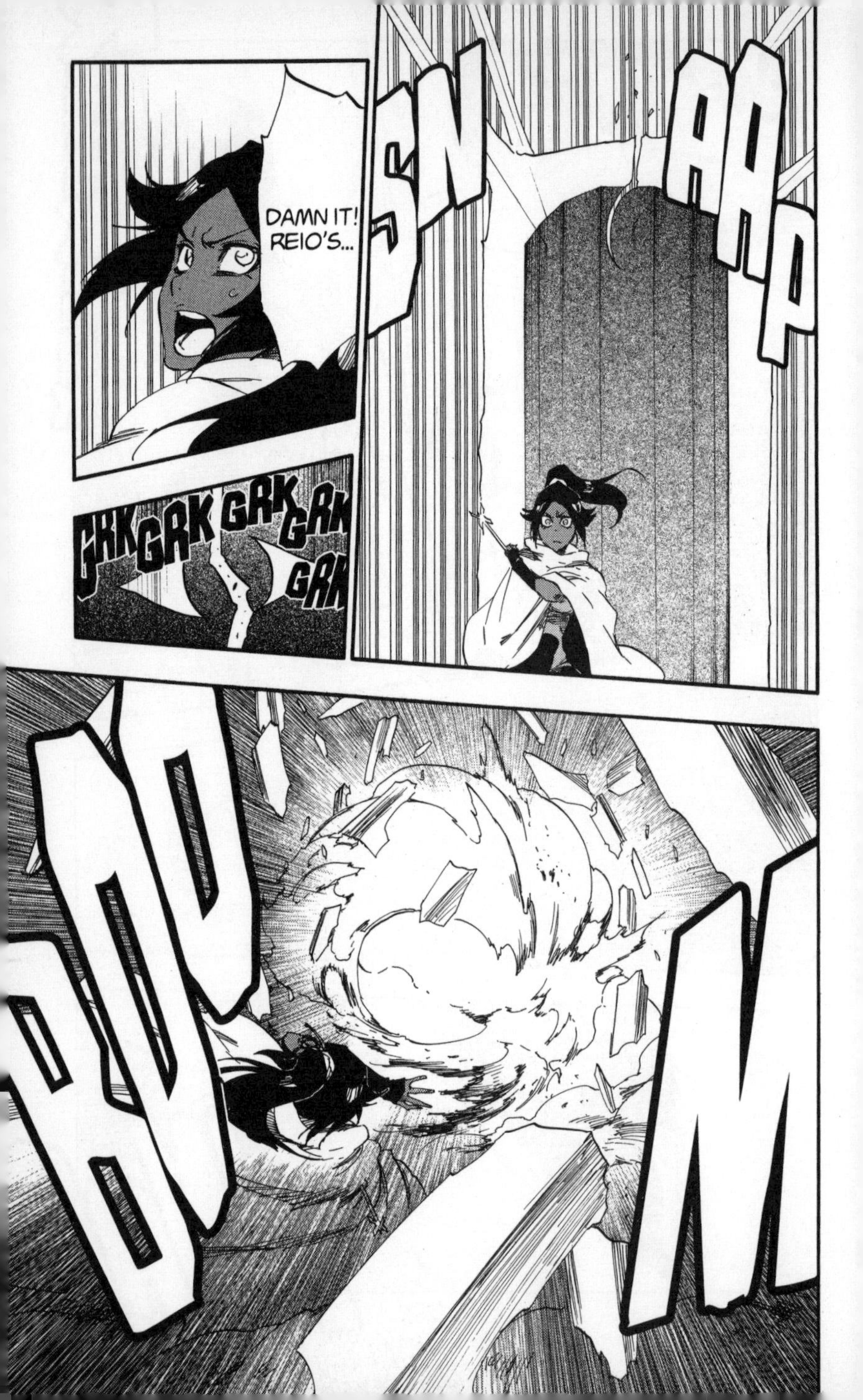
SNAAP
DAMN IT! REIO'S...
GRK GRK GRK GRK GRK
BOOM

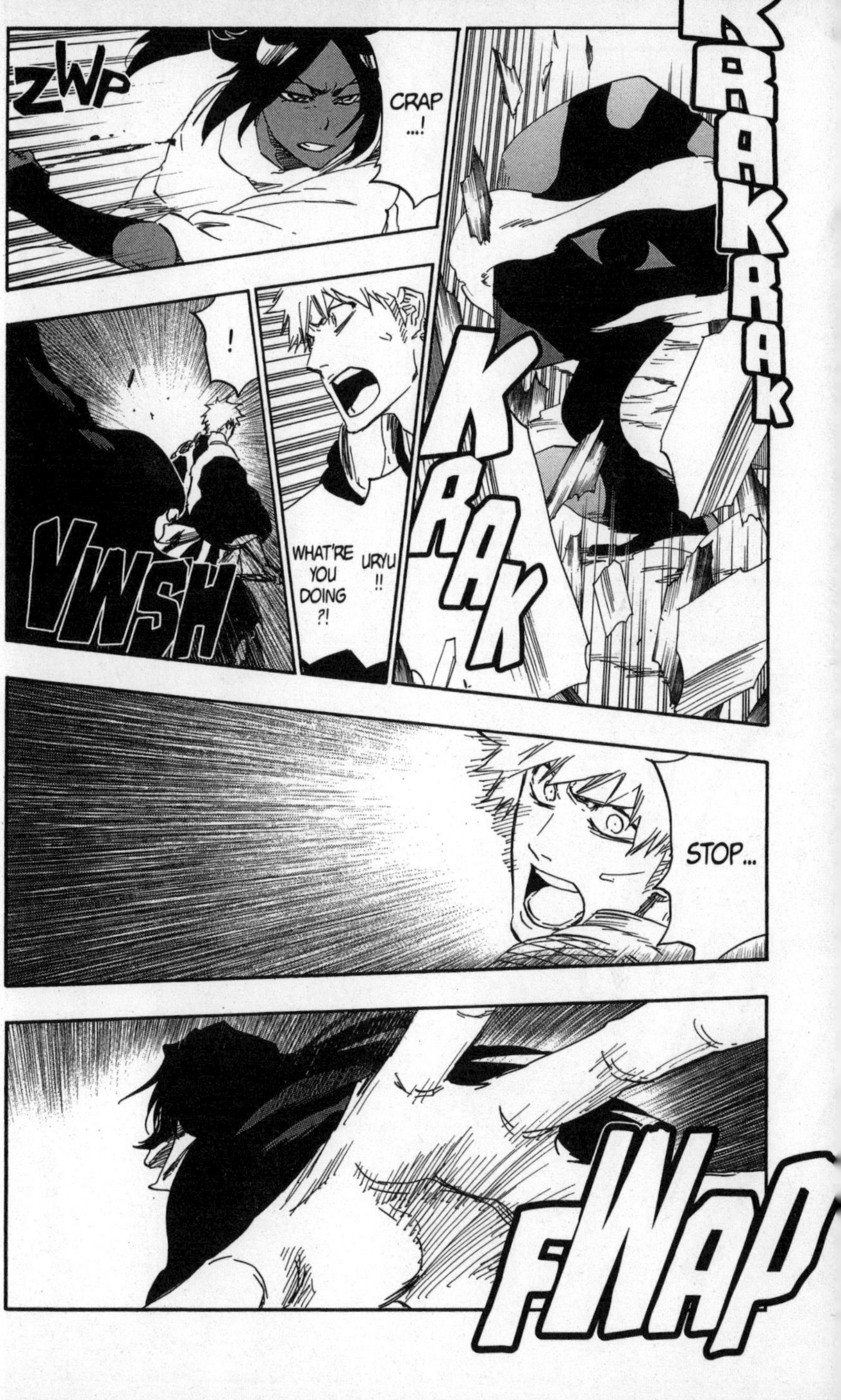
KRAKRAK
KRAK
ZWP
CRAP ...!
URYU !!
WHAT'RE YOU DOING ?!
!
VWSH
STOP...
FWAP

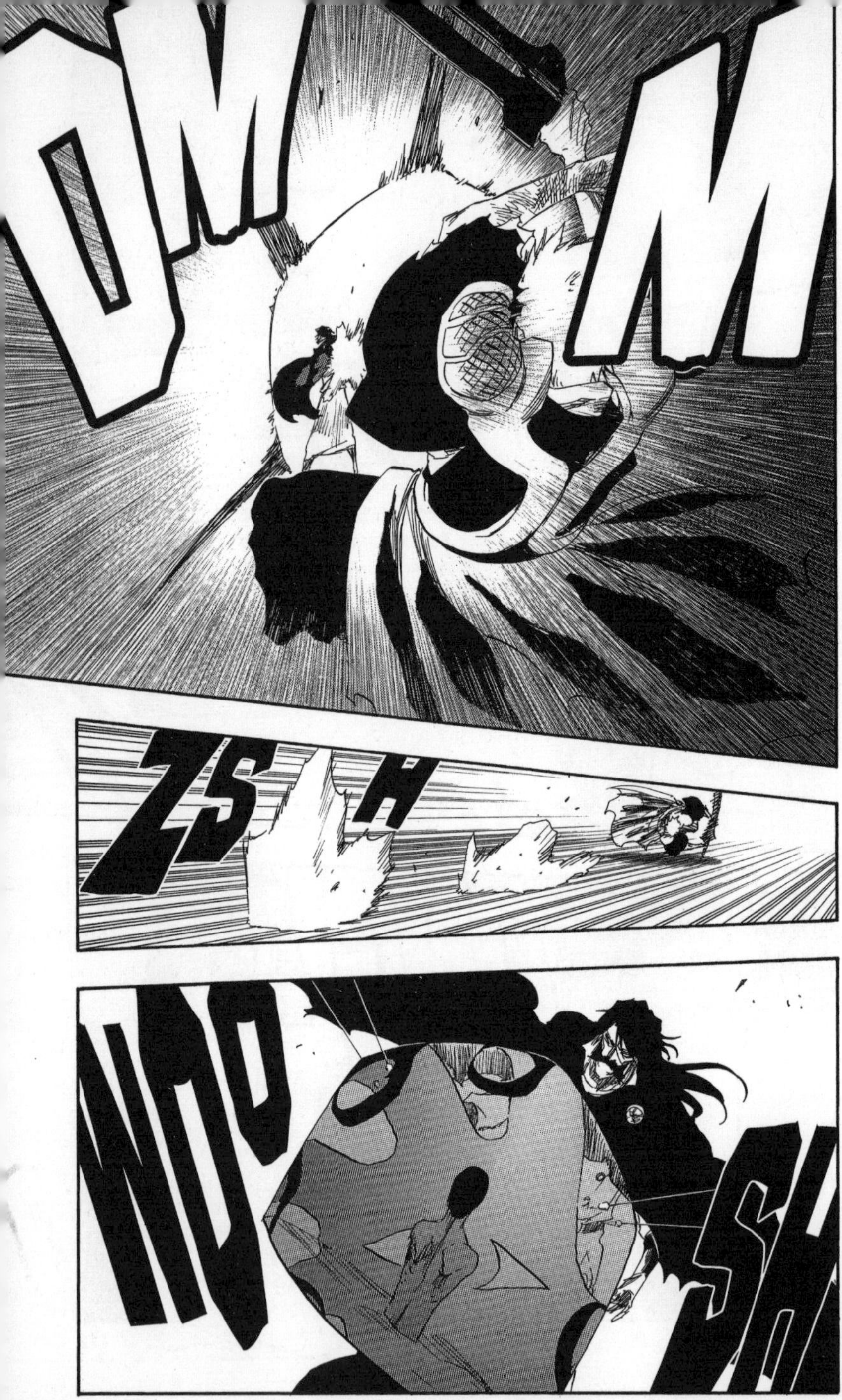

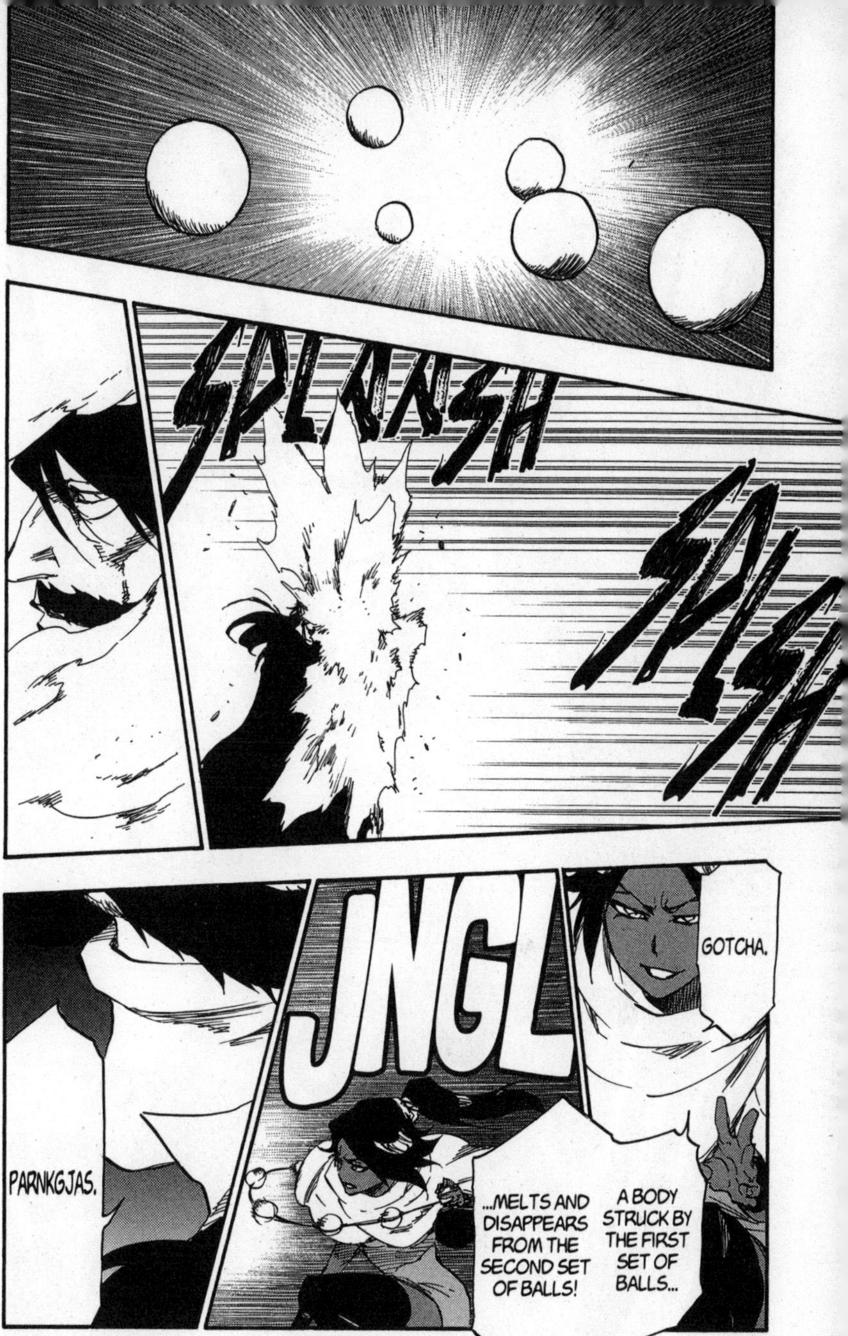
SPLASH
SPLASH
GOTCHA.
JNGL
A BODY STRUCK BY THE FIRST SET OF BALLS...
...MELTS AND DISAPPEARS FROM THE SECOND SET OF BALLS!
PARNKGJAS.

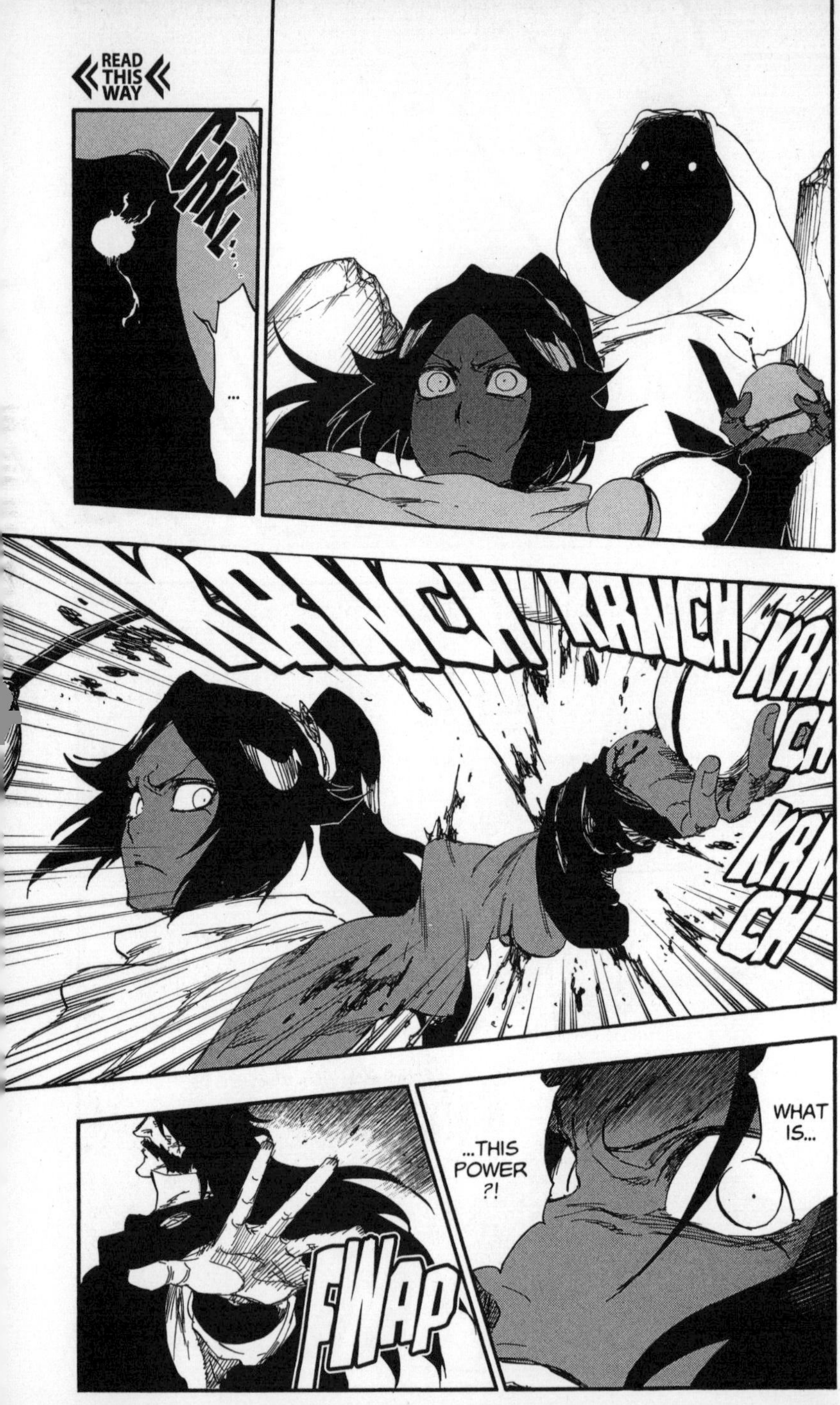
READ THIS WAY
CRKL...
...
KRNCH
KRNCH
KRNCH
KRNCH
WHAT IS...
...THIS POWER ?!
FWAP

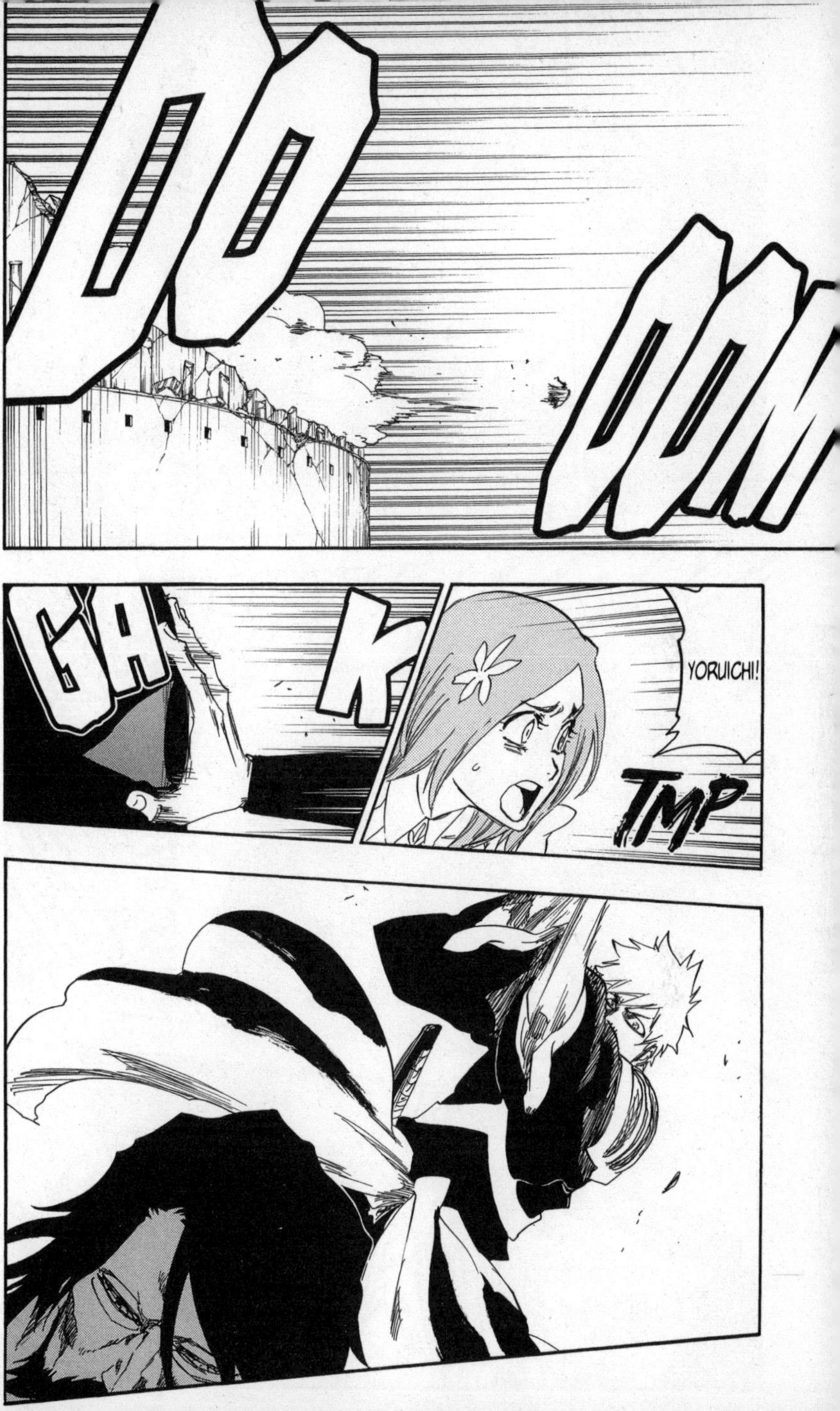
DO
DOM
YORUICHI!
TMP
GA
K

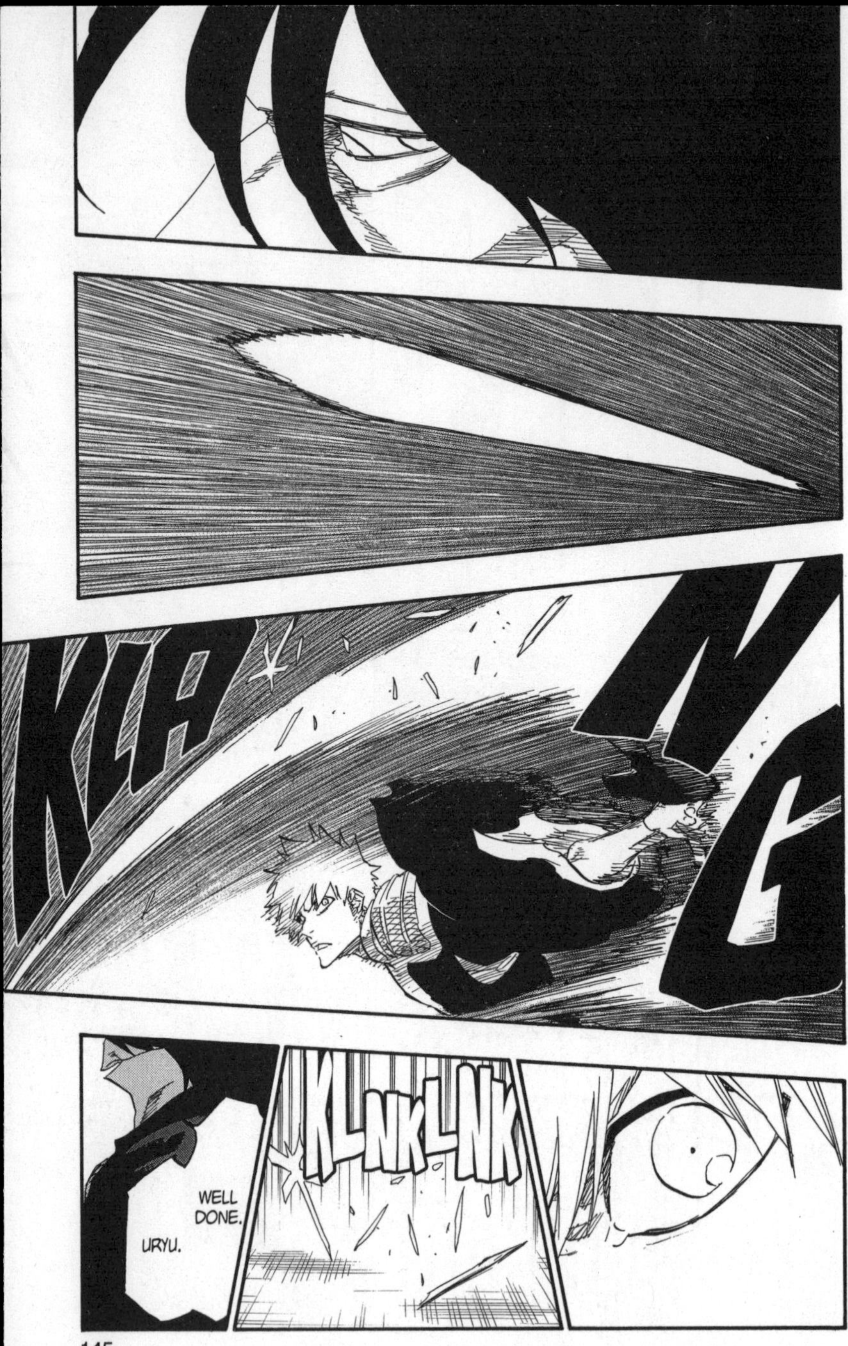
KLANG
KLNKLNK
WELL DONE,
URYU.

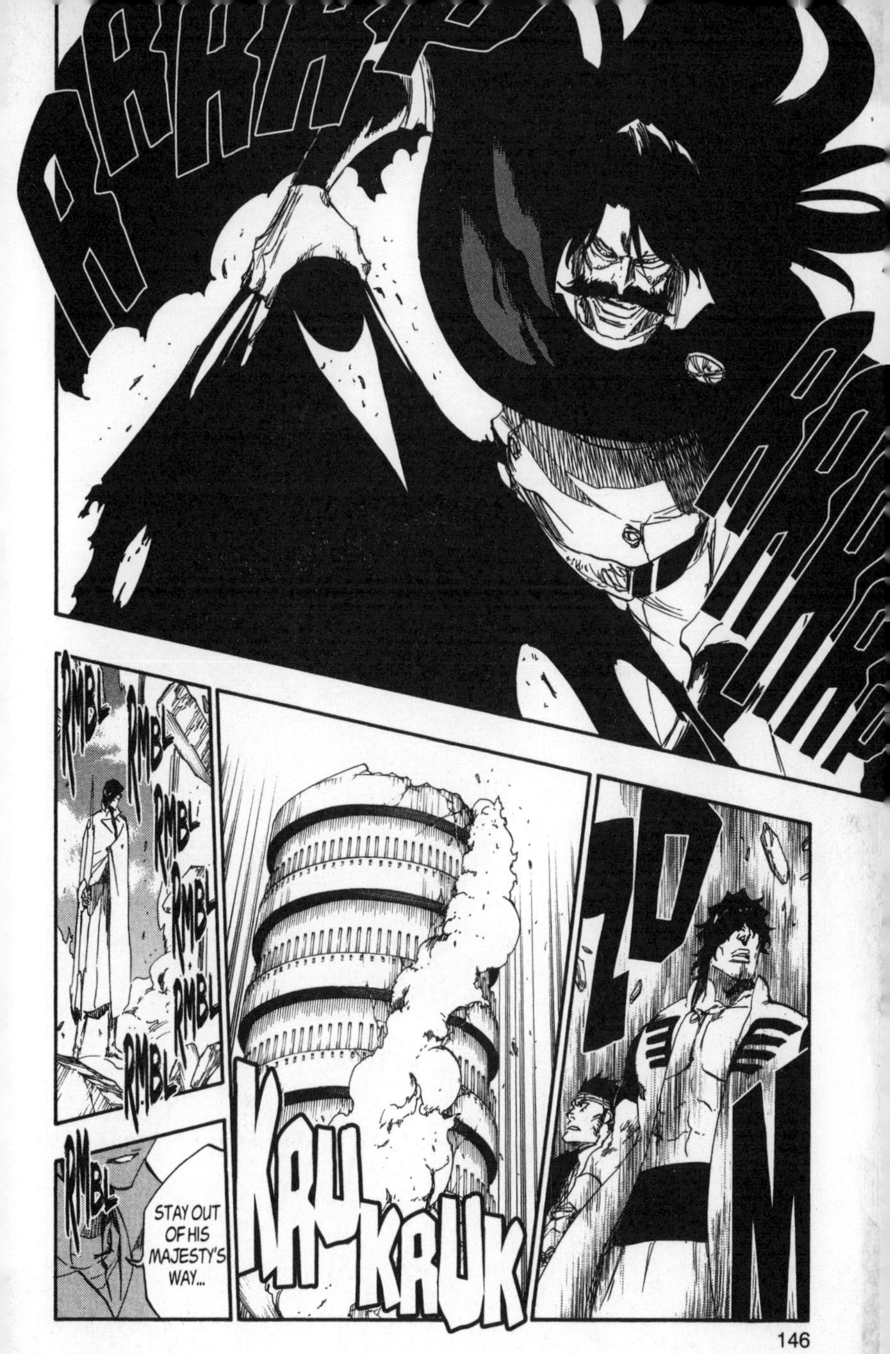
KRUK
RMBL RMBL RMBL RMBL RMBL RMBL RMBL
RMBL
STAY OUT OF HIS MAJESTY'S WAY...

BLEACH 619.

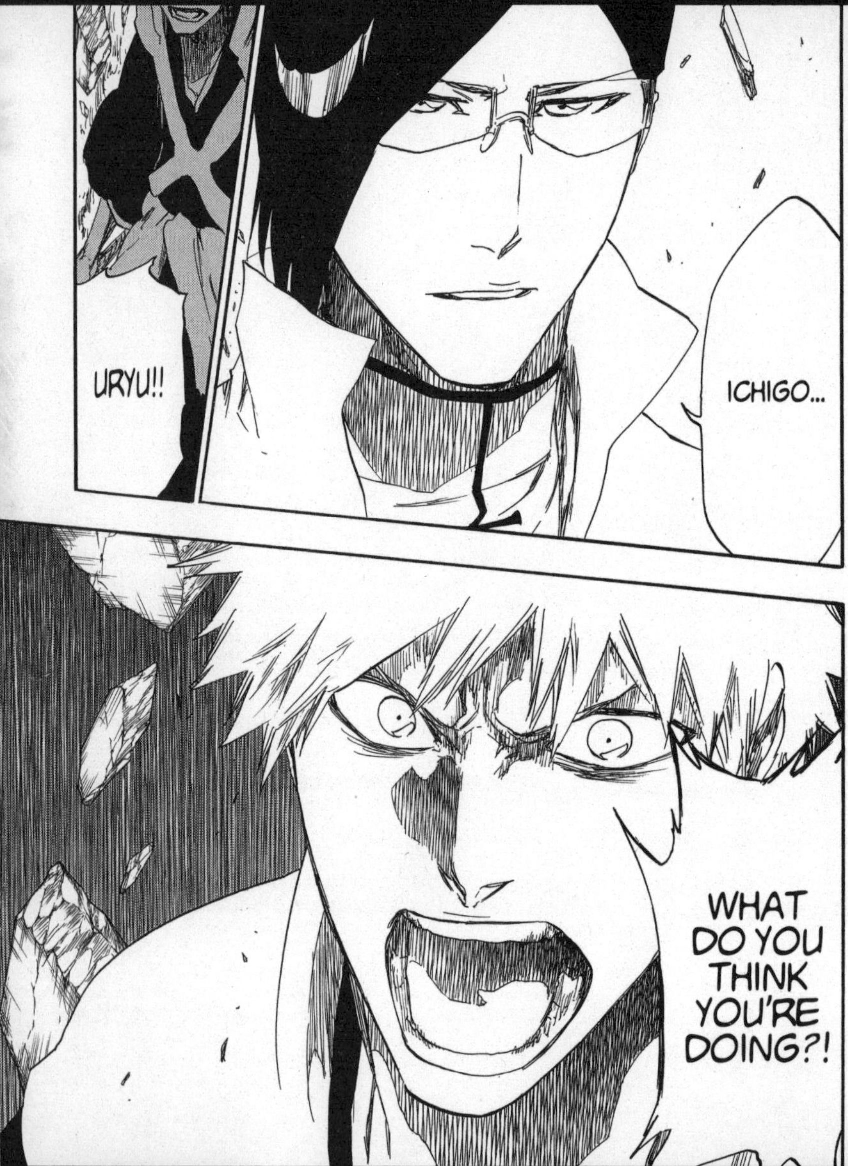
ICHIGO...
URYU!!
WHAT DO YOU THINK YOU'RE DOING?!

The Betrayer

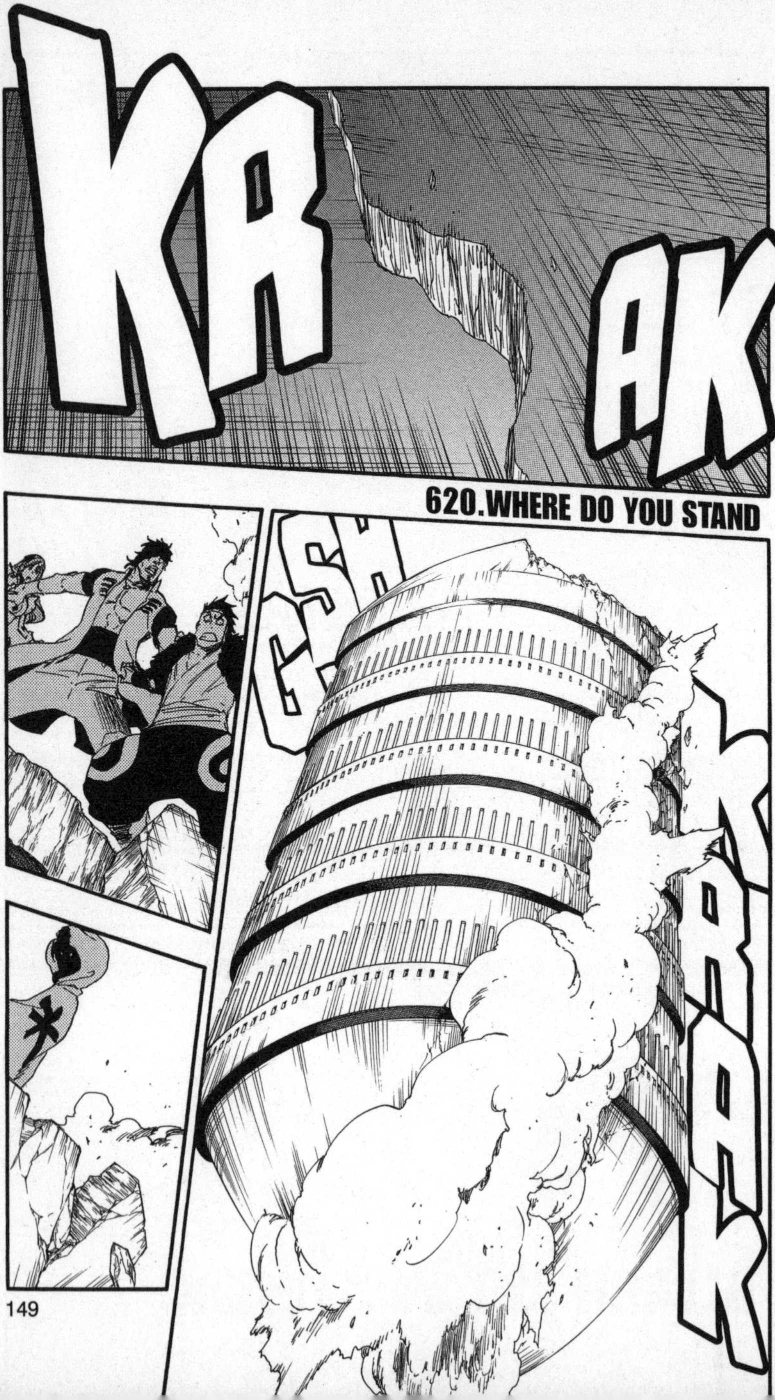
KRAAK
GSH

620. WHERE DO YOU STAND

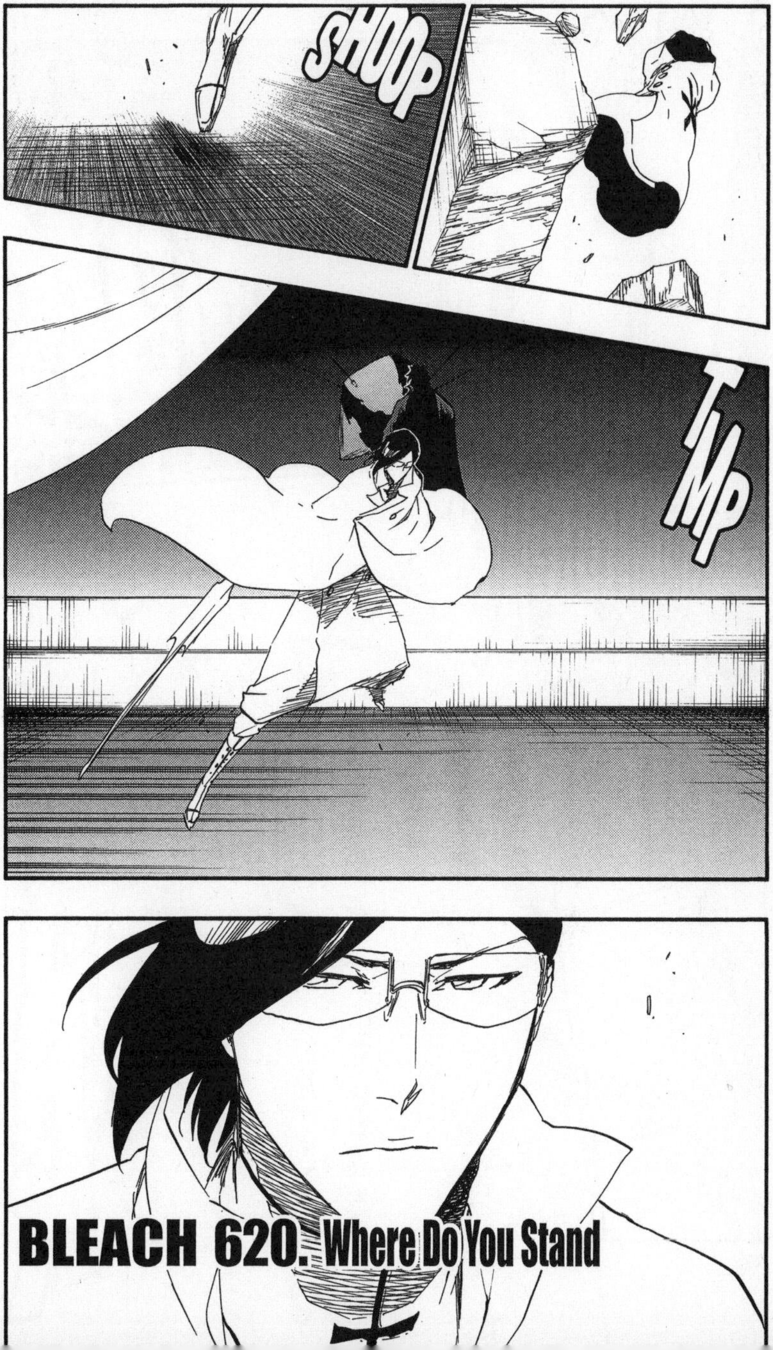
SHOOP
TMP
BLEACH 620. Where Do You Stand

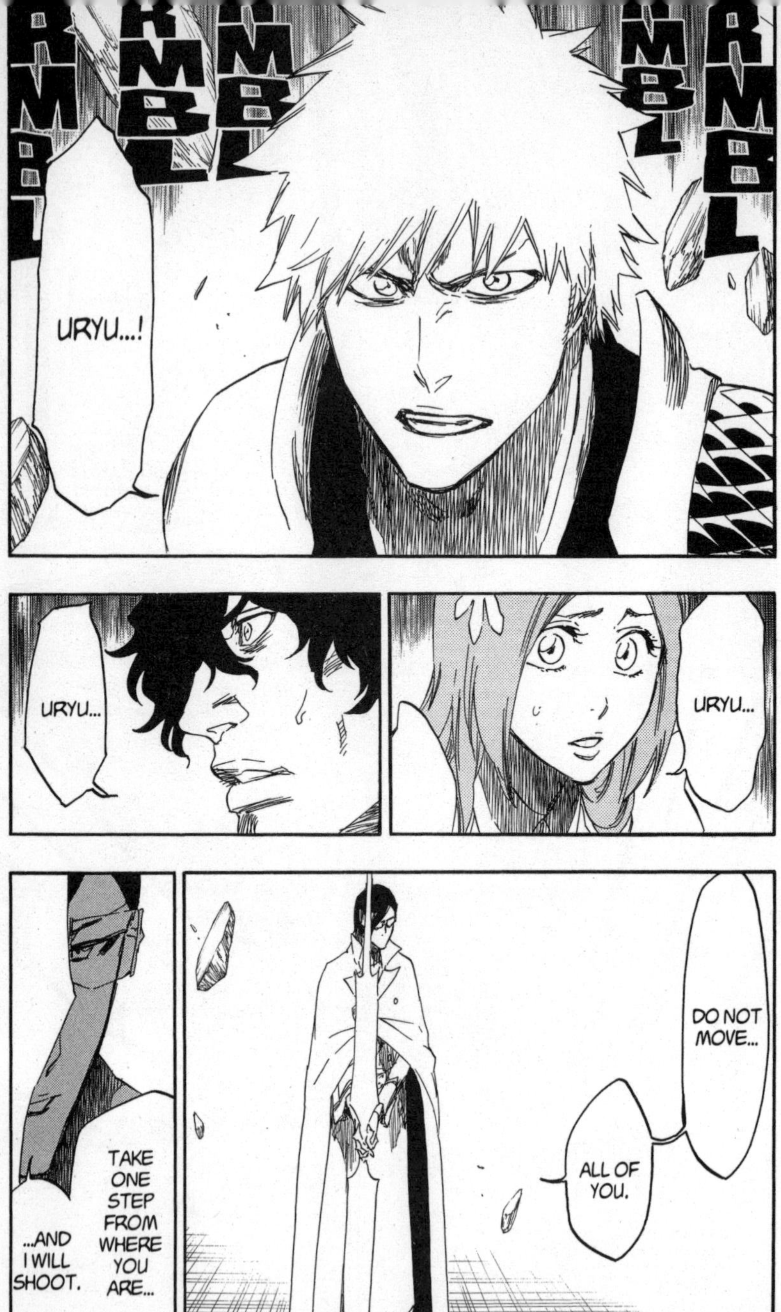
RMMBL
RMMBL
RMMBL
RMMBL
URYU...!
URYU...
URYU...
DO NOT MOVE...
ALL OF YOU.
TAKE ONE STEP FROM WHERE YOU ARE...
...AND I WILL SHOOT.

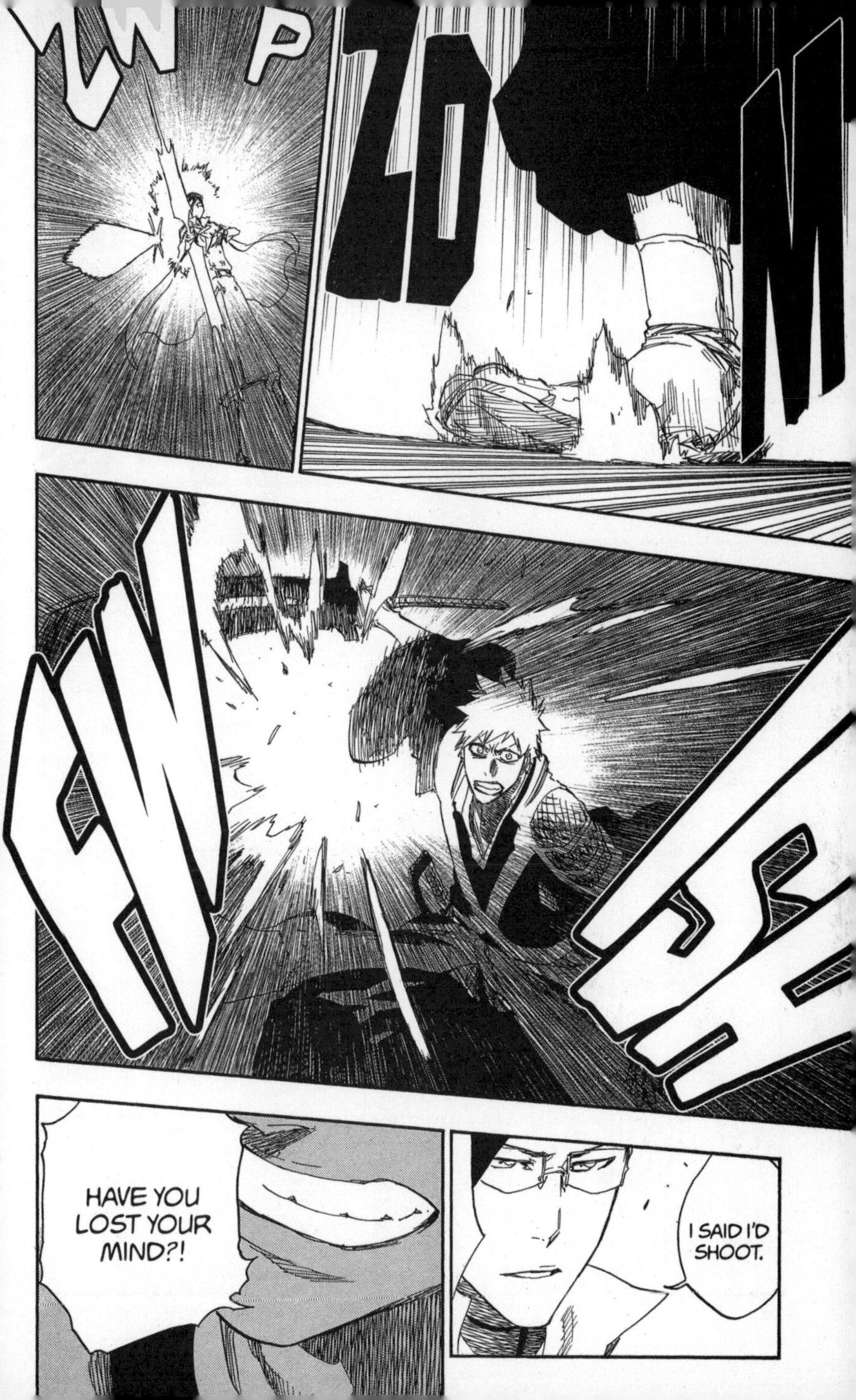
I SAID I'D SHOOT.
HAVE YOU LOST YOUR MIND?!

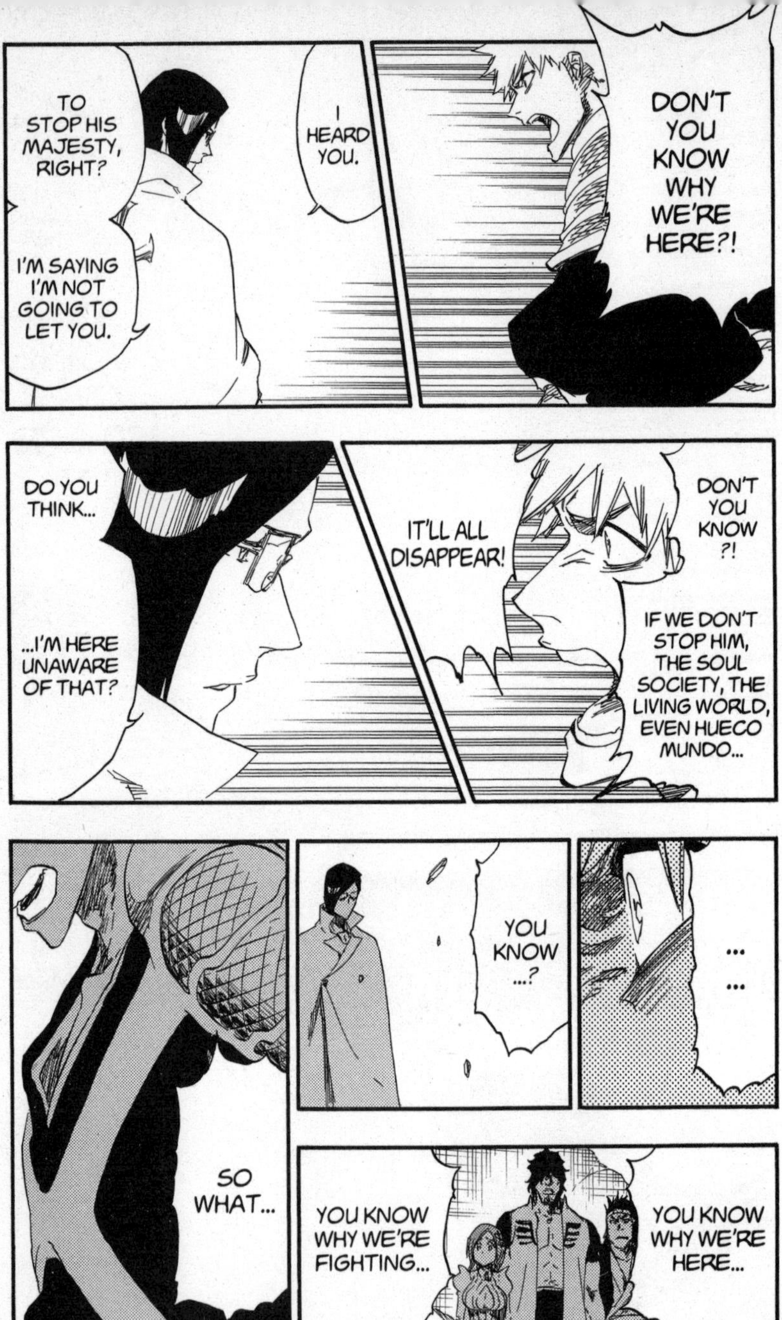
DON'T YOU KNOW WHY WE'RE HERE?!
I HEARD YOU.
TO STOP HIS MAJESTY, RIGHT?
I'M SAYING I'M NOT GOING TO LET YOU.
DON'T YOU KNOW?!
IF WE DON'T STOP HIM, THE SOUL SOCIETY, THE LIVING WORLD, EVEN HUECO MUNDO...
IT'LL ALL DISAPPEAR!
DO YOU THINK...
...I'M HERE UNAWARE OF THAT?
...
...
YOU KNOW ...?
YOU KNOW WHY WE'RE HERE...
YOU KNOW WHY WE'RE FIGHTING...
SO WHAT...

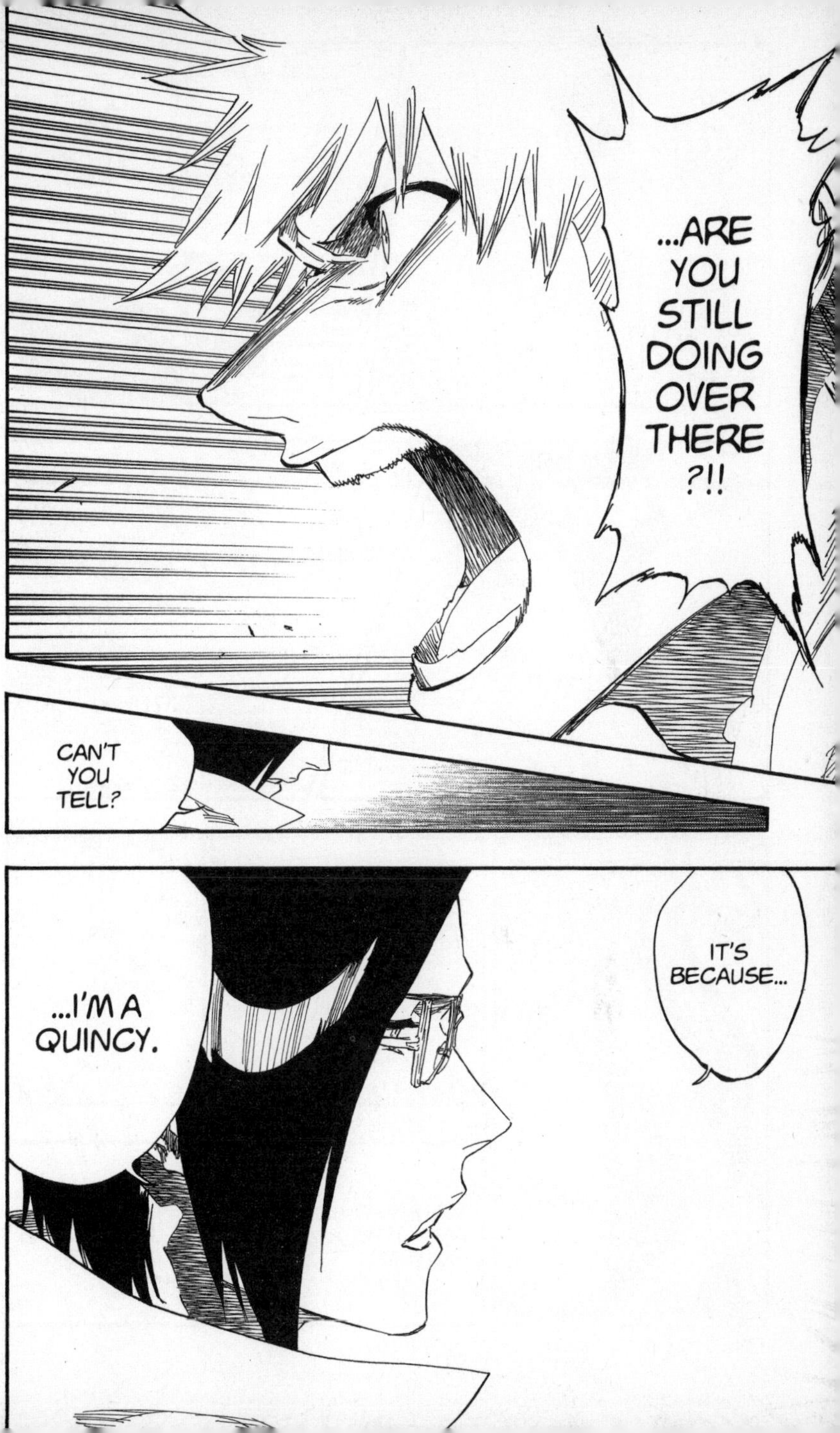
...ARE YOU STILL DOING OVER THERE?!!
CAN'T YOU TELL?
IT'S BECAUSE...
...I'M A QUINCY.

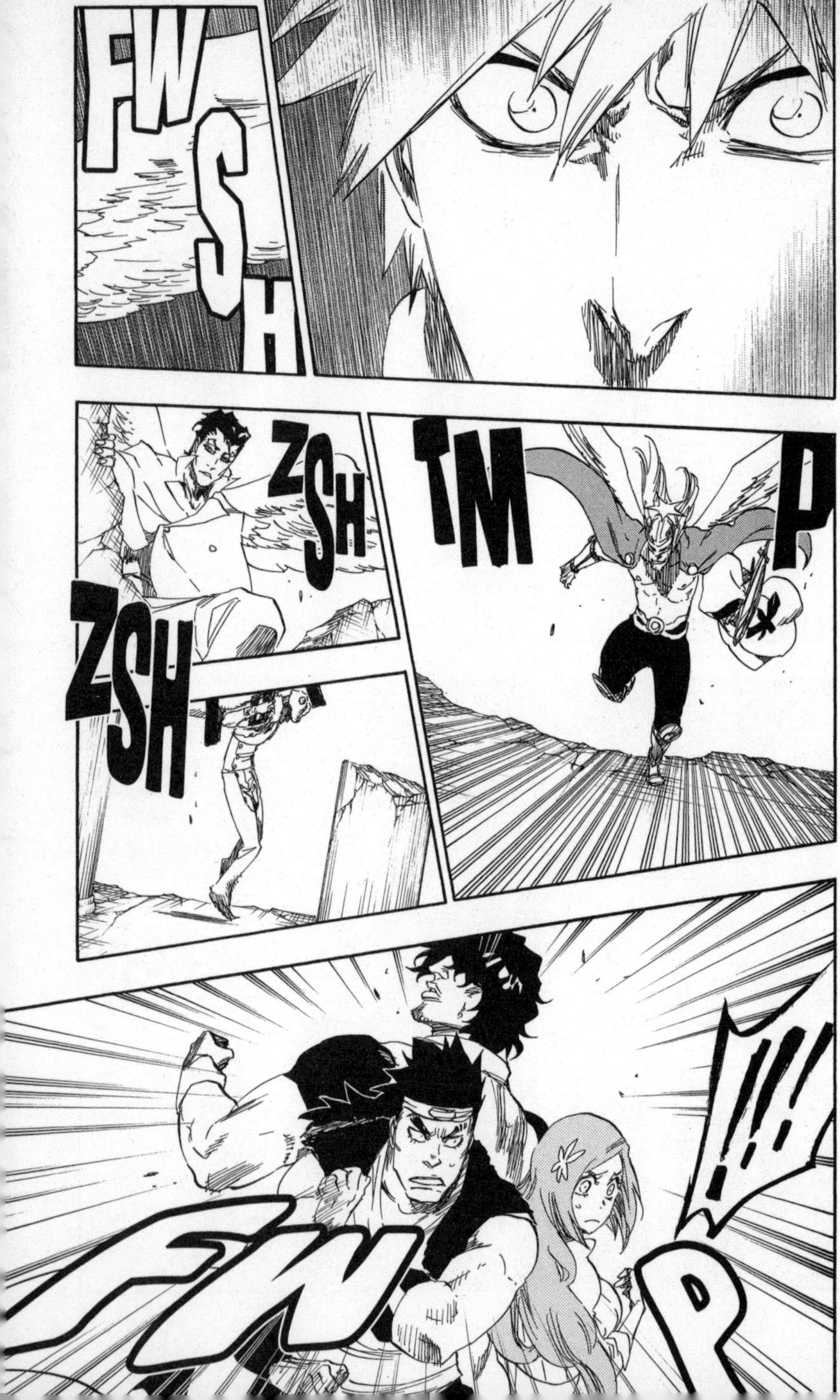
FWSH
TMP
ZSH
ZSH
!!
FWP

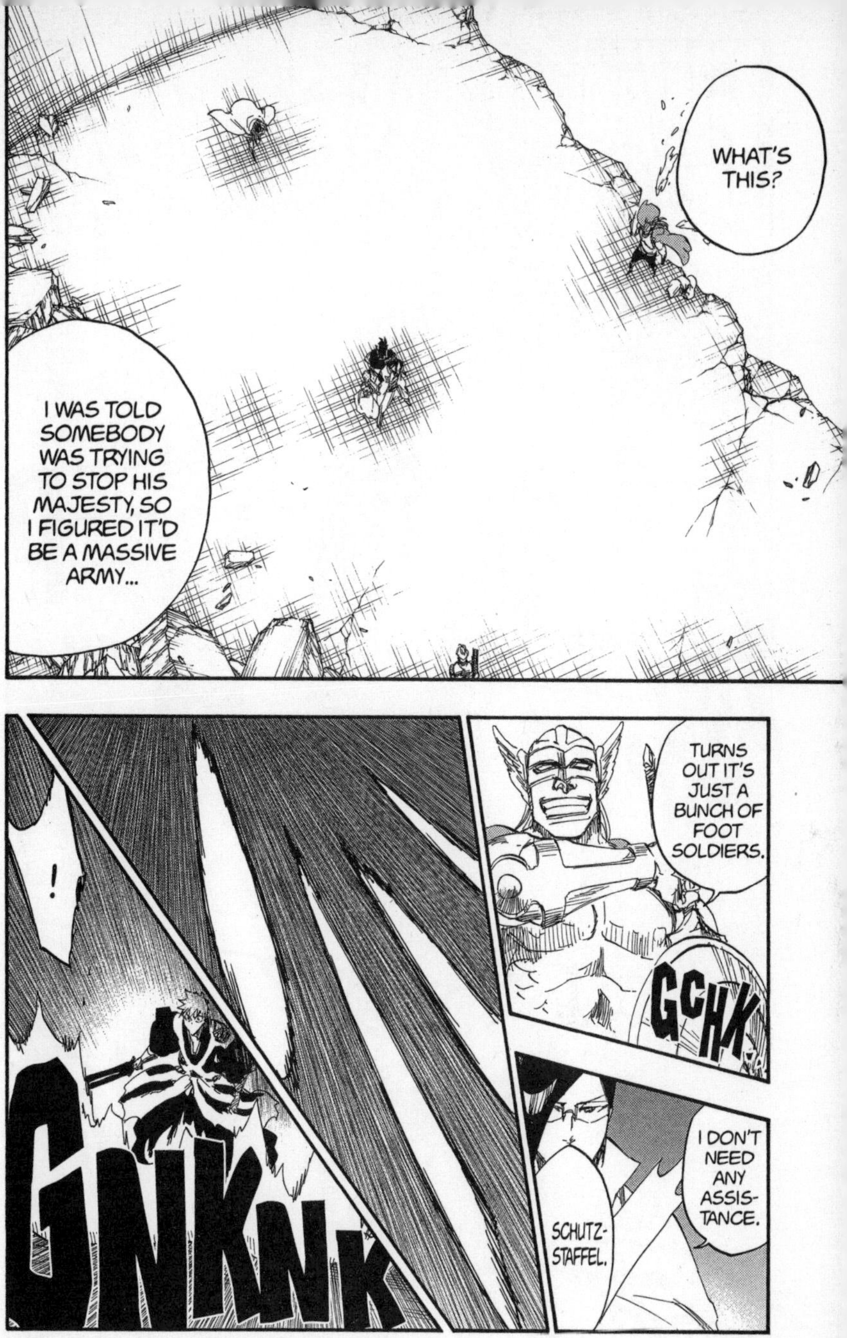
WHAT'S THIS?
I WAS TOLD SOMEBODY WAS TRYING TO STOP HIS MAJESTY, SO I FIGURED IT'D BE A MASSIVE ARMY...
TURNS OUT IT'S JUST A BUNCH OF FOOT SOLDIERS.
GCHK
I DON'T NEED ANY ASSIS-TANCE.
SCHUTZ-STAFFEL.
!
GNKNK

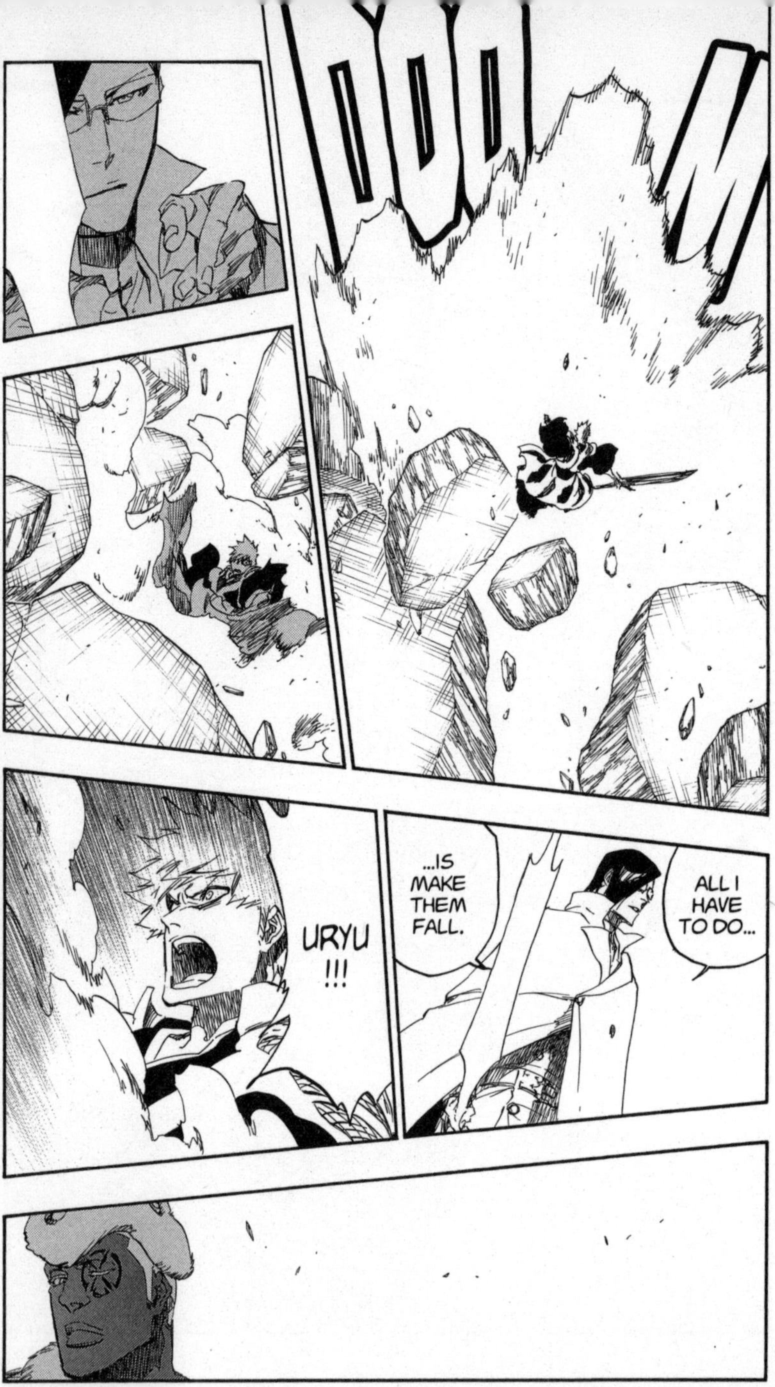
DOOOM
ALL I HAVE TO DO...
...IS MAKE THEM FALL.
URYU !!!

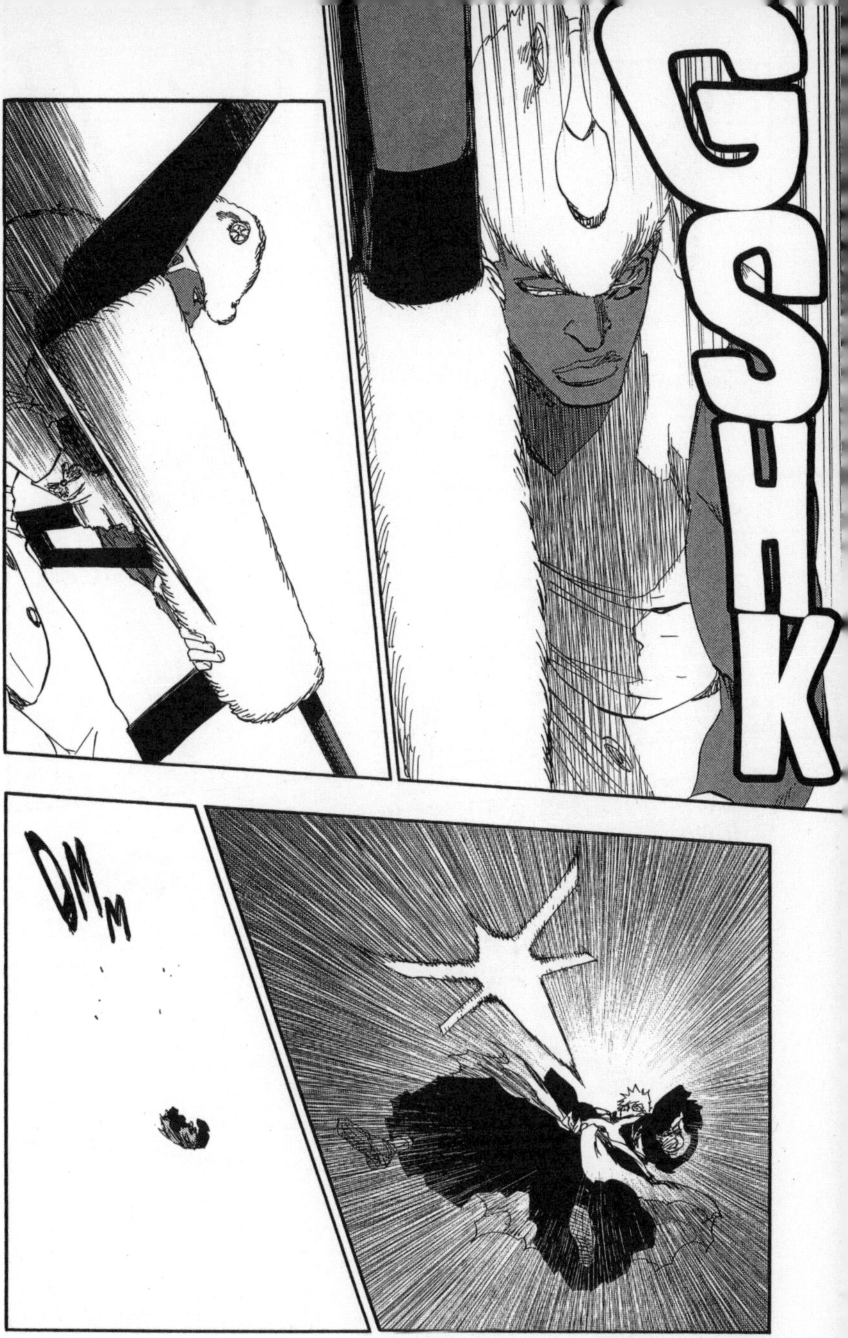
GSHK
DMM

READ THIS WAY

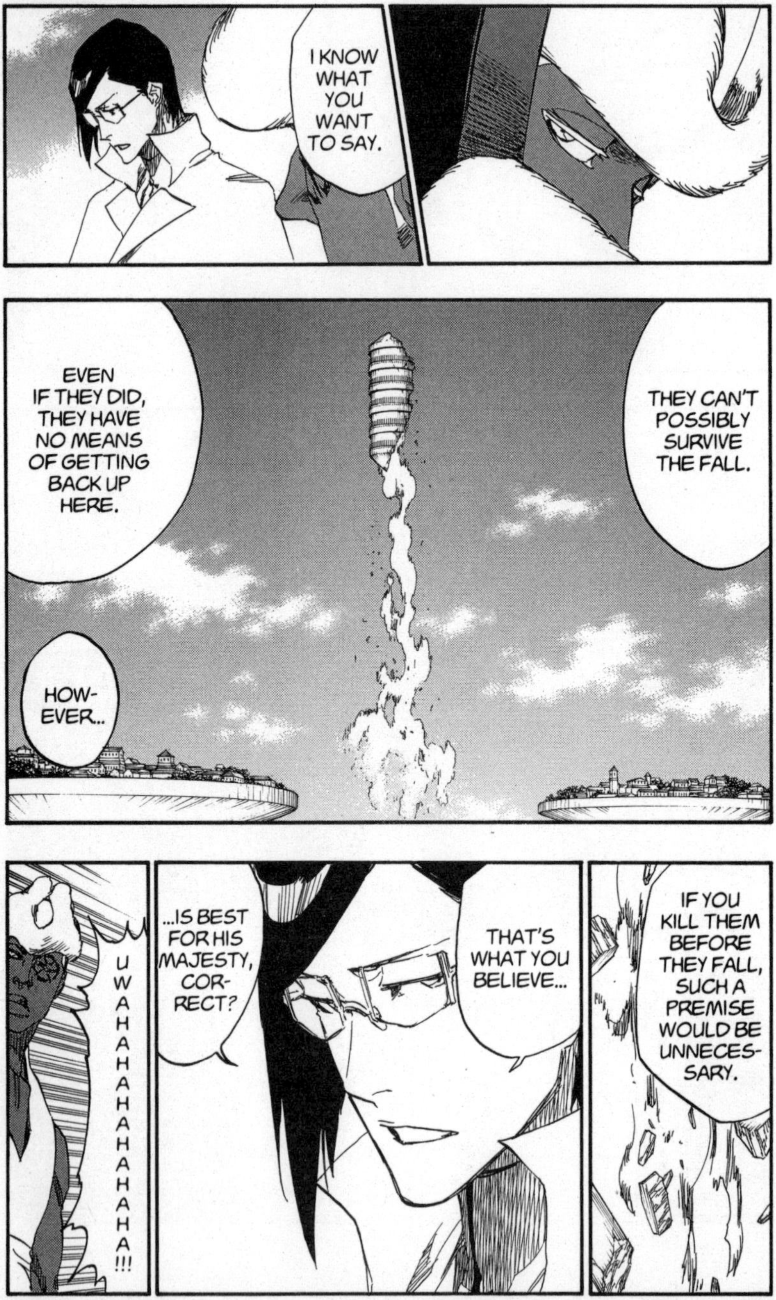
I KNOW WHAT YOU WANT TO SAY.
THEY CAN'T POSSIBLY SURVIVE THE FALL.
EVEN IF THEY DID, THEY HAVE NO MEANS OF GETTING BACK UP HERE.
HOW-EVER...
IF YOU KILL THEM BEFORE THEY FALL, SUCH A PREMISE WOULD BE UNNECES-SARY.
THAT'S WHAT YOU BELIEVE...
...IS BEST FOR HIS MAJESTY, COR-RECT?
UWAHAHAHAHAHAHAHA!!!

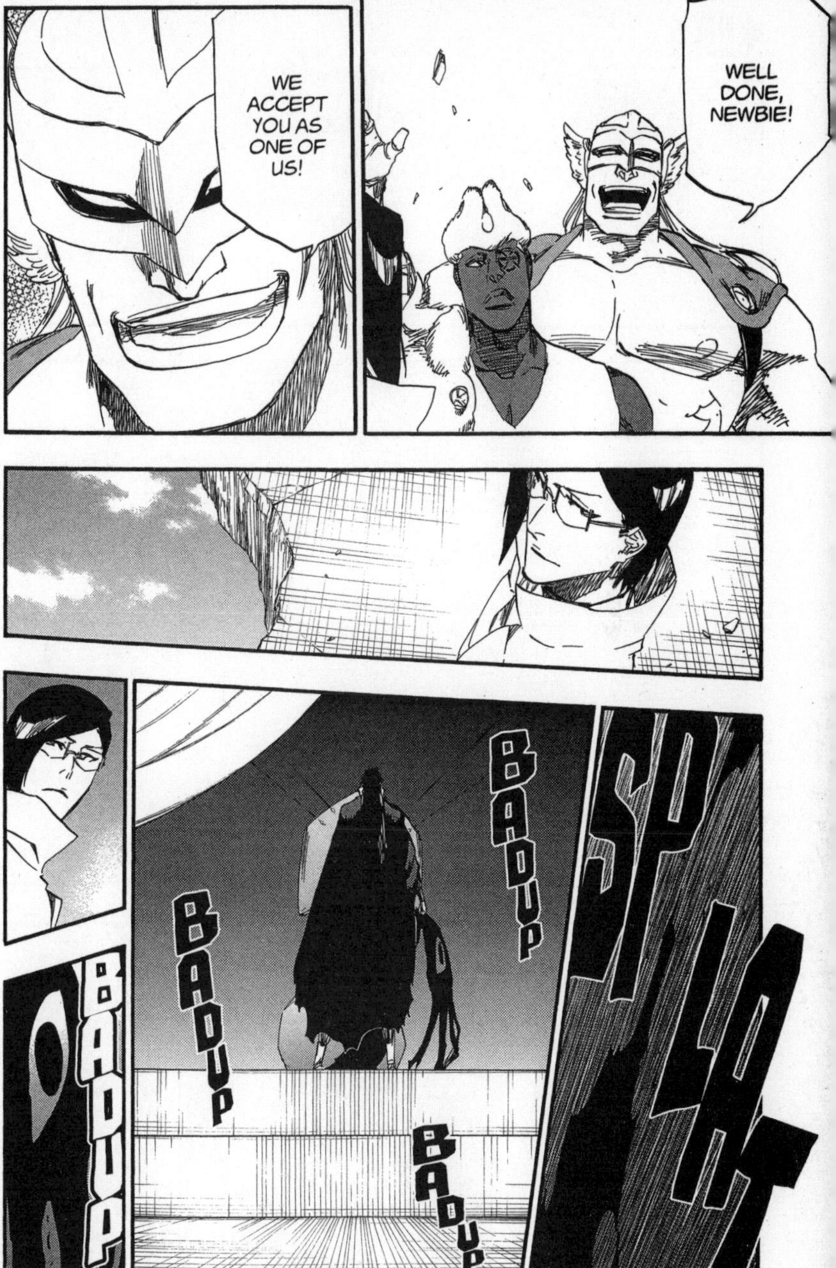
WELL DONE, NEWBIE!
WE ACCEPT YOU AS ONE OF US!
BADUP
BADUP
BADUP
BADUP
BADUP

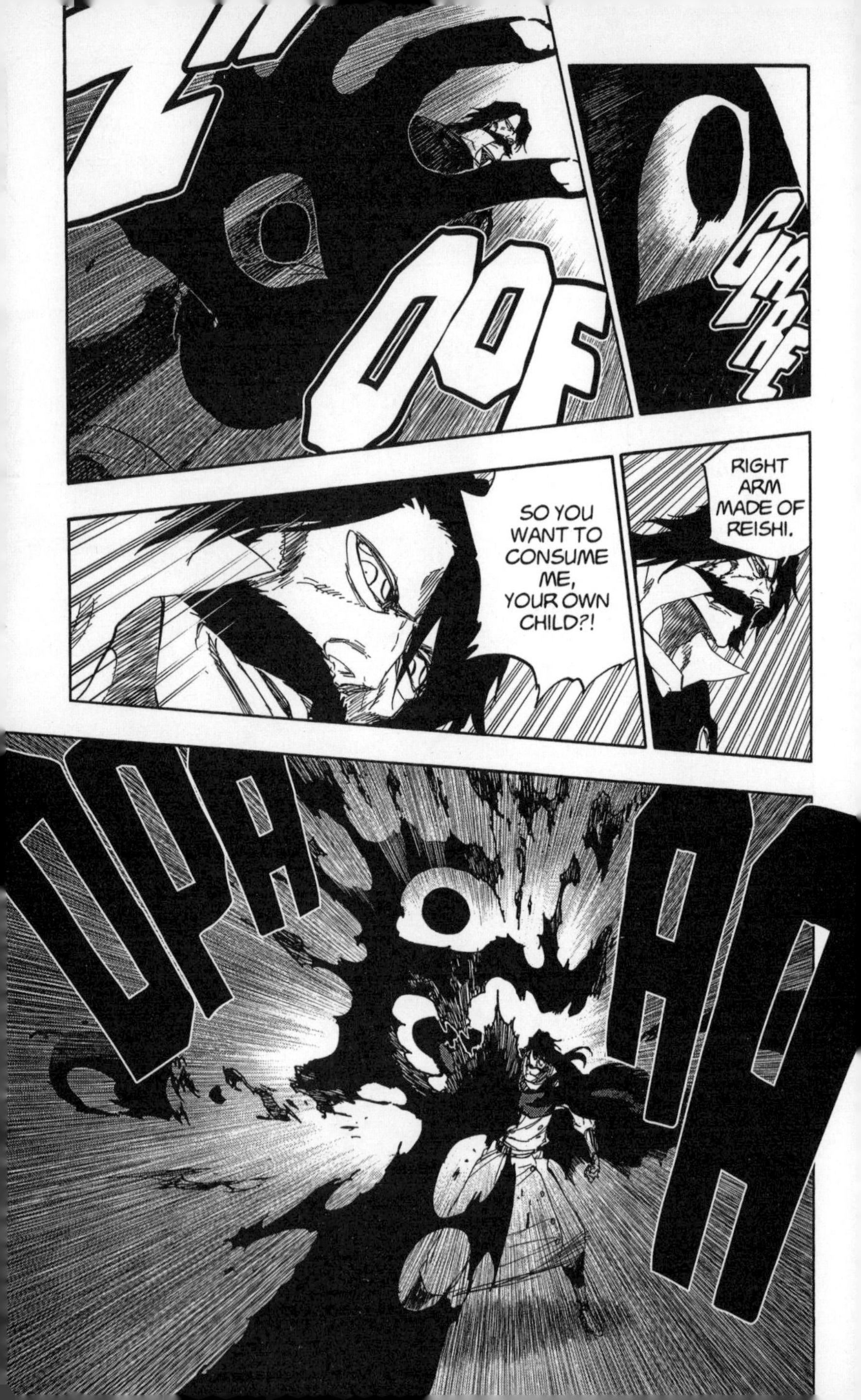
OOF
RIGHT ARM MADE OF REISHI.
SO YOU WANT TO CONSUME ME, YOUR OWN CHILD?!

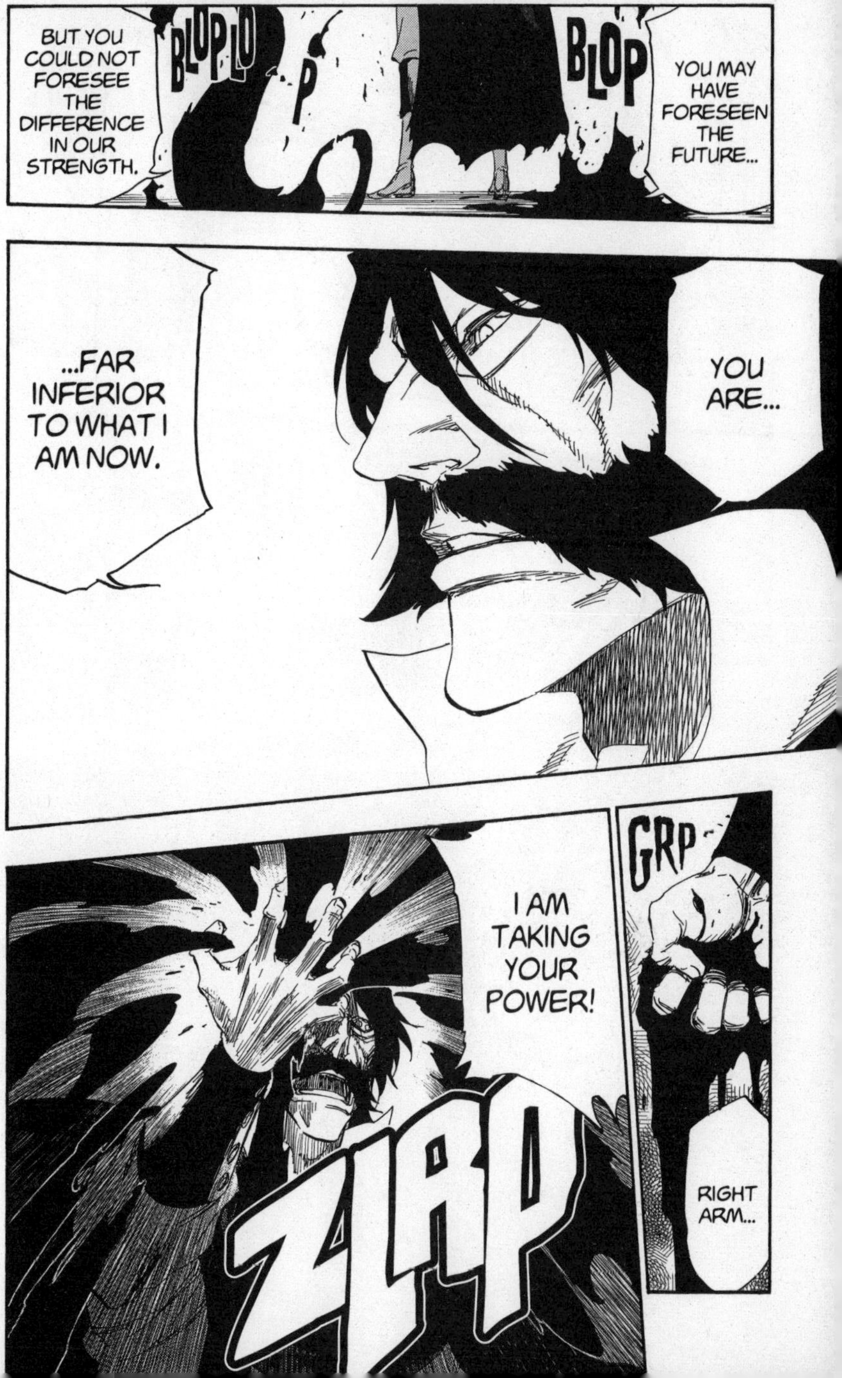
YOU MAY HAVE FORESEEN THE FUTURE...
BLOP
BLOPLOP
BUT YOU COULD NOT FORESEE THE DIFFERENCE IN OUR STRENGTH.
YOU ARE...
...FAR INFERIOR TO WHAT I AM NOW.
GRP
RIGHT ARM...
I AM TAKING YOUR POWER!

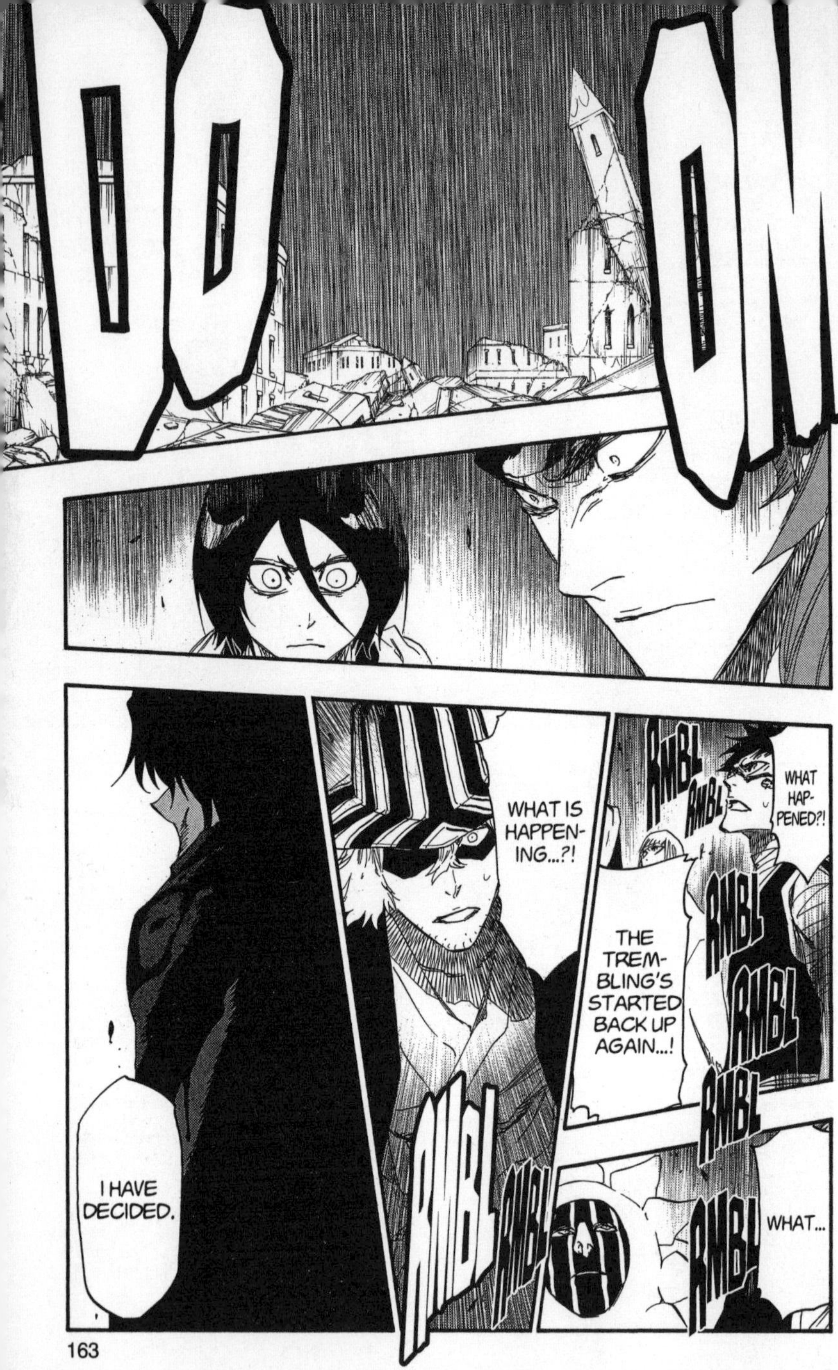
DOOM
RMBL RMBL
WHAT HAPPENED?!
THE TREMBLING'S STARTED BACK UP AGAIN...!
RMBL RMBL RMBL
RMBL
WHAT...
WHAT IS HAPPENING...?!
RMBL RMBL
I HAVE DECIDED.

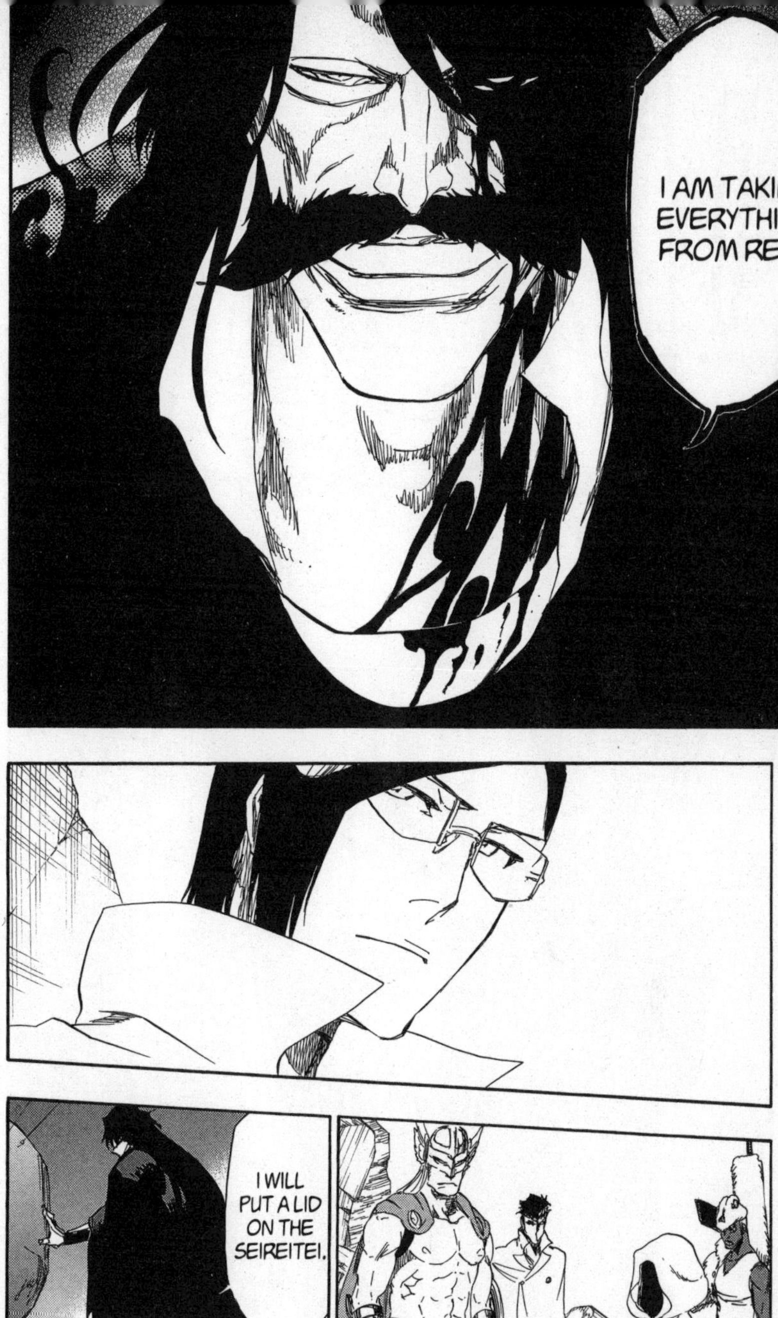
I AM TAKING EVERYTHING FROM REIO.
I WILL PUT A LID ON THE SEIREITEI.

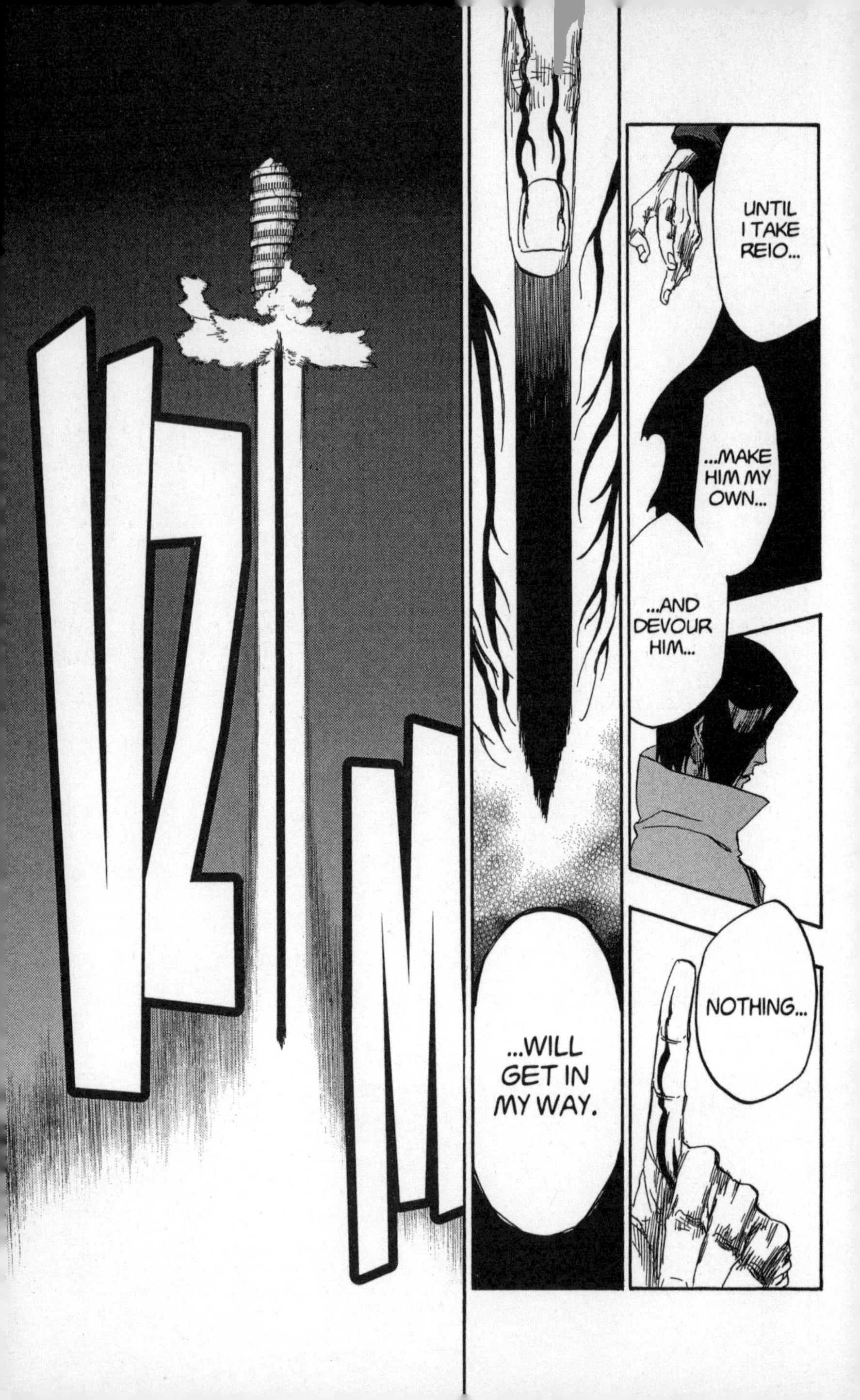
UNTIL I TAKE REIO...
...MAKE HIM MY OWN...
...AND DEVOUR HIM...
NOTHING...
...WILL GET IN MY WAY.

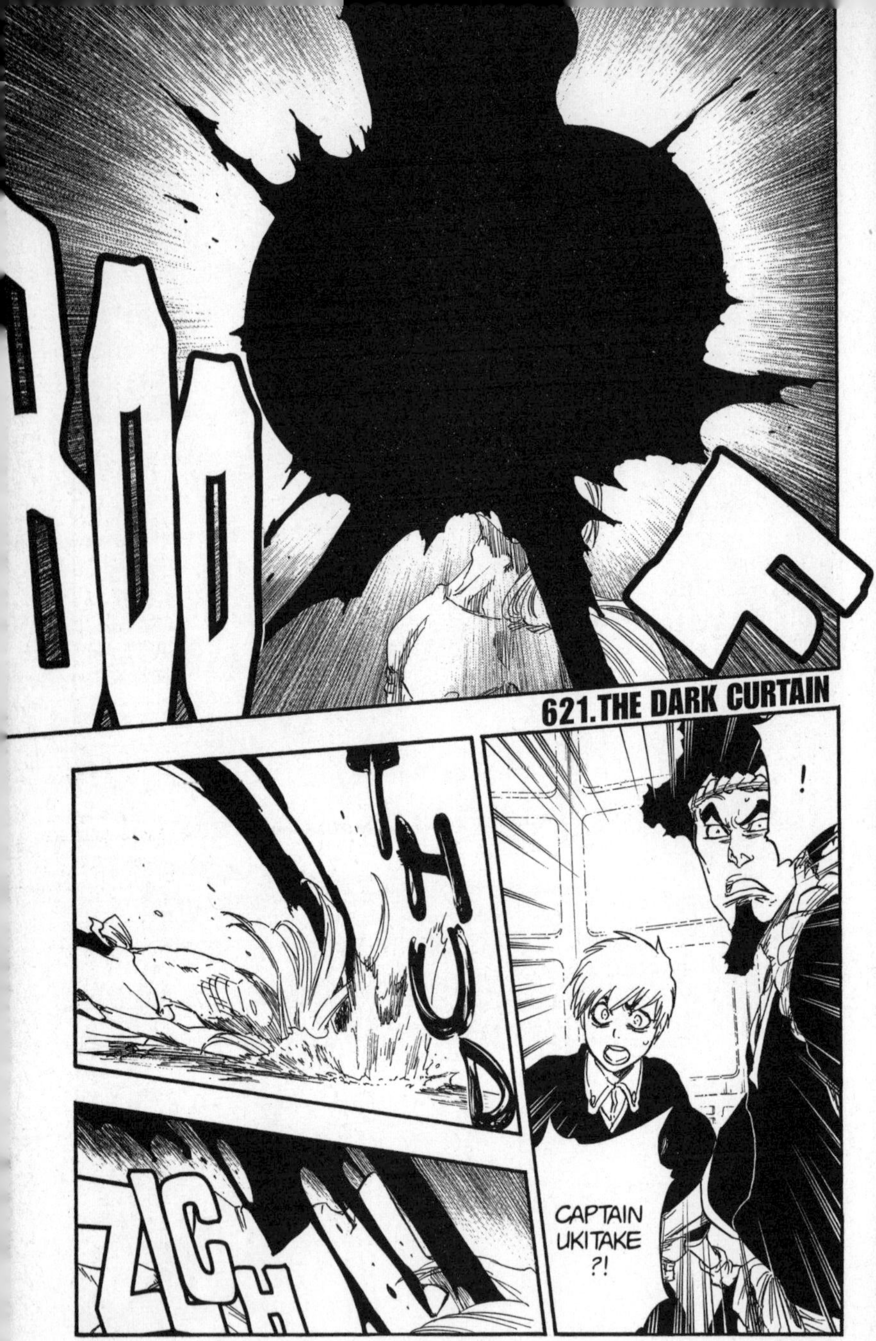
621. THE DARK CURTAIN
!
CAPTAIN UKITAKE ?!

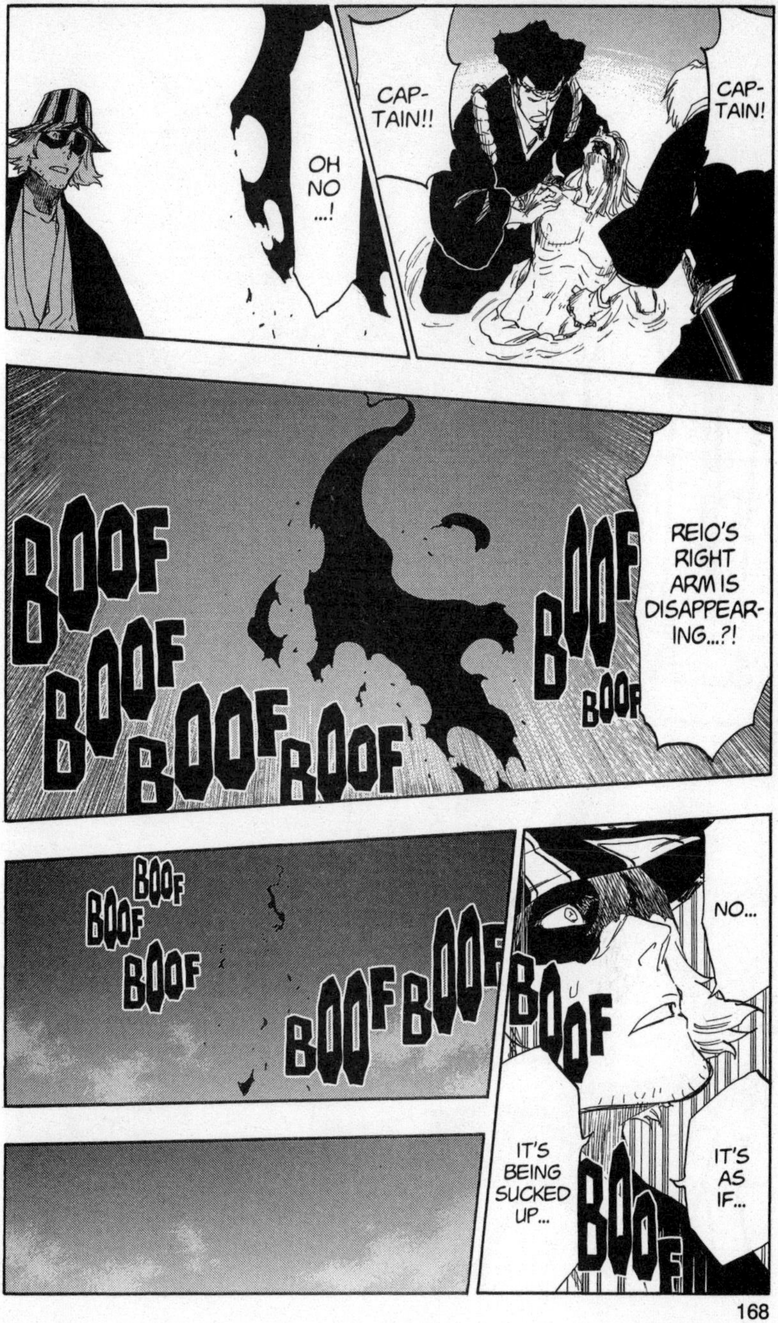
CAP-
TAIN!
CAP-
TAIN!!
OH
NO
...!
REIO'S
RIGHT
ARM IS
DISAPPEAR-
ING...?!
BOOF
BOOF
BOOF
BOOF
BOOF
BOOF
BOOF
NO...
IT'S
AS
IF...
IT'S
BEING
SUCKED
UP...
BOOF
BOOF
BOOF
BOOF
BOOF
BOOF
BOOF
BOOF
BOOF

READ THIS WAY

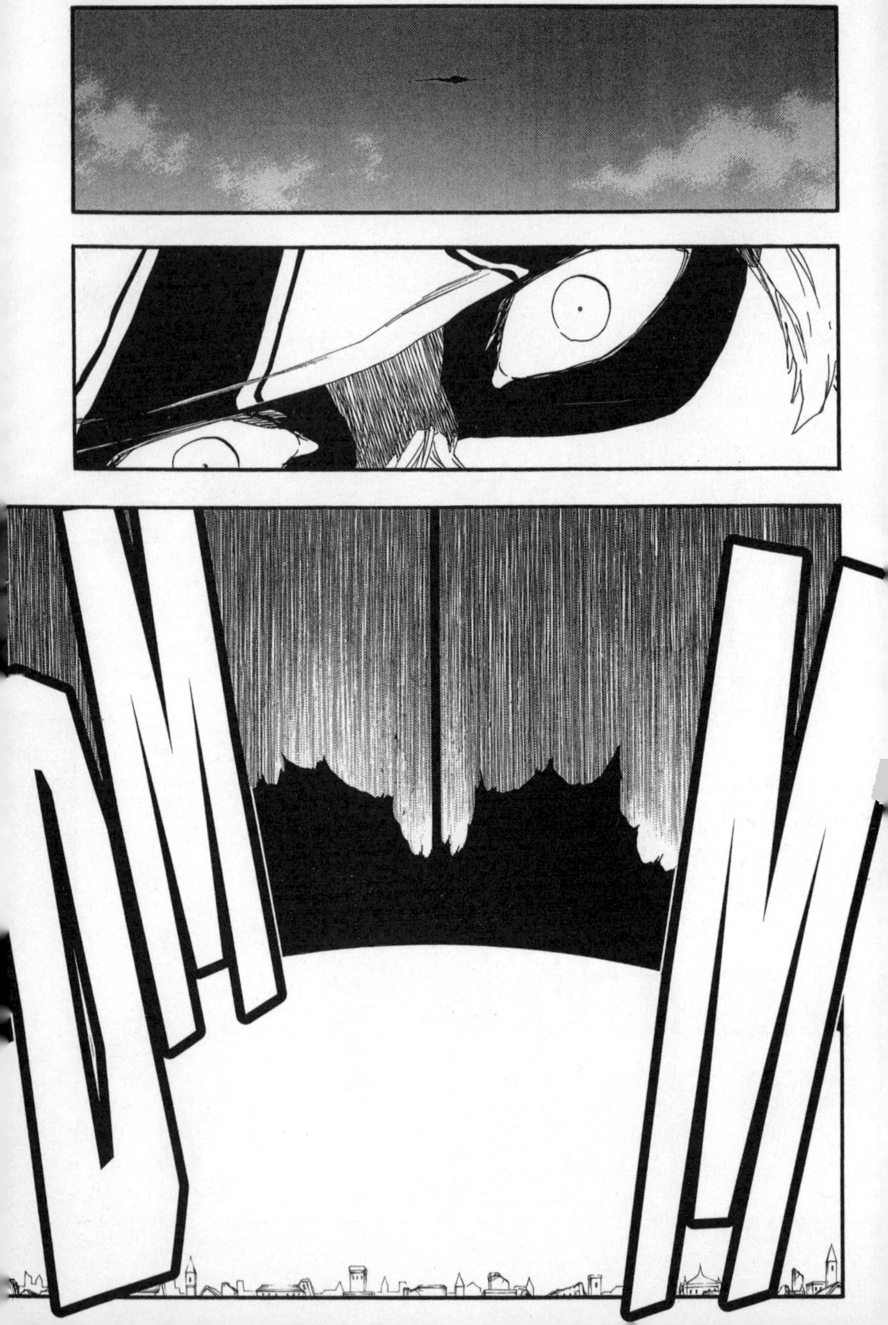

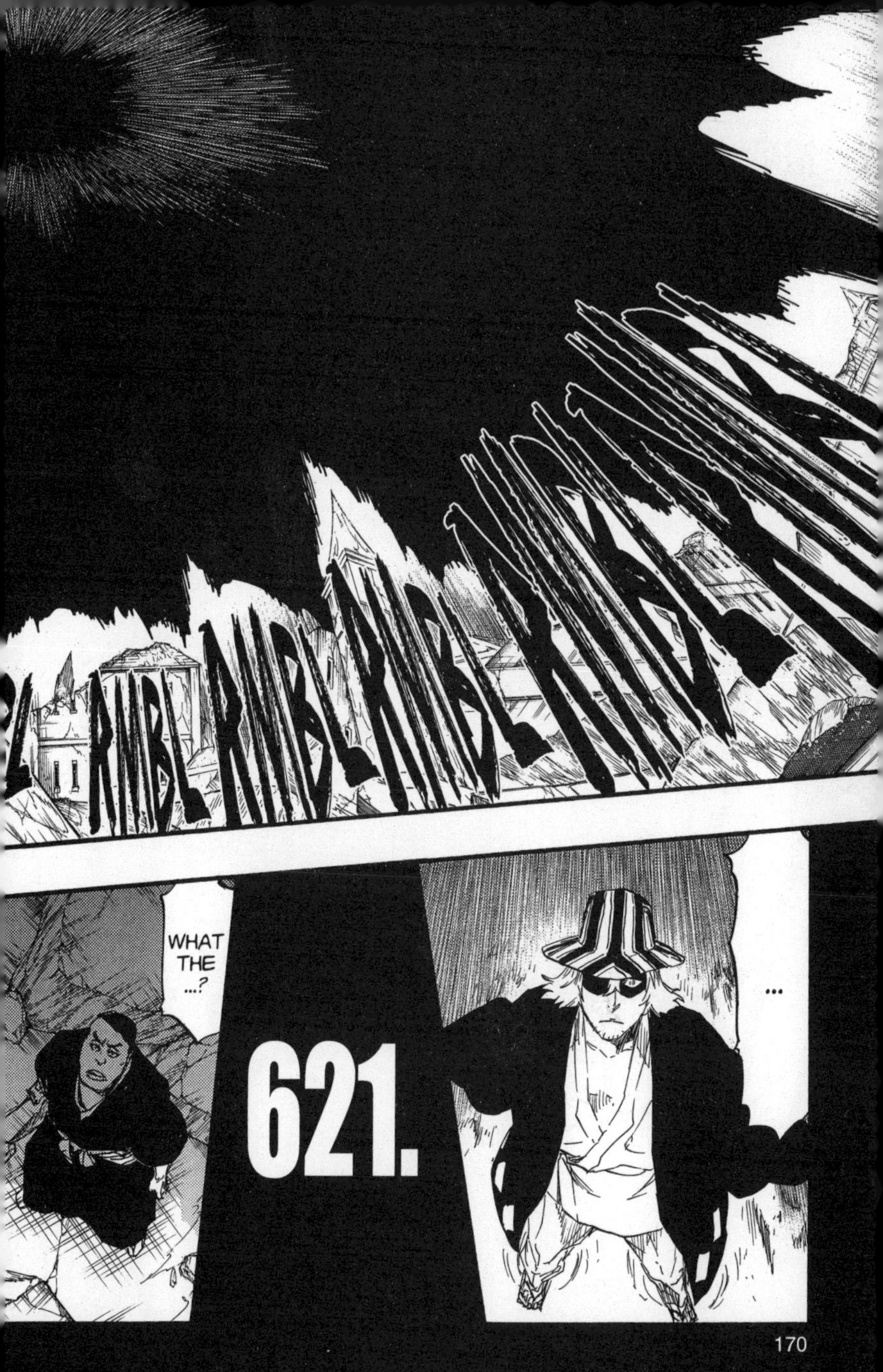
RMBL RMBL RMBL RMBL
...
621.
WHAT THE ...?

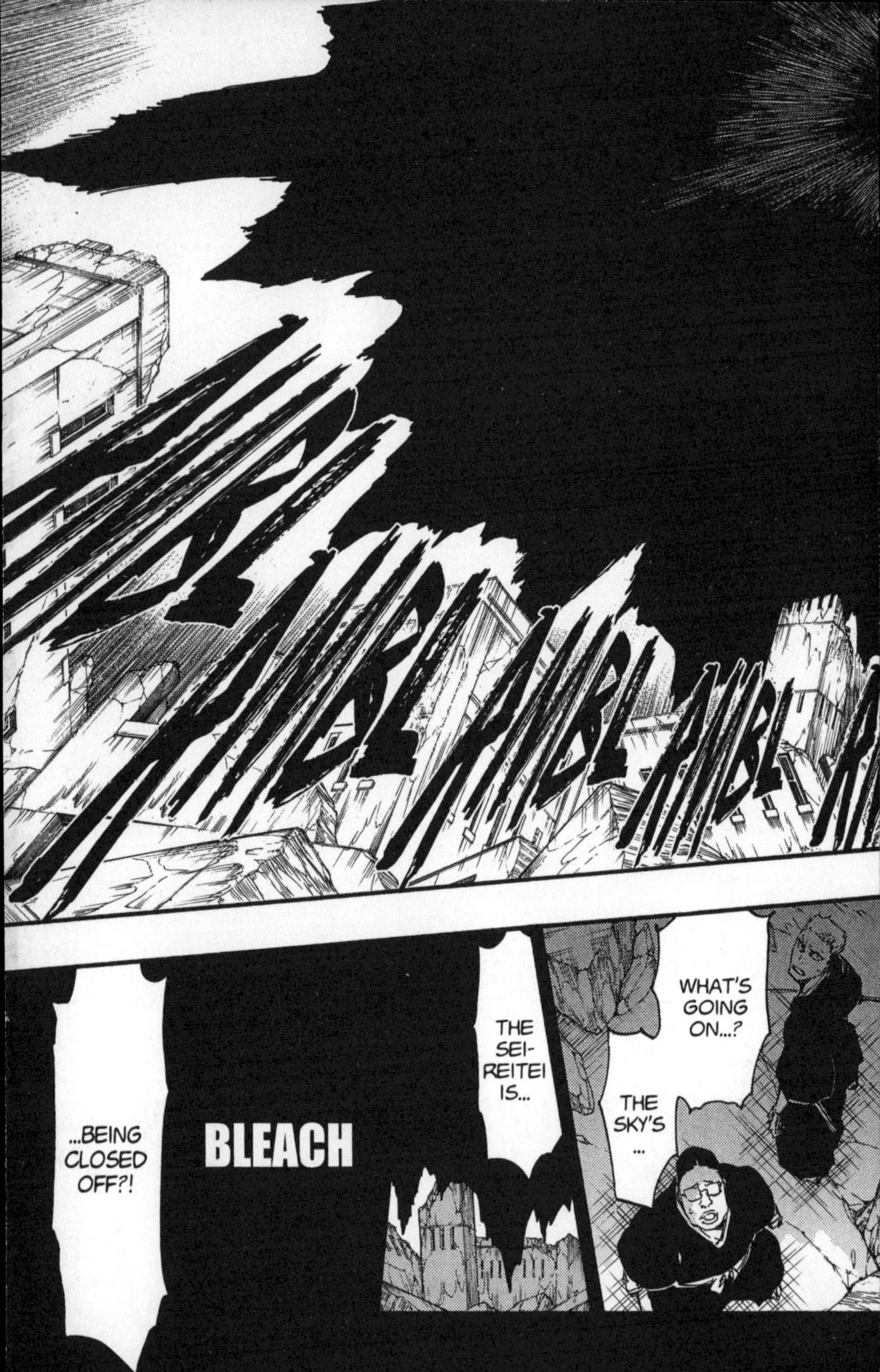
WHAT'S GOING ON...?
THE SKY'S ...
THE SEI-REITEI IS...
...BEING CLOSED OFF?!
BLEACH

THE DARK CURTAIN

READ THIS WAY

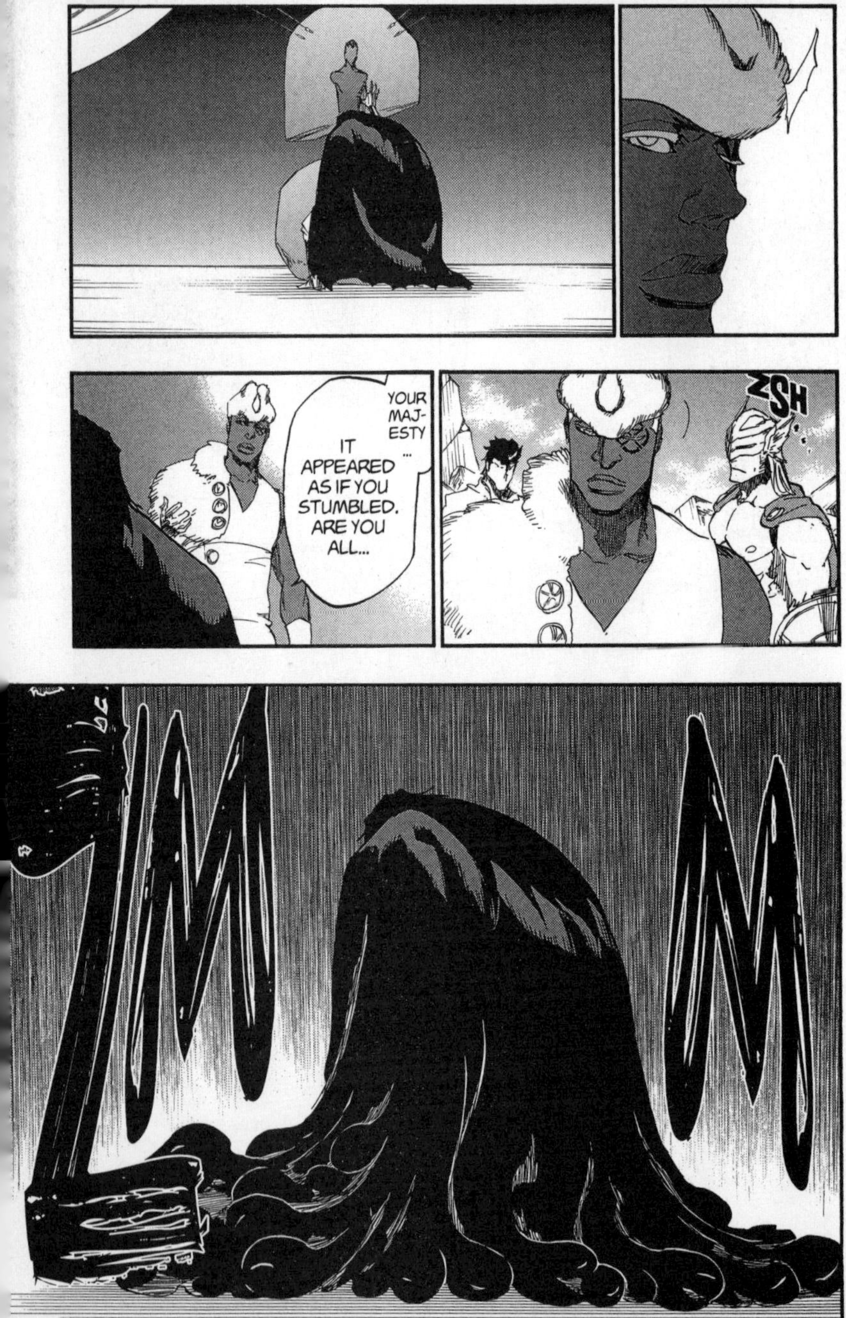
ZSH
YOUR MAJESTY...
IT APPEARED AS IF YOU STUMBLED. ARE YOU ALL...

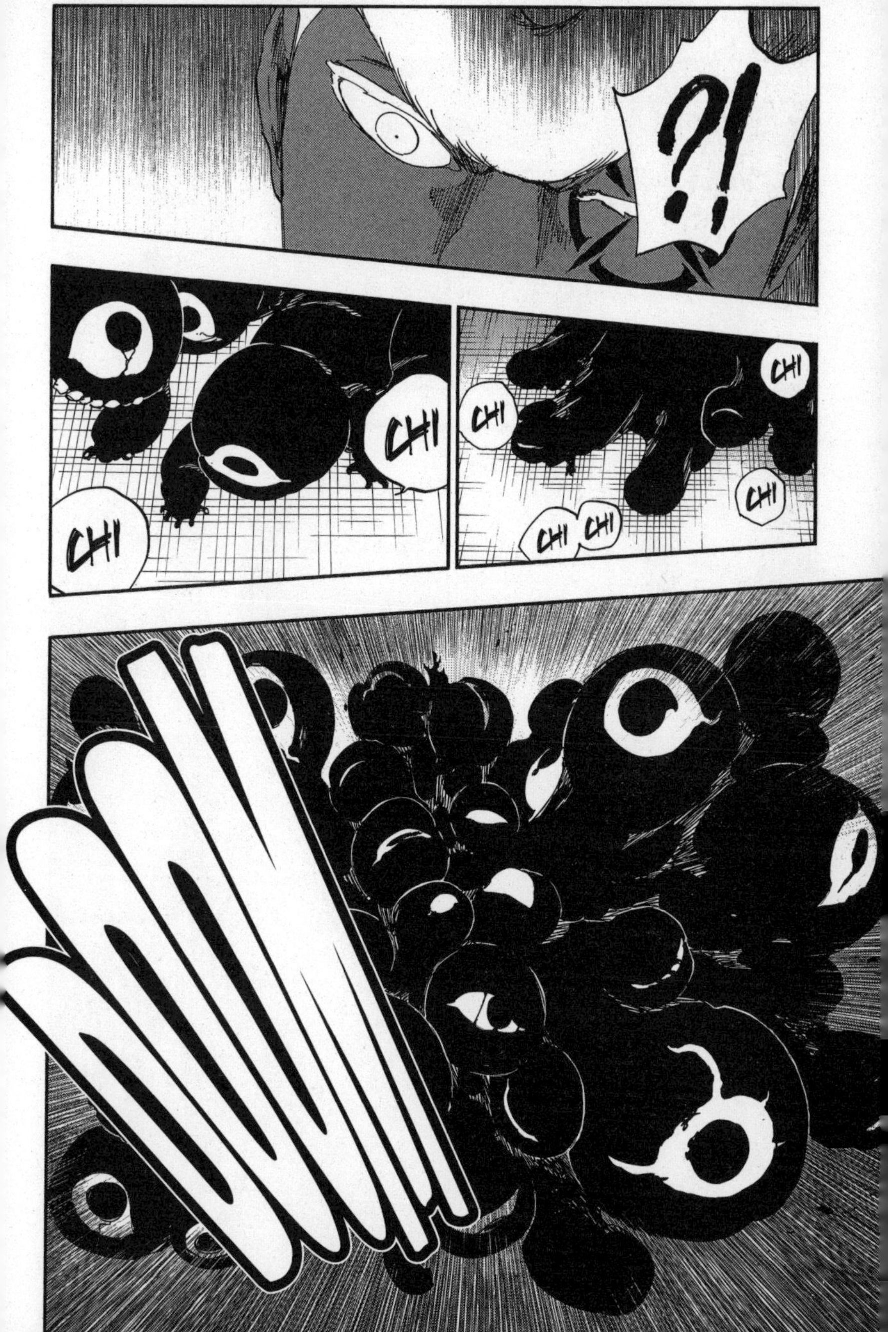
?!
CHI
CHI
CHI
CHI
CHI
CHI
CHI

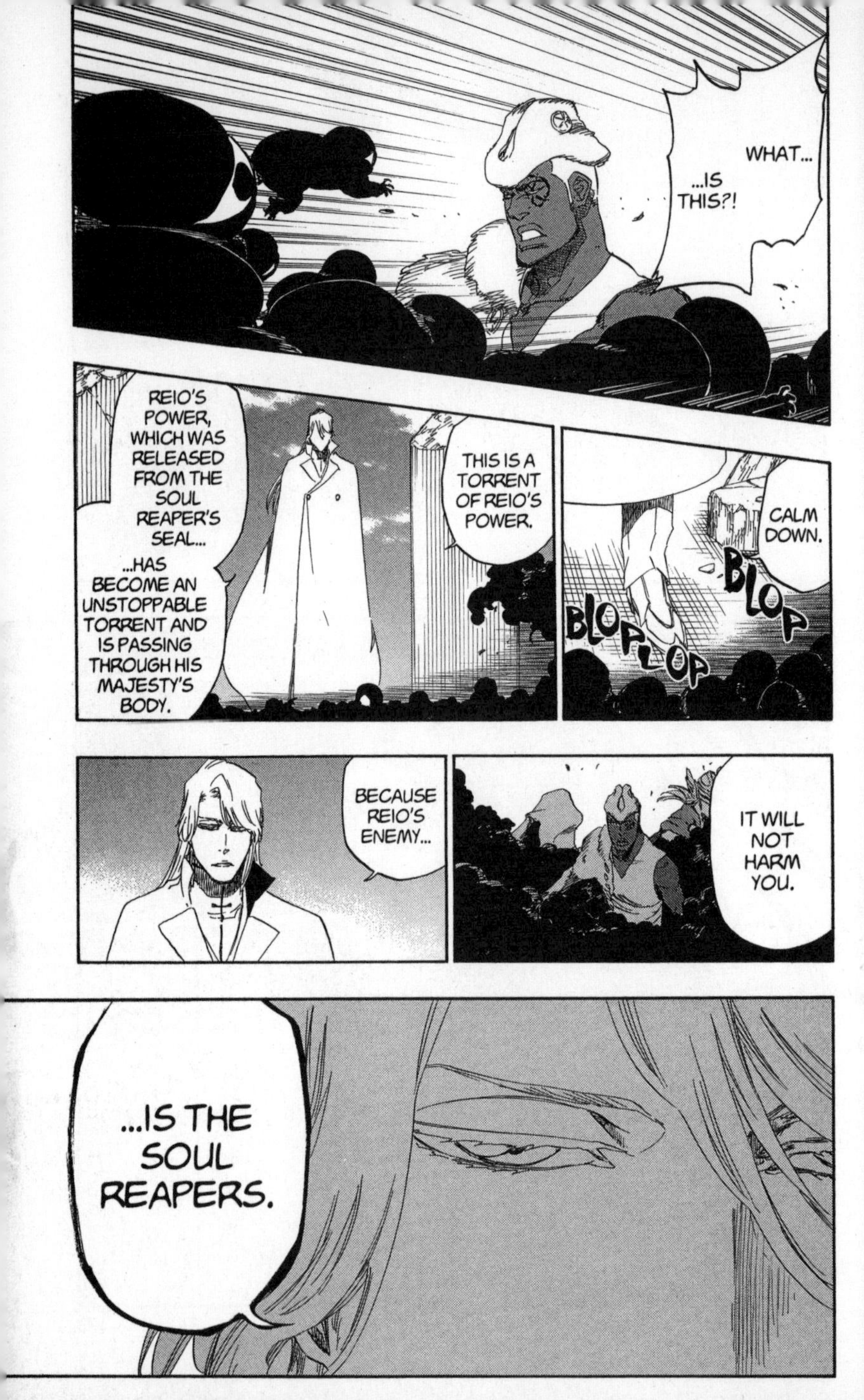
WHAT...
...IS THIS?!
CALM DOWN.
BLOP
BLOPLOP
THIS IS A TORRENT OF REIO'S POWER.
REIO'S POWER, WHICH WAS RELEASED FROM THE SOUL REAPER'S SEAL...
...HAS BECOME AN UNSTOPPABLE TORRENT AND IS PASSING THROUGH HIS MAJESTY'S BODY.
IT WILL NOT HARM YOU.
BECAUSE REIO'S ENEMY...
...IS THE SOUL REAPERS.

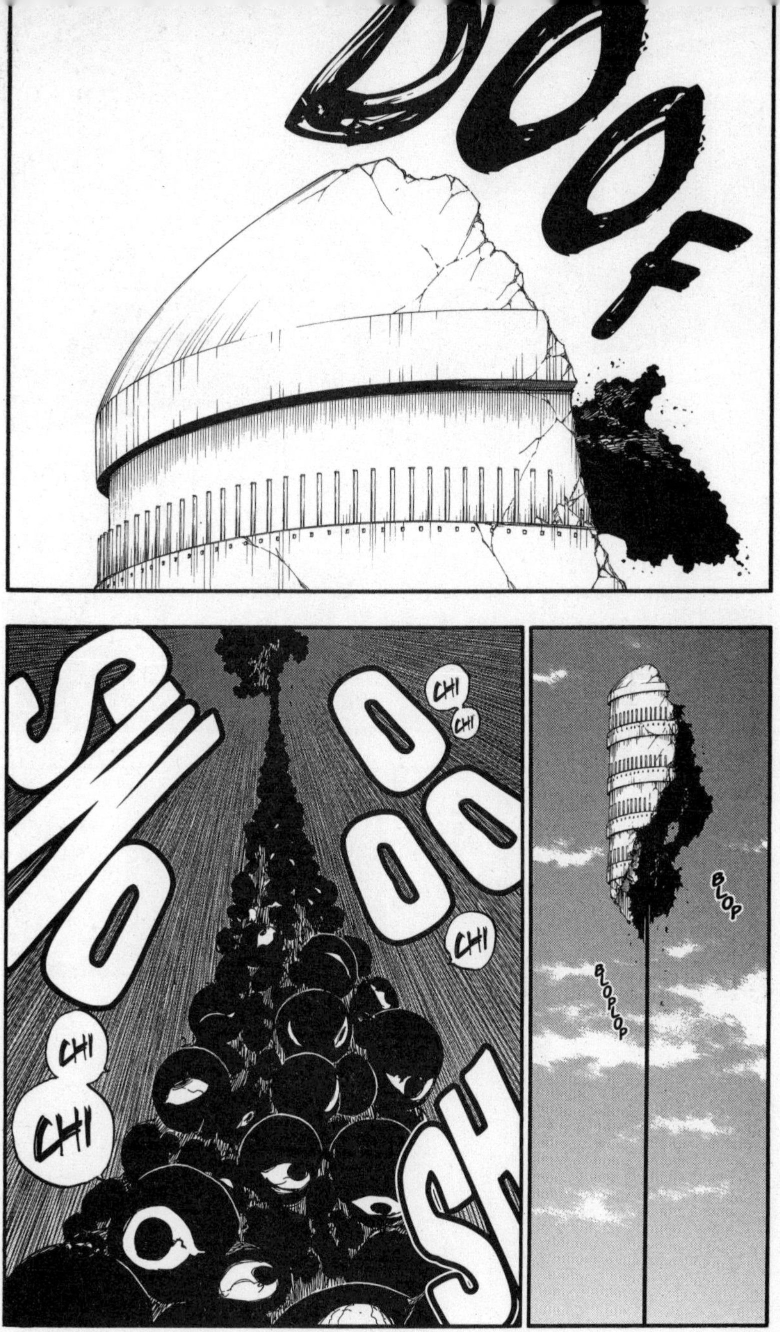
DOOF
BLOP
BLOPLOP
CHI
CHI
OOO
CHI
SH
SHOO
CHI
CHI

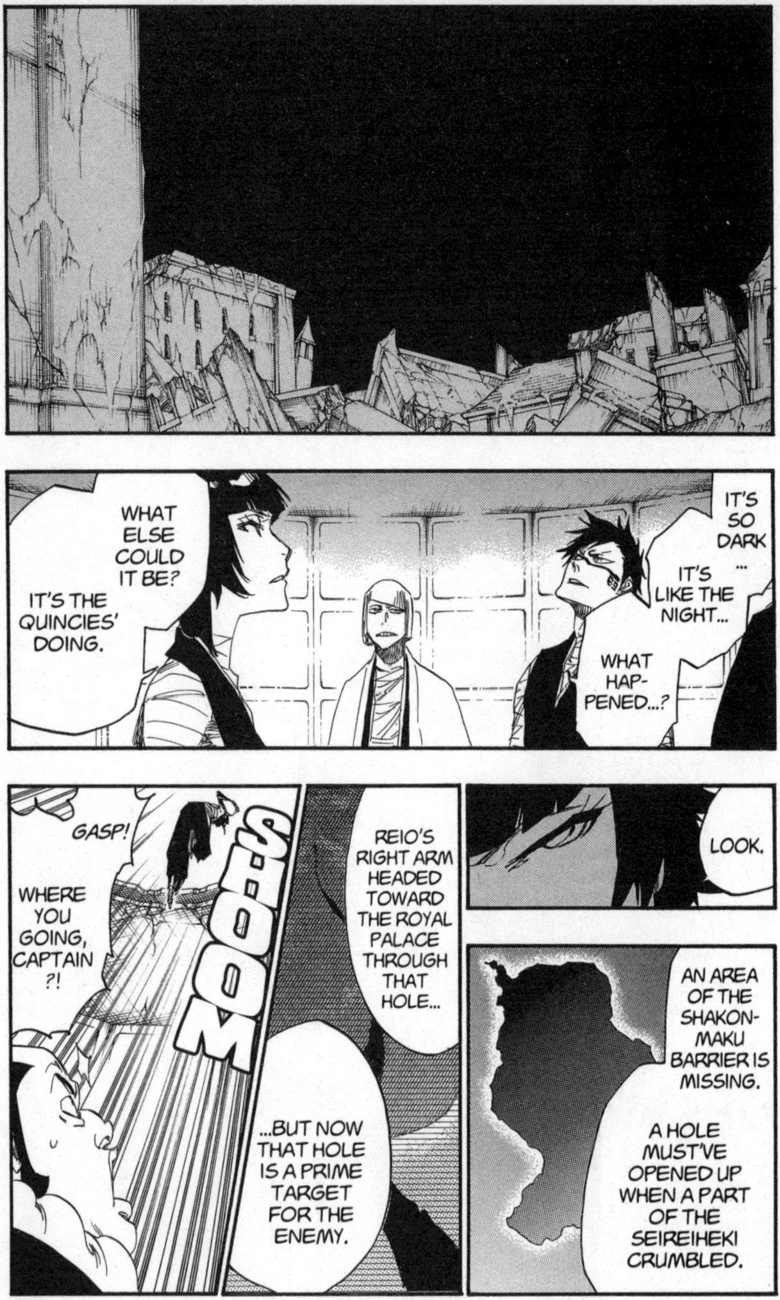
IT'S SO DARK ...
IT'S LIKE THE NIGHT...
WHAT HAP-PENED...?
WHAT ELSE COULD IT BE?
IT'S THE QUINCIES' DOING.
LOOK.
AN AREA OF THE SHAKON-MAKU BARRIER IS MISSING.
A HOLE MUST'VE OPENED UP WHEN A PART OF THE SEIREIHEKI CRUMBLED.
REIO'S RIGHT ARM HEADED TOWARD THE ROYAL PALACE THROUGH THAT HOLE...
...BUT NOW THAT HOLE IS A PRIME TARGET FOR THE ENEMY.
SHOOM
GASP!
WHERE YOU GOING, CAPTAIN ?!

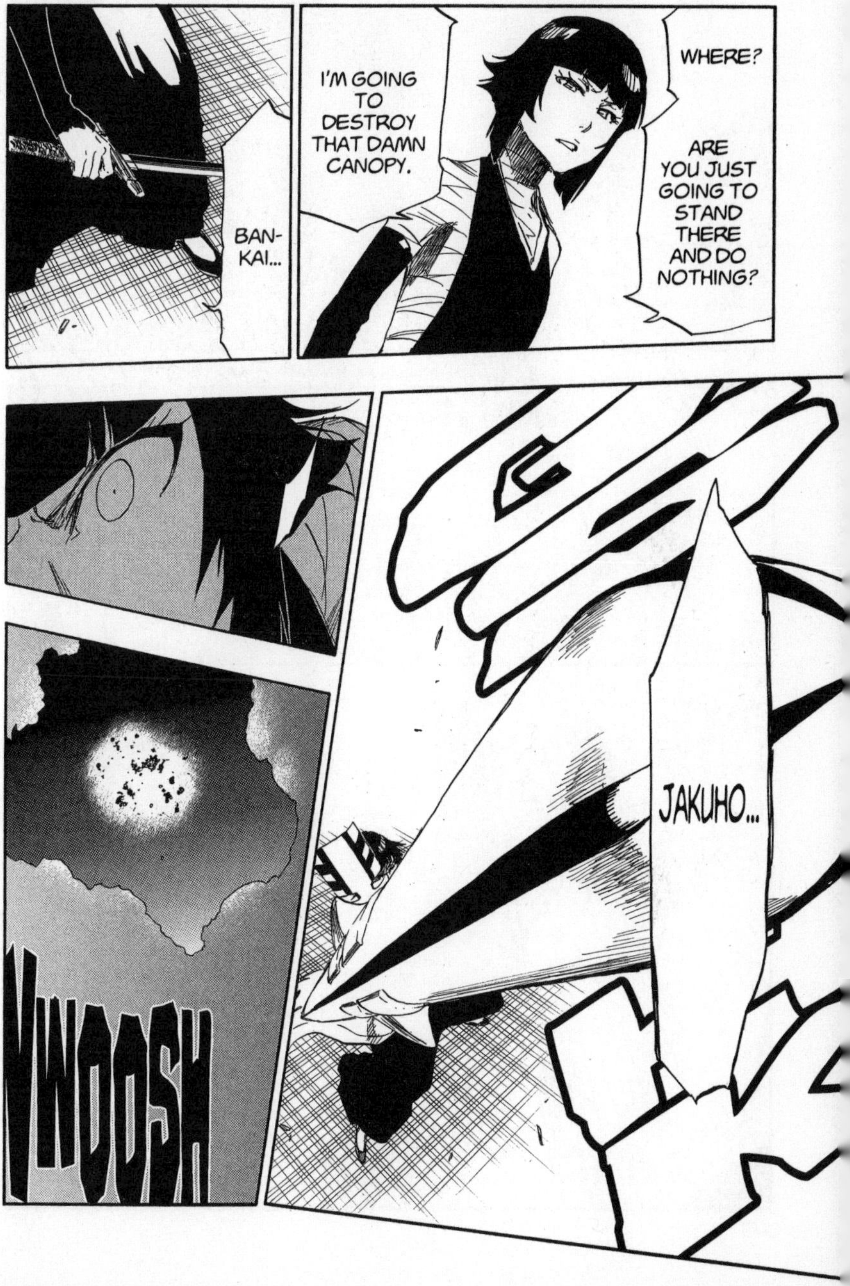
WHERE?
ARE YOU JUST GOING TO STAND THERE AND DO NOTHING?
I'M GOING TO DESTROY THAT DAMN CANOPY.
BAN-KAI...
JAKUHO...
WHOOSH

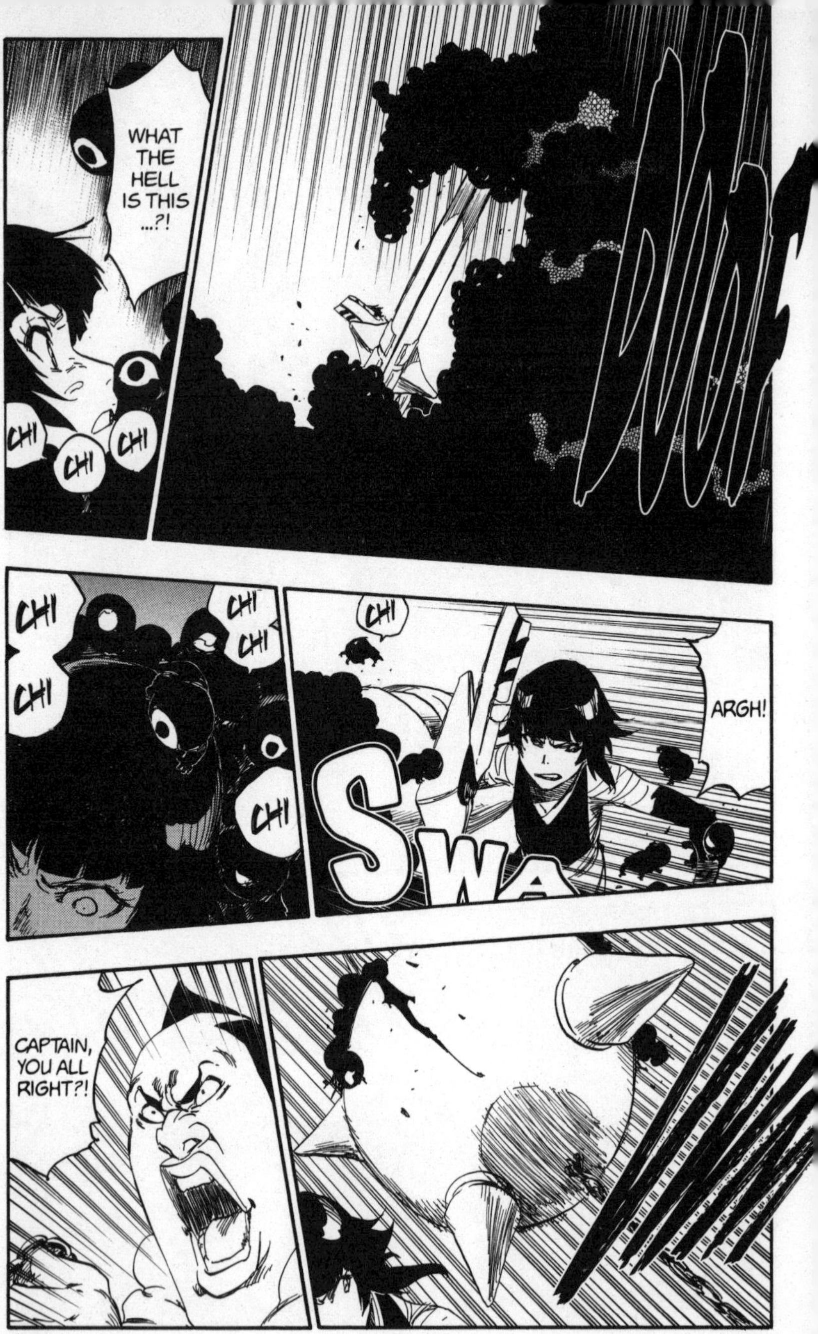
WHAT THE HELL IS THIS ...?!
CHI
CHI
CHI
CHI
ARGH!
SWA
CHI
CHI
CHI
CHI
CHI
CAPTAIN, YOU ALL RIGHT?!

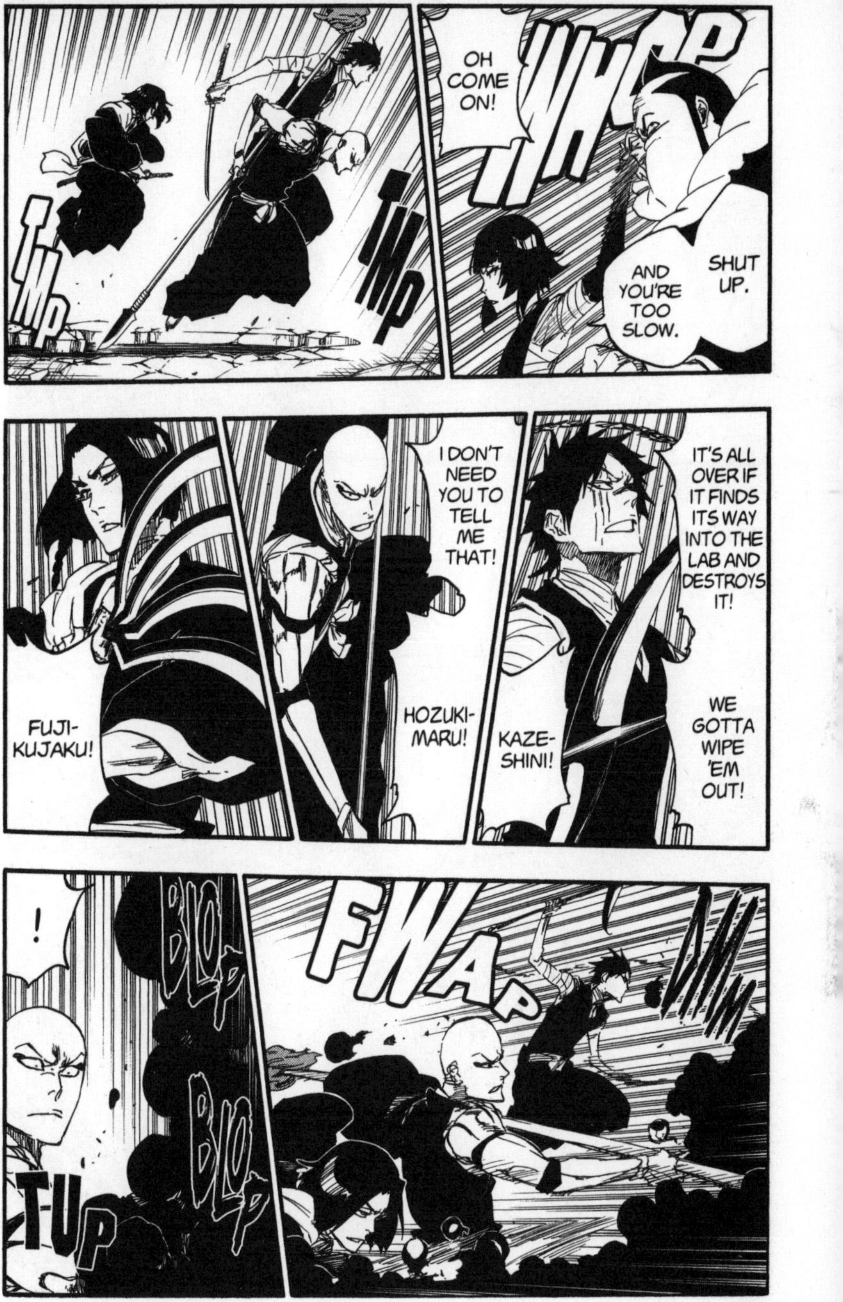
OH COME ON!
SHUT UP.
AND YOU'RE TOO SLOW.
TMP
TMP
IT'S ALL OVER IF IT FINDS ITS WAY INTO THE LAB AND DESTROYS IT!
WE GOTTA WIPE 'EM OUT!
KAZE-SHINI!
I DON'T NEED YOU TO TELL ME THAT!
HOZUKI-MARU!
FUJI-KUJAKU!
FWAP
!
BLOP
BLOP
TUP

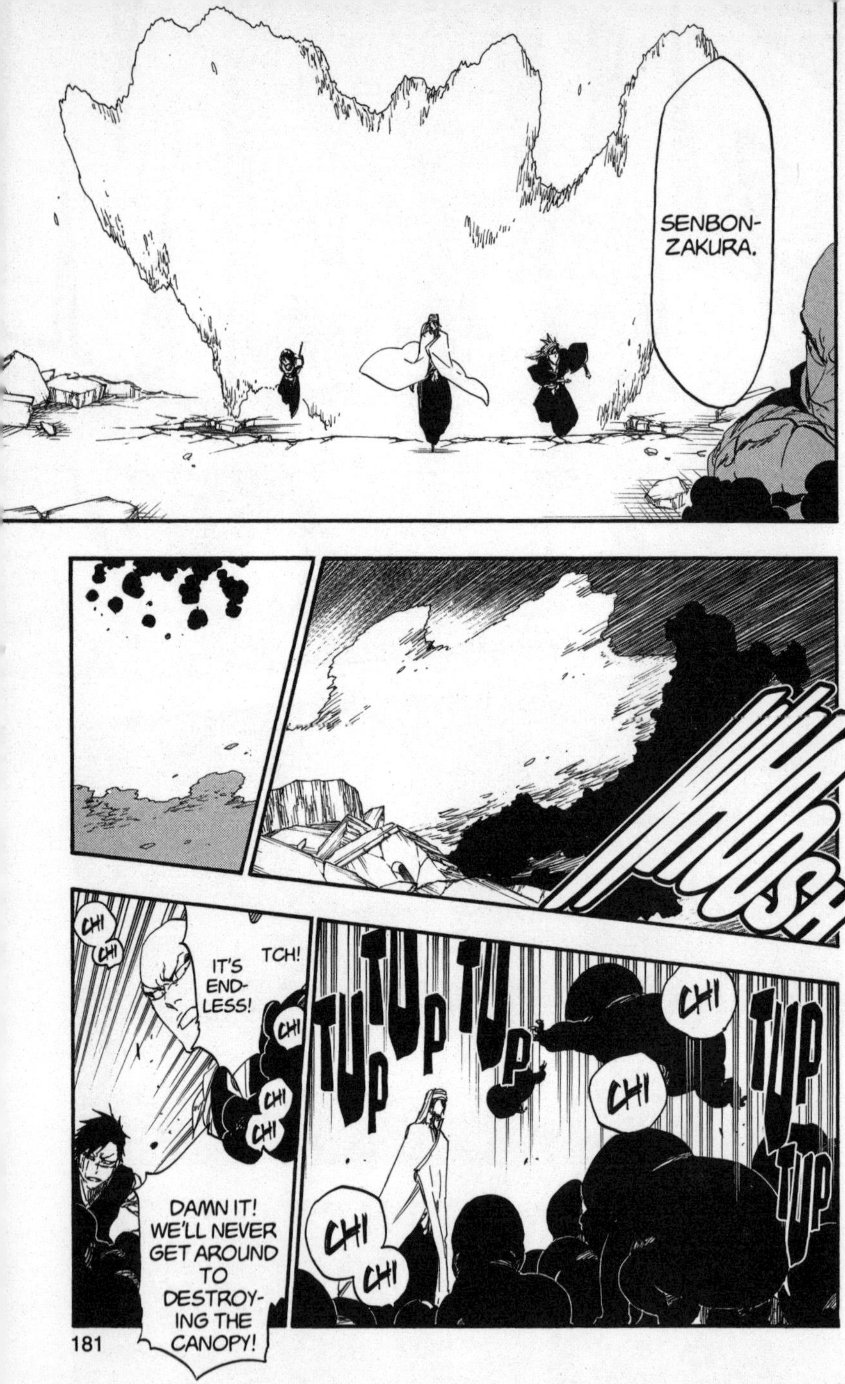
SENBON-ZAKURA.
WHOOSH
TUP TUP TUP TUP
CHI
CHI
TUP
TUP
CHI
CHI
TCH!
IT'S ENDLESS!
CHI CHI
CHI
CHI
CHI
DAMN IT! WE'LL NEVER GET AROUND TO DESTROYING THE CANOPY!

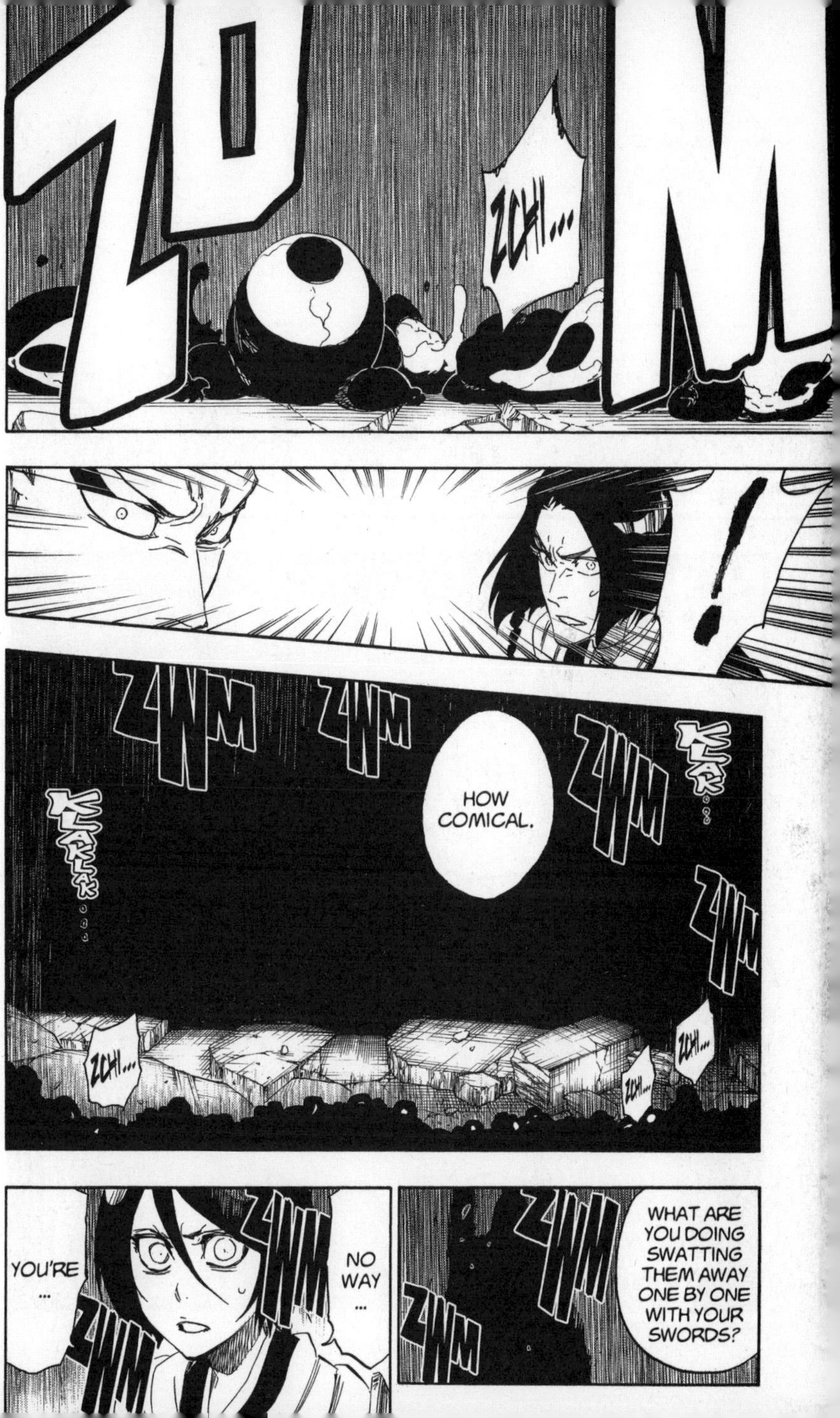
ZOOM
ZCHI...
!
KLAK...
ZWM
ZWM
ZWM
ZWM
HOW COMICAL.
KLAKLAK...
ZCHI...
ZCHI...
ZCHI...
WHAT ARE YOU DOING SWATTING THEM AWAY ONE BY ONE WITH YOUR SWORDS?
ZWM
ZWM
NO WAY...
ZWM
ZWM
YOU'RE...

READ THIS WAY

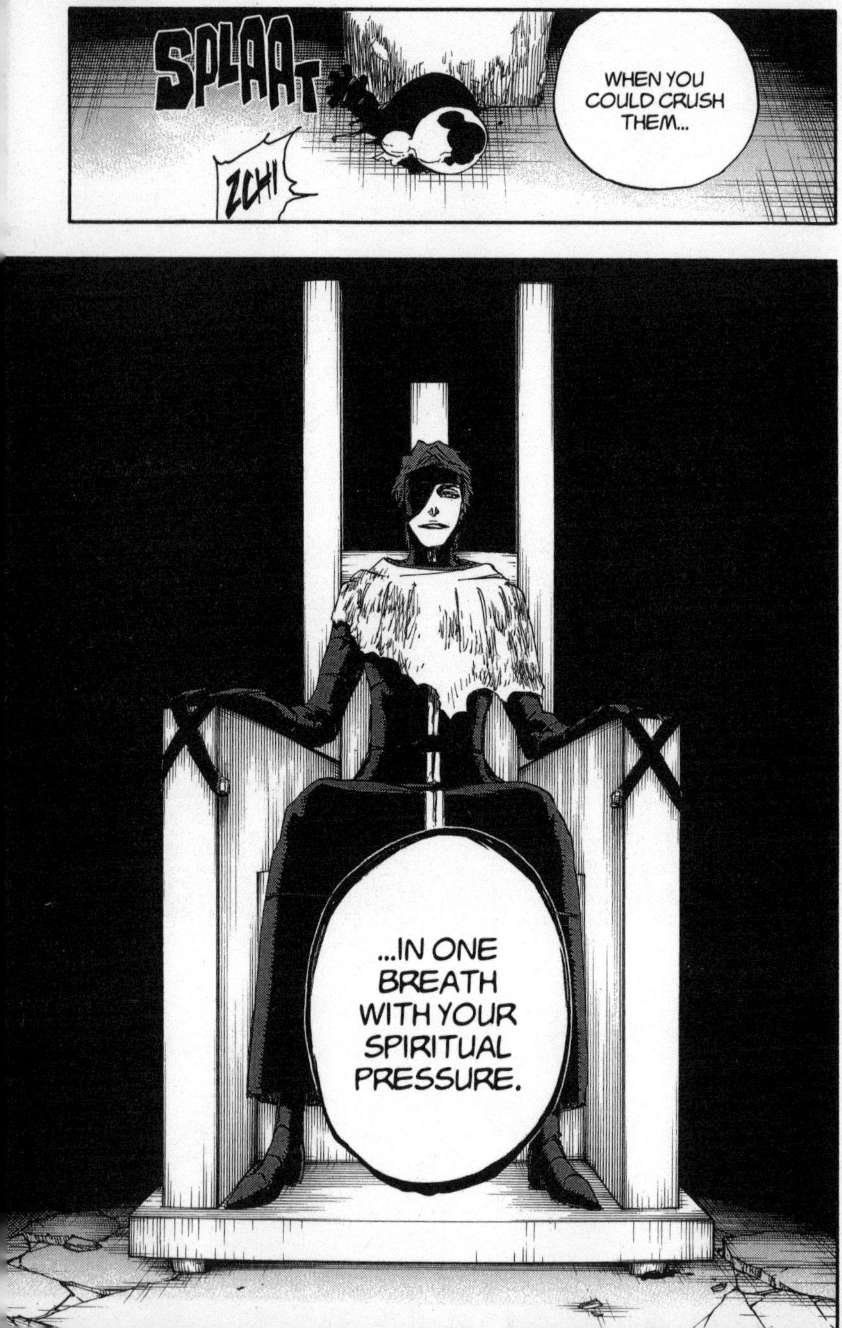
WHEN YOU COULD CRUSH THEM...
SPLAAT
ZCHI
...IN ONE BREATH WITH YOUR SPIRITUAL PRESSURE.

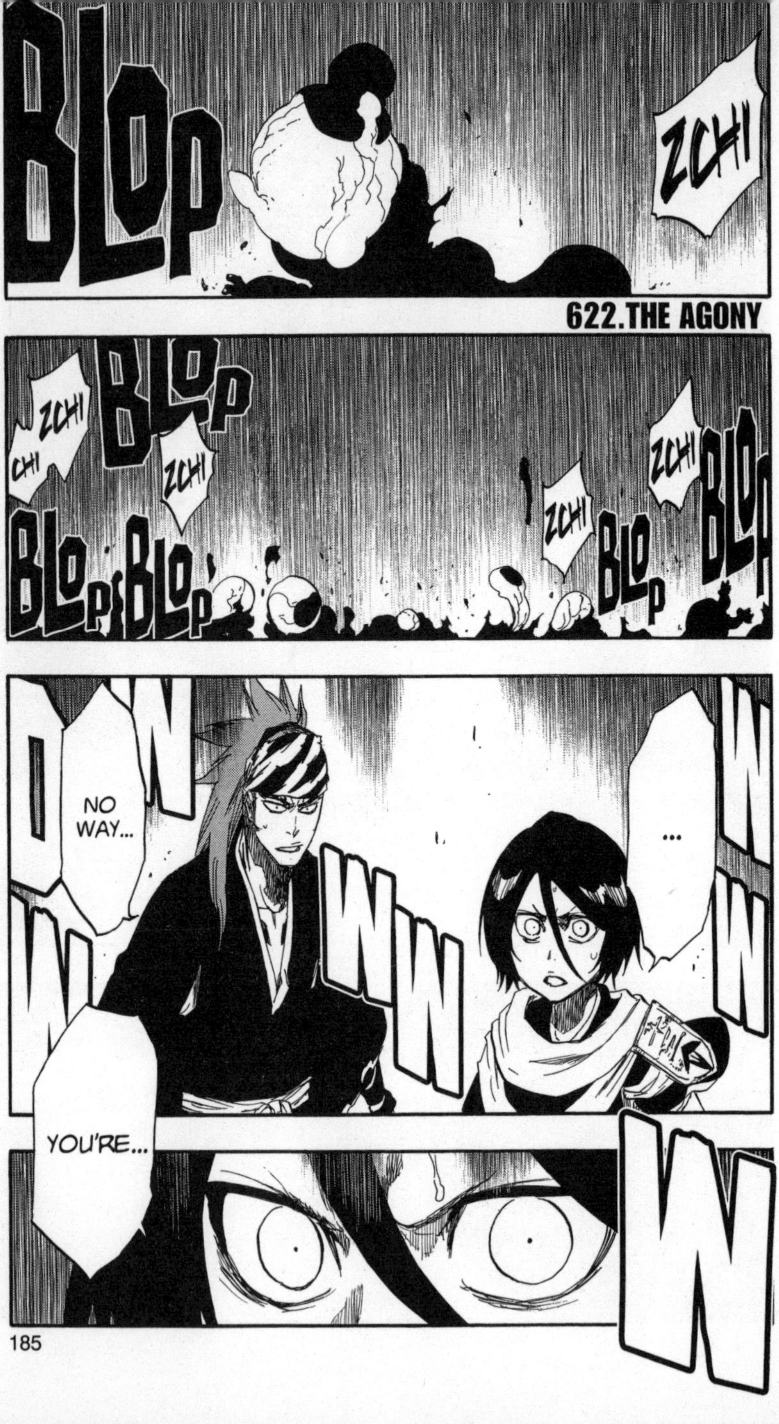
ZCHI
BLOP
622. THE AGONY
BLOP
ZCHI
BLOP
ZCHI
BLOP
ZCHI
ZCHI
BLOP
ZCHI
CHI
BLOP
BLOP
WN
WN
...
WN
NO WAY...
WN
WN
YOU'RE...

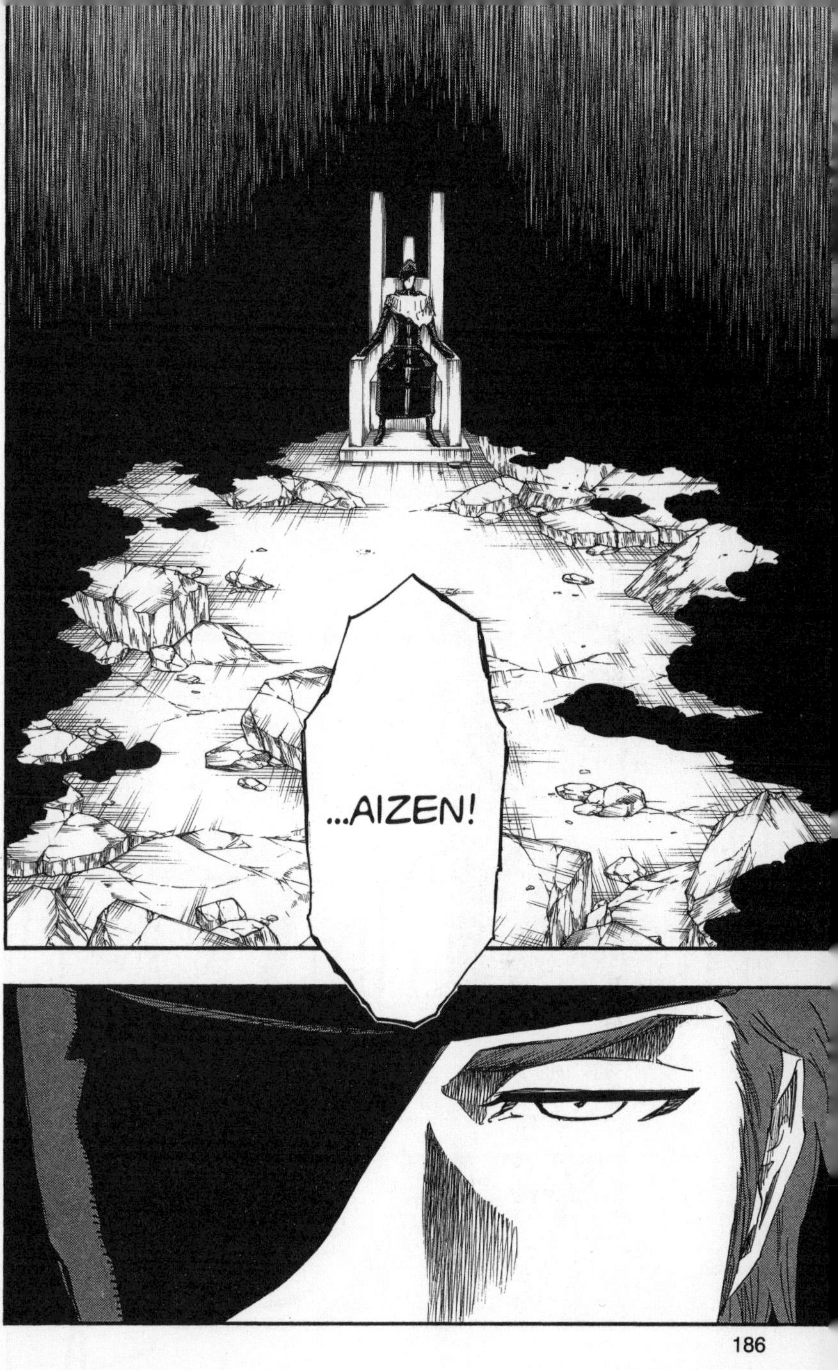
...AIZEN!

READ THIS WAY

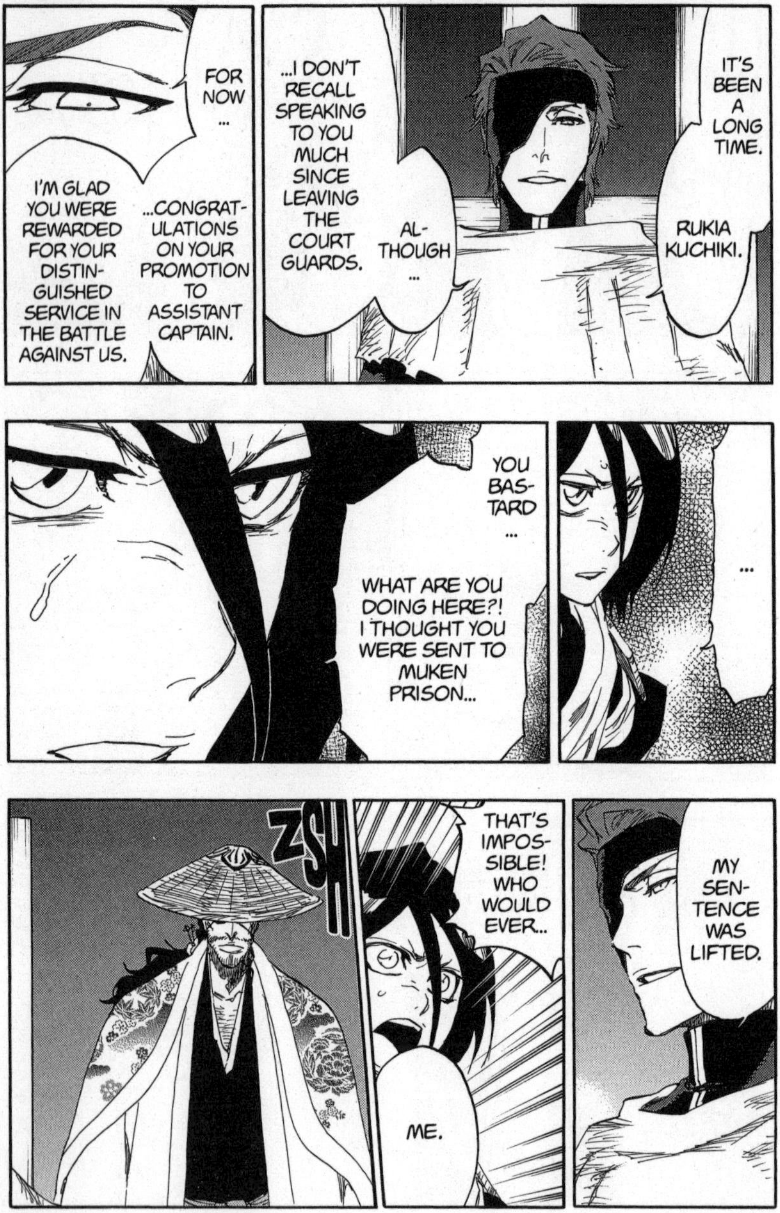

IT'S BEEN A LONG TIME.
RUKIA KUCHIKI.
...I DON'T RECALL SPEAKING TO YOU MUCH SINCE LEAVING THE COURT GUARDS.
ALTHOUGH...
FOR NOW...
...CONGRATULATIONS ON YOUR PROMOTION TO ASSISTANT CAPTAIN.
I'M GLAD YOU WERE REWARDED FOR YOUR DISTINGUISHED SERVICE IN THE BATTLE AGAINST US.
...
YOU BASTARD...
WHAT ARE YOU DOING HERE?! I THOUGHT YOU WERE SENT TO MUKEN PRISON...
MY SENTENCE WAS LIFTED.
THAT'S IMPOSSIBLE! WHO WOULD EVER...
ZSH
ME.

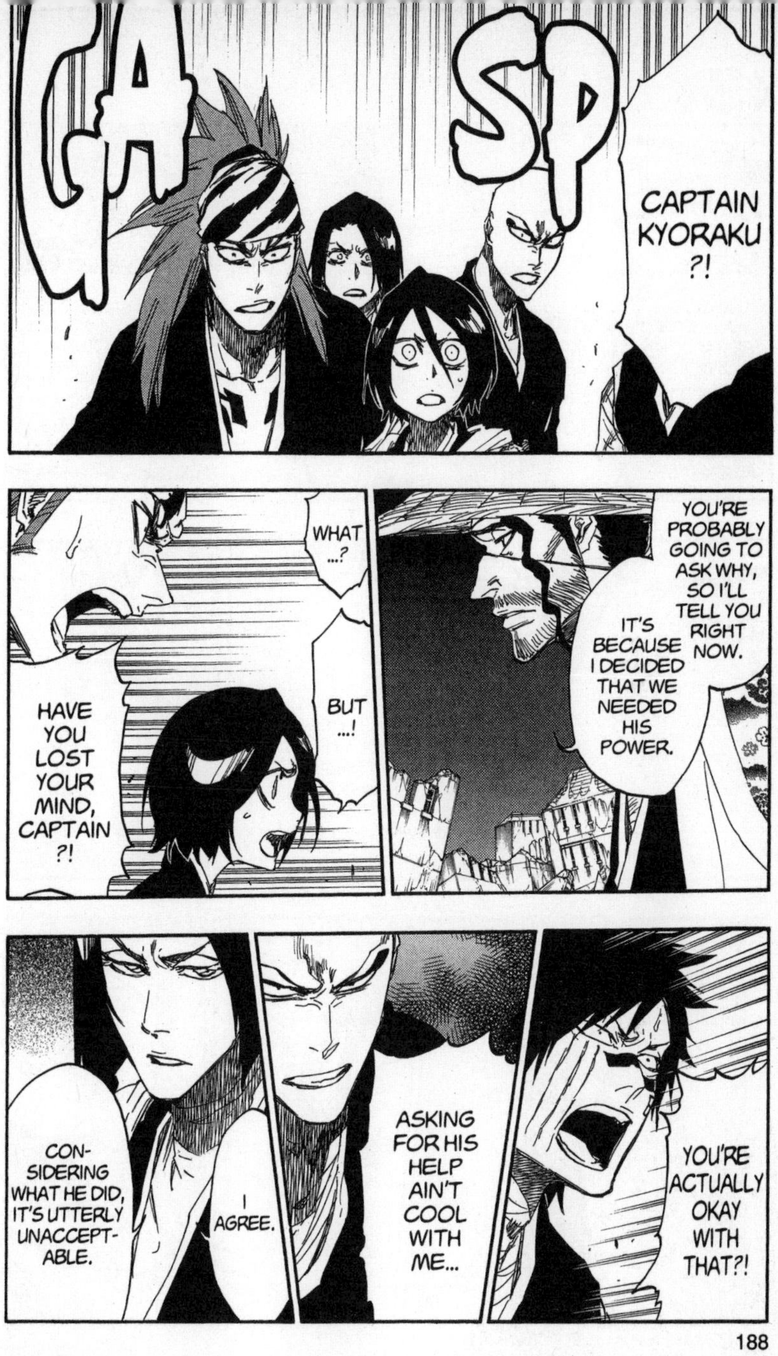
GASP
CAPTAIN KYORAKU?!
YOU'RE PROBABLY GOING TO ASK WHY, SO I'LL TELL YOU RIGHT NOW.
IT'S BECAUSE I DECIDED THAT WE NEEDED HIS POWER.
WHAT...?
BUT...!
HAVE YOU LOST YOUR MIND, CAPTAIN?!
YOU'RE ACTUALLY OKAY WITH THAT?!
ASKING FOR HIS HELP AIN'T COOL WITH ME...
I AGREE.
CONSIDERING WHAT HE DID, IT'S UTTERLY UNACCEPTABLE.

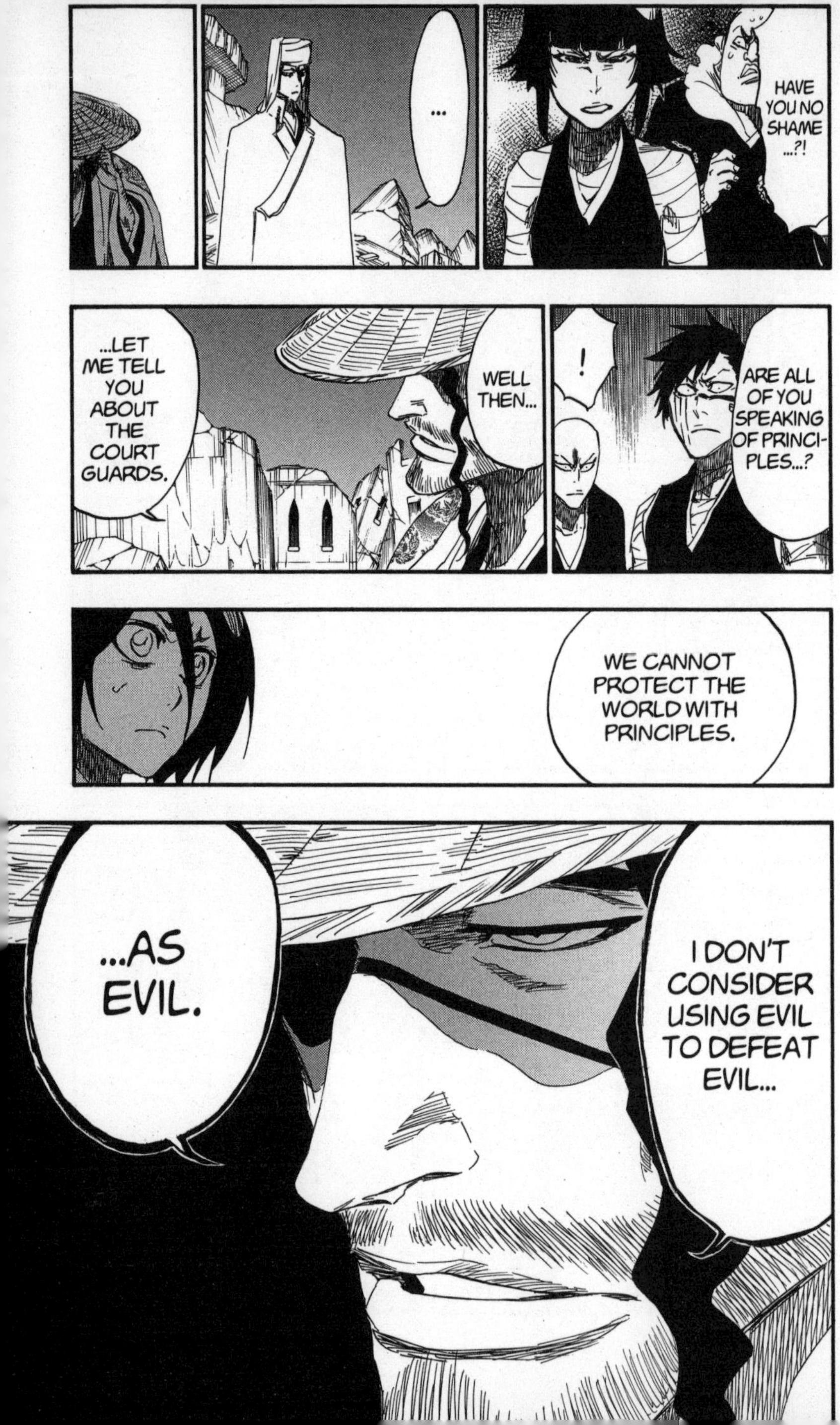
HAVE YOU NO SHAME ...?!
...
ARE ALL OF YOU SPEAKING OF PRINCIPLES...?
!
WELL THEN...
...LET ME TELL YOU ABOUT THE COURT GUARDS.
WE CANNOT PROTECT THE WORLD WITH PRINCIPLES.
I DON'T CONSIDER USING EVIL TO DEFEAT EVIL...
...AS EVIL.

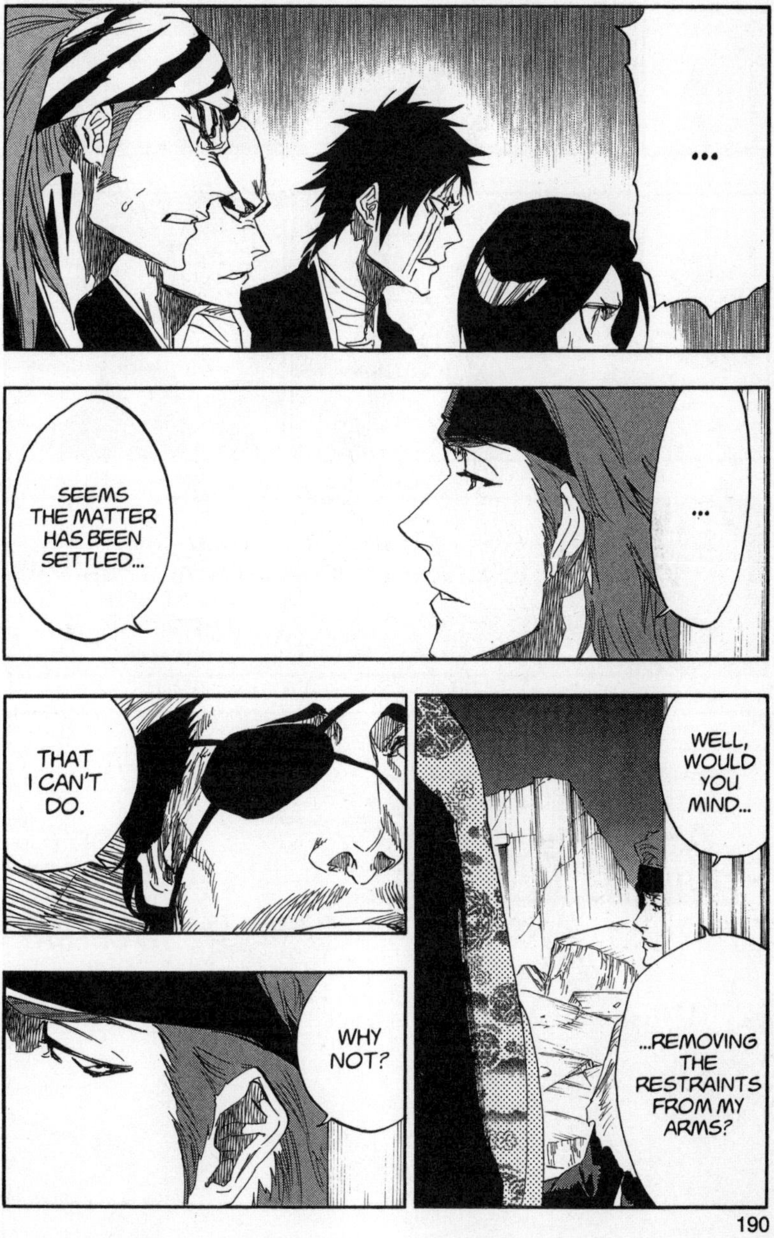
…
…
SEEMS THE MATTER HAS BEEN SETTLED...
WELL, WOULD YOU MIND...
...REMOVING THE RESTRAINTS FROM MY ARMS?
THAT I CAN'T DO.
WHY NOT?

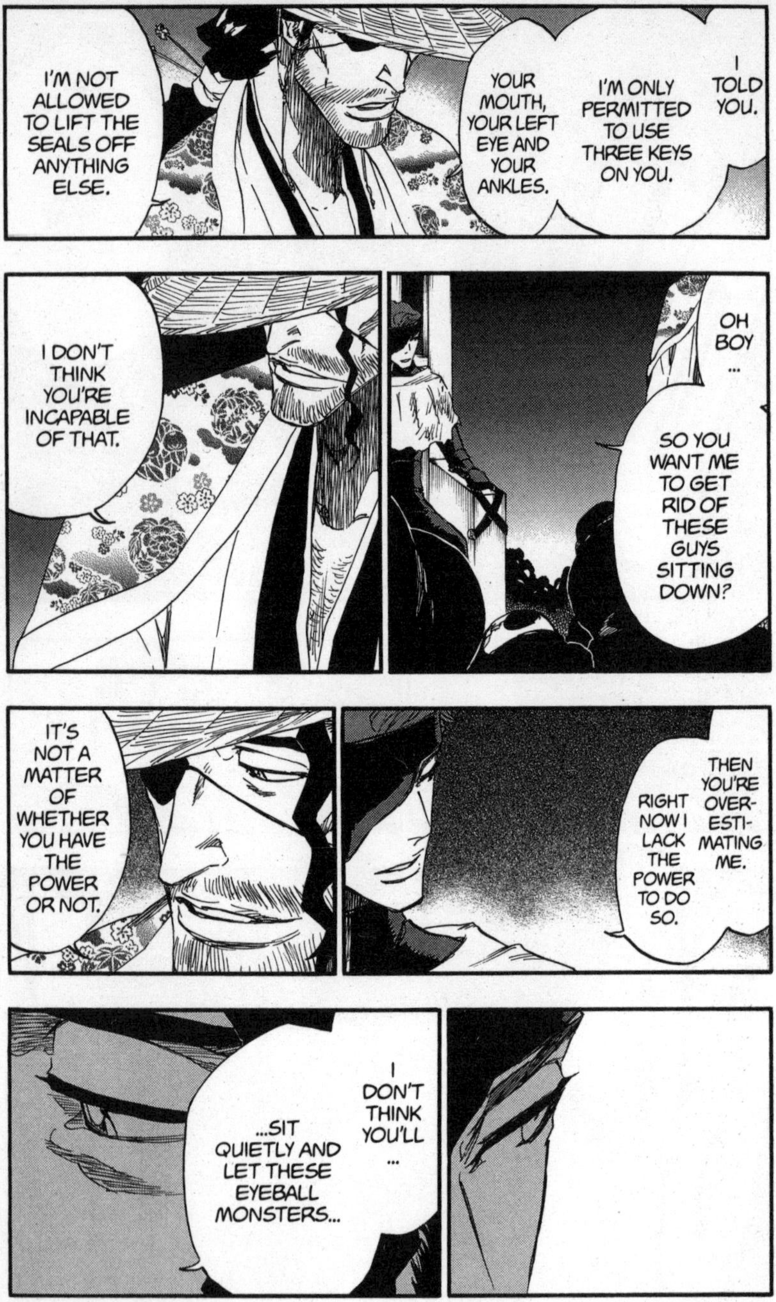
I TOLD YOU.
I'M ONLY PERMITTED TO USE THREE KEYS ON YOU.
YOUR MOUTH, YOUR LEFT EYE AND YOUR ANKLES.
I'M NOT ALLOWED TO LIFT THE SEALS OFF ANYTHING ELSE.
OH BOY ...
SO YOU WANT ME TO GET RID OF THESE GUYS SITTING DOWN?
I DON'T THINK YOU'RE INCAPABLE OF THAT.
THEN YOU'RE OVER-ESTIMATING ME.
RIGHT NOW I LACK THE POWER TO DO SO.
IT'S NOT A MATTER OF WHETHER YOU HAVE THE POWER OR NOT.
I DON'T THINK YOU'LL ...
...SIT QUIETLY AND LET THESE EYEBALL MONSTERS...

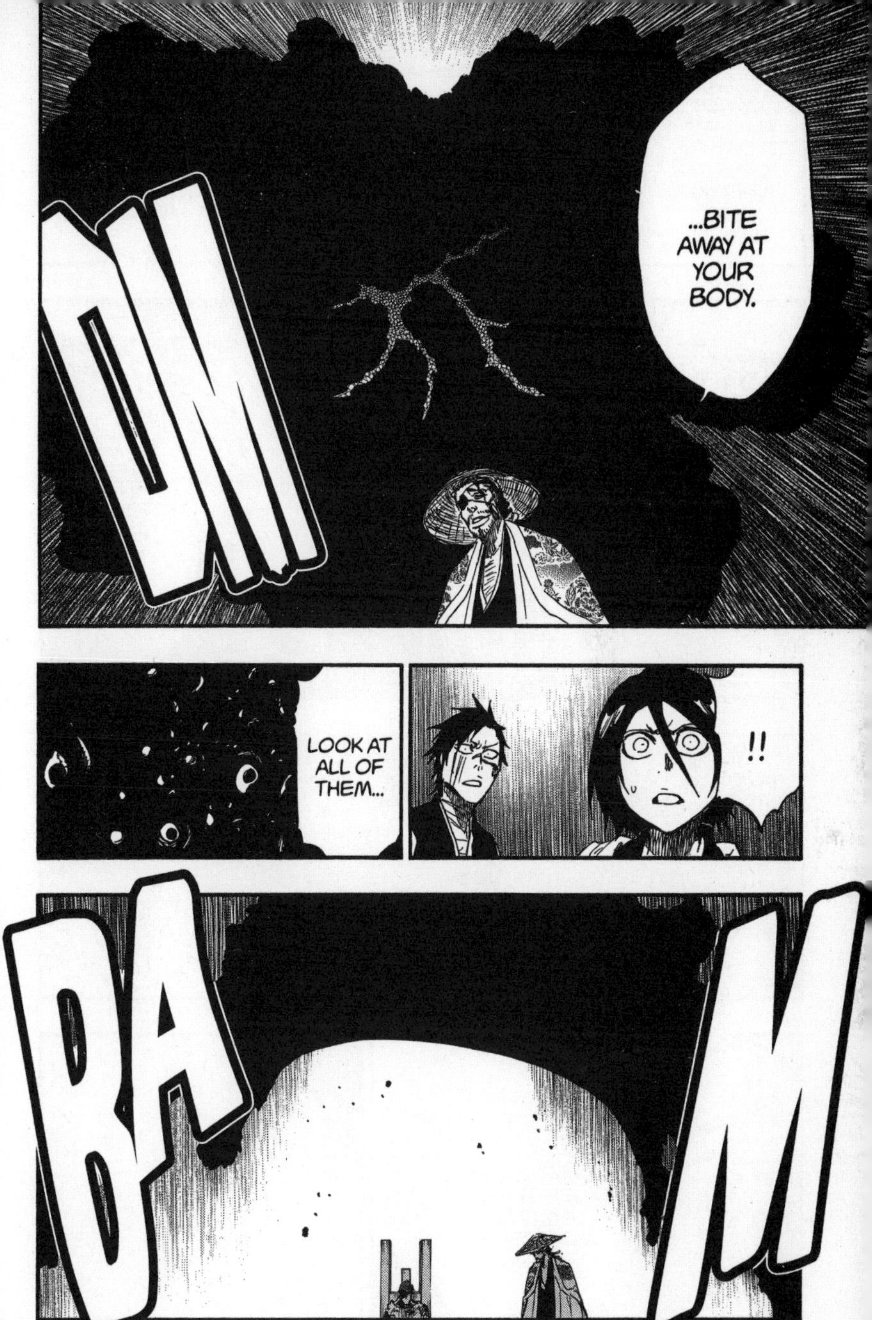
...BITE AWAY AT YOUR BODY.
DUM
!!
LOOK AT ALL OF THEM...
BAM

READ THIS WAY

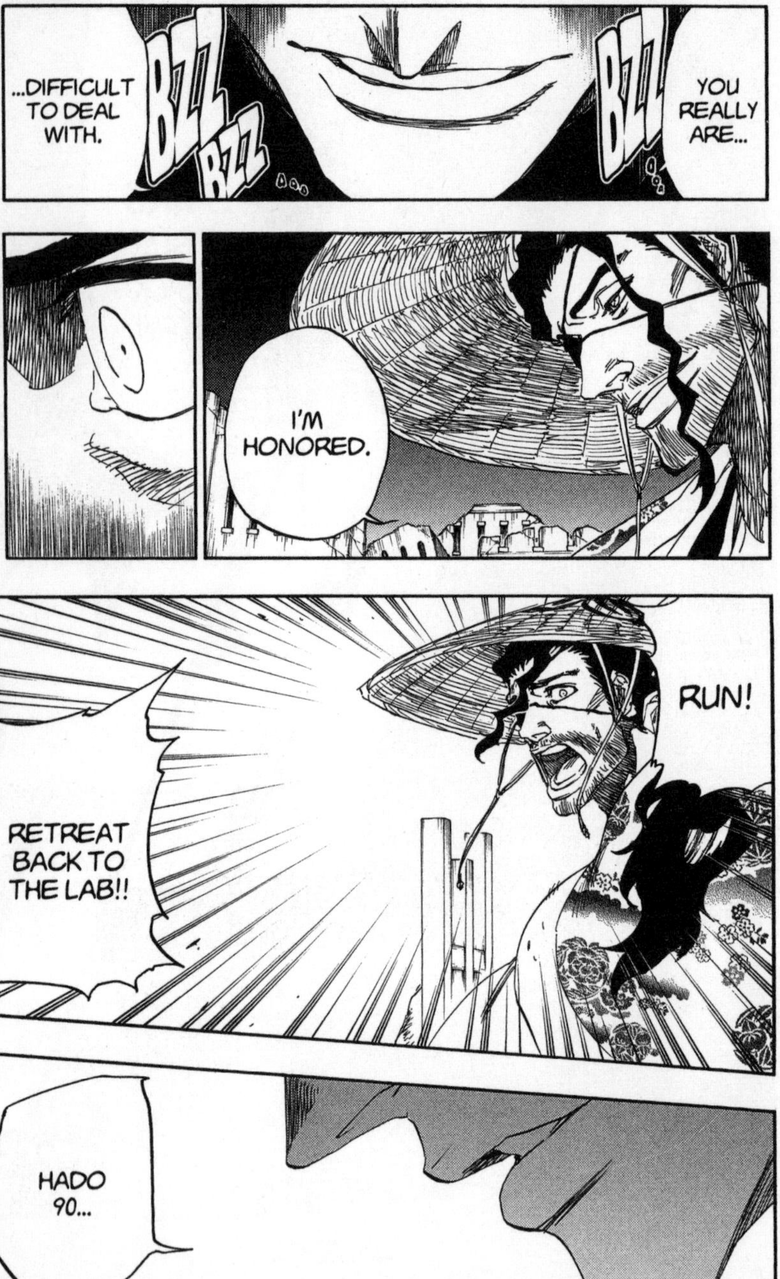
YOU REALLY ARE...
BZZ
...DIFFICULT TO DEAL WITH.
BZZ
BZZ
I'M HONORED.
RUN!
RETREAT BACK TO THE LAB!!
HADO 90...

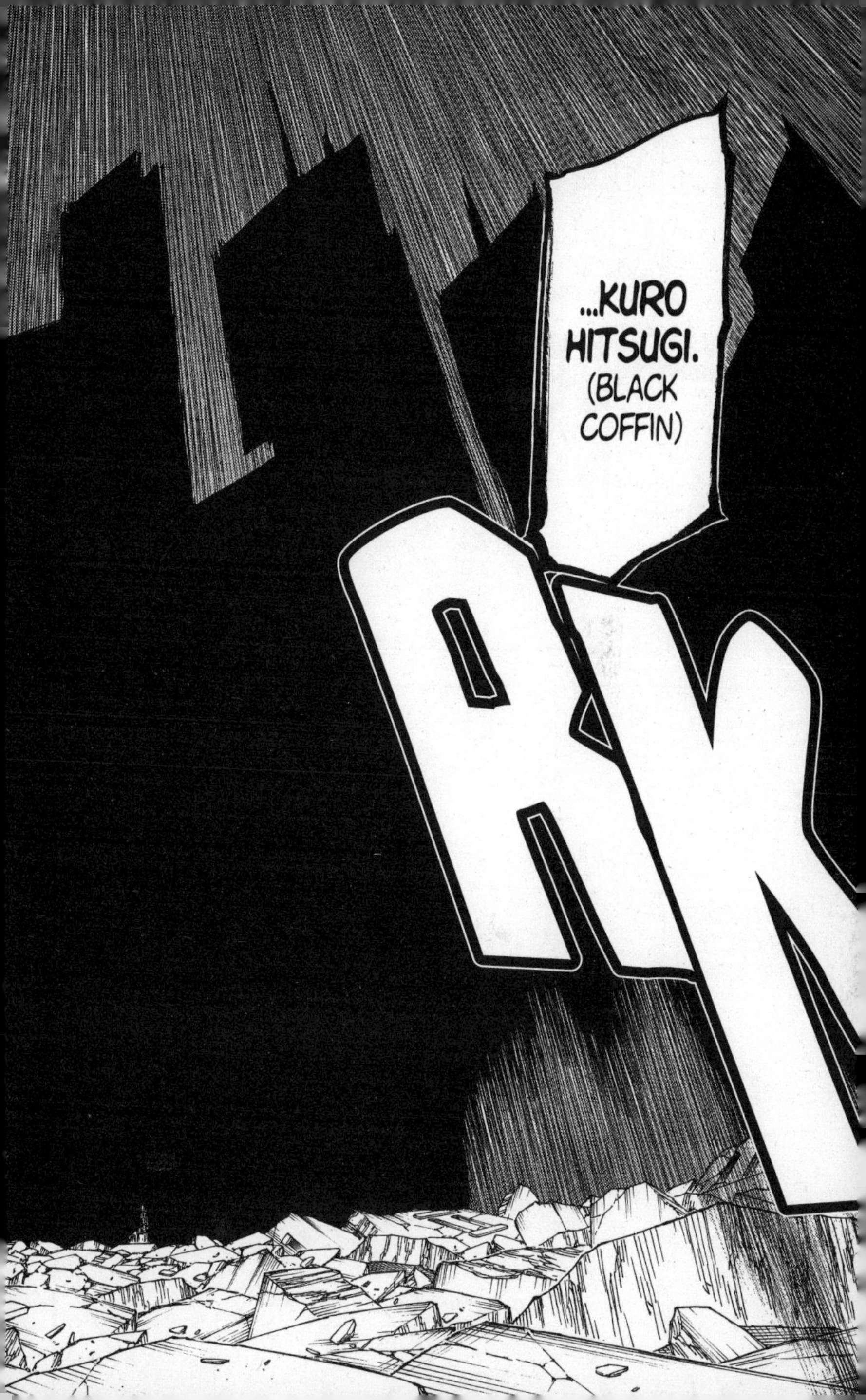
...KURO HITSUGI. (BLACK COFFIN)
RK

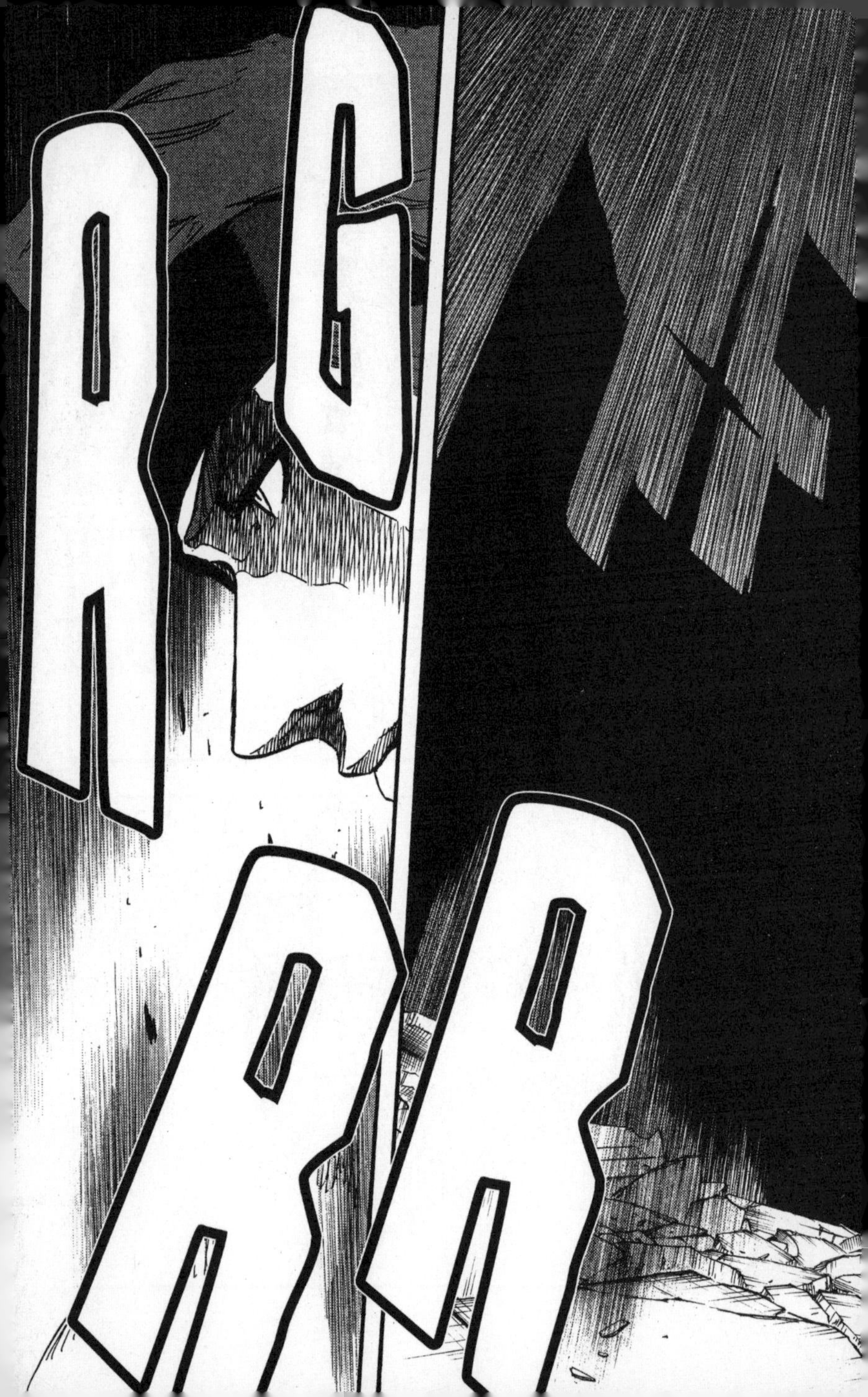

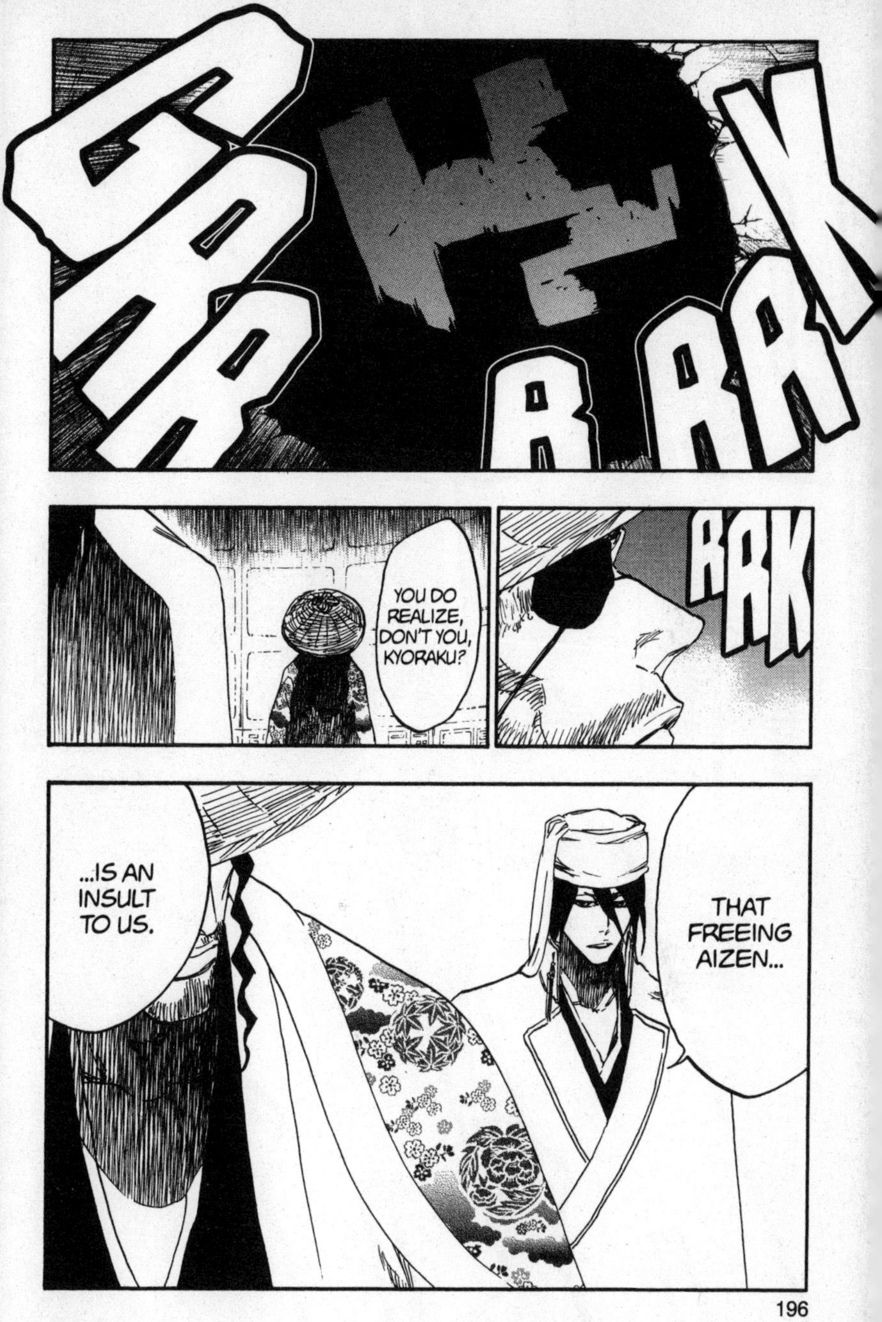
GRRRRRK
RRK
YOU DO REALIZE, DON'T YOU, KYORAKU?
THAT FREEING AIZEN...
...IS AN INSULT TO US.

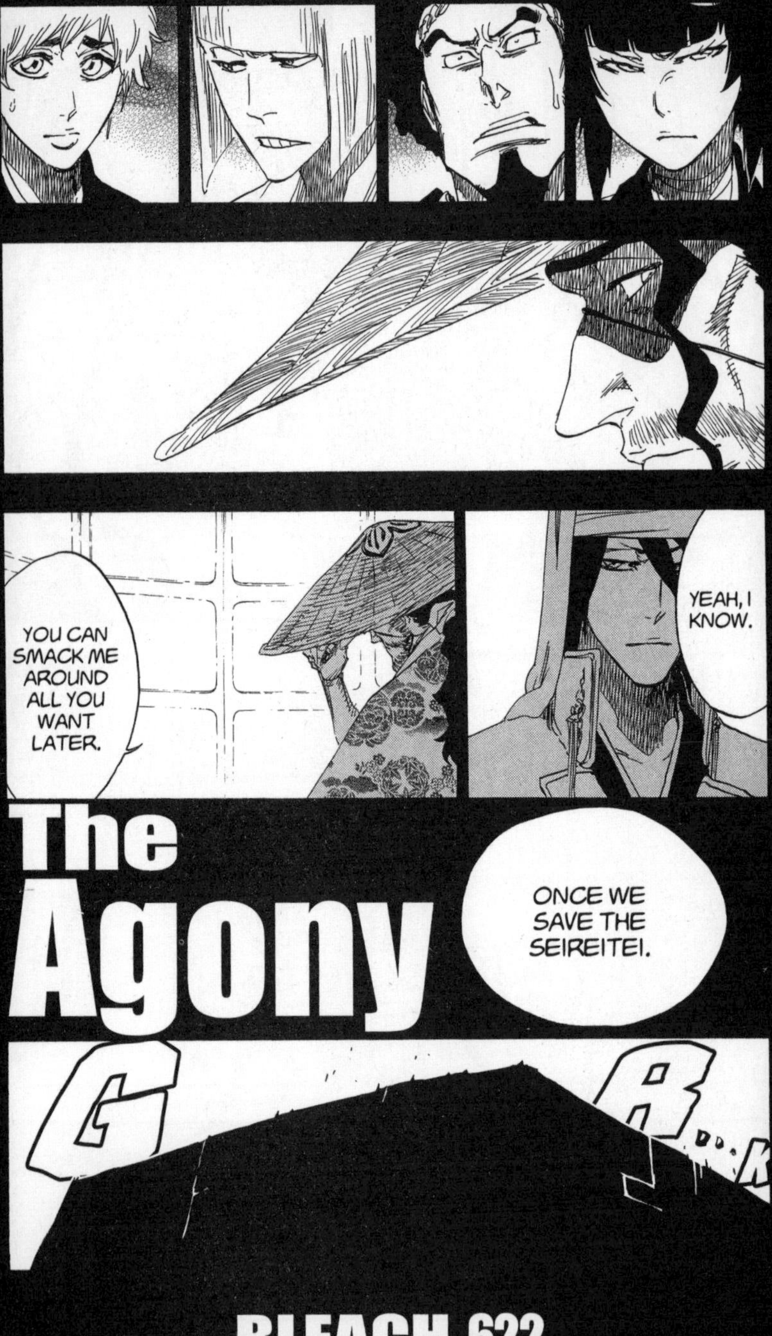
YEAH, I KNOW.
YOU CAN SMACK ME AROUND ALL YOU WANT LATER.
ONCE WE SAVE THE SEIREITEI.
The Agony
BLEACH 622.

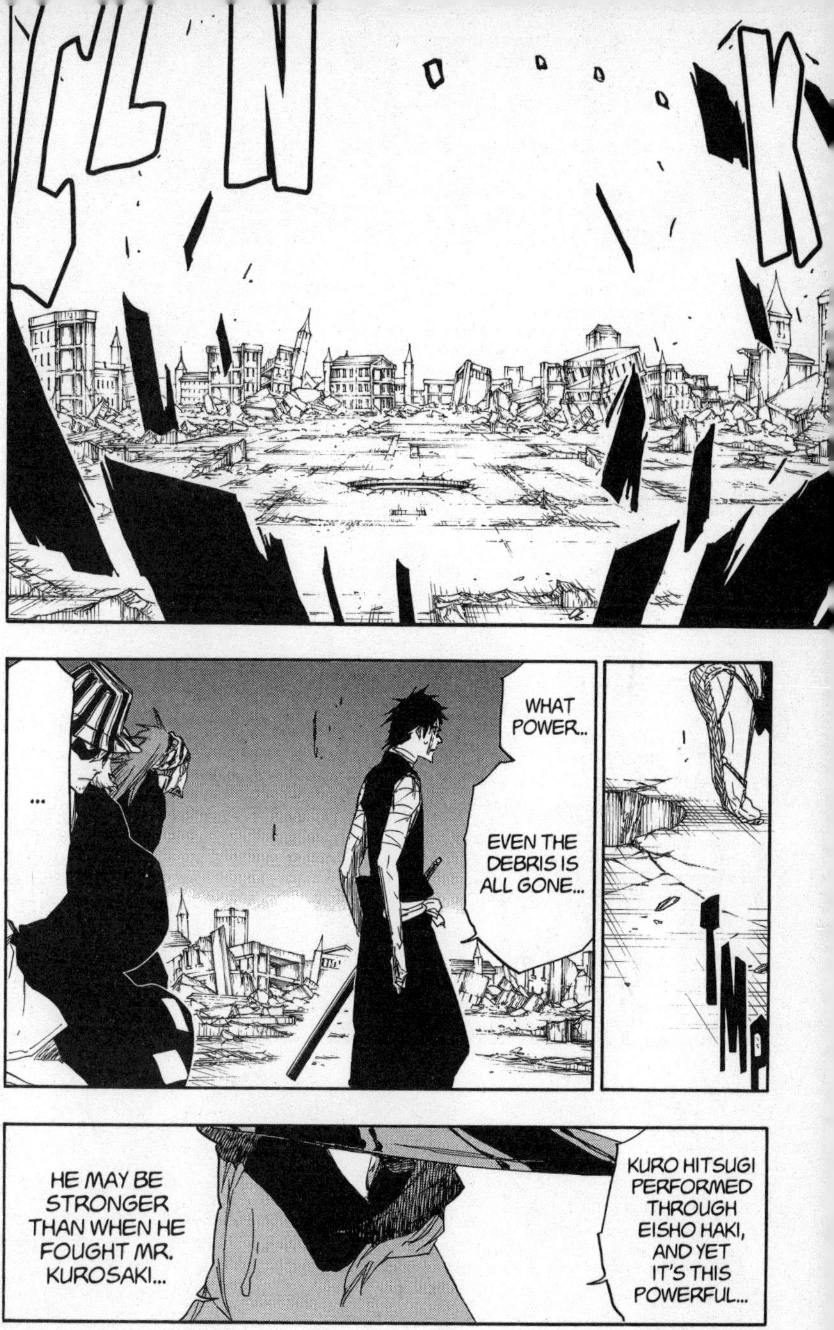
CLINK
TMP
WHAT POWER...
EVEN THE DEBRIS IS ALL GONE...
...
KURO HITSUGI PERFORMED THROUGH EISHO HAKI, AND YET IT'S THIS POWERFUL...
HE MAY BE STRONGER THAN WHEN HE FOUGHT MR. KUROSAKI...

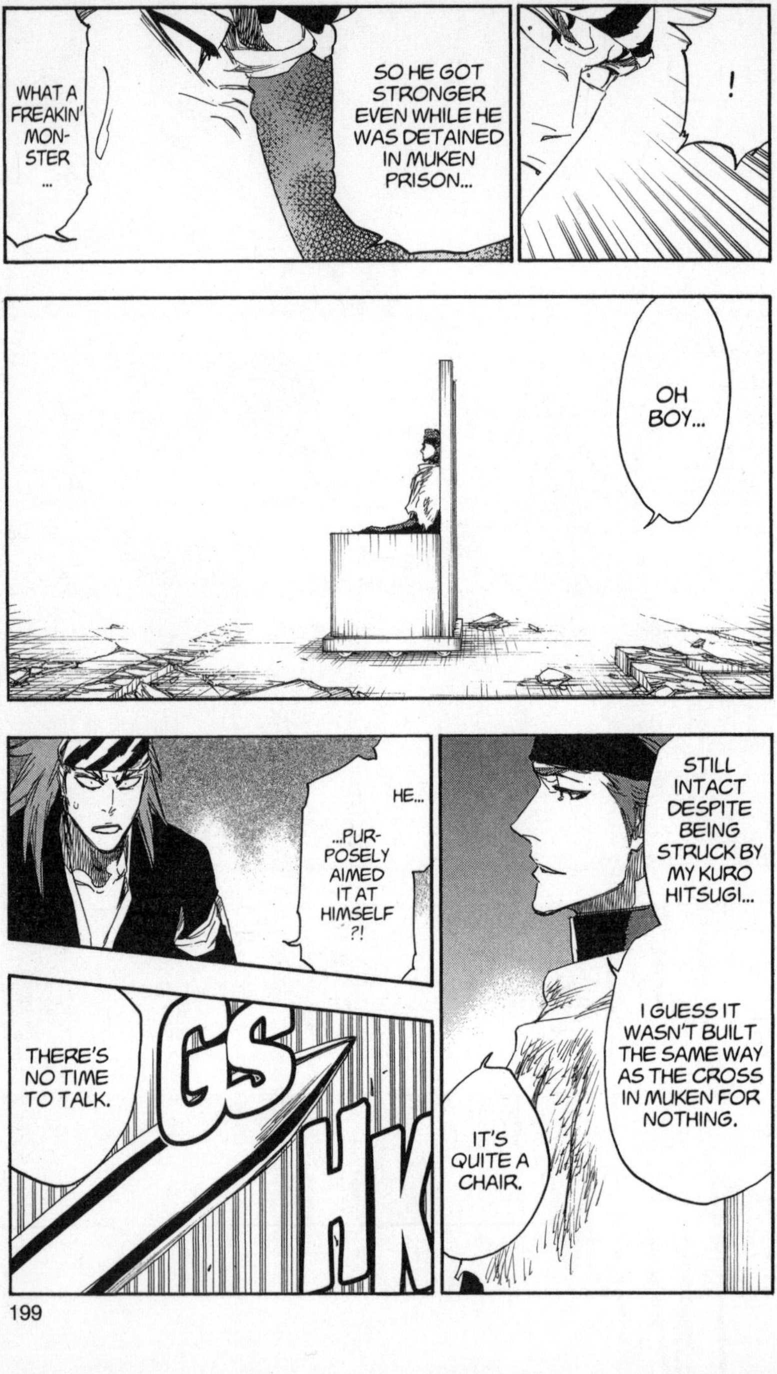
!
SO HE GOT STRONGER EVEN WHILE HE WAS DETAINED IN MUKEN PRISON...
WHAT A FREAKIN' MONSTER...
OH BOY...
STILL INTACT DESPITE BEING STRUCK BY MY KURO HITSUGI...
I GUESS IT WASN'T BUILT THE SAME WAY AS THE CROSS IN MUKEN FOR NOTHING.
IT'S QUITE A CHAIR.
HE...
...PURPOSELY AIMED IT AT HIMSELF ?!
GSHK
THERE'S NO TIME TO TALK.

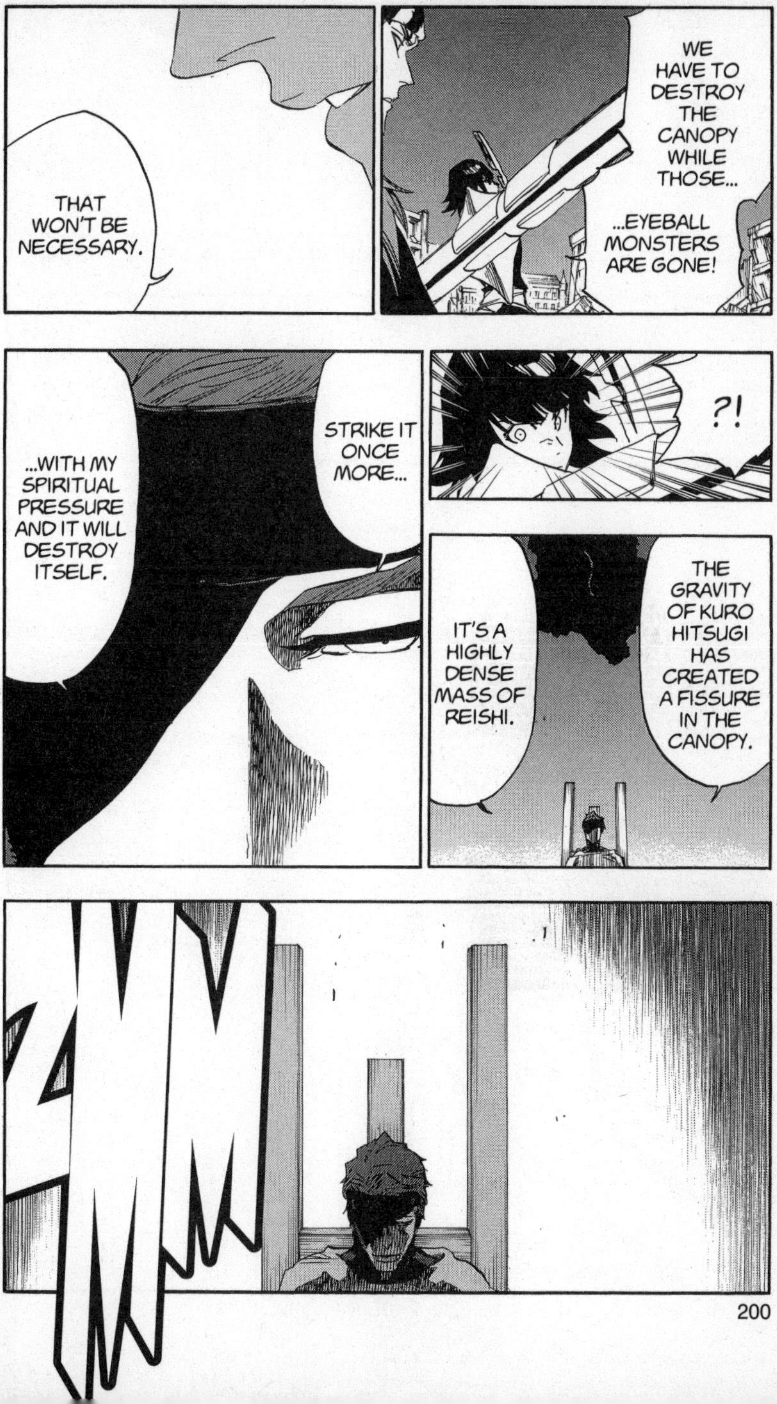
WE HAVE TO DESTROY THE CANOPY WHILE THOSE...
...EYEBALL MONSTERS ARE GONE!
THAT WON'T BE NECESSARY.
?!
THE GRAVITY OF KURO HITSUGI HAS CREATED A FISSURE IN THE CANOPY.
IT'S A HIGHLY DENSE MASS OF REISHI.
STRIKE IT ONCE MORE...
...WITH MY SPIRITUAL PRESSURE AND IT WILL DESTROY ITSELF.
ZMM

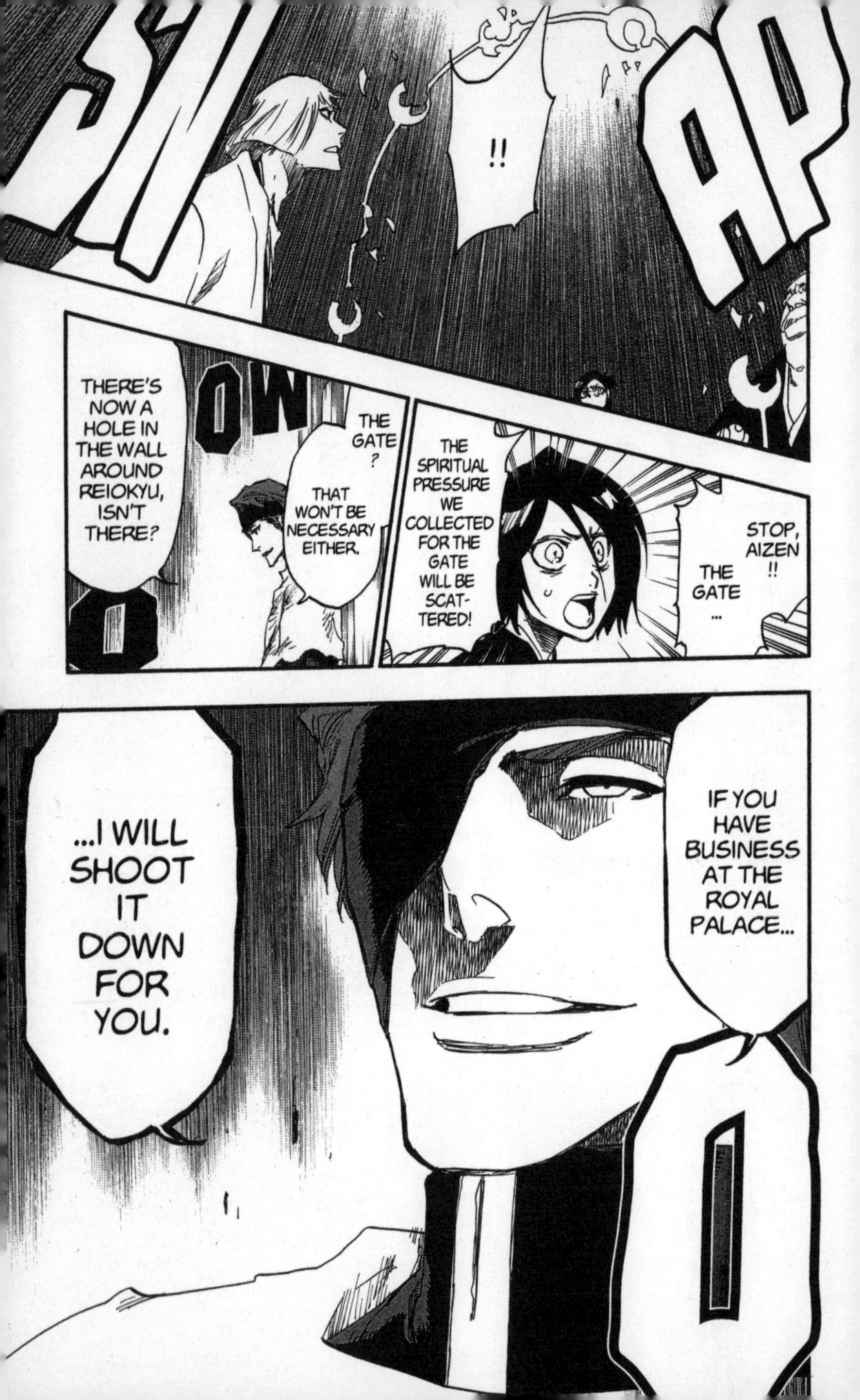
!!
STOP, AIZEN !!
THE GATE ...
THE SPIRITUAL PRESSURE WE COLLECTED FOR THE GATE WILL BE SCATTERED!
THE GATE?
THAT WON'T BE NECESSARY EITHER.
THERE'S NOW A HOLE IN THE WALL AROUND REIOKYU, ISN'T THERE?
IF YOU HAVE BUSINESS AT THE ROYAL PALACE...
...I WILL SHOOT IT DOWN FOR YOU.

CONTINUED IN BLEACH 69

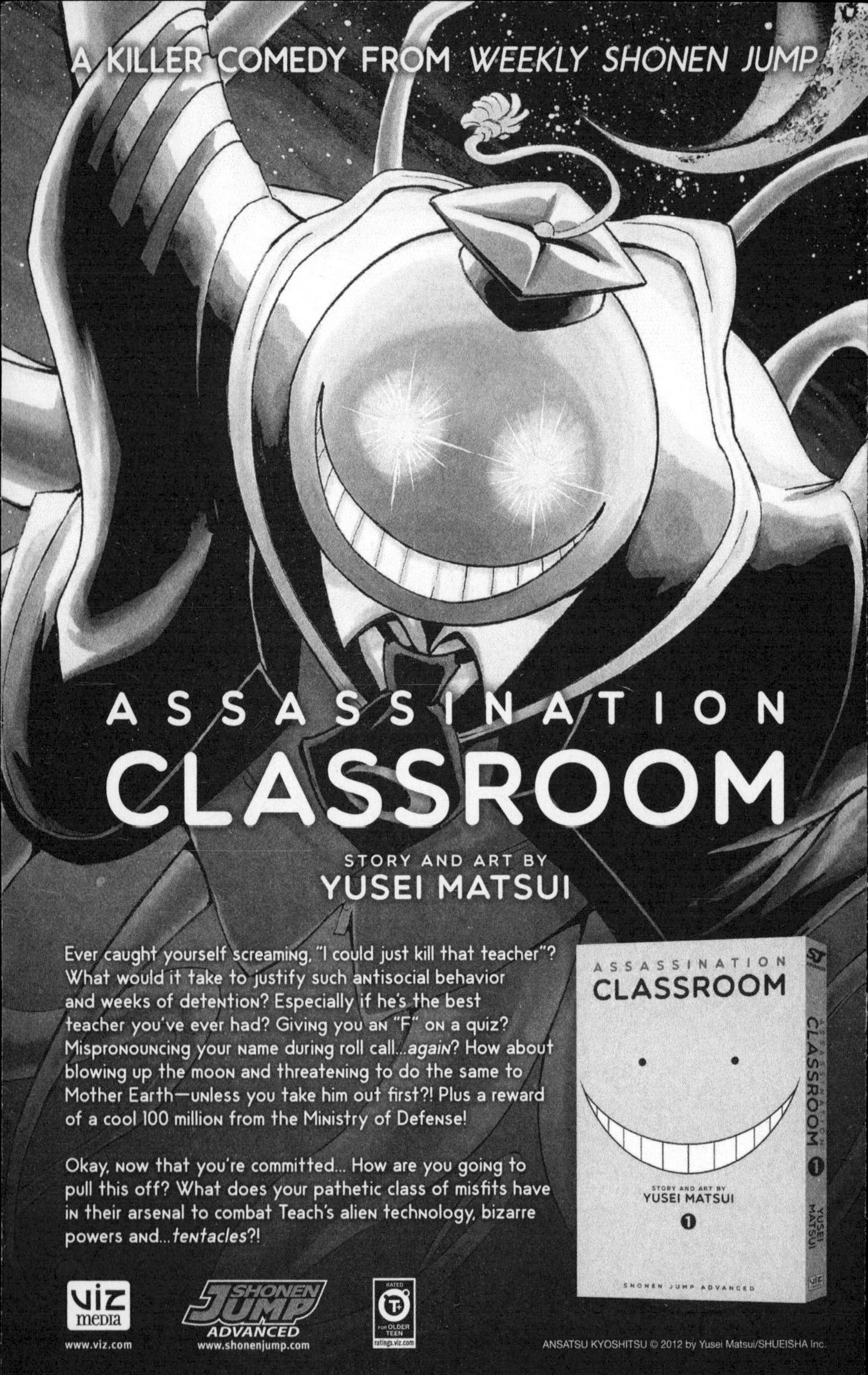
A KILLER COMEDY FROM *WEEKLY SHONEN JUMP*
ASSASSINATION
CLASSROOM
STORY AND ART BY
YUSEI MATSUI
Ever caught yourself screaming, "I could just kill that teacher"? What would it take to justify such antisocial behavior and weeks of detention? Especially if he's the best teacher you've ever had? Giving you an "F" on a quiz? Mispronouncing your name during roll call...*again*? How about blowing up the moon and threatening to do the same to Mother Earth—unless you take him out first?! Plus a reward of a cool 100 million from the Ministry of Defense!
Okay, now that you're committed... How are you going to pull this off? What does your pathetic class of misfits have in their arsenal to combat Teach's alien technology, bizarre powers and...*tentacles*?!
ASSASSINATION
CLASSROOM
STORY AND ART BY
YUSEI MATSUI
1
SHONEN JUMP ADVANCED
viz media
www.viz.com
SHONEN JUMP ADVANCED
www.shonenjump.com
RATED T+ FOR OLDER TEEN
ratings.viz.com
ANSATSU KYOSHITSU © 2012 by Yusei Matsui/SHUEISHA Inc.

NARUTO

Story and Art by
Masashi Kishimoto

Naruto is determined to become the greatest ninja ever!

Twelve years ago the Village Hidden in the Leaves was attacked by a fearsome threat. A nine-tailed fox spirit claimed the life of the village leader, the Hokage, and many others. Today, the village is at peace and a troublemaking kid named Naruto is struggling to graduate from Ninja Academy. His goal may be to become the next Hokage, but his true destiny will be much more complicated. The adventure begins now!

WORLD'S BEST SELLING MANGA!

www.shonenjump.com   www.viz.com

You're Reading in the Wrong Direction!!

Whoops! Guess what? You're starting at the wrong end of the comic!

...It's true! In keeping with the original Japanese format, **Bleach** is meant to be read from right to left, starting in the upper-right corner.

Unlike English, which is read from left to right, Japanese is read from right to left, meaning that action, sound effects and word-balloon order are completely reversed... something which can make readers unfamiliar with Japanese feel pretty backwards themselves. For this reason, manga or Japanese comics published in the U.S. in English have sometimes been published "flopped"—that is, printed in exact reverse order, as though seen from the other side of a mirror.

By flopping pages, U.S. publishers can avoid confusing readers, but the compromise is not without its downside. For one thing, a character in a flopped manga series who once wore in the original Japanese version a T-shirt emblazoned with "M A Y" (as in "the merry month of") now wears one which reads "Y A M"! Additionally, many manga creators in Japan are themselves unhappy with the process, as some feel the mirror-imaging of their art skews their original intentions.

We are proud to bring you Tite Kubo's **Bleach** in the original unflopped format. For now, though, turn to the other side of the book and let the adventure begin...!

—Editor

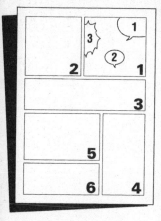